OCCULTED

Amy Rose   Ryan Estrada   Jeongmin Lee

IRON CIRCUS COMICS

AUTHORS
Amy Rose, Ryan Estrada

ARTIST
Jeongmin Lee

PROOFREADER
Abby Lehrke

PUBLISHER
C. Spike Trotman

ART DIRECTOR
Matt Sheridan

PRINT TECHNICIAN & ADDITIONAL DESIGN
Hye Mardikian

ISBN: 978-1-945820-76-2 (print) • 978-1-63899-110-6 (ebook)

First Edition: May 2023
Printed in China

IRON CIRCUS COMICS
strange and amazing

329 WEST 18TH STREET, SUITE 604 | CHICAGO, IL 60616 | IRONCIRCUS.COM | INQUIRY@IRONCIRCUS.COM

Names: Rose, Amy, 1987- author. | Estrada, Ryan, 1980- author. | Lee, Jeongmin, 1989- illustrator. |
    Spike, 1978- publisher. | Sheridan, Matt, art director. | Mardikian, Hye, designer.
Title: Occulted / Amy Rose, Ryan Estrada [authors], Jeongmin Lee, [illustrator] ; proofreader, Abby
    Lehrke ; publisher, C. Spike Trotman ; art director, Matt Sheridan ; print technician & additional
    design, Hye Mardikian.
Description: First edition. | Chicago, IL : Iron Circus Comics, 2023. | Interest age level: 010-012.
    | Summary: Survivor Amy Rose recounts her upbringing in an abusive cult which forbade independent
    learning, and how she discovered books in a secret library that opened up her world and inspired her
    to escape.--Publisher.
Identifiers: ISBN: 9781638991090
Subjects: LCSH: Rose, Amy, 1987---Comic books, strips, etc. | Cult members--Biography--Comic
    books, strips, etc. | Cults--United States--Comic books, strips, etc. | Childhood--Comic books,
    strips, etc. | Psychological abuse--Comic books, strips, etc. | Intellectual freedom--Comic books,
    strips, etc. | Libraries--Comic books, strips, etc. | Escapes--Comic books, strips, etc. | CYAC: Rose,
    Amy, 1987---Cartoons and comics. | Cult members--Biography--Cartoons and comics. | Cults-- United
    States--Cartoons and comics. | Children--Cartoons and comics. | Psychological abuse--Cartoons and
    comics. | Intellectual freedom--Cartoons and comics. | Libraries-- Cartoons and comics. | Escapes--
    Cartoons and comics. | LCGFT: Graphic novels. | Autobiographies. | BISAC: JUVENILE NONFICTION / Comics
    & Graphic Novels / Biography & Memoir. | JUVENILE NONFICTION / Health & Daily Living / Mental Health.
    | JUVENILE NONFICTION / Social Topics / Physical & Emotional Abuse.
Classification: LCC: BL2525 .R67 2023 | DDC: 200.973--dc23

CHAPTERS

For Momma

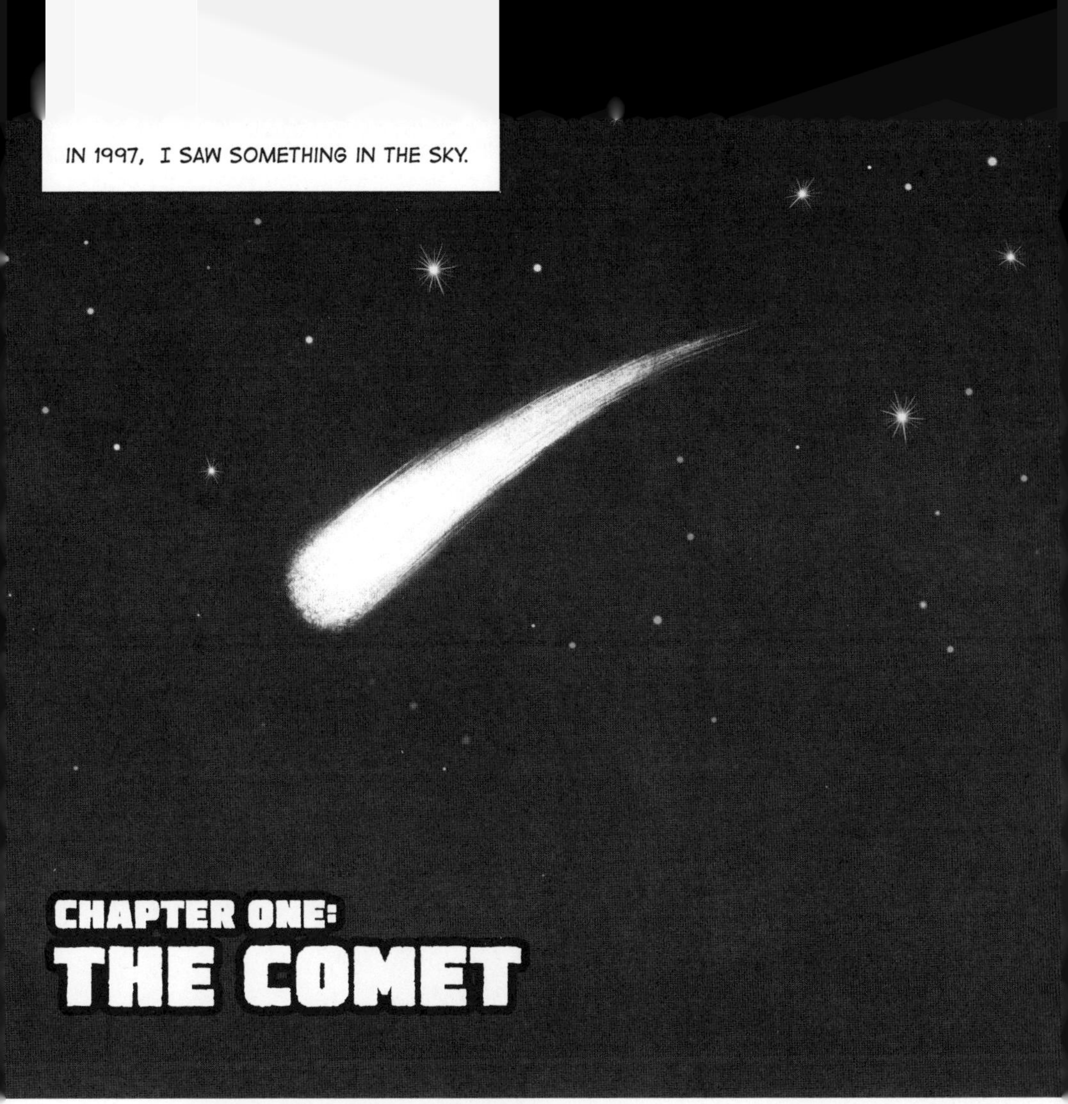
IN 1997, I SAW SOMETHING IN THE SKY.
CHAPTER ONE:
THE COMET

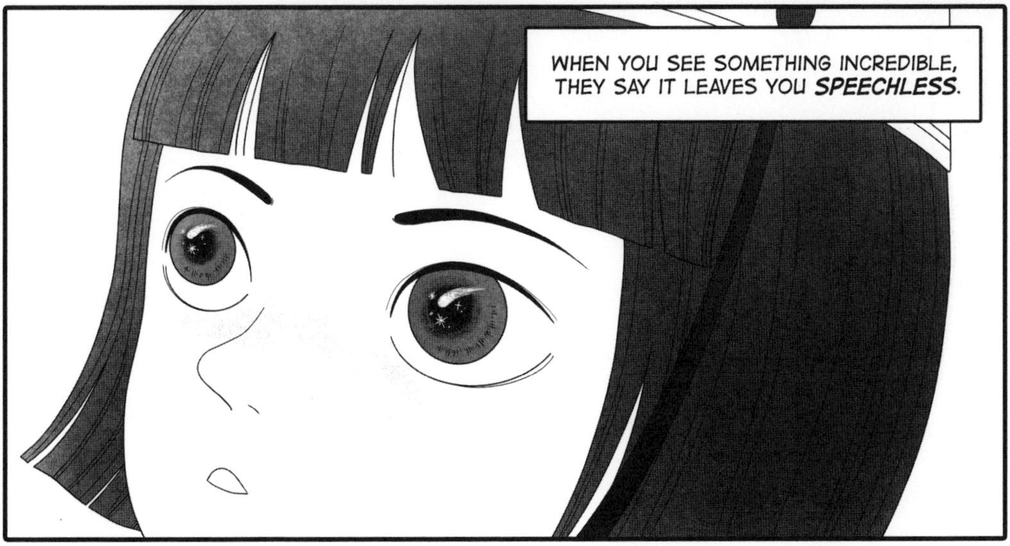
WHEN YOU SEE SOMETHING INCREDIBLE, THEY SAY IT LEAVES YOU *SPEECHLESS*.

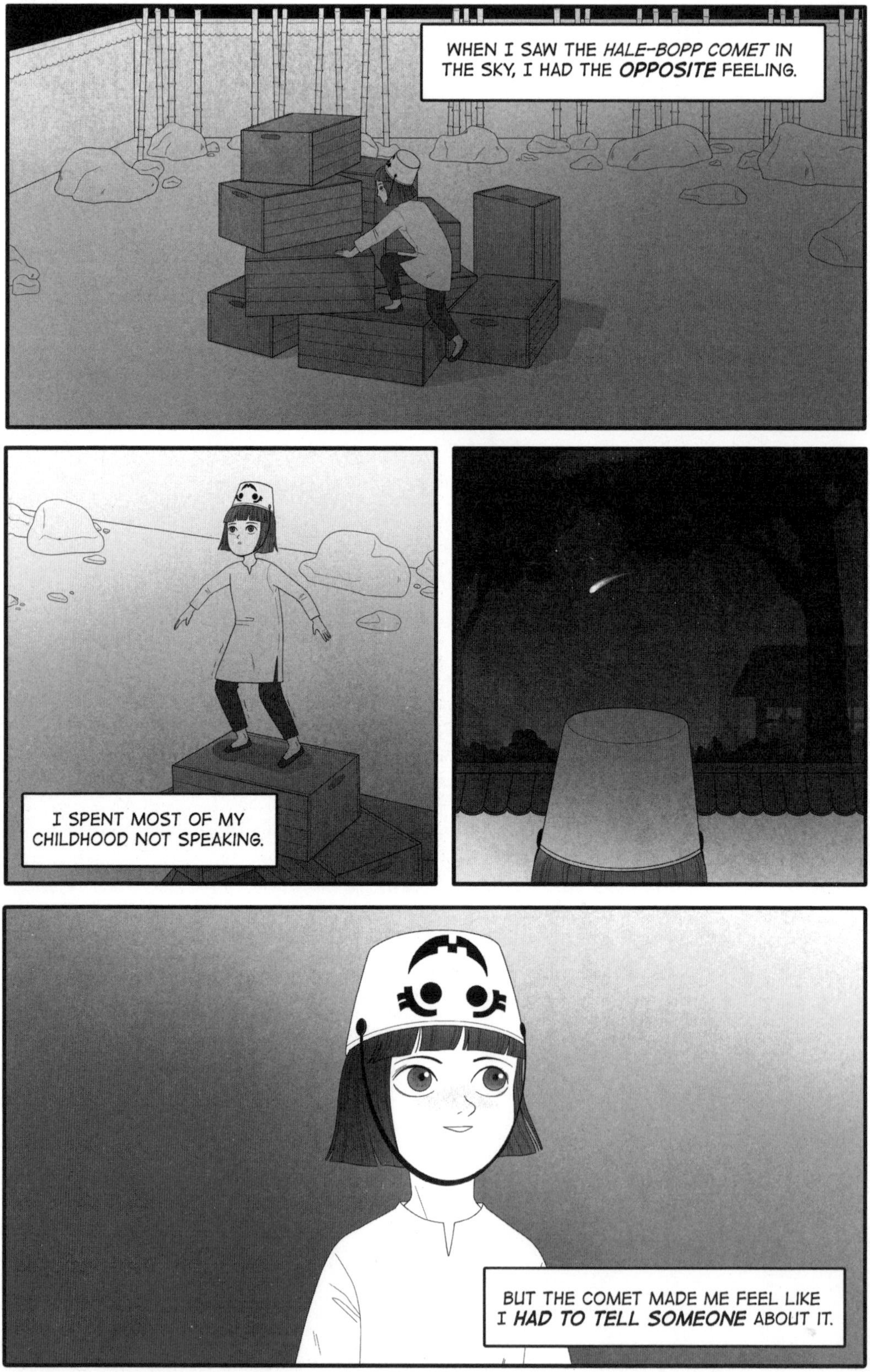
WHEN I SAW THE *HALE-BOPP COMET* IN THE SKY, I HAD THE ***OPPOSITE*** FEELING.
I SPENT MOST OF MY CHILDHOOD NOT SPEAKING.
BUT THE COMET MADE ME FEEL LIKE I ***HAD TO TELL SOMEONE*** ABOUT IT.

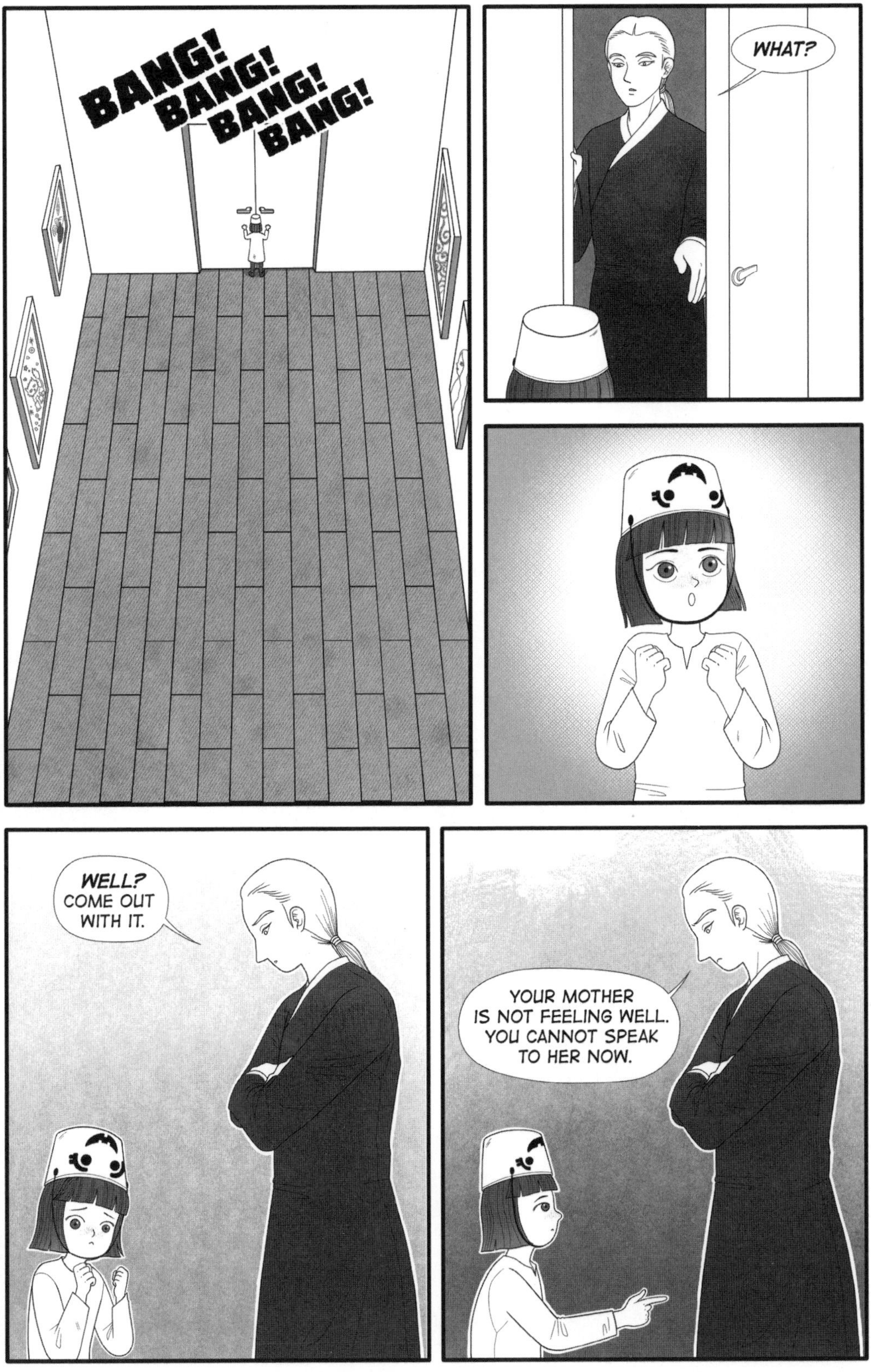
BANG! BANG! BANG! BANG!
WHAT?
WELL? COME OUT WITH IT.
YOUR MOTHER IS NOT FEELING WELL. YOU CANNOT SPEAK TO HER NOW.

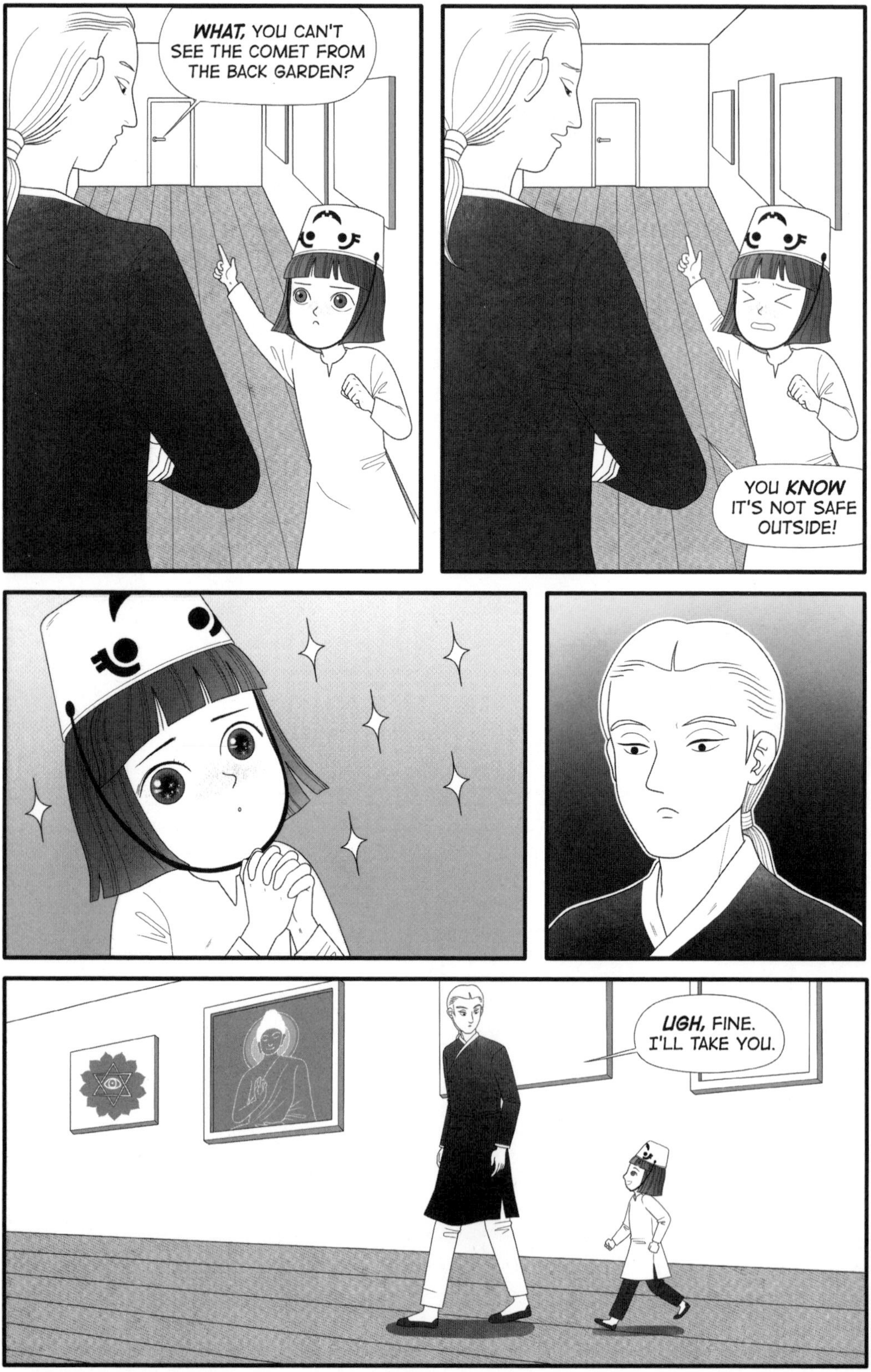
WHAT, YOU CAN'T SEE THE COMET FROM THE BACK GARDEN?
YOU KNOW IT'S NOT SAFE OUTSIDE!
UGH, FINE. I'LL TAKE YOU.

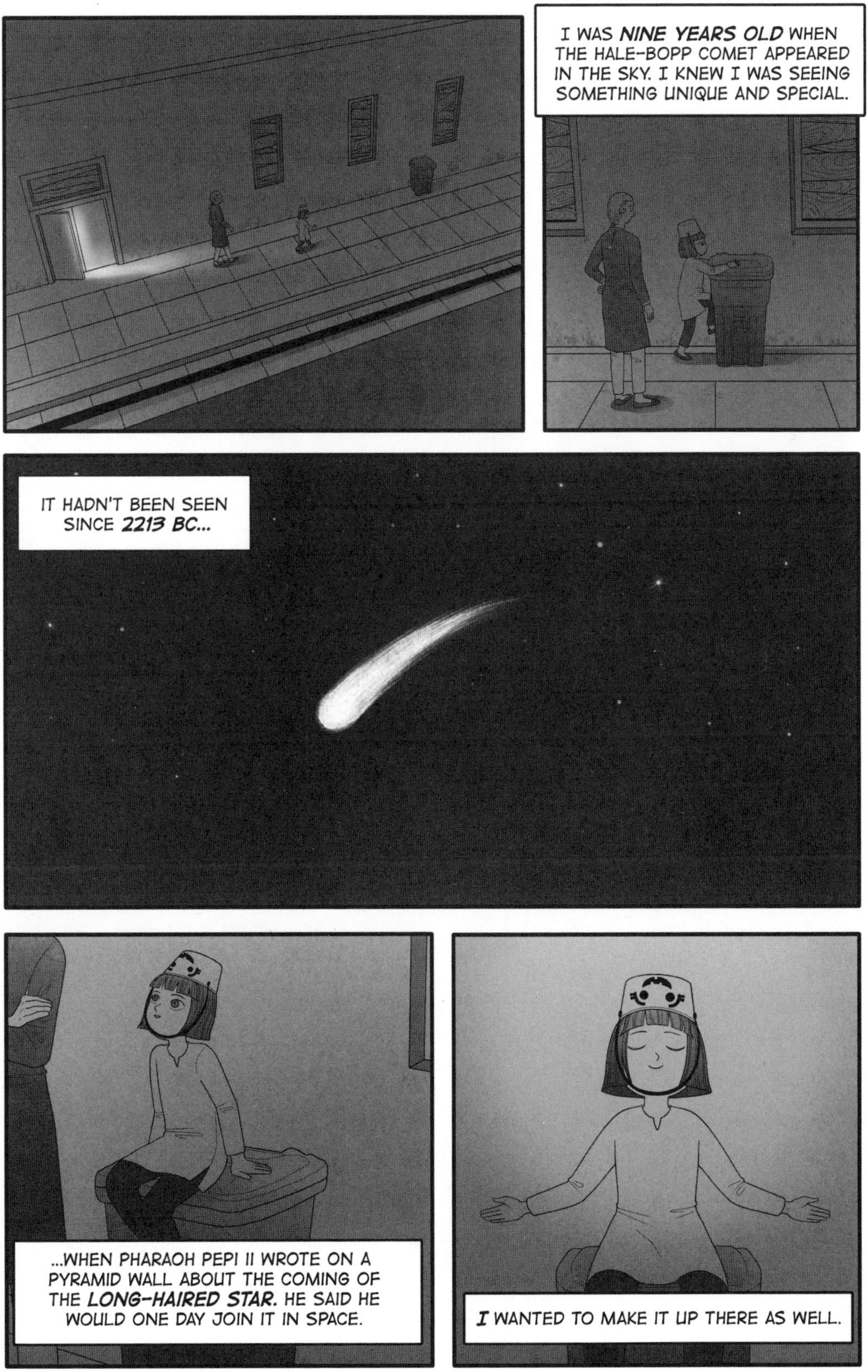
I WAS NINE YEARS OLD WHEN THE HALE-BOPP COMET APPEARED IN THE SKY. I KNEW I WAS SEEING SOMETHING UNIQUE AND SPECIAL.
IT HADN'T BEEN SEEN SINCE 2213 BC...
...WHEN PHARAOH PEPI II WROTE ON A PYRAMID WALL ABOUT THE COMING OF THE LONG-HAIRED STAR. HE SAID HE WOULD ONE DAY JOIN IT IN SPACE.
I WANTED TO MAKE IT UP THERE AS WELL.

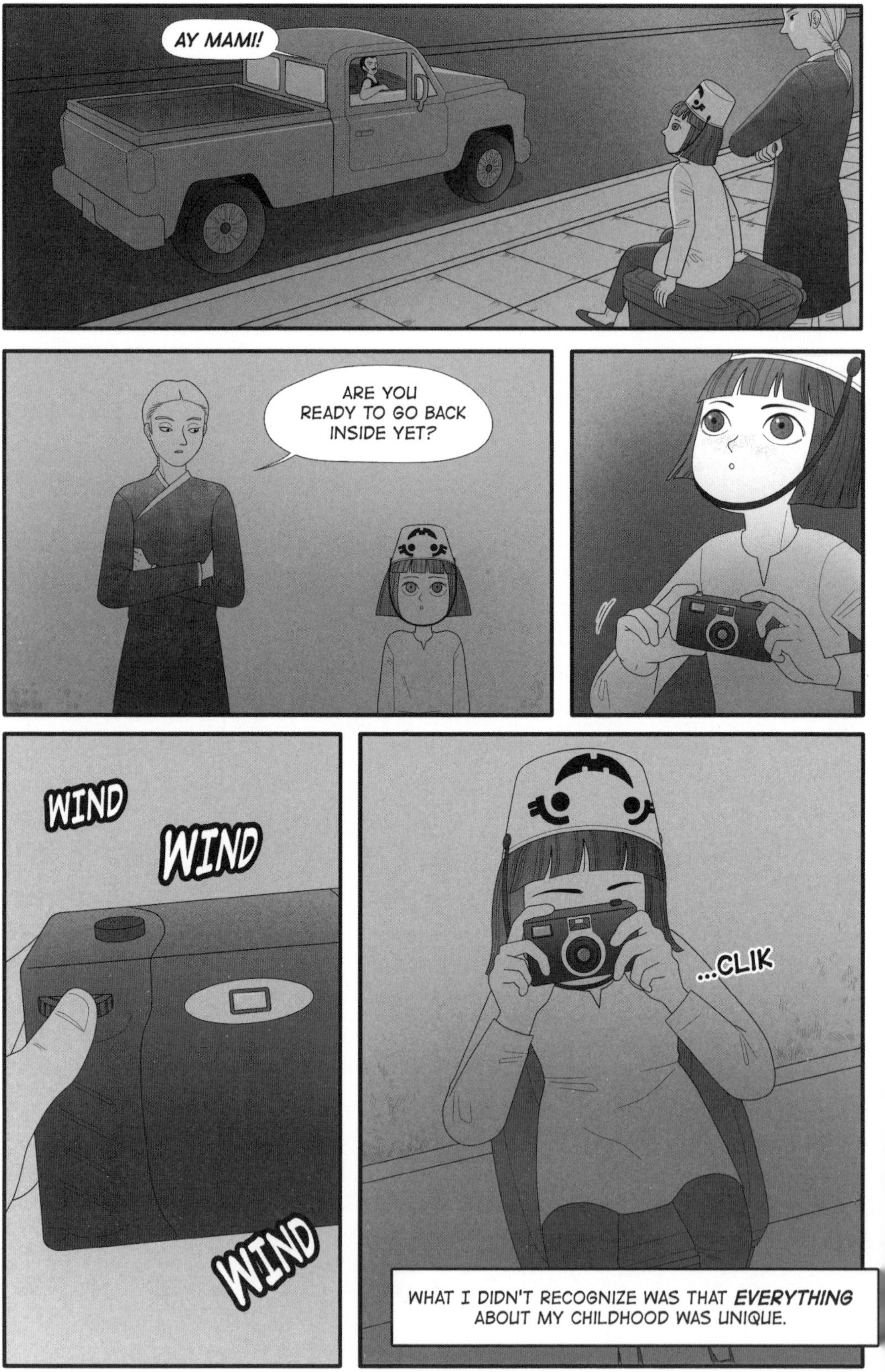
AY MAMI!
ARE YOU READY TO GO BACK INSIDE YET?
WIND
WIND
WIND
...CLIK
WHAT I DIDN'T RECOGNIZE WAS THAT *EVERYTHING* ABOUT MY CHILDHOOD WAS UNIQUE.

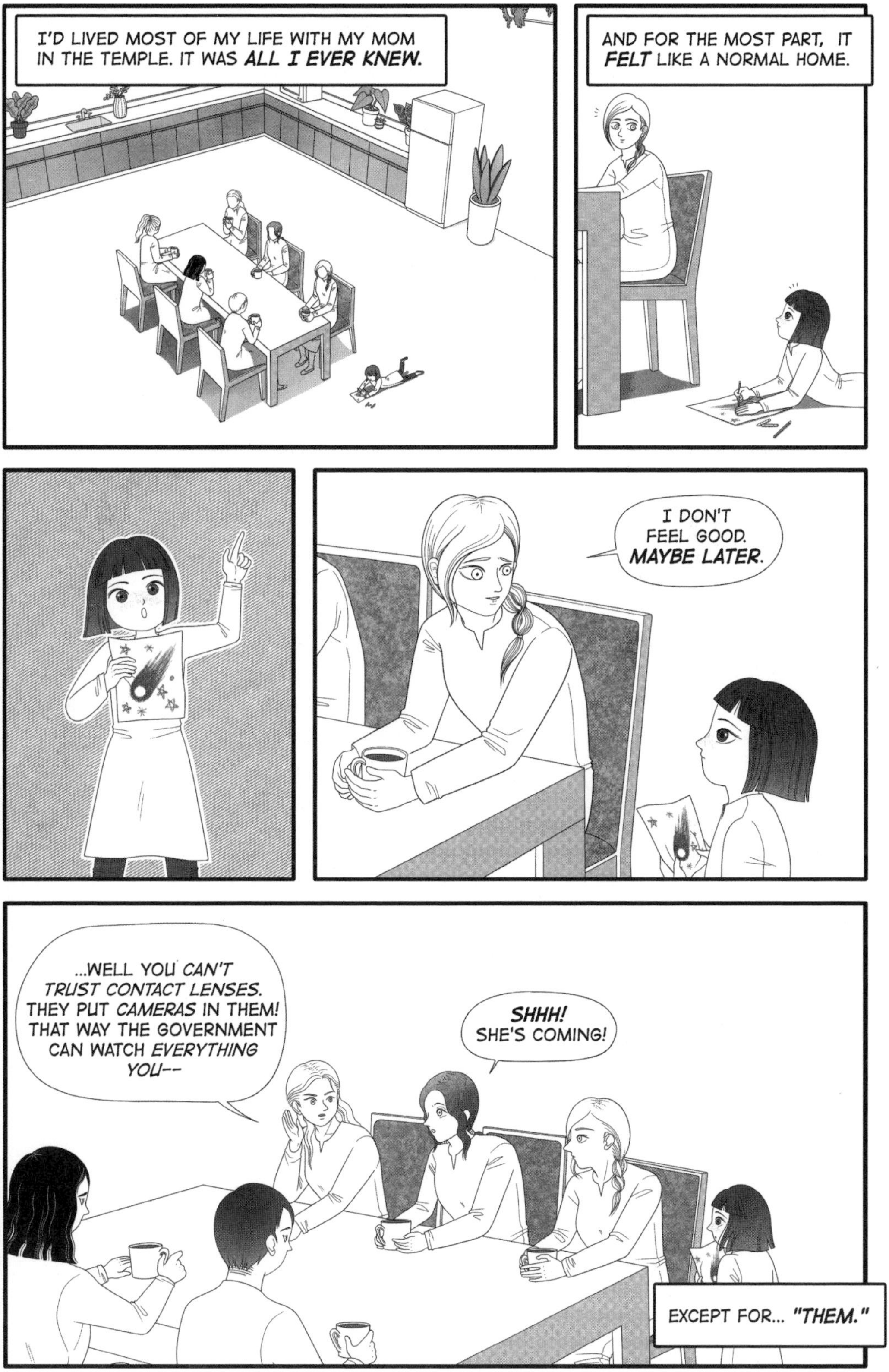
I'D LIVED MOST OF MY LIFE WITH MY MOM IN THE TEMPLE. IT WAS ALL I EVER KNEW.
AND FOR THE MOST PART, IT FELT LIKE A NORMAL HOME.
I DON'T FEEL GOOD. MAYBE LATER.
...WELL YOU CAN'T TRUST CONTACT LENSES. THEY PUT CAMERAS IN THEM! THAT WAY THE GOVERNMENT CAN WATCH EVERYTHING YOU--
SHHH! SHE'S COMING!
EXCEPT FOR... "THEM."

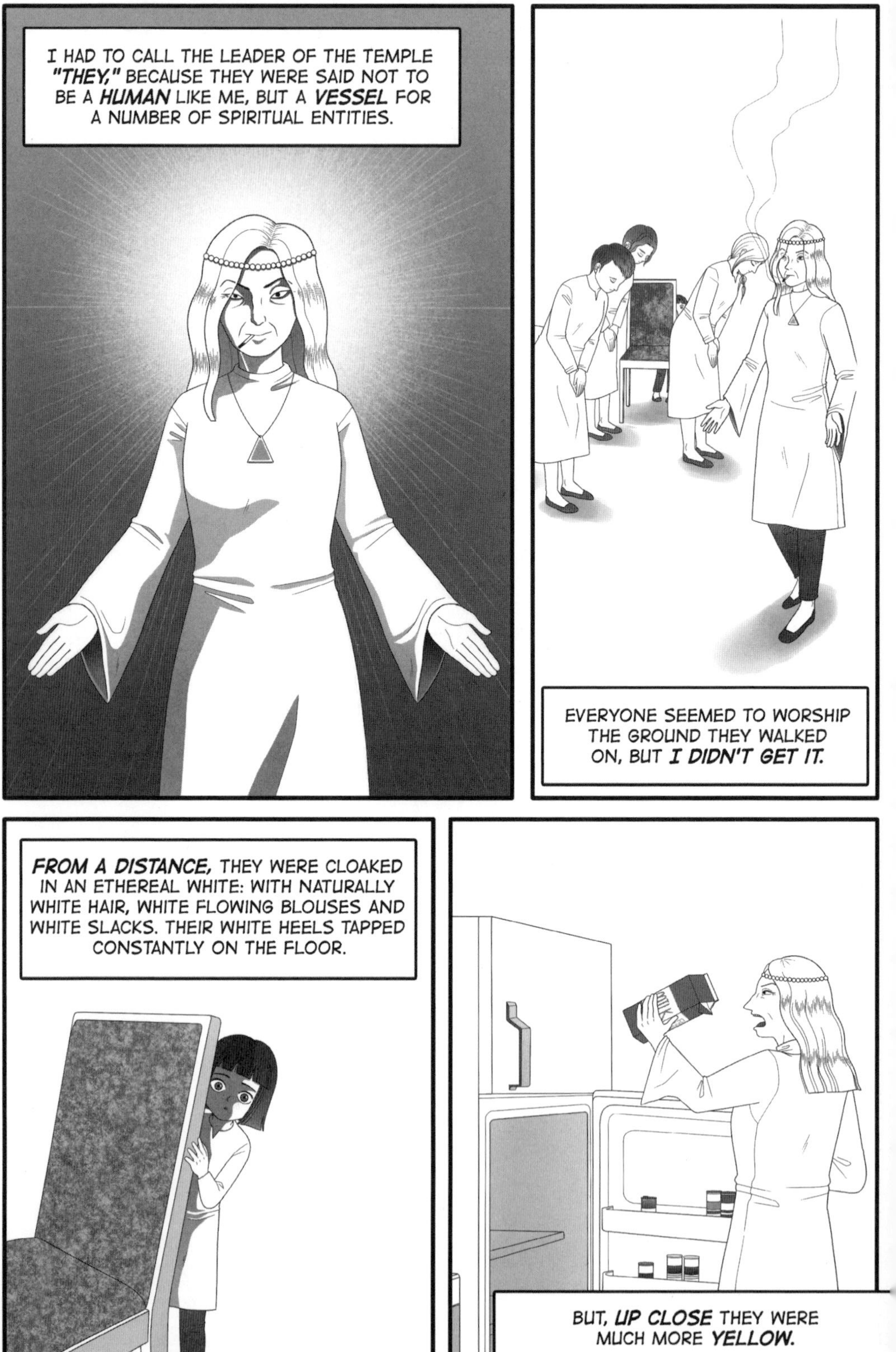
I HAD TO CALL THE LEADER OF THE TEMPLE "THEY," BECAUSE THEY WERE SAID NOT TO BE A HUMAN LIKE ME, BUT A VESSEL FOR A NUMBER OF SPIRITUAL ENTITIES.
EVERYONE SEEMED TO WORSHIP THE GROUND THEY WALKED ON, BUT I DIDN'T GET IT.
FROM A DISTANCE, THEY WERE CLOAKED IN AN ETHEREAL WHITE: WITH NATURALLY WHITE HAIR, WHITE FLOWING BLOUSES AND WHITE SLACKS. THEIR WHITE HEELS TAPPED CONSTANTLY ON THE FLOOR.
BUT, UP CLOSE THEY WERE MUCH MORE YELLOW.

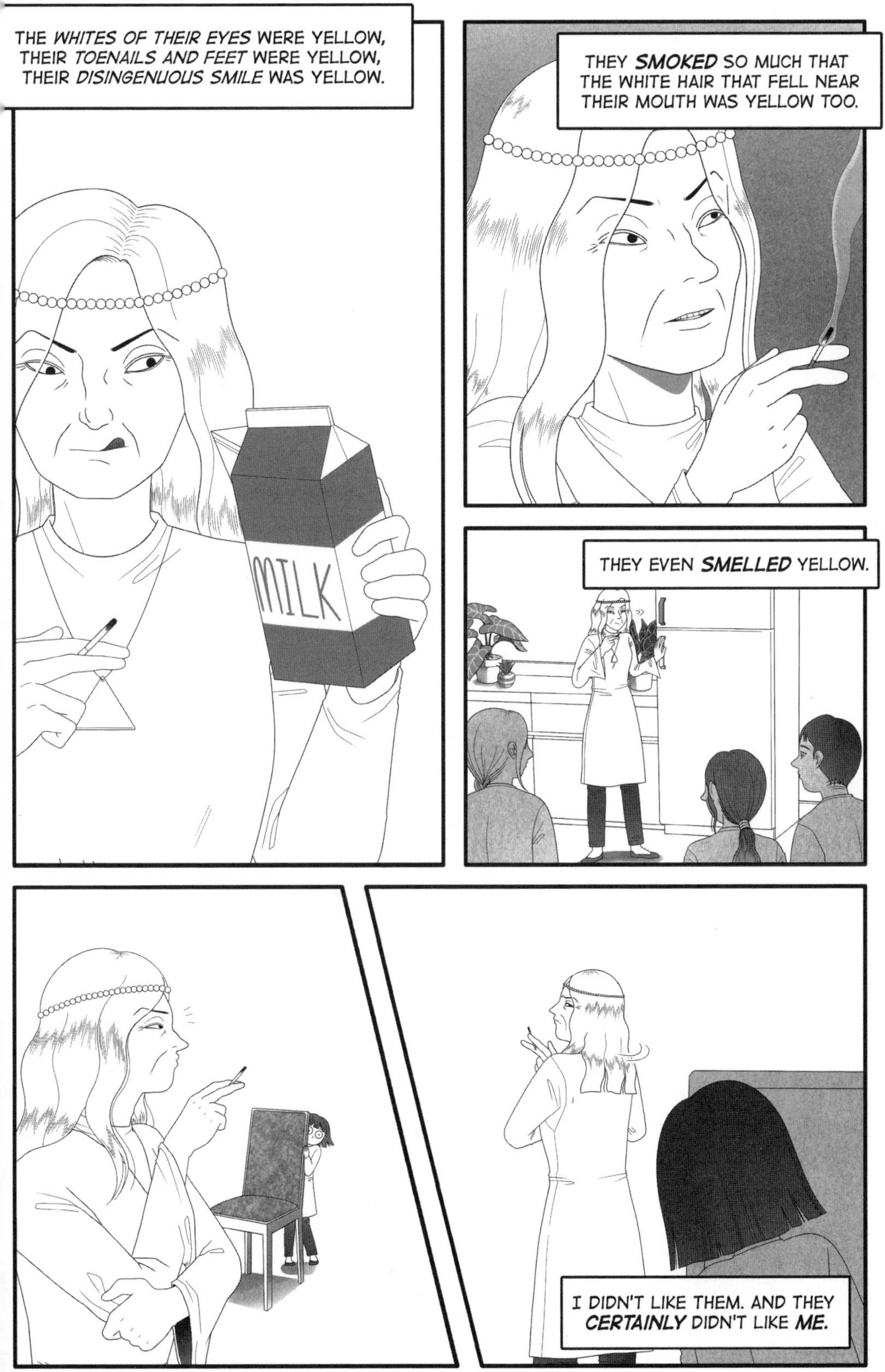
THE *WHITES OF THEIR EYES* WERE YELLOW, THEIR *TOENAILS AND FEET* WERE YELLOW, THEIR *DISINGENUOUS SMILE* WAS YELLOW.
MILK
THEY ***SMOKED*** SO MUCH THAT THE WHITE HAIR THAT FELL NEAR THEIR MOUTH WAS YELLOW TOO.
THEY EVEN ***SMELLED*** YELLOW.
I DIDN'T LIKE THEM. AND THEY ***CERTAINLY*** DIDN'T LIKE ***ME.***

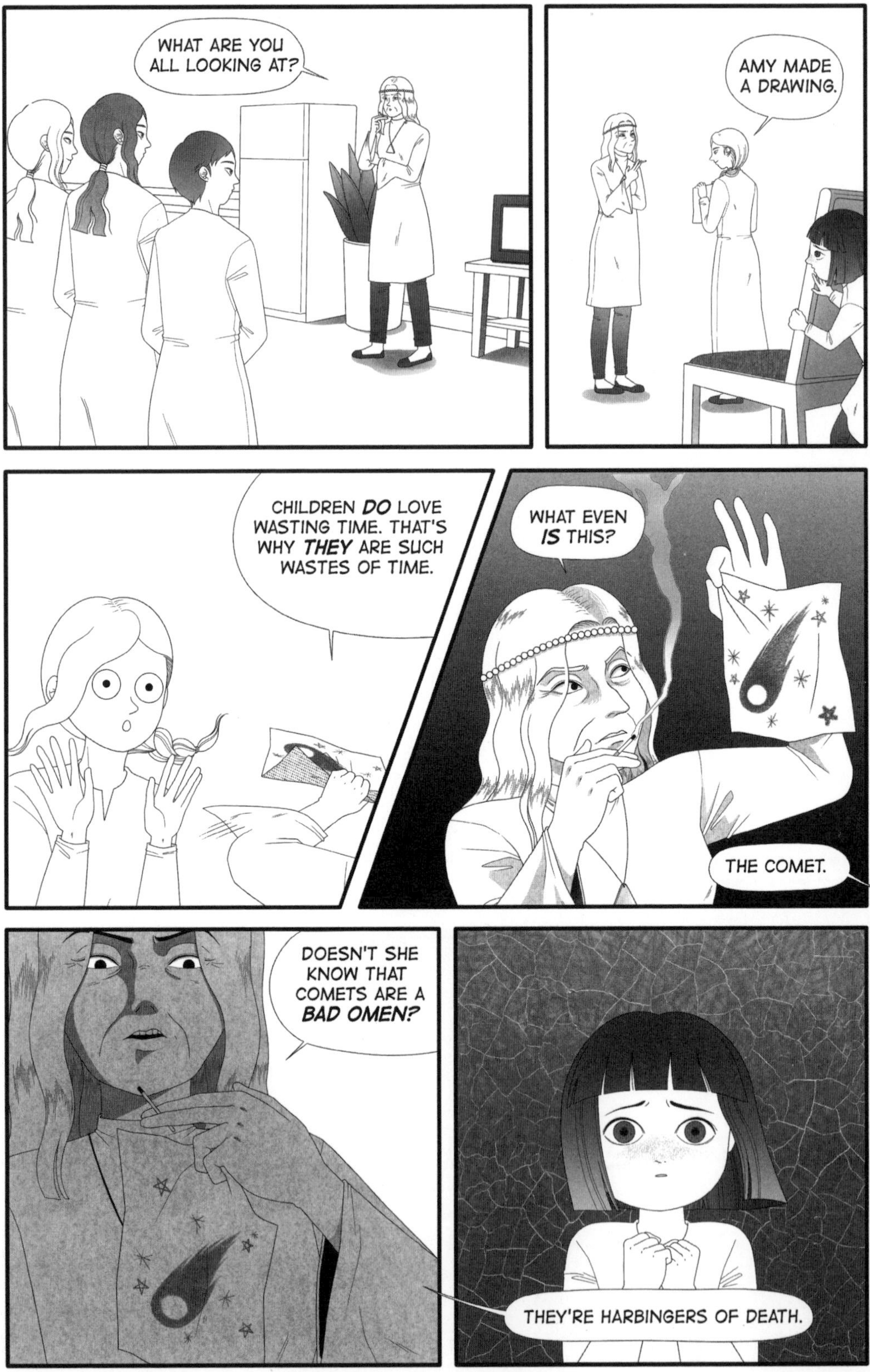
WHAT ARE YOU ALL LOOKING AT?
AMY MADE A DRAWING.
CHILDREN DO LOVE WASTING TIME. THAT'S WHY THEY ARE SUCH WASTES OF TIME.
WHAT EVEN IS THIS?
THE COMET.
DOESN'T SHE KNOW THAT COMETS ARE A BAD OMEN?
THEY'RE HARBINGERS OF DEATH.

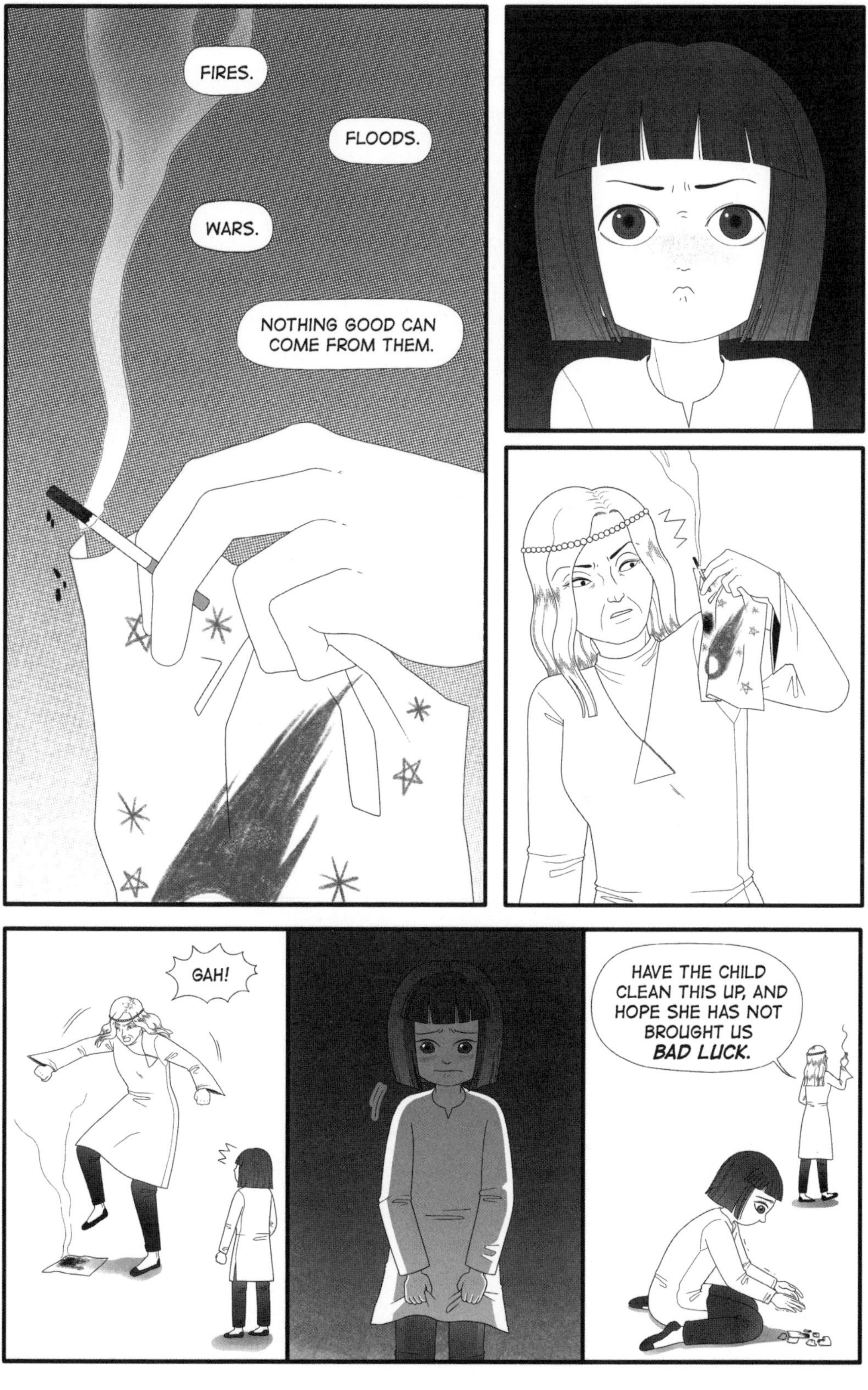
FIRES.
FLOODS.
WARS.
NOTHING GOOD CAN COME FROM THEM.
GAH!
HAVE THE CHILD CLEAN THIS UP, AND HOPE SHE HAS NOT BROUGHT US BAD LUCK.

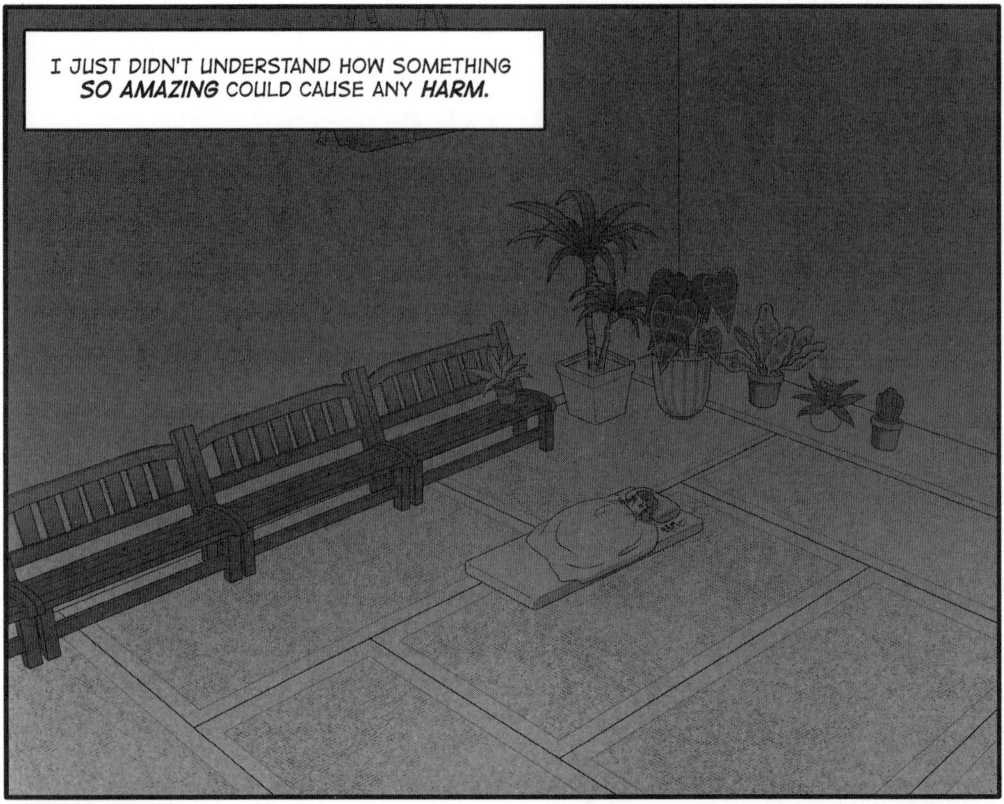
I JUST DIDN'T UNDERSTAND HOW SOMETHING SO AMAZING COULD CAUSE ANY HARM.

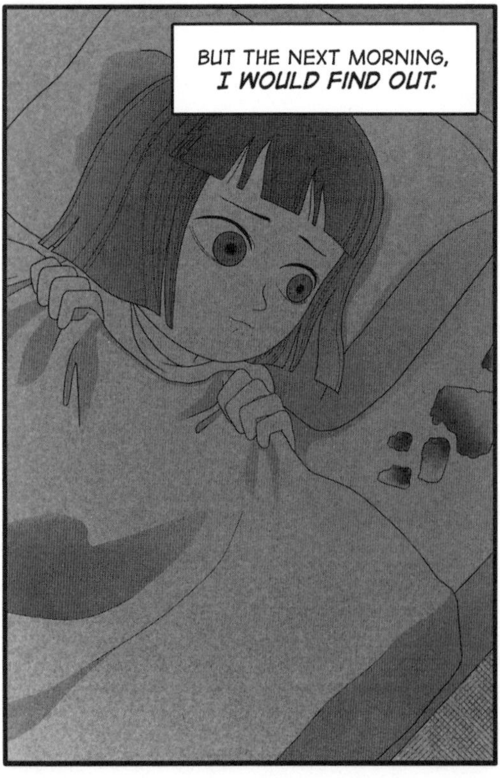
BUT THE NEXT MORNING, I WOULD FIND OUT.

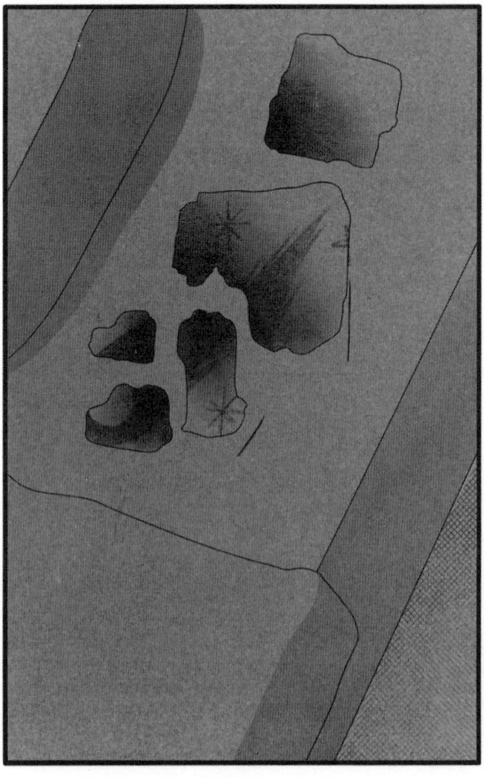

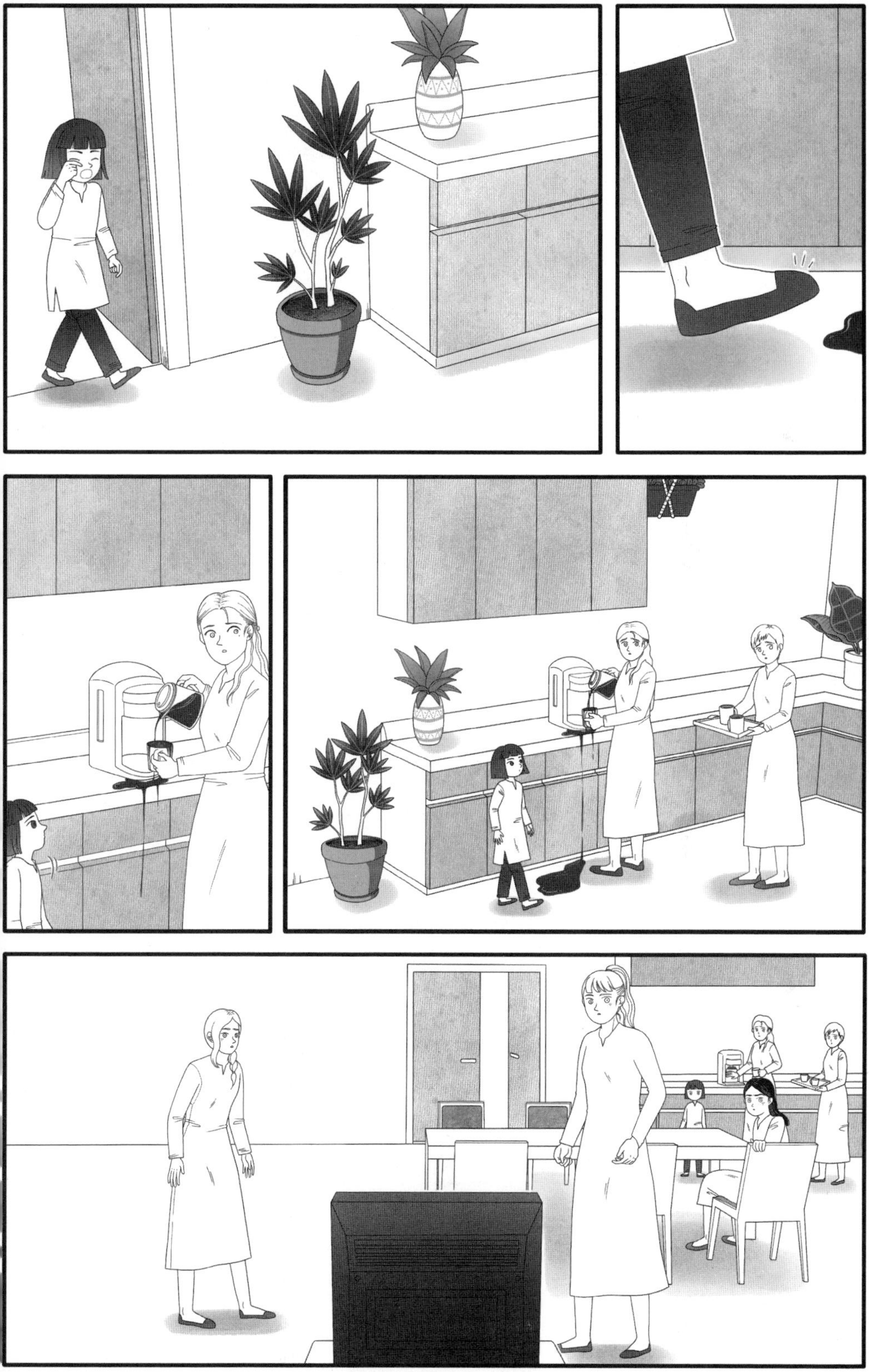

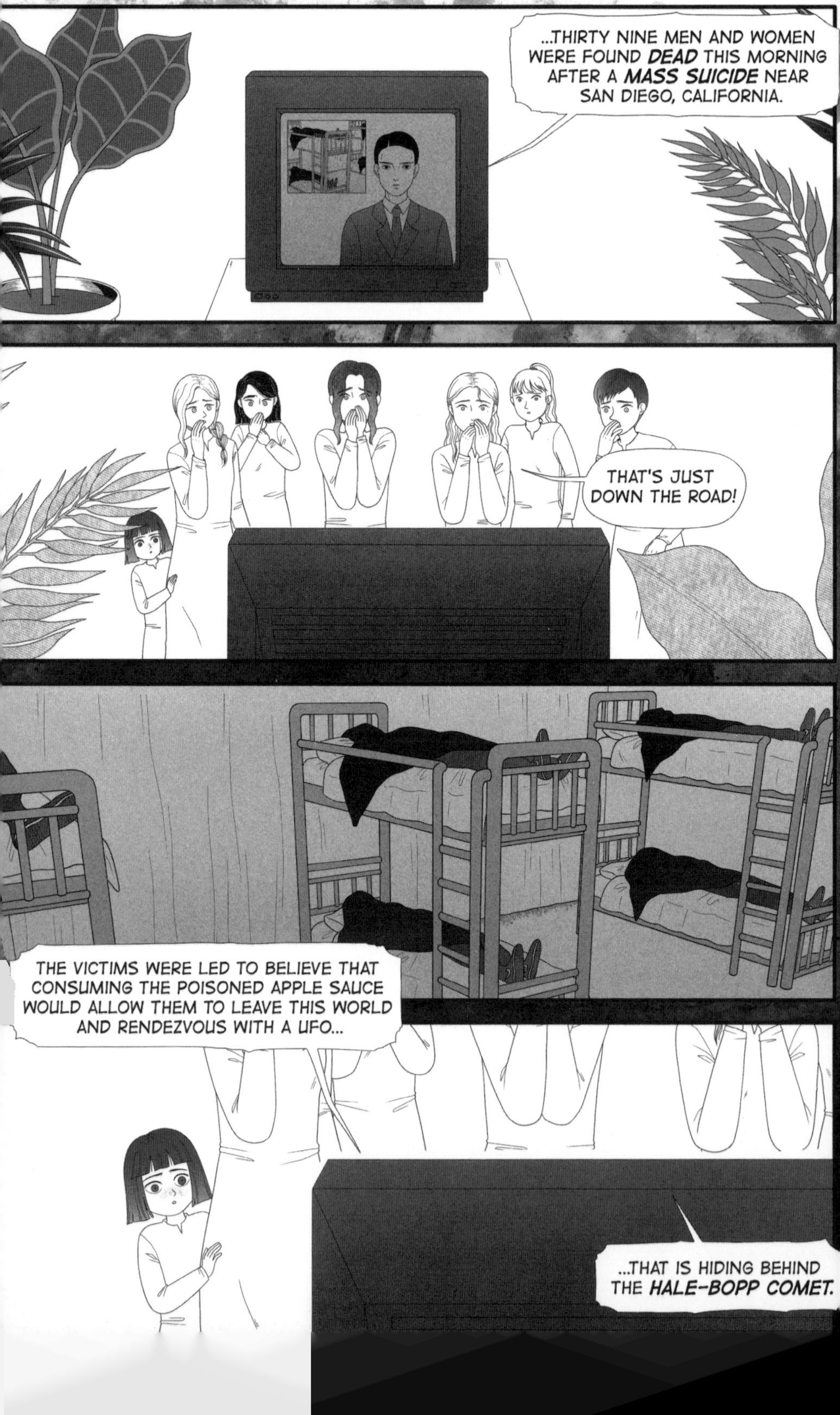
...THIRTY NINE MEN AND WOMEN WERE FOUND DEAD THIS MORNING AFTER A MASS SUICIDE NEAR SAN DIEGO, CALIFORNIA.
THAT'S JUST DOWN THE ROAD!
THE VICTIMS WERE LED TO BELIEVE THAT CONSUMING THE POISONED APPLE SAUCE WOULD ALLOW THEM TO LEAVE THIS WORLD AND RENDEZVOUS WITH A UFO...
...THAT IS HIDING BEHIND THE HALE-BOPP COMET.

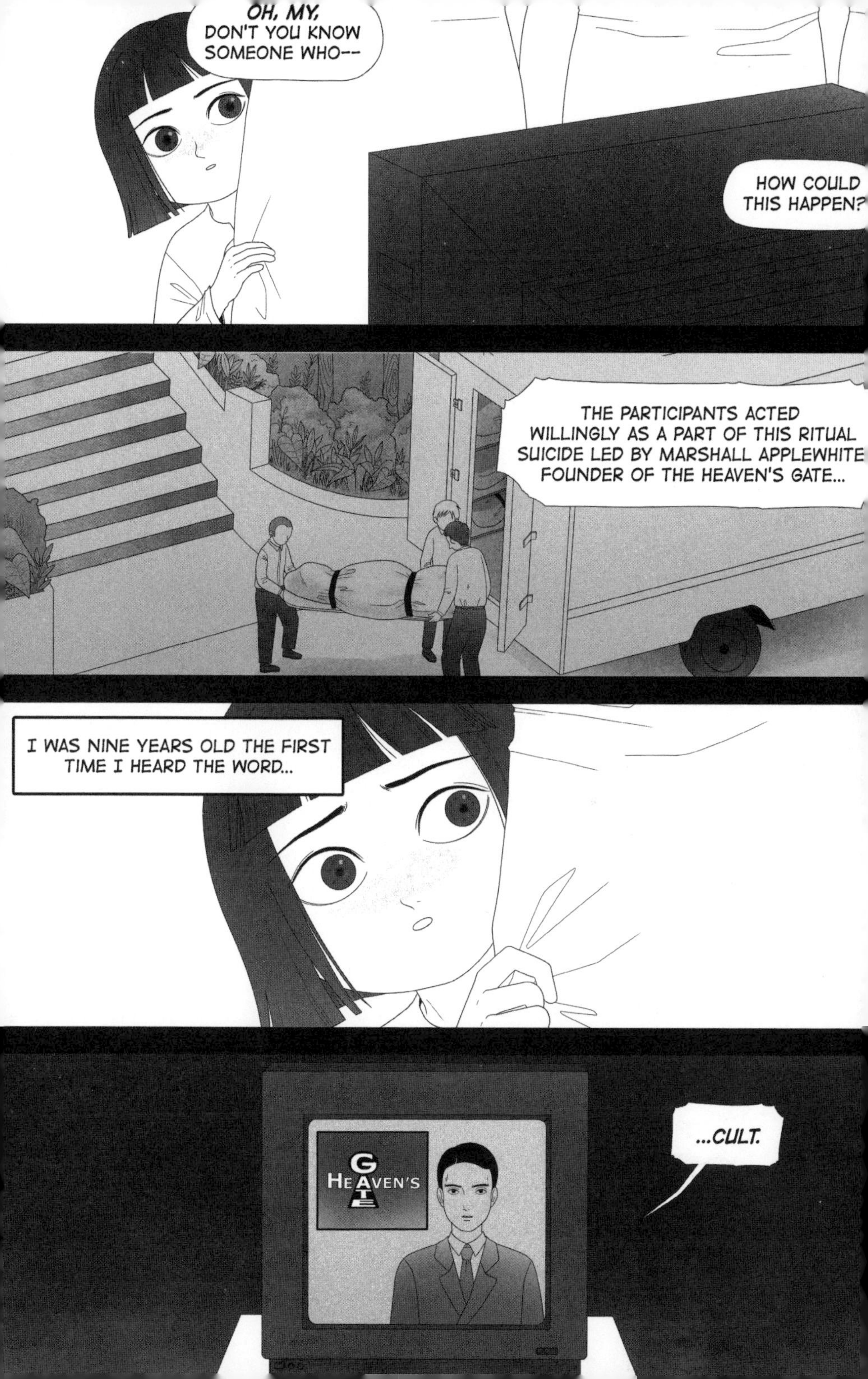
OH, MY, DON'T YOU KNOW SOMEONE WHO--
HOW COULD THIS HAPPEN?
THE PARTICIPANTS ACTED WILLINGLY AS A PART OF THIS RITUAL SUICIDE LED BY MARSHALL APPLEWHITE FOUNDER OF THE HEAVEN'S GATE...
I WAS NINE YEARS OLD THE FIRST TIME I HEARD THE WORD...
HEAVEN'S GATE
...CULT.

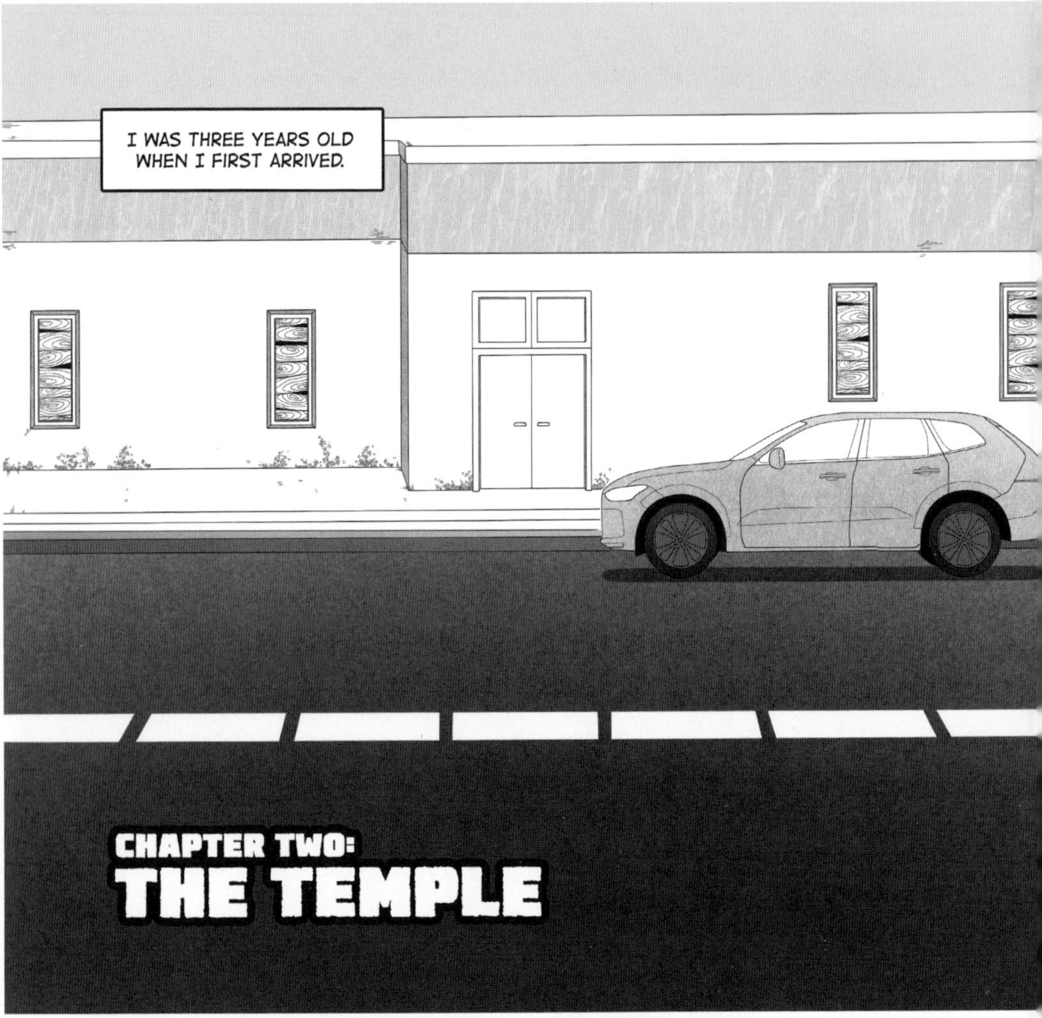
I WAS THREE YEARS OLD WHEN I FIRST ARRIVED.
CHAPTER TWO:
THE TEMPLE

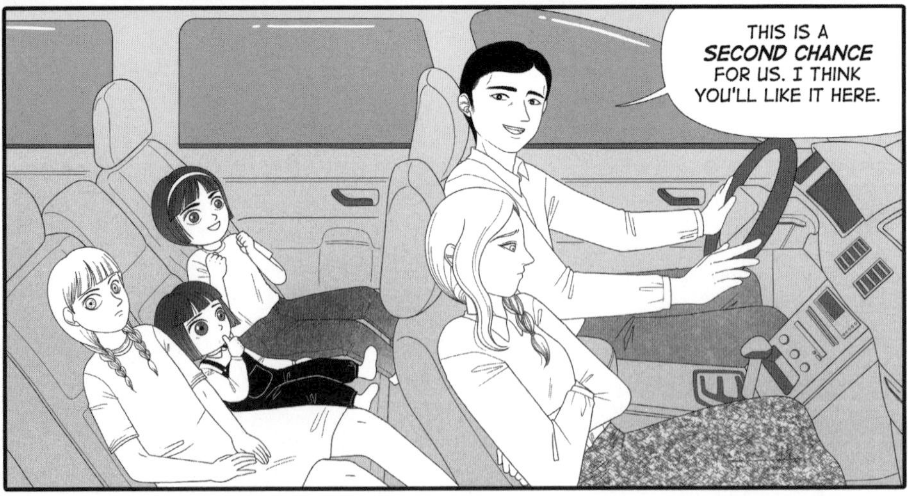
THIS IS A *SECOND CHANCE* FOR US. I THINK YOU'LL LIKE IT HERE.

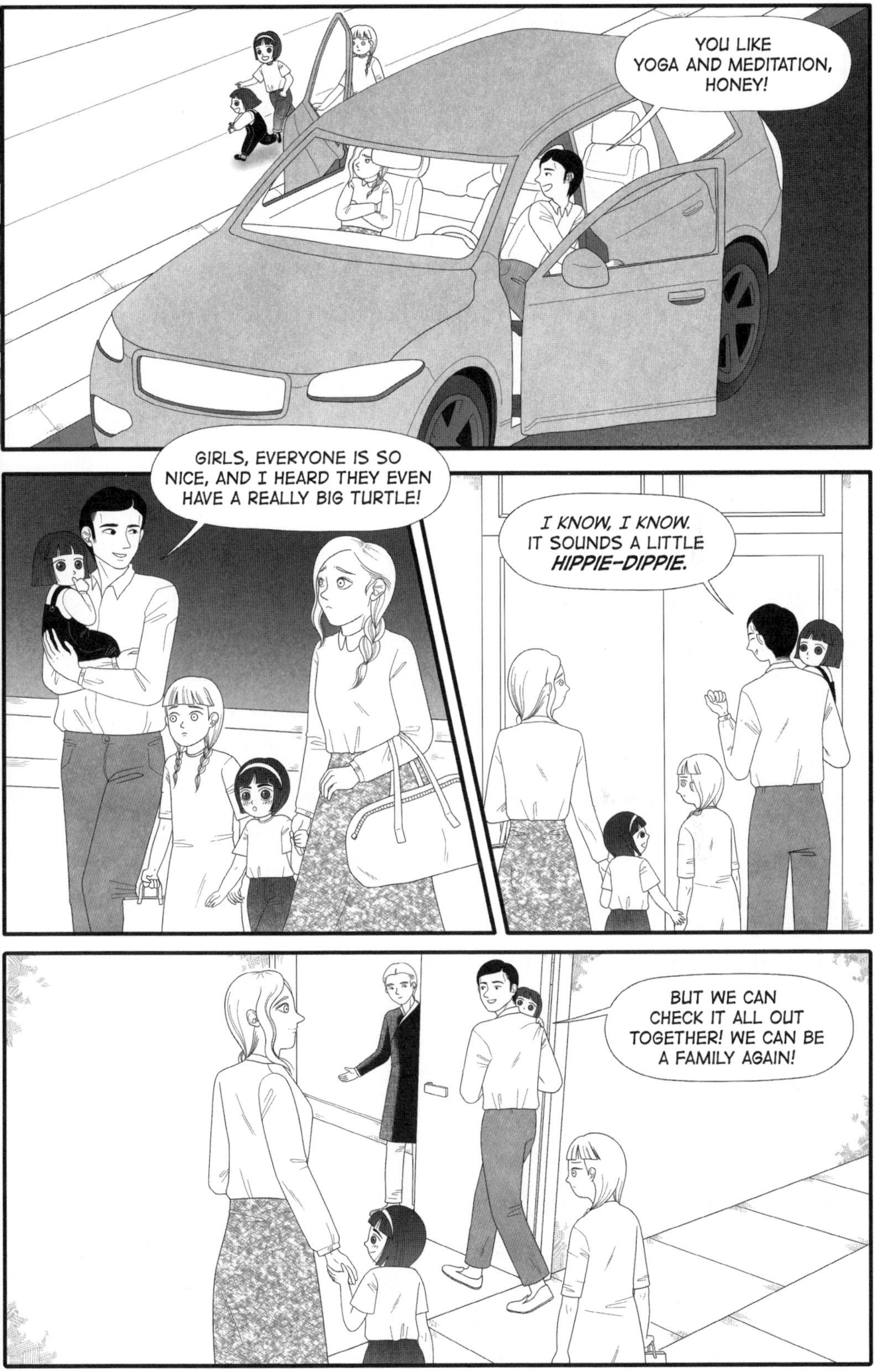
YOU LIKE YOGA AND MEDITATION, HONEY!
GIRLS, EVERYONE IS SO NICE, AND I HEARD THEY EVEN HAVE A REALLY BIG TURTLE!
I KNOW, I KNOW. IT SOUNDS A LITTLE *HIPPIE-DIPPIE.*
BUT WE CAN CHECK IT ALL OUT TOGETHER! WE CAN BE A FAMILY AGAIN!

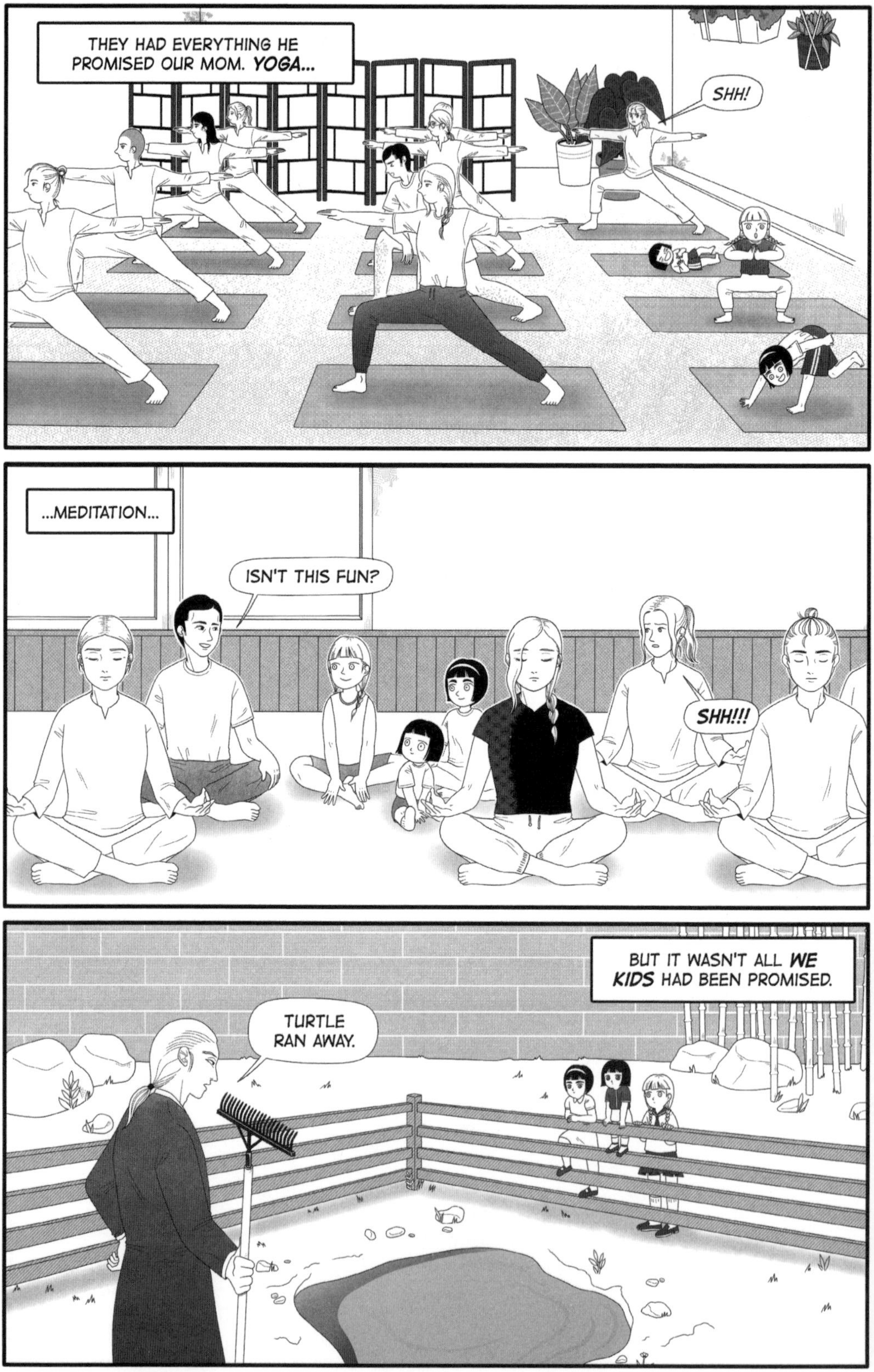
THEY HAD EVERYTHING HE PROMISED OUR MOM. ***YOGA...***
SHH!
...MEDITATION...
ISN'T THIS FUN?
SHH!!!
BUT IT WASN'T ALL ***WE KIDS*** HAD BEEN PROMISED.
TURTLE RAN AWAY.

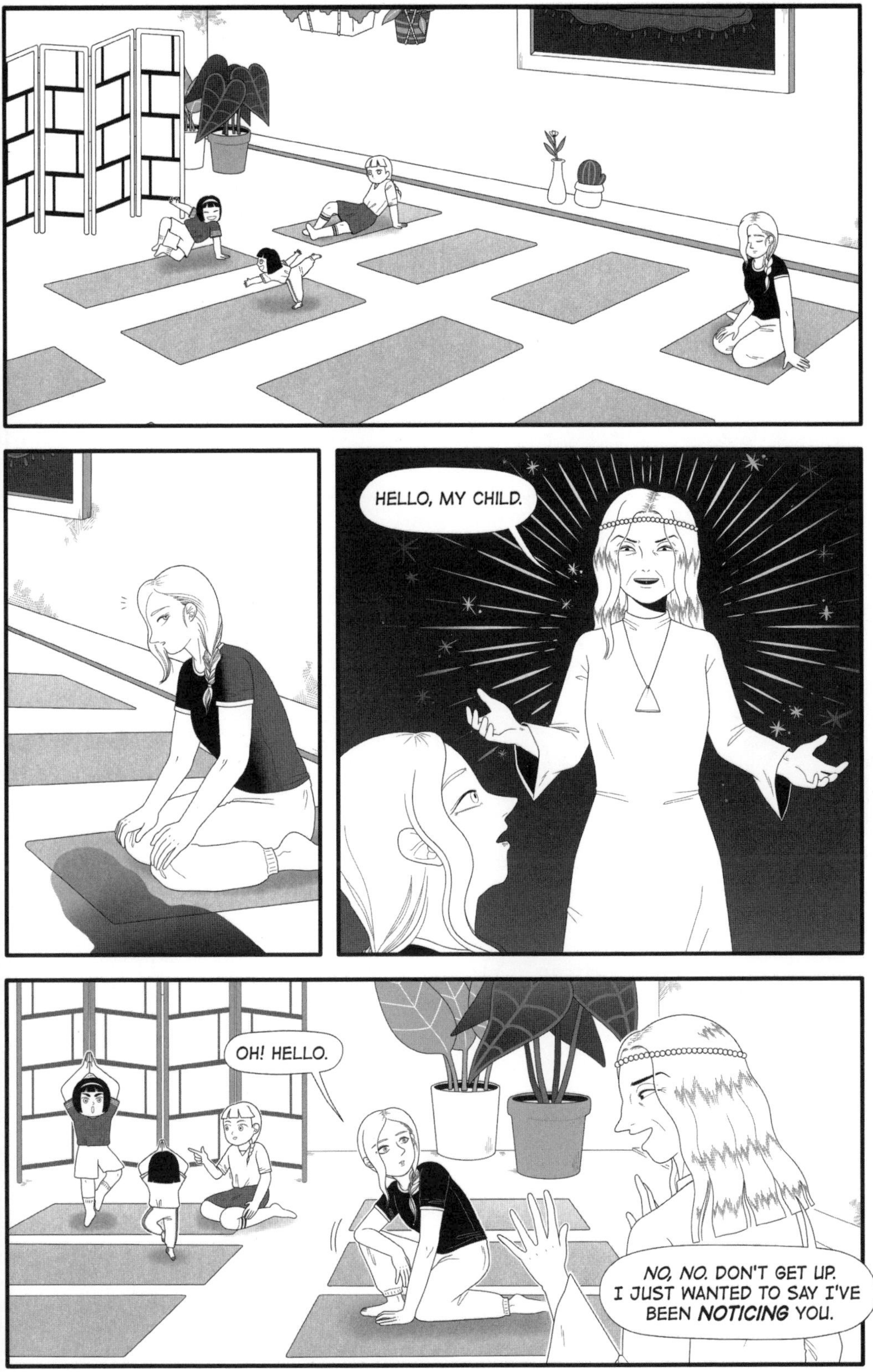
HELLO, MY CHILD.
OH! HELLO.
NO, NO. DON'T GET UP. I JUST WANTED TO SAY I'VE BEEN NOTICING YOU.

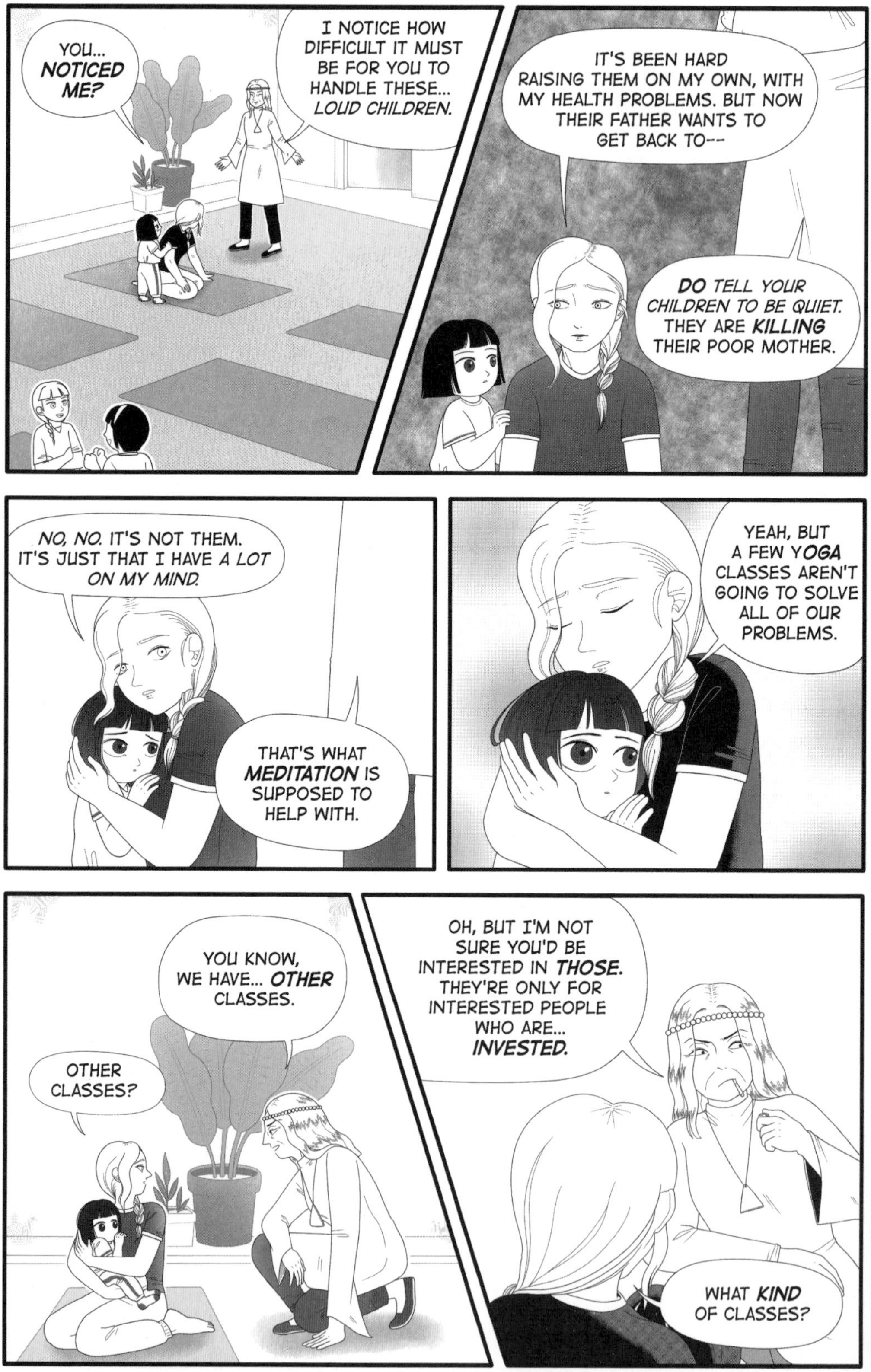
YOU... NOTICED ME?
I NOTICE HOW DIFFICULT IT MUST BE FOR YOU TO HANDLE THESE... LOUD CHILDREN.
IT'S BEEN HARD RAISING THEM ON MY OWN, WITH MY HEALTH PROBLEMS. BUT NOW THEIR FATHER WANTS TO GET BACK TO--
DO TELL YOUR CHILDREN TO BE QUIET. THEY ARE KILLING THEIR POOR MOTHER.
NO, NO. IT'S NOT THEM. IT'S JUST THAT I HAVE A LOT ON MY MIND.
THAT'S WHAT MEDITATION IS SUPPOSED TO HELP WITH.
YEAH, BUT A FEW YOGA CLASSES AREN'T GOING TO SOLVE ALL OF OUR PROBLEMS.
YOU KNOW, WE HAVE... OTHER CLASSES.
OTHER CLASSES?
OH, BUT I'M NOT SURE YOU'D BE INTERESTED IN THOSE. THEY'RE ONLY FOR INTERESTED PEOPLE WHO ARE... INVESTED.
WHAT KIND OF CLASSES?

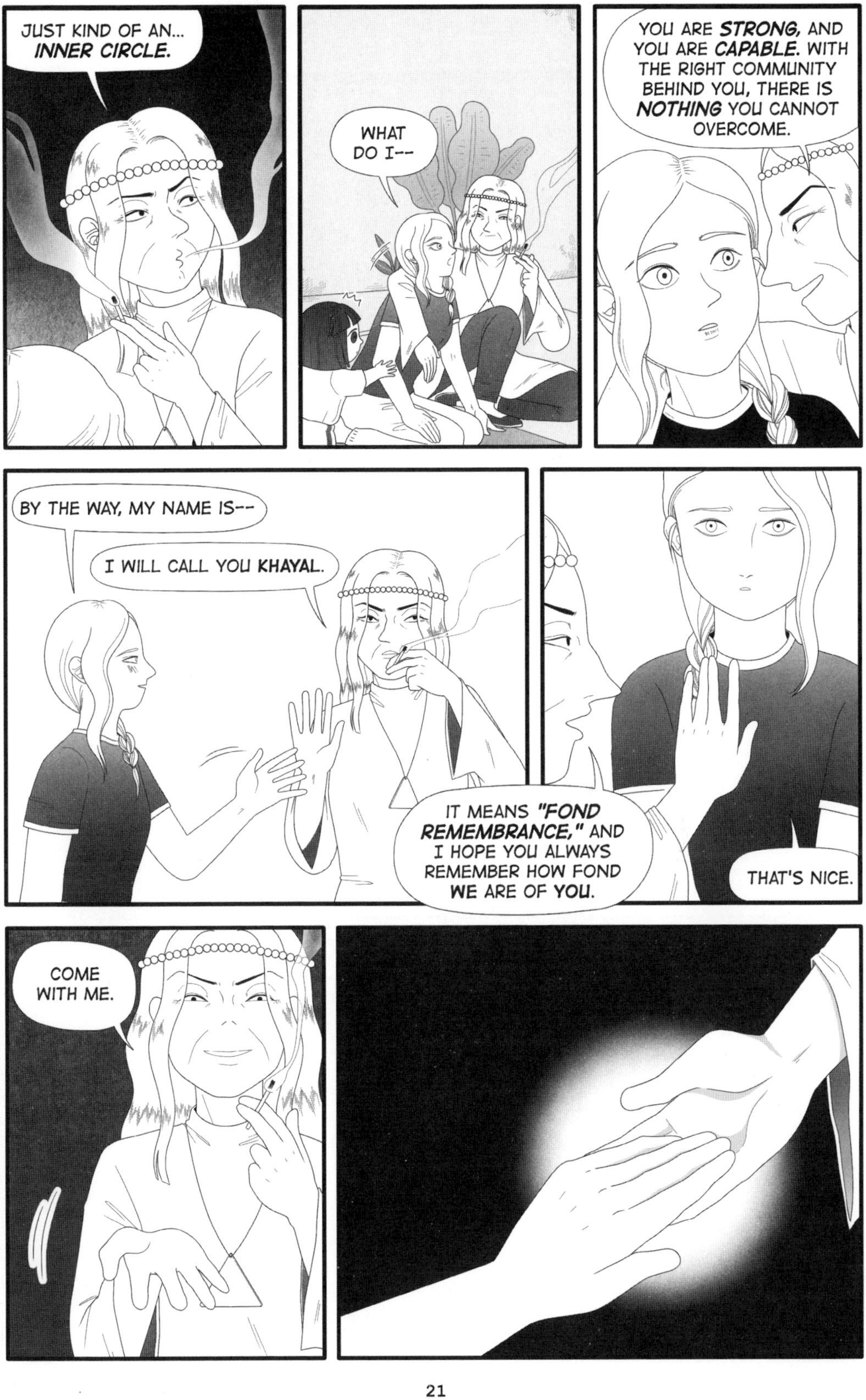
JUST KIND OF AN... *INNER CIRCLE.*
WHAT DO I--
YOU ARE ***STRONG,*** AND YOU ARE ***CAPABLE.*** WITH THE RIGHT COMMUNITY BEHIND YOU, THERE IS ***NOTHING*** YOU CANNOT OVERCOME.
BY THE WAY, MY NAME IS--
I WILL CALL YOU **KHAYAL.**
IT MEANS ***"FOND REMEMBRANCE,"*** AND I HOPE YOU ALWAYS REMEMBER HOW FOND **WE** ARE OF **YOU.**
THAT'S NICE.
COME WITH ME.

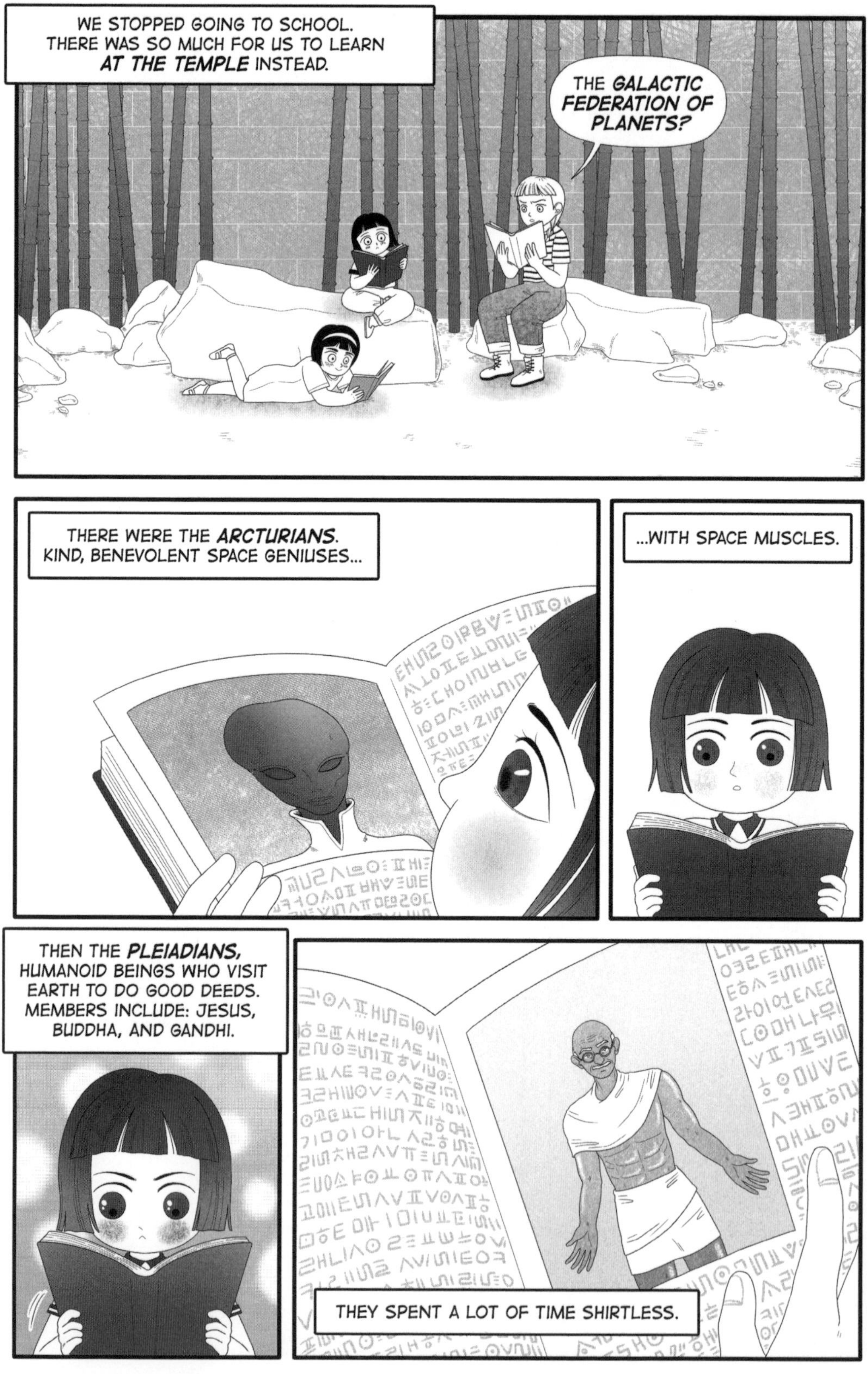
WE STOPPED GOING TO SCHOOL. THERE WAS SO MUCH FOR US TO LEARN *AT THE TEMPLE* INSTEAD.
THE *GALACTIC FEDERATION OF PLANETS?*
THERE WERE THE *ARCTURIANS*. KIND, BENEVOLENT SPACE GENIUSES...
...WITH SPACE MUSCLES.
THEN THE *PLEIADIANS,* HUMANOID BEINGS WHO VISIT EARTH TO DO GOOD DEEDS. MEMBERS INCLUDE: JESUS, BUDDHA, AND GANDHI.
THEY SPENT A LOT OF TIME SHIRTLESS.

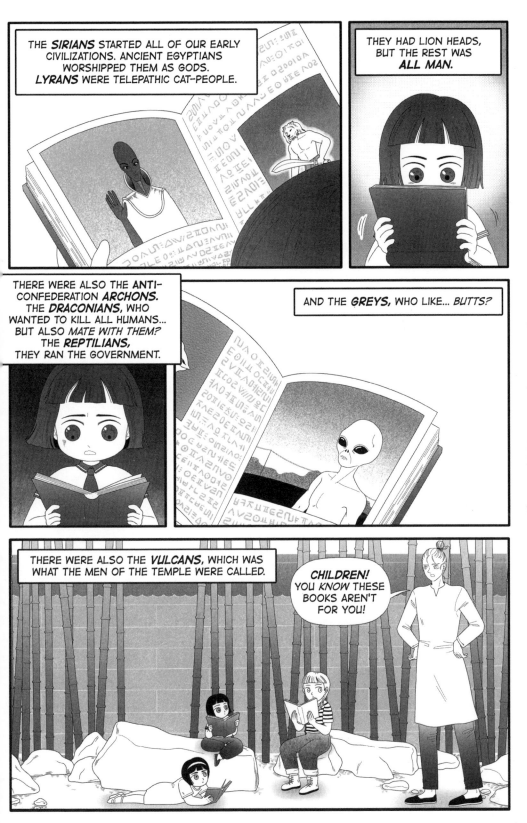

THE **SIRIANS** STARTED ALL OF OUR EARLY CIVILIZATIONS. ANCIENT EGYPTIANS WORSHIPPED THEM AS GODS. *LYRANS* WERE TELEPATHIC CAT-PEOPLE.

THEY HAD LION HEADS, BUT THE REST WAS ***ALL MAN.***

THERE WERE ALSO THE **ANTI-CONFEDERATION ARCHONS.** THE *DRACONIANS,* WHO WANTED TO KILL ALL HUMANS... BUT ALSO *MATE WITH THEM?* THE **REPTILIANS,** THEY RAN THE GOVERNMENT.

AND THE **GREYS,** WHO LIKE... *BUTTS?*

THERE WERE ALSO THE **VULCANS,** WHICH WAS WHAT THE MEN OF THE TEMPLE WERE CALLED.

CHILDREN! YOU *KNOW* THESE BOOKS AREN'T FOR YOU!

23

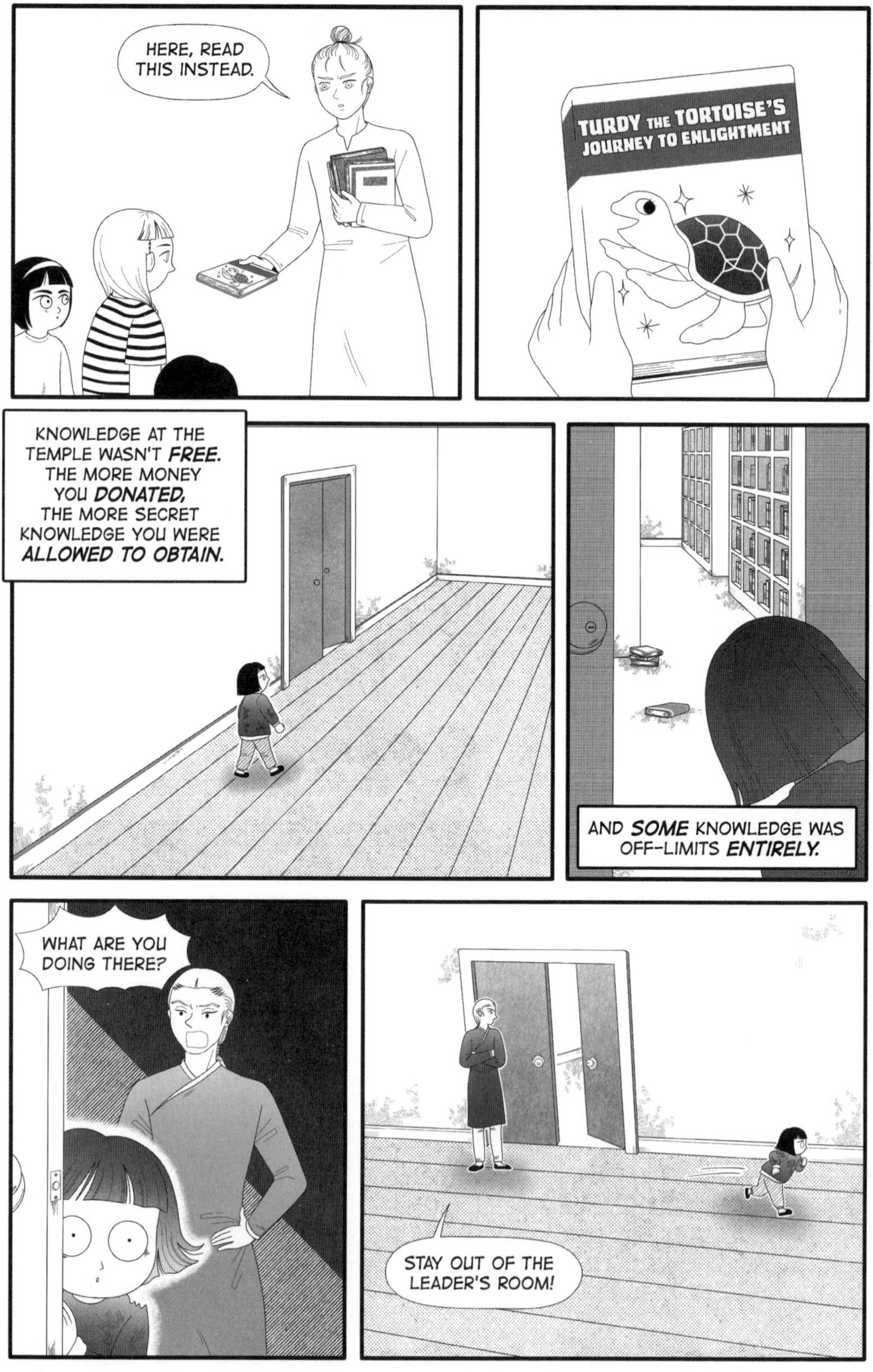
HERE, READ THIS INSTEAD.
TURDY THE TORTOISE'S JOURNEY TO ENLIGHTMENT
KNOWLEDGE AT THE TEMPLE WASN'T FREE. THE MORE MONEY YOU DONATED, THE MORE SECRET KNOWLEDGE YOU WERE ALLOWED TO OBTAIN.
AND SOME KNOWLEDGE WAS OFF-LIMITS ENTIRELY.
WHAT ARE YOU DOING THERE?
STAY OUT OF THE LEADER'S ROOM!

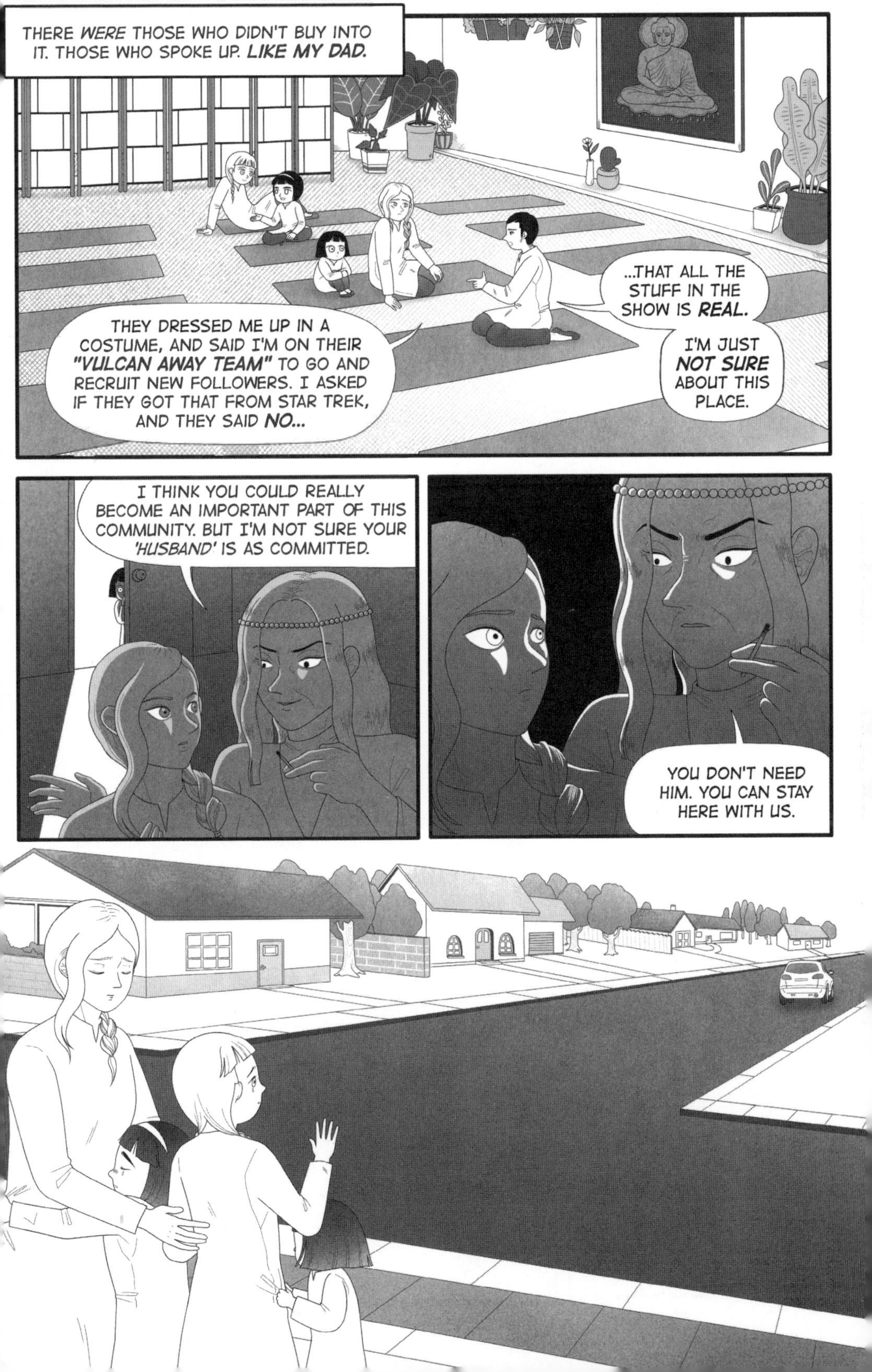

THERE WERE THOSE WHO DIDN'T BUY INTO IT. THOSE WHO SPOKE UP. LIKE MY DAD.
THEY DRESSED ME UP IN A COSTUME, AND SAID I'M ON THEIR "VULCAN AWAY TEAM" TO GO AND RECRUIT NEW FOLLOWERS. I ASKED IF THEY GOT THAT FROM STAR TREK, AND THEY SAID NO...
...THAT ALL THE STUFF IN THE SHOW IS REAL.
I'M JUST NOT SURE ABOUT THIS PLACE.
I THINK YOU COULD REALLY BECOME AN IMPORTANT PART OF THIS COMMUNITY. BUT I'M NOT SURE YOUR 'HUSBAND' IS AS COMMITTED.
YOU DON'T NEED HIM. YOU CAN STAY HERE WITH US.

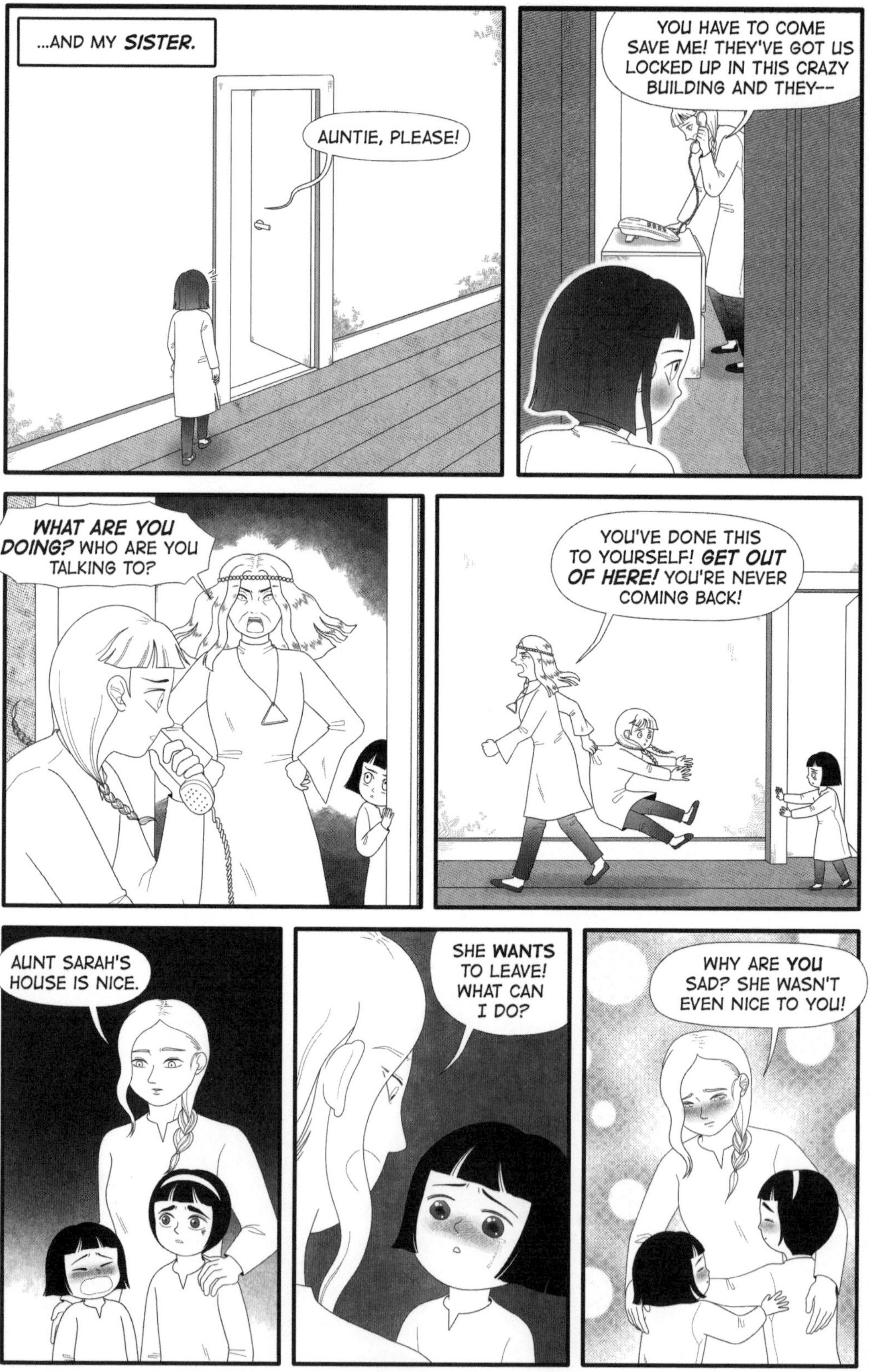
...AND MY SISTER.
AUNTIE, PLEASE!
YOU HAVE TO COME SAVE ME! THEY'VE GOT US LOCKED UP IN THIS CRAZY BUILDING AND THEY--
WHAT ARE YOU DOING? WHO ARE YOU TALKING TO?
YOU'VE DONE THIS TO YOURSELF! GET OUT OF HERE! YOU'RE NEVER COMING BACK!
AUNT SARAH'S HOUSE IS NICE.
SHE WANTS TO LEAVE! WHAT CAN I DO?
WHY ARE YOU SAD? SHE WASN'T EVEN NICE TO YOU!

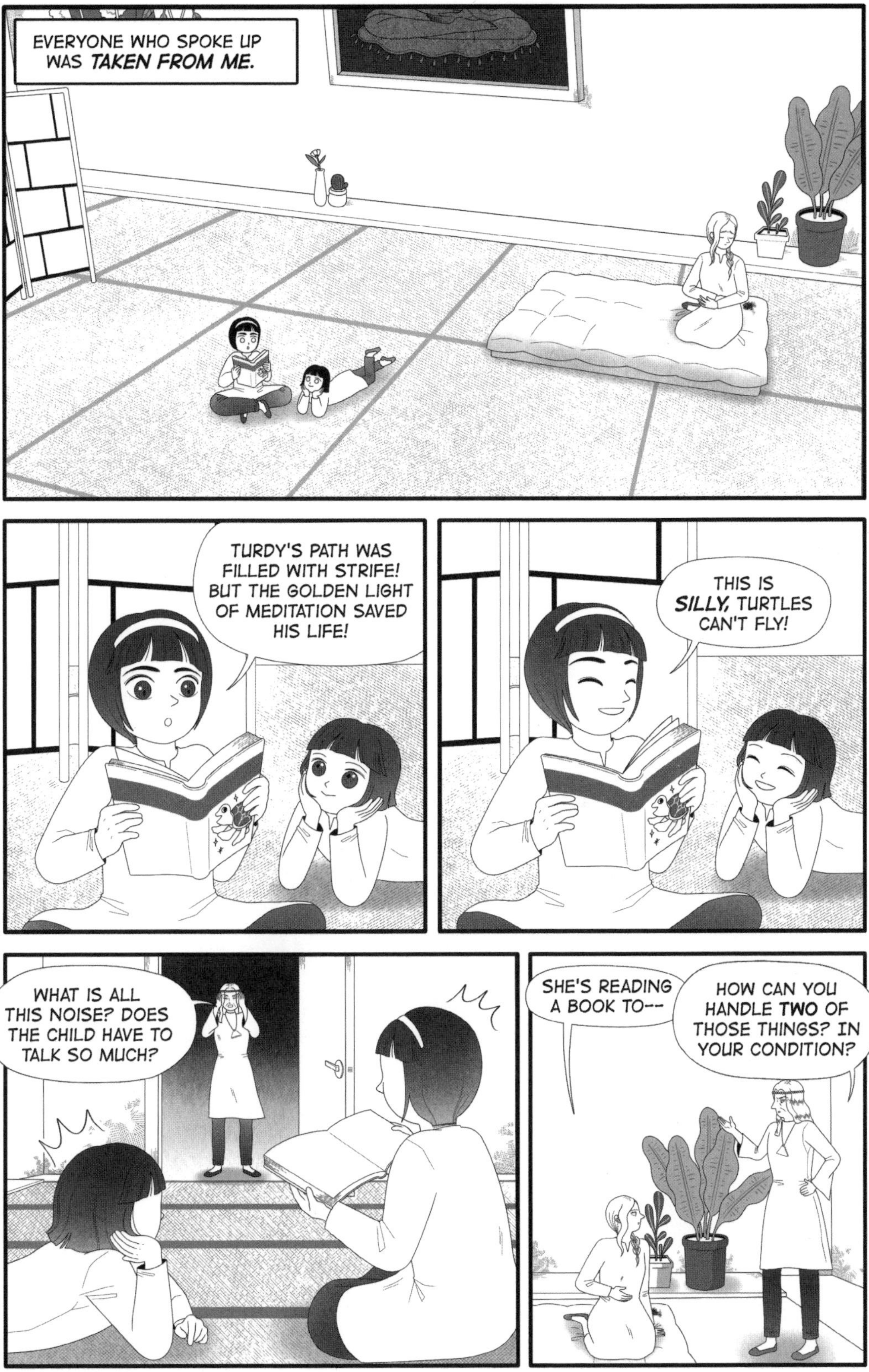
EVERYONE WHO SPOKE UP WAS *TAKEN FROM ME.*
TURDY'S PATH WAS FILLED WITH STRIFE! BUT THE GOLDEN LIGHT OF MEDITATION SAVED HIS LIFE!
THIS IS *SILLY,* TURTLES CAN'T FLY!
WHAT IS ALL THIS NOISE? DOES THE CHILD HAVE TO TALK SO MUCH?
SHE'S READING A BOOK TO--
HOW CAN YOU HANDLE **TWO** OF THOSE THINGS? IN YOUR CONDITION?

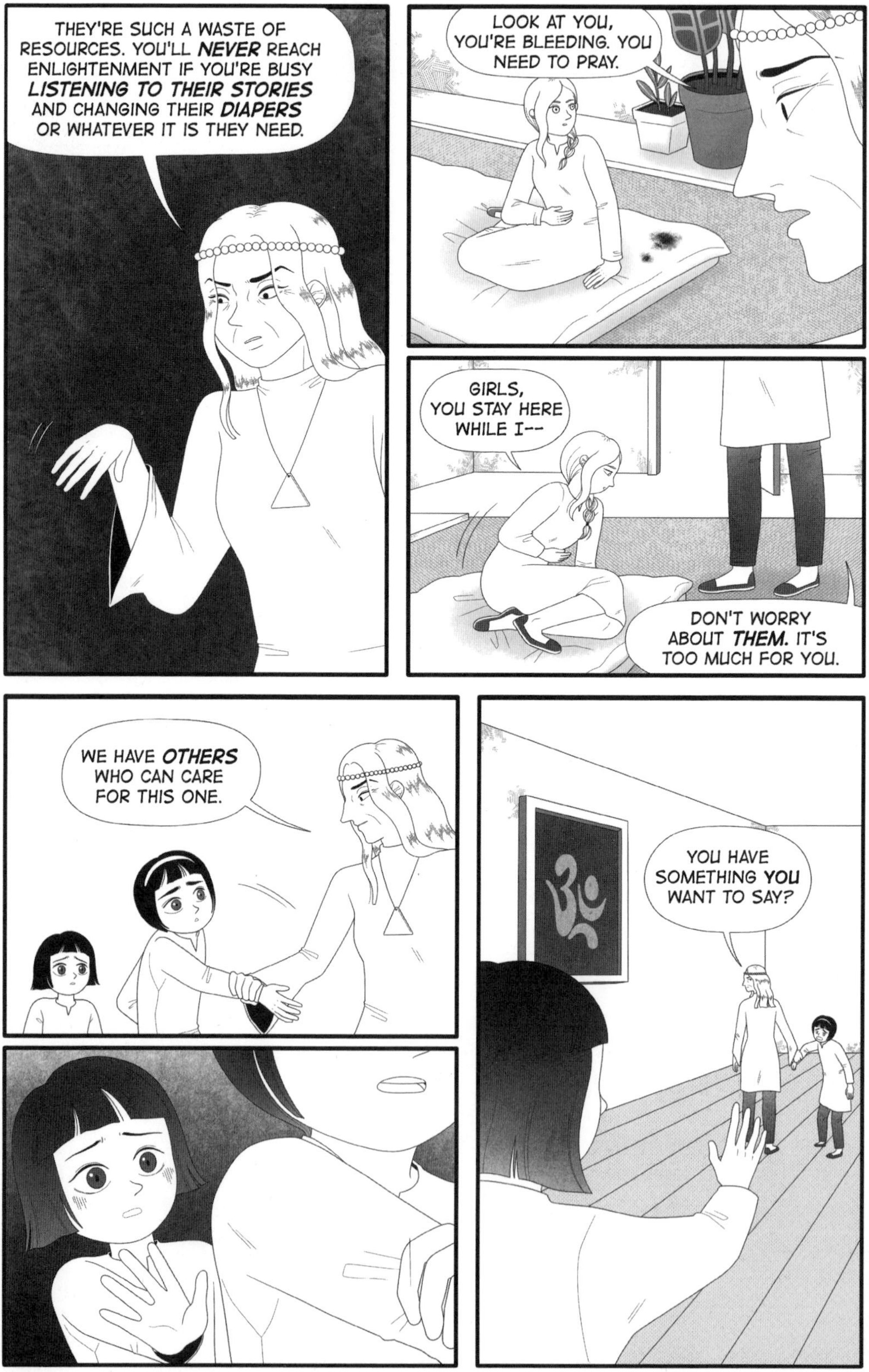
THEY'RE SUCH A WASTE OF RESOURCES. YOU'LL NEVER REACH ENLIGHTENMENT IF YOU'RE BUSY LISTENING TO THEIR STORIES AND CHANGING THEIR DIAPERS OR WHATEVER IT IS THEY NEED.
LOOK AT YOU, YOU'RE BLEEDING. YOU NEED TO PRAY.
GIRLS, YOU STAY HERE WHILE I--
DON'T WORRY ABOUT THEM. IT'S TOO MUCH FOR YOU.
WE HAVE OTHERS WHO CAN CARE FOR THIS ONE.
YOU HAVE SOMETHING YOU WANT TO SAY?

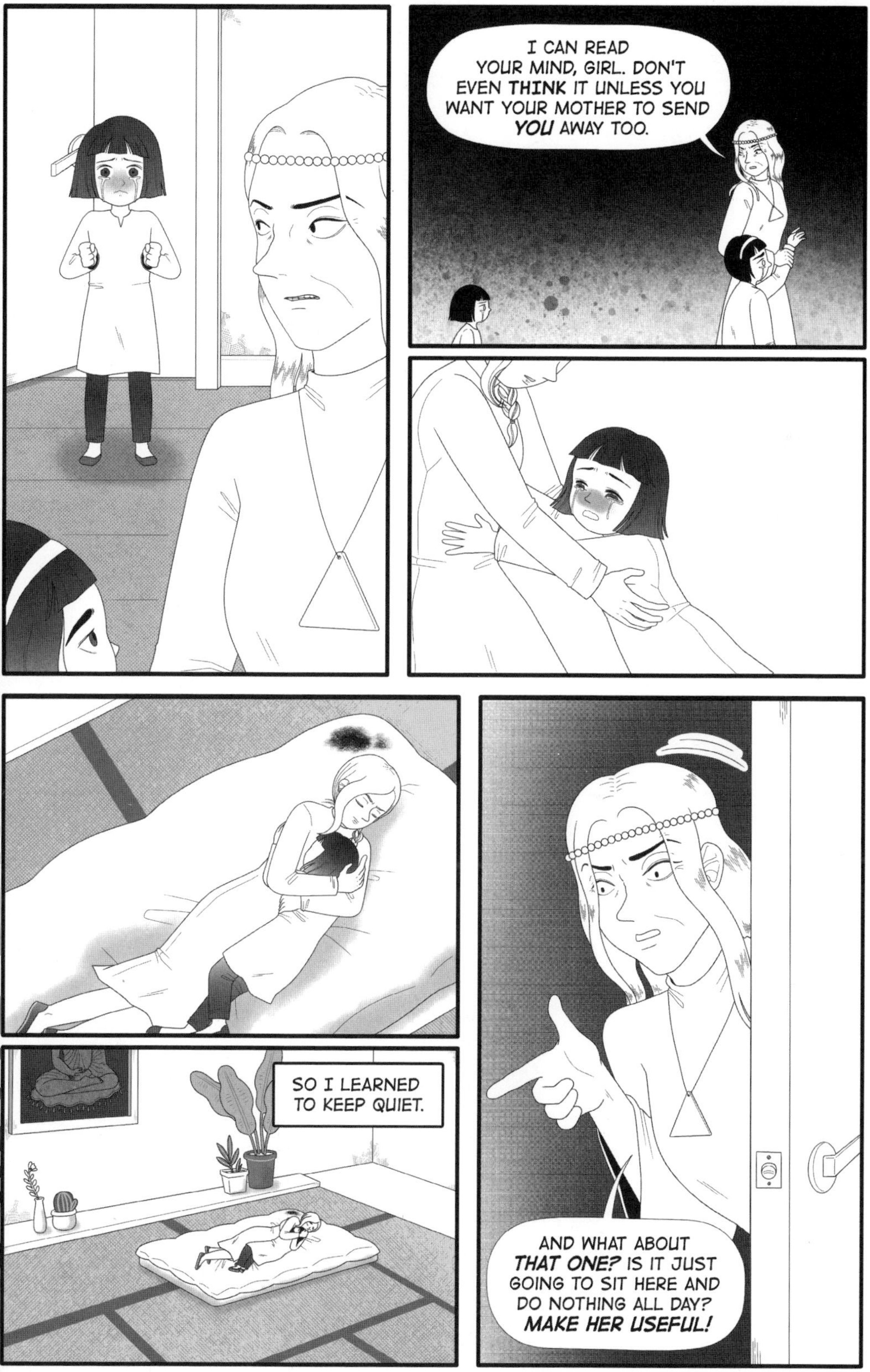
I CAN READ YOUR MIND, GIRL.. DON'T EVEN **THINK** IT UNLESS YOU WANT YOUR MOTHER TO SEND ***YOU*** AWAY TOO.
SO I LEARNED TO KEEP QUIET.
AND WHAT ABOUT ***THAT ONE?*** IS IT JUST GOING TO SIT HERE AND DO NOTHING ALL DAY? ***MAKE HER USEFUL!***

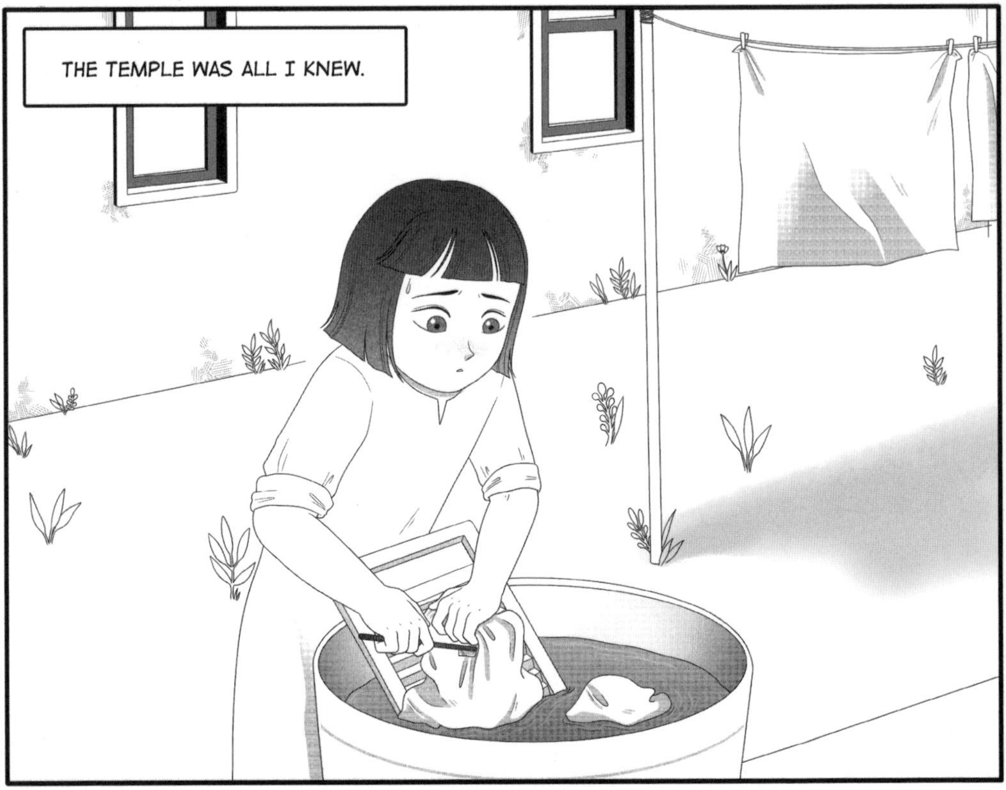
THE TEMPLE WAS ALL I KNEW.

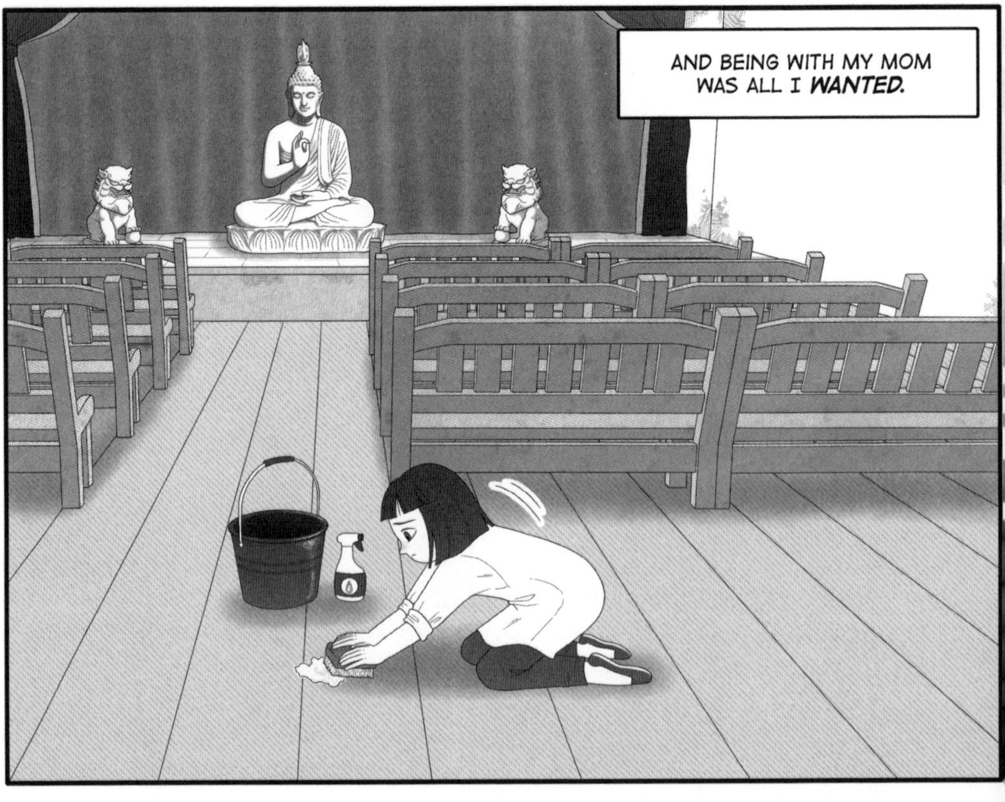
AND BEING WITH MY MOM WAS ALL I *WANTED.*

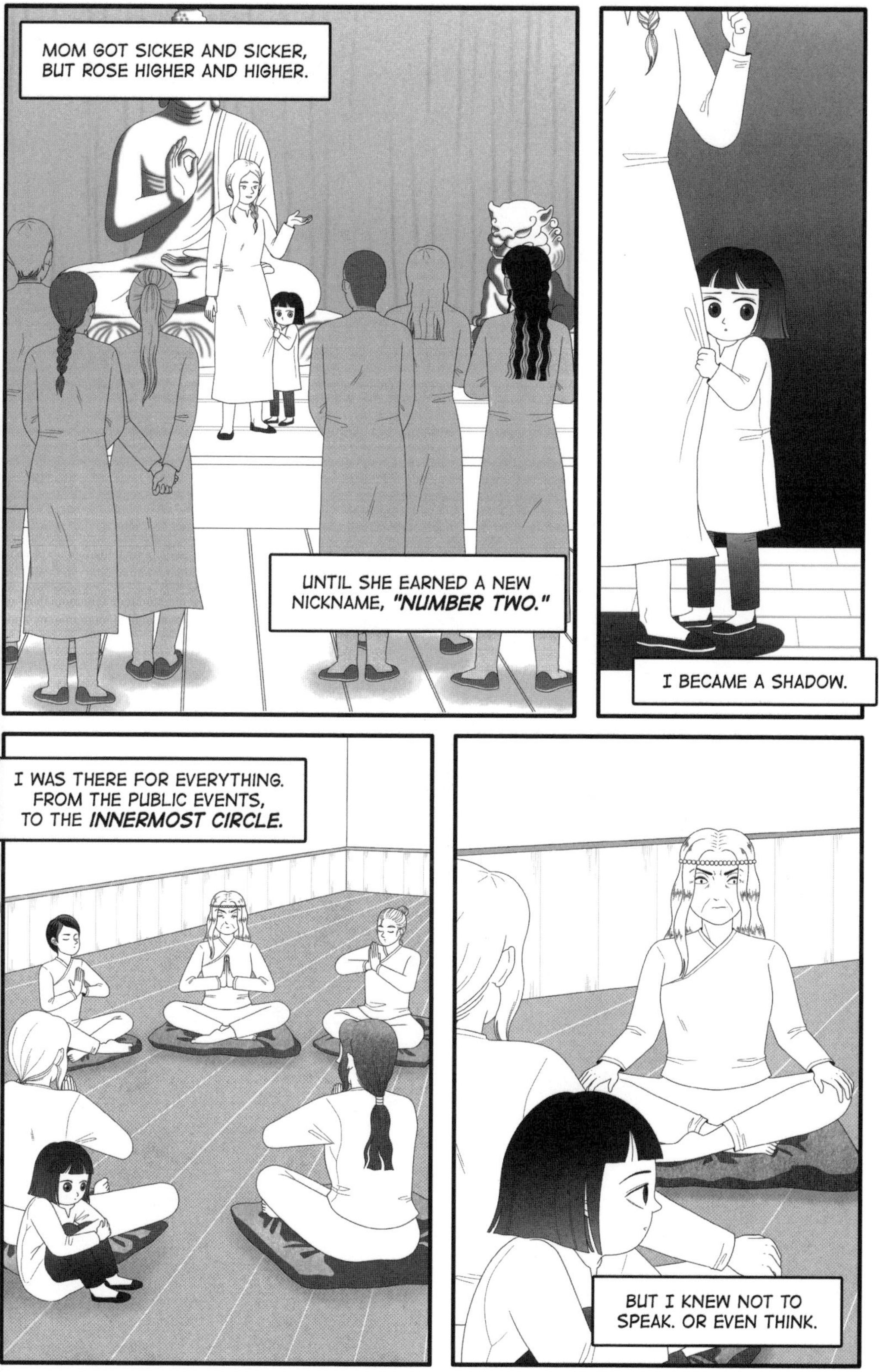
MOM GOT SICKER AND SICKER, BUT ROSE HIGHER AND HIGHER.
UNTIL SHE EARNED A NEW NICKNAME, ***"NUMBER TWO."***
I BECAME A SHADOW.
I WAS THERE FOR EVERYTHING. FROM THE PUBLIC EVENTS, TO THE ***INNERMOST CIRCLE.***
BUT I KNEW NOT TO SPEAK. OR EVEN THINK.

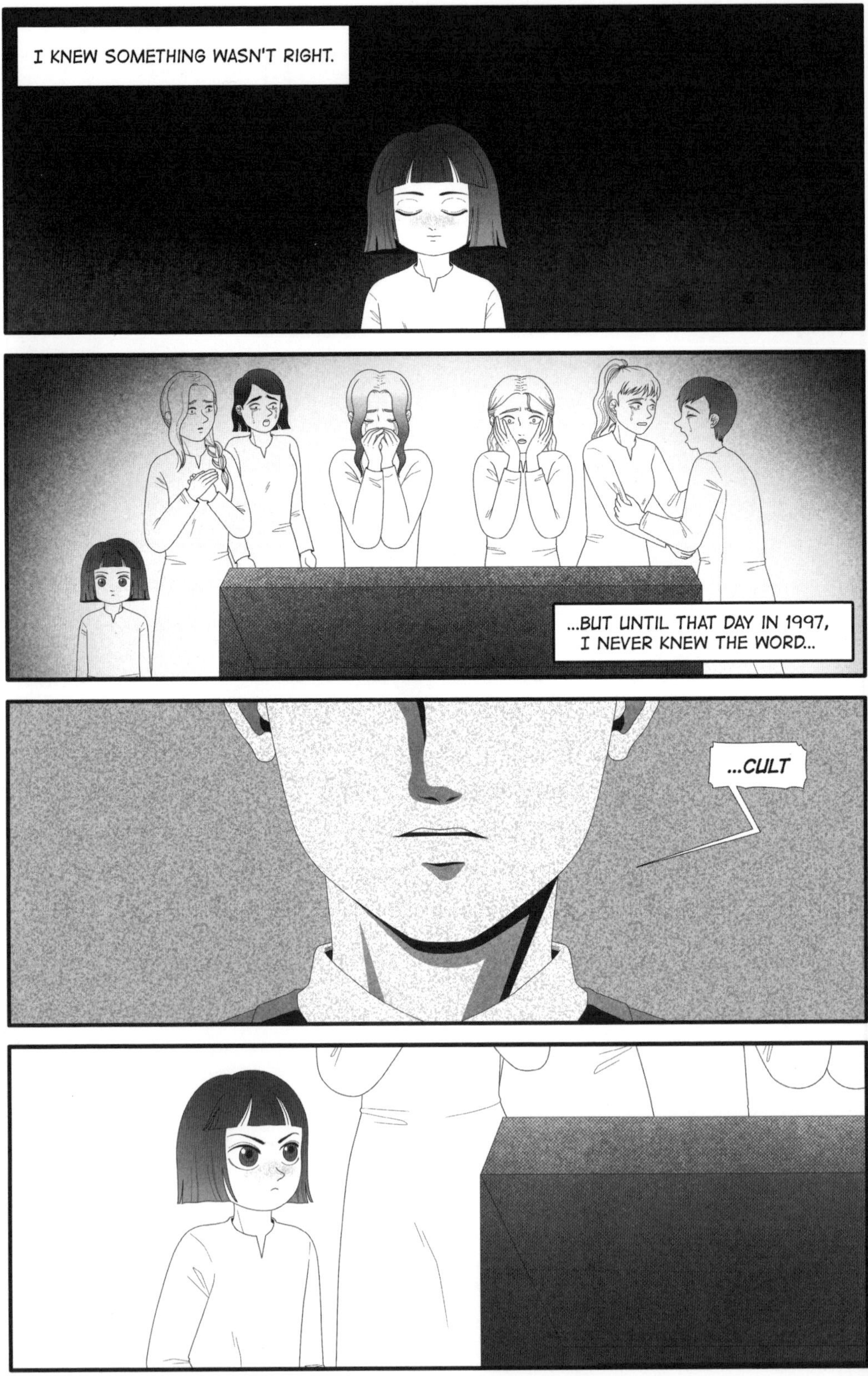
I KNEW SOMETHING WASN'T RIGHT.
...BUT UNTIL THAT DAY IN 1997, I NEVER KNEW THE WORD...
...CULT

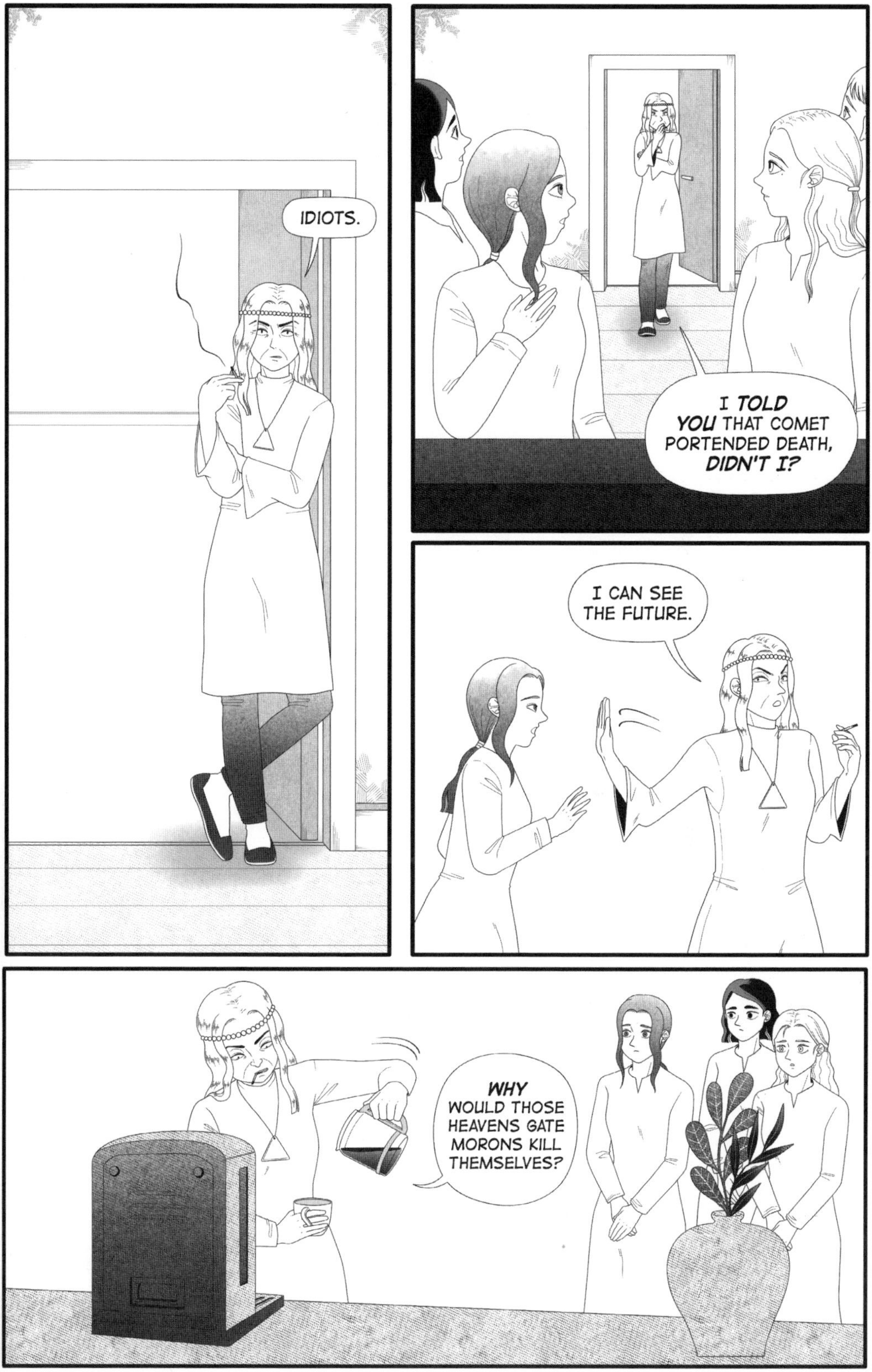
IDIOTS.
I TOLD YOU THAT COMET PORTENDED DEATH, DIDN'T I?
I CAN SEE THE FUTURE.
WHY WOULD THOSE HEAVENS GATE MORONS KILL THEMSELVES?

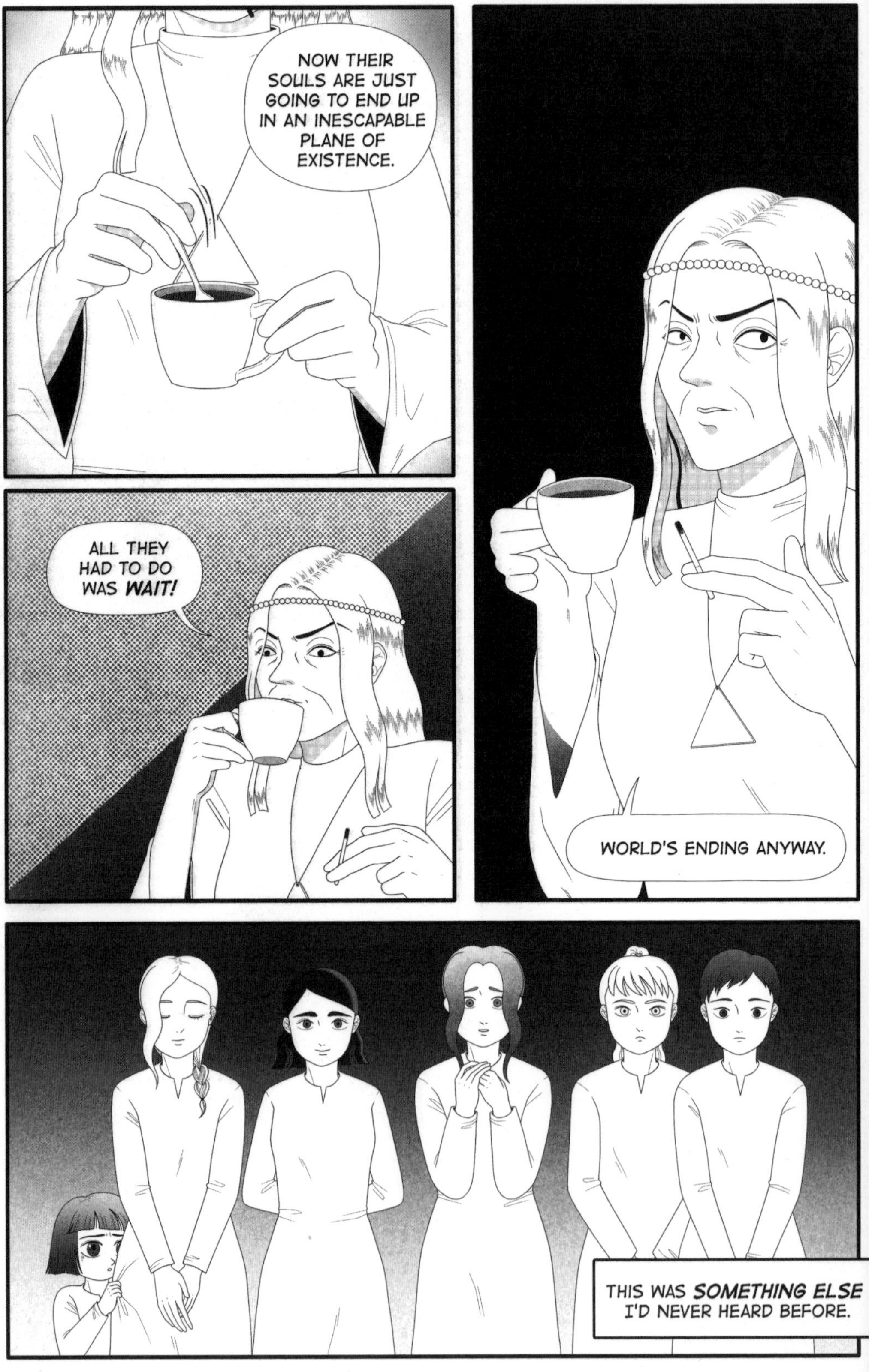
NOW THEIR SOULS ARE JUST GOING TO END UP IN AN INESCAPABLE PLANE OF EXISTENCE.
ALL THEY HAD TO DO WAS *WAIT!*
WORLD'S ENDING ANYWAY.
THIS WAS *SOMETHING ELSE* I'D NEVER HEARD BEFORE.

CHAPTER THREE:
THE PROPHECY

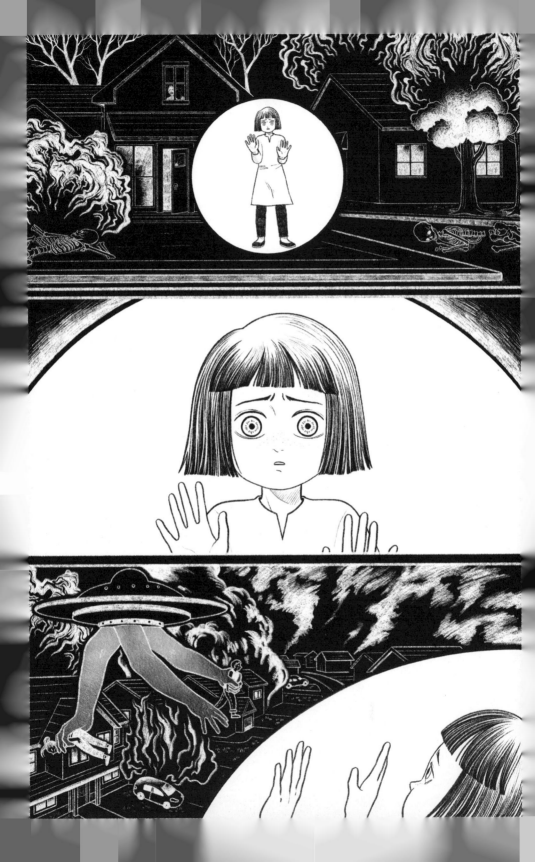

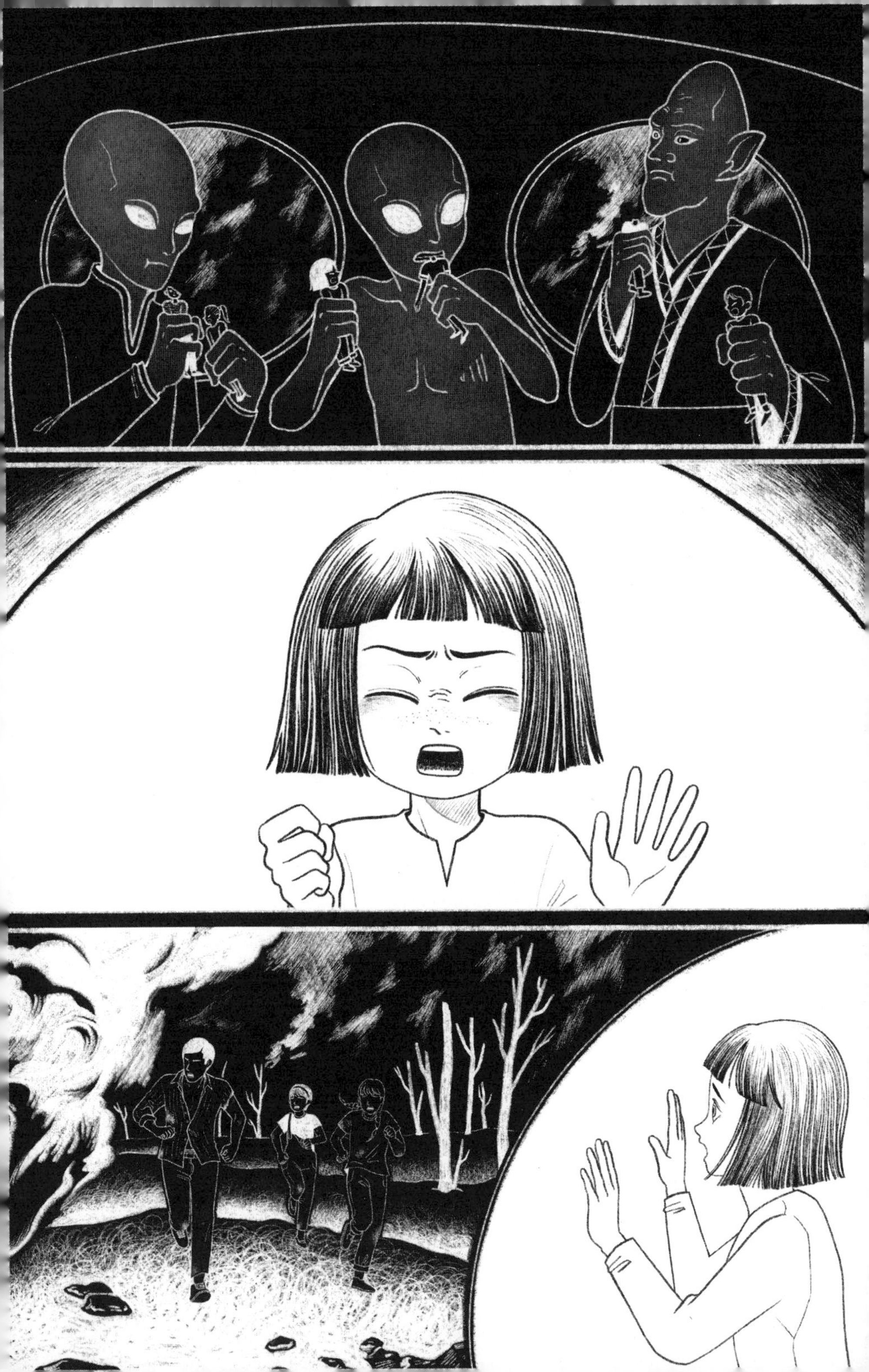

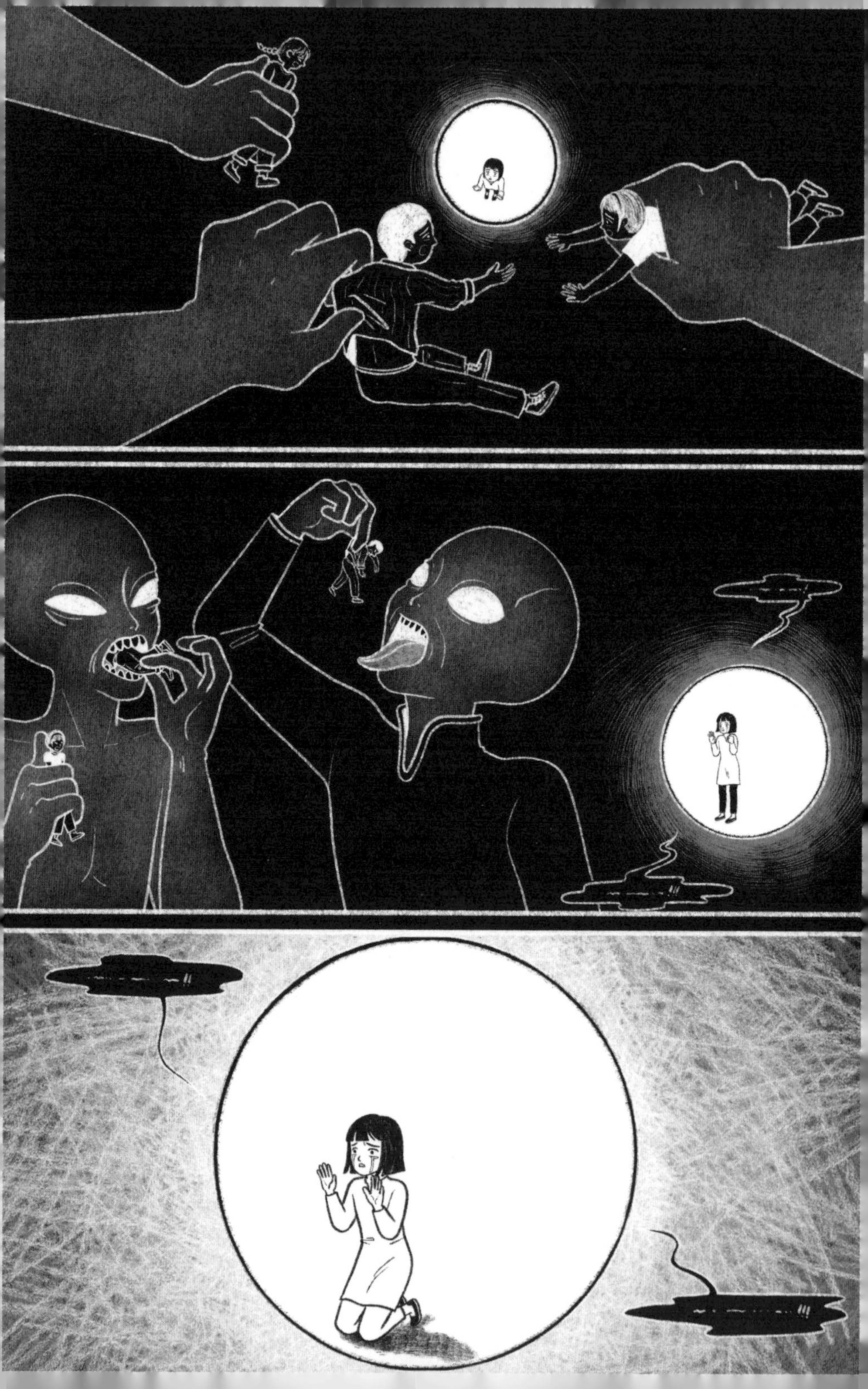

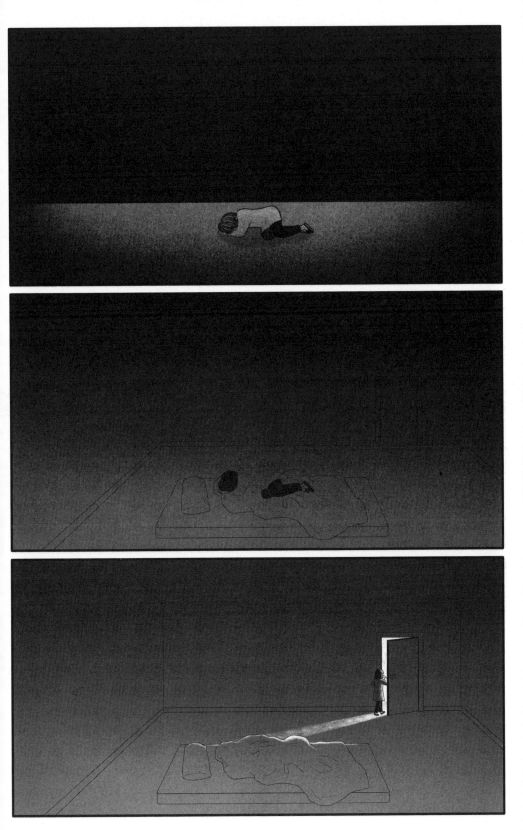

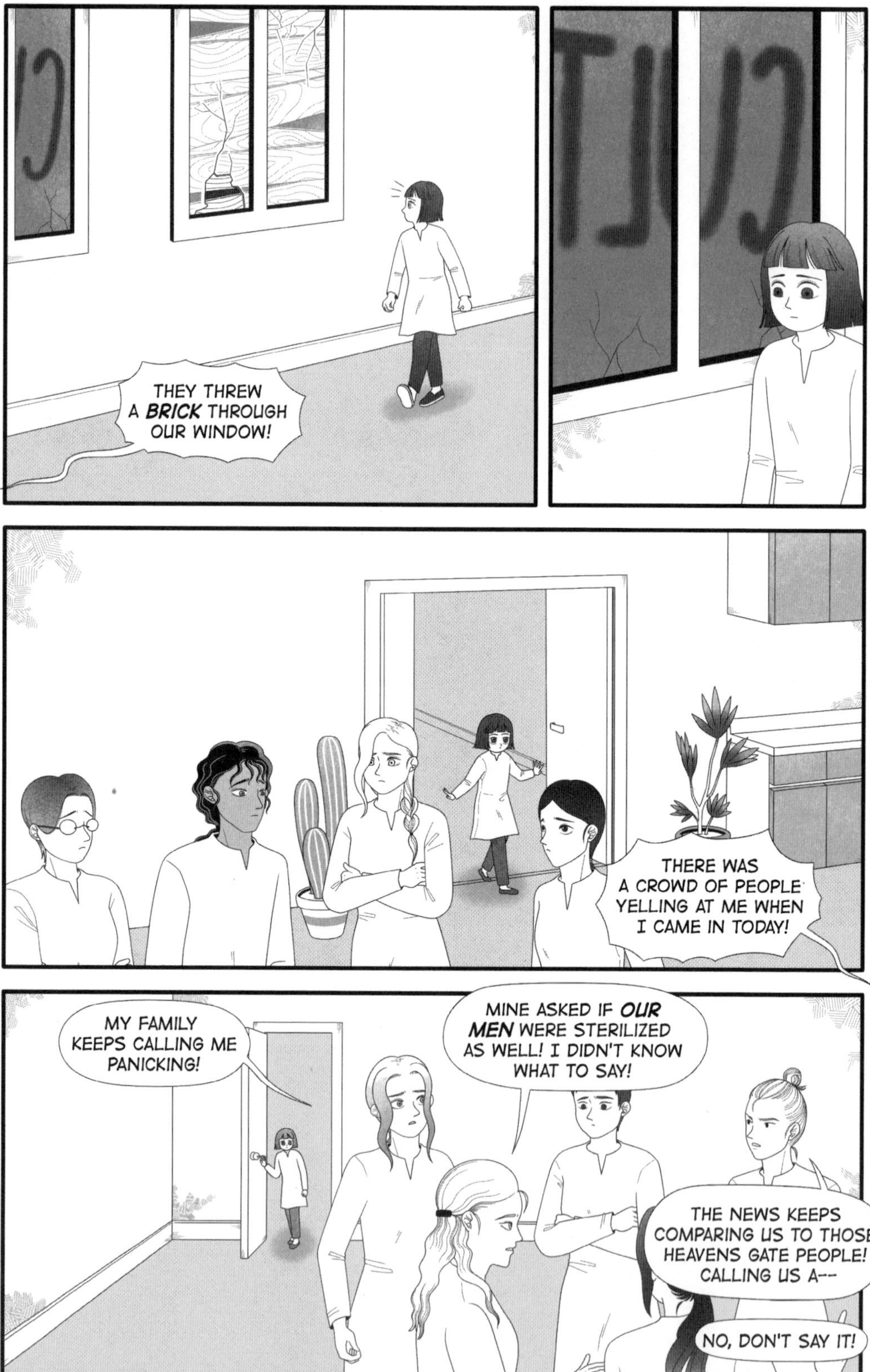
THEY THREW A BRICK THROUGH OUR WINDOW!
CULT
THERE WAS A CROWD OF PEOPLE YELLING AT ME WHEN I CAME IN TODAY!
MY FAMILY KEEPS CALLING ME PANICKING!
MINE ASKED IF OUR MEN WERE STERILIZED AS WELL! I DIDN'T KNOW WHAT TO SAY!
THE NEWS KEEPS COMPARING US TO THOSE HEAVENS GATE PEOPLE! CALLING US A--
NO, DON'T SAY IT!

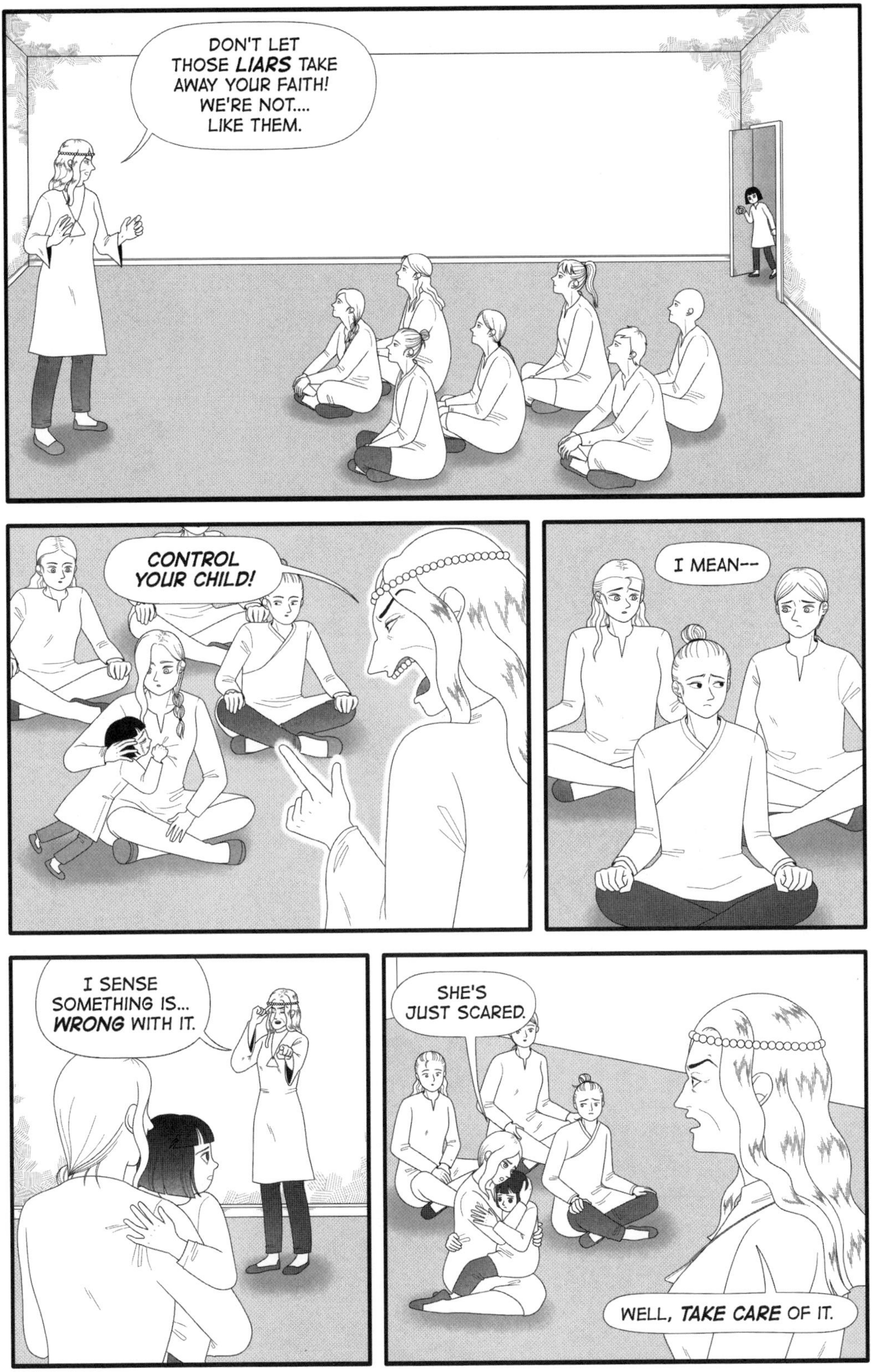
DON'T LET THOSE LIARS TAKE AWAY YOUR FAITH! WE'RE NOT.... LIKE THEM.
CONTROL YOUR CHILD!
I MEAN--
I SENSE SOMETHING IS... WRONG WITH IT.
SHE'S JUST SCARED.
WELL, TAKE CARE OF IT.

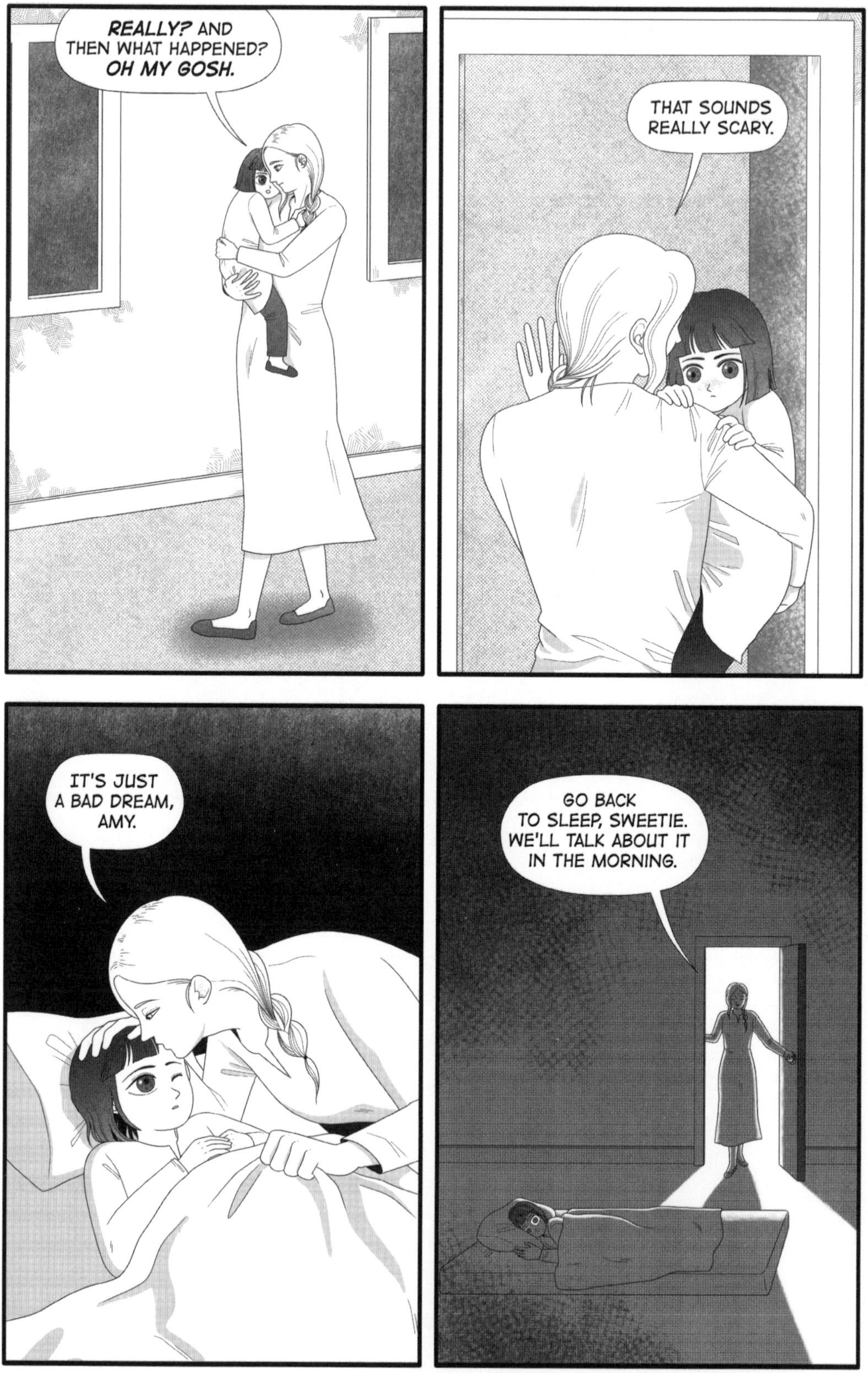
REALLY? AND THEN WHAT HAPPENED? OH MY GOSH.
THAT SOUNDS REALLY SCARY.
IT'S JUST A BAD DREAM, AMY.
GO BACK TO SLEEP, SWEETIE. WE'LL TALK ABOUT IT IN THE MORNING.

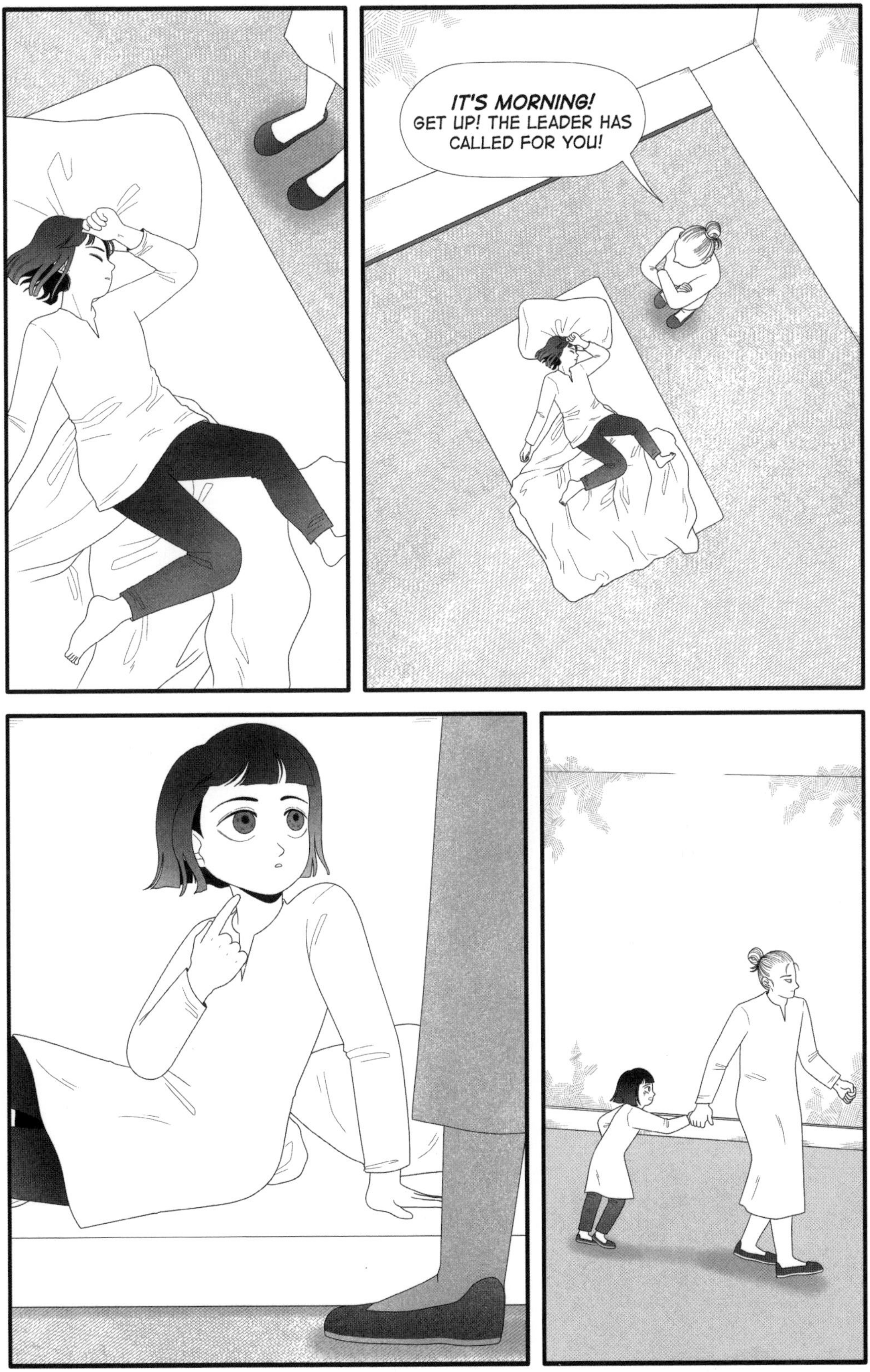
IT'S MORNING! GET UP! THE LEADER HAS CALLED FOR YOU!

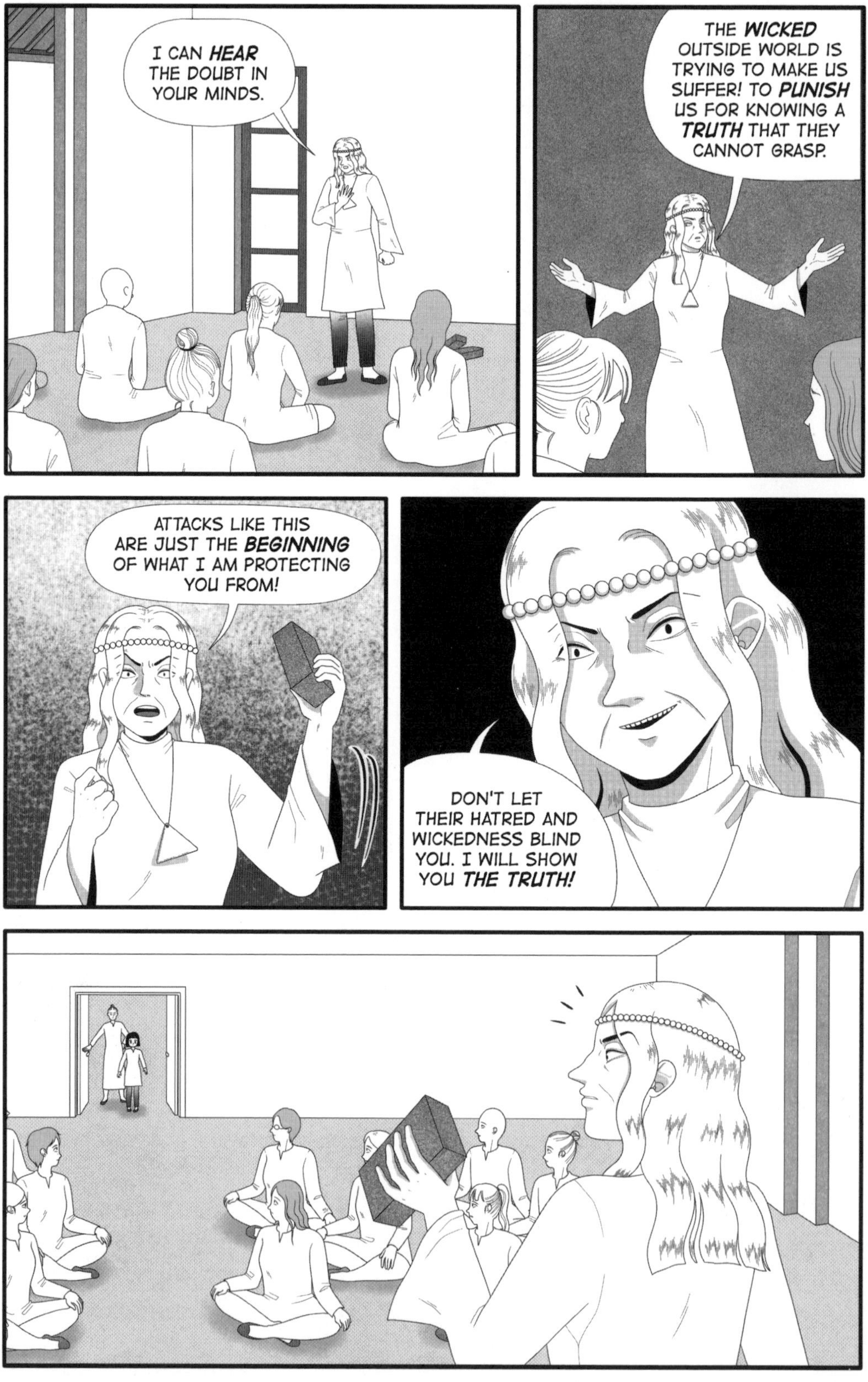
I CAN *HEAR* THE DOUBT IN YOUR MINDS.
THE *WICKED* OUTSIDE WORLD IS TRYING TO MAKE US SUFFER! TO *PUNISH* US FOR KNOWING A *TRUTH* THAT THEY CANNOT GRASP.
ATTACKS LIKE THIS ARE JUST THE *BEGINNING* OF WHAT I AM PROTECTING YOU FROM!
DON'T LET THEIR HATRED AND WICKEDNESS BLIND YOU. I WILL SHOW YOU *THE TRUTH!*

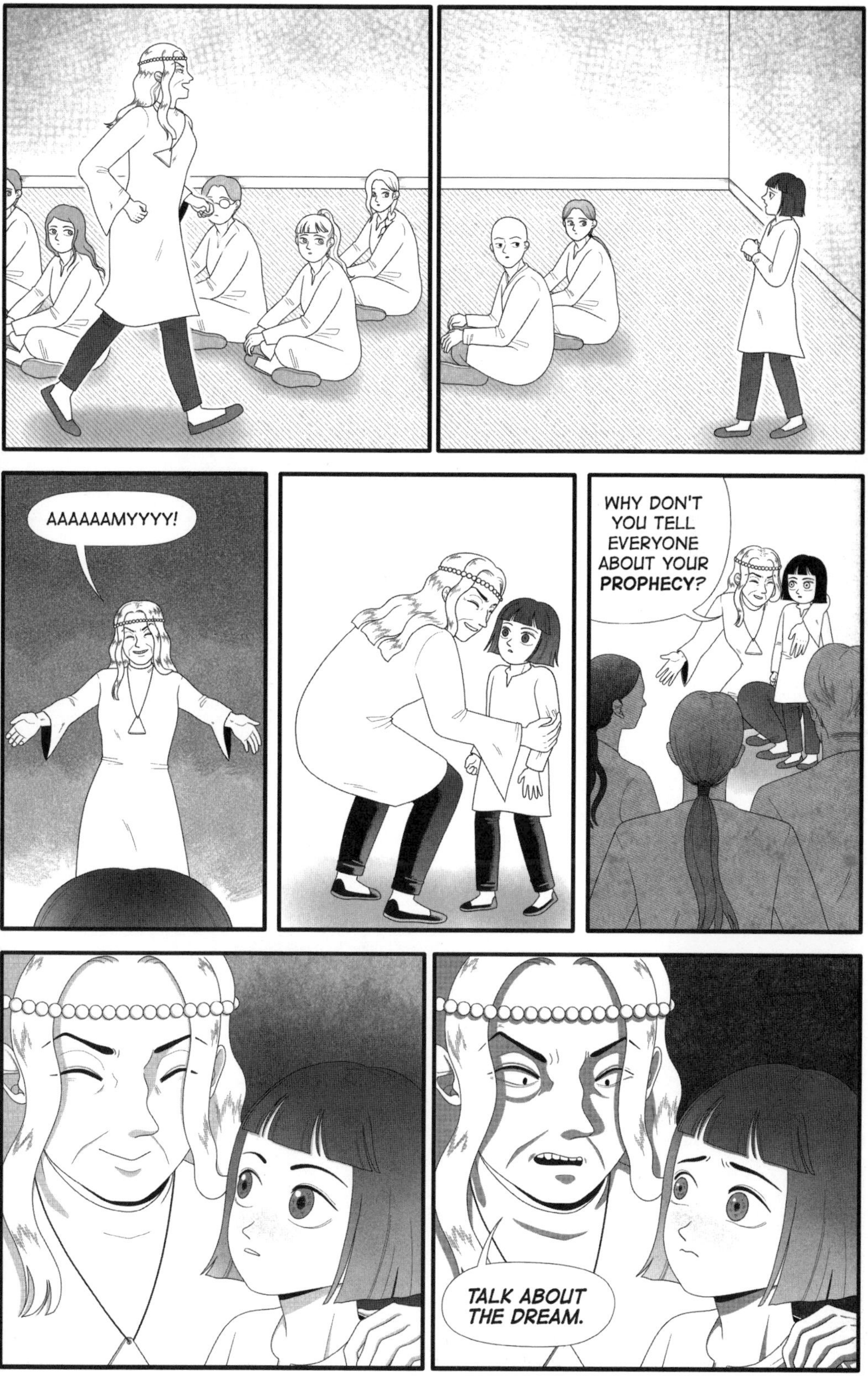
AAAAAAMYYYY!
WHY DON'T YOU TELL EVERYONE ABOUT YOUR PROPHECY?
TALK ABOUT THE DREAM.

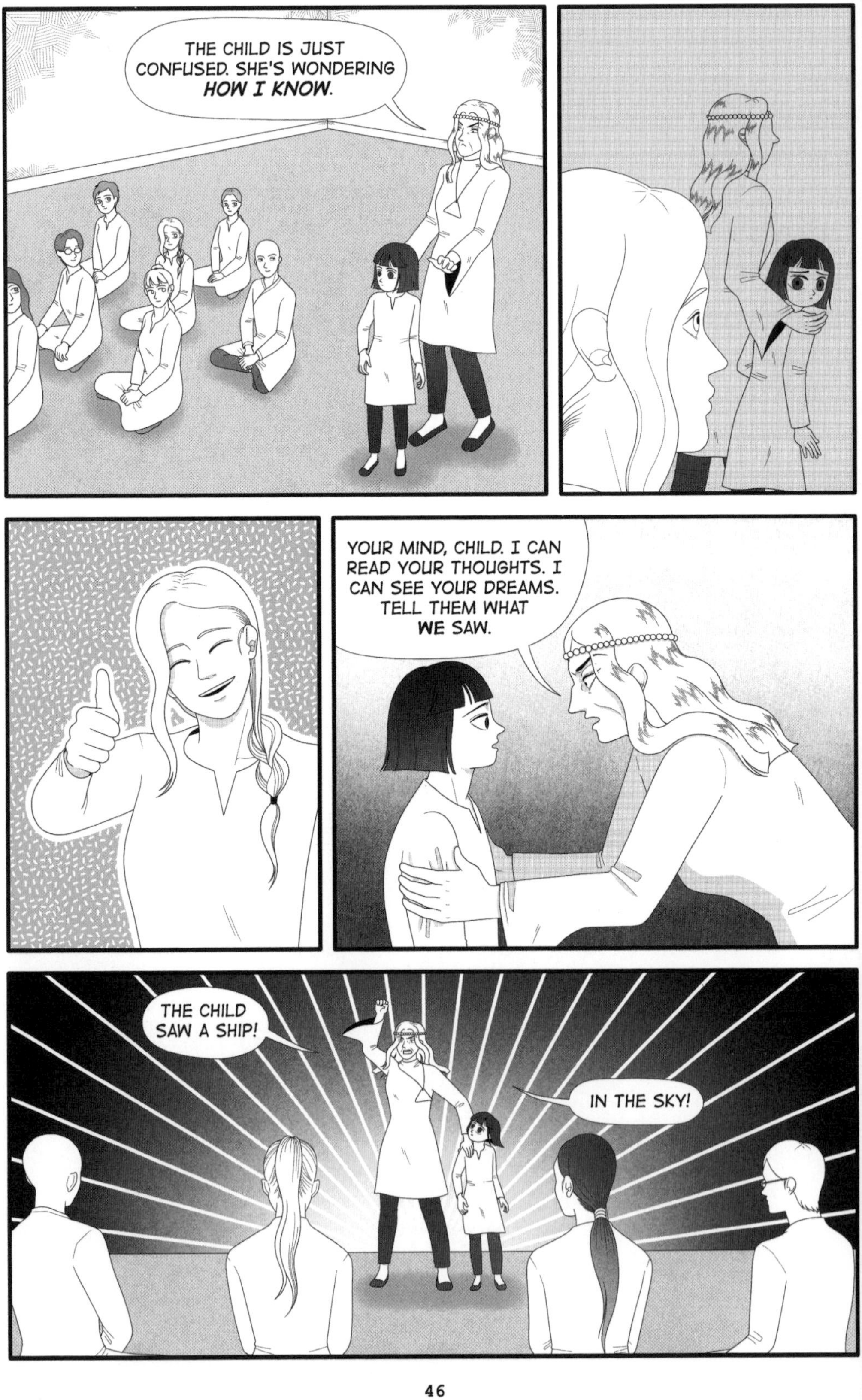
THE CHILD IS JUST CONFUSED. SHE'S WONDERING *HOW I KNOW*.
YOUR MIND, CHILD. I CAN READ YOUR THOUGHTS. I CAN SEE YOUR DREAMS. TELL THEM WHAT **WE** SAW.
THE CHILD SAW A SHIP!
IN THE SKY!

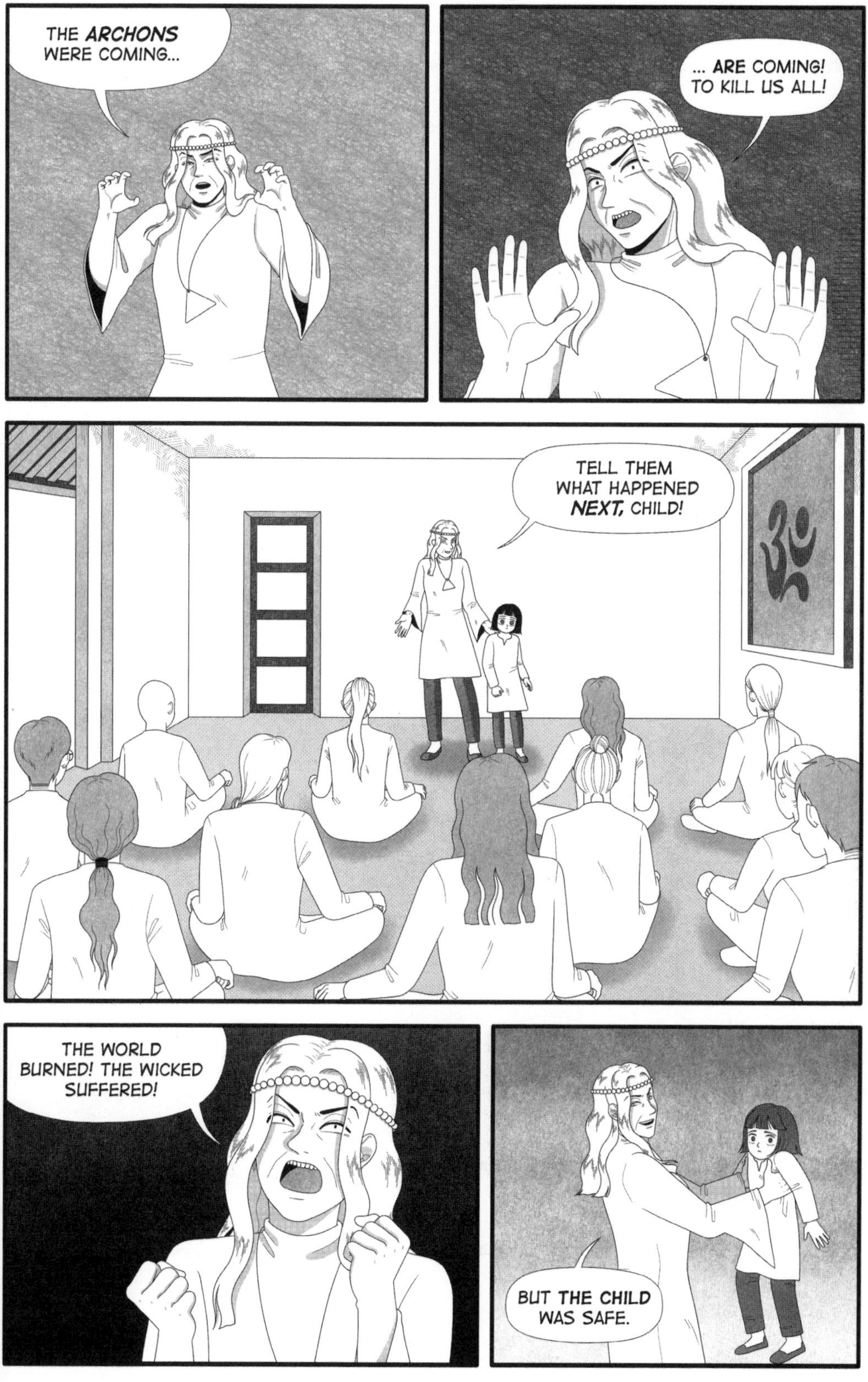
THE ARCHONS WERE COMING...
... ARE COMING! TO KILL US ALL!
TELL THEM WHAT HAPPENED NEXT, CHILD!
THE WORLD BURNED! THE WICKED SUFFERED!
BUT THE CHILD WAS SAFE.

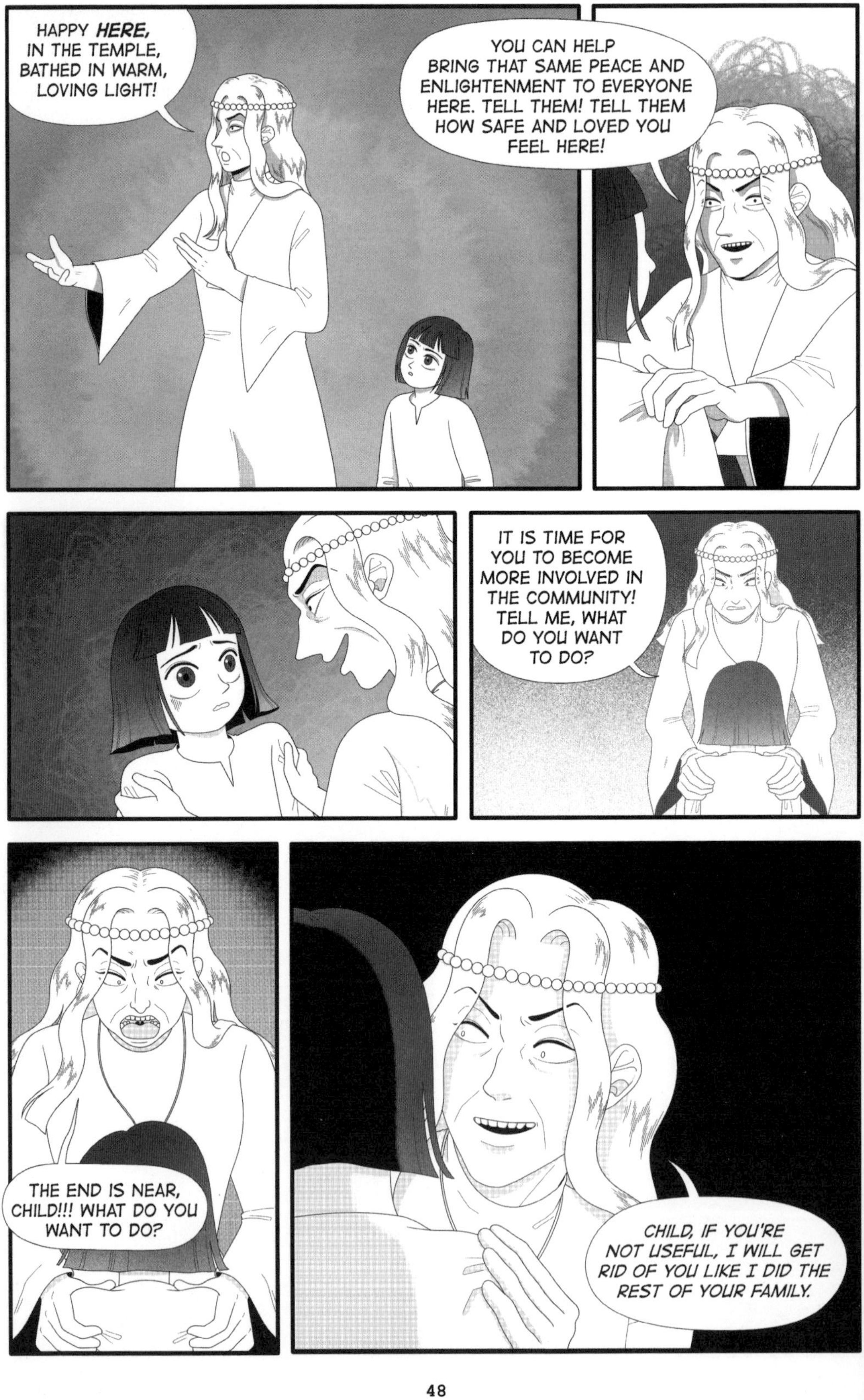
HAPPY **HERE,** IN THE TEMPLE, BATHED IN WARM, LOVING LIGHT!
YOU CAN HELP BRING THAT SAME PEACE AND ENLIGHTENMENT TO EVERYONE HERE. TELL THEM! TELL THEM HOW SAFE AND LOVED YOU FEEL HERE!
IT IS TIME FOR YOU TO BECOME MORE INVOLVED IN THE COMMUNITY! TELL ME, WHAT DO YOU WANT TO DO?
THE END IS NEAR, CHILD!!! WHAT DO YOU WANT TO DO?
CHILD, IF YOU'RE NOT USEFUL, I WILL GET RID OF YOU LIKE I DID THE REST OF YOUR FAMILY.

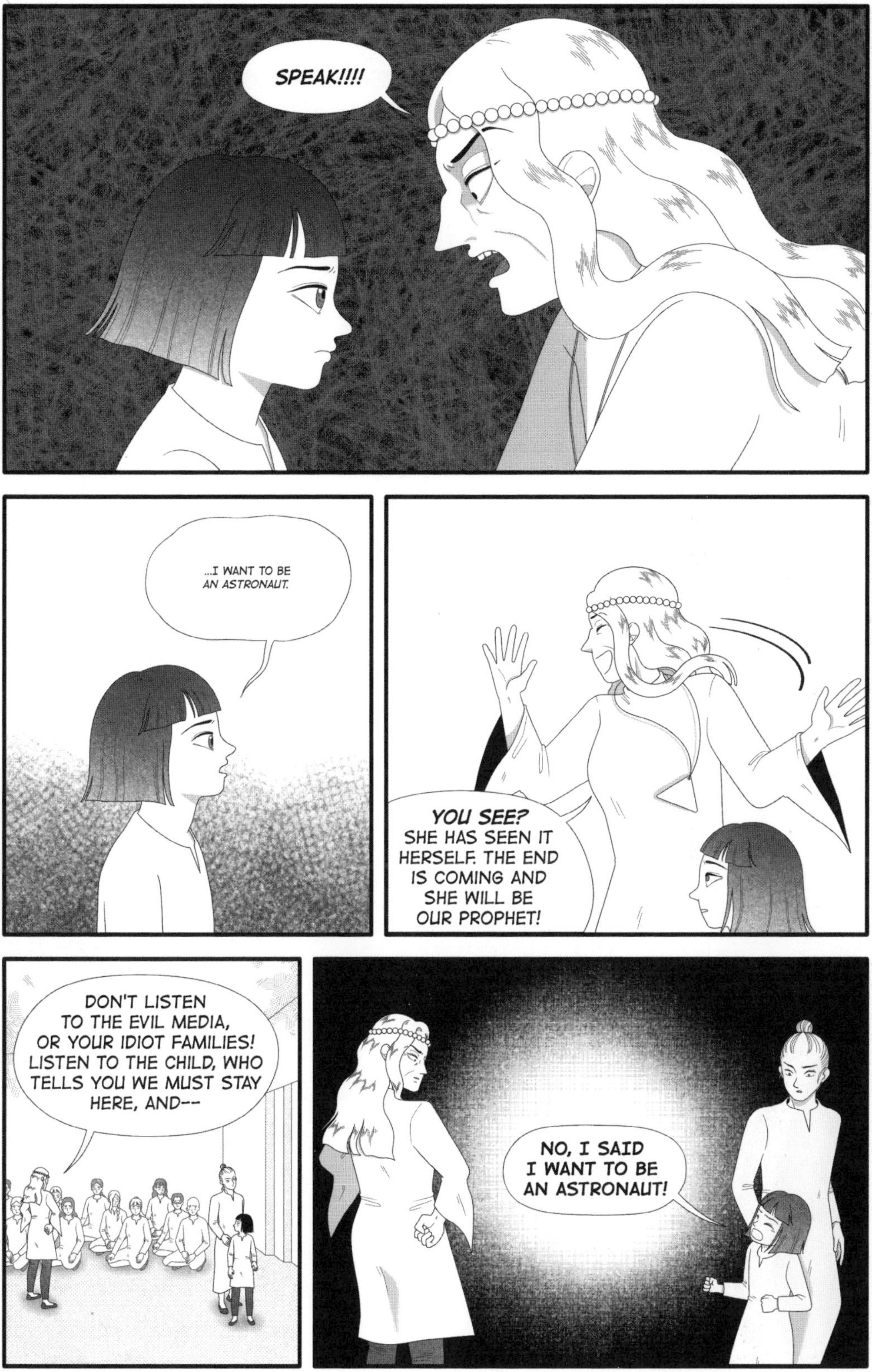
SPEAK!!!!
...I WANT TO BE AN ASTRONAUT.
YOU SEE? SHE HAS SEEN IT HERSELF. THE END IS COMING AND SHE WILL BE OUR PROPHET!
DON'T LISTEN TO THE EVIL MEDIA, OR YOUR IDIOT FAMILIES! LISTEN TO THE CHILD, WHO TELLS YOU WE MUST STAY HERE, AND--
NO, I SAID I WANT TO BE AN ASTRONAUT!

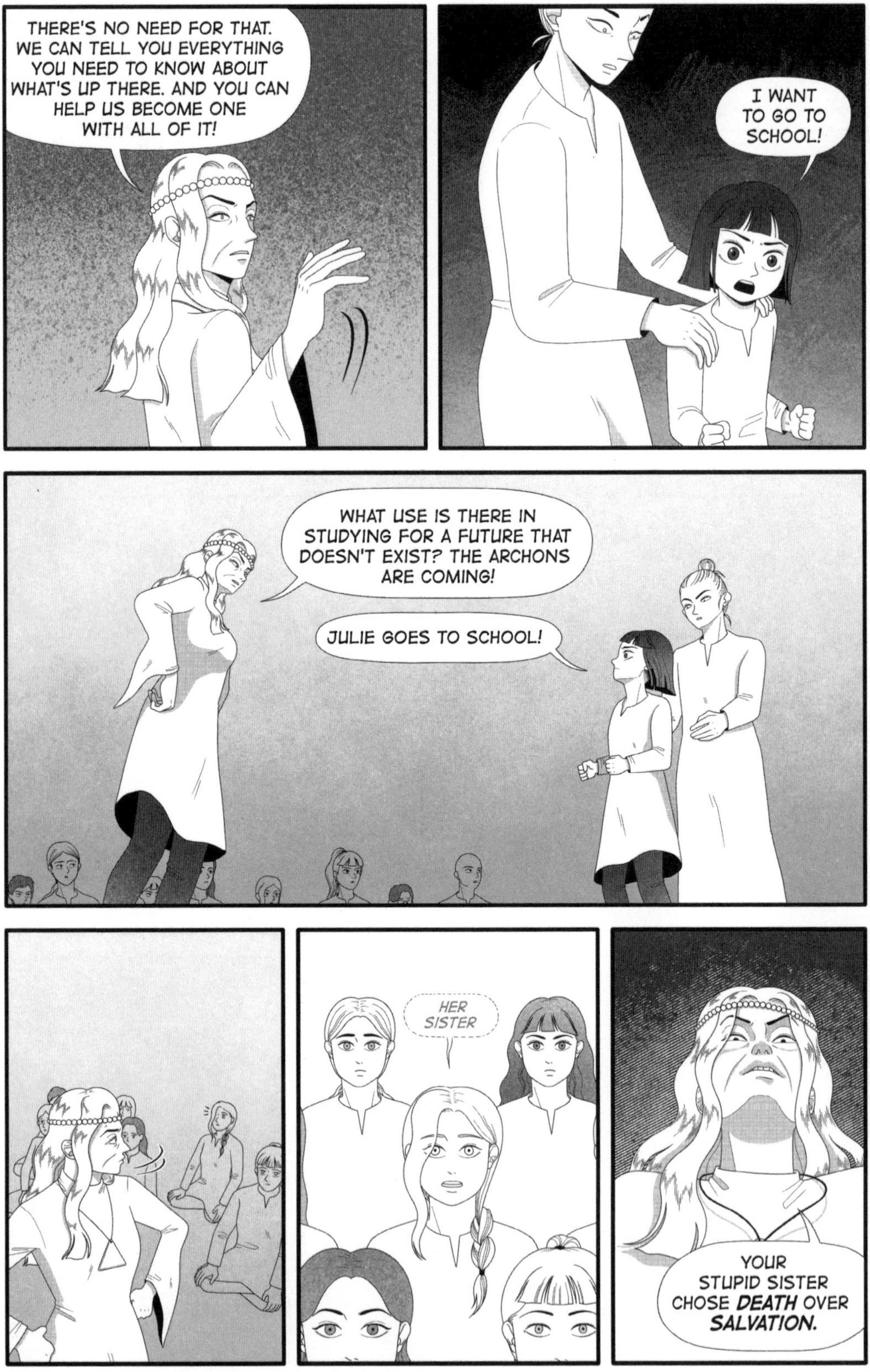
THERE'S NO NEED FOR THAT. WE CAN TELL YOU EVERYTHING YOU NEED TO KNOW ABOUT WHAT'S UP THERE. AND YOU CAN HELP US BECOME ONE WITH ALL OF IT!
I WANT TO GO TO SCHOOL!
WHAT USE IS THERE IN STUDYING FOR A FUTURE THAT DOESN'T EXIST? THE ARCHONS ARE COMING!
JULIE GOES TO SCHOOL!
HER SISTER
YOUR STUPID SISTER CHOSE DEATH OVER SALVATION.

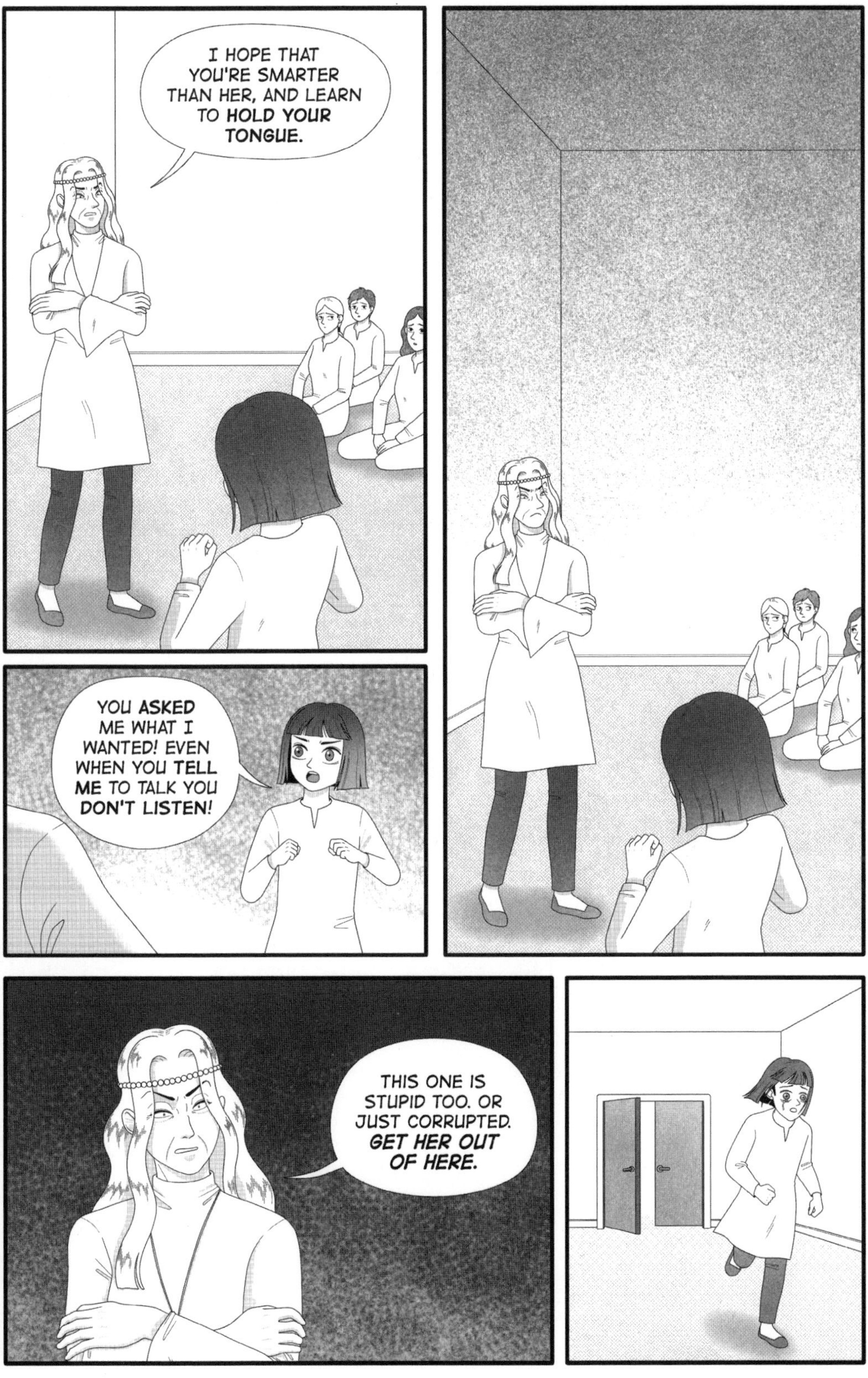
I HOPE THAT YOU'RE SMARTER THAN HER, AND LEARN TO **HOLD YOUR TONGUE.**
YOU **ASKED** ME WHAT I WANTED! EVEN WHEN YOU **TELL ME** TO TALK YOU **DON'T LISTEN!**
THIS ONE IS STUPID TOO. OR JUST CORRUPTED. ***GET HER OUT OF HERE.***

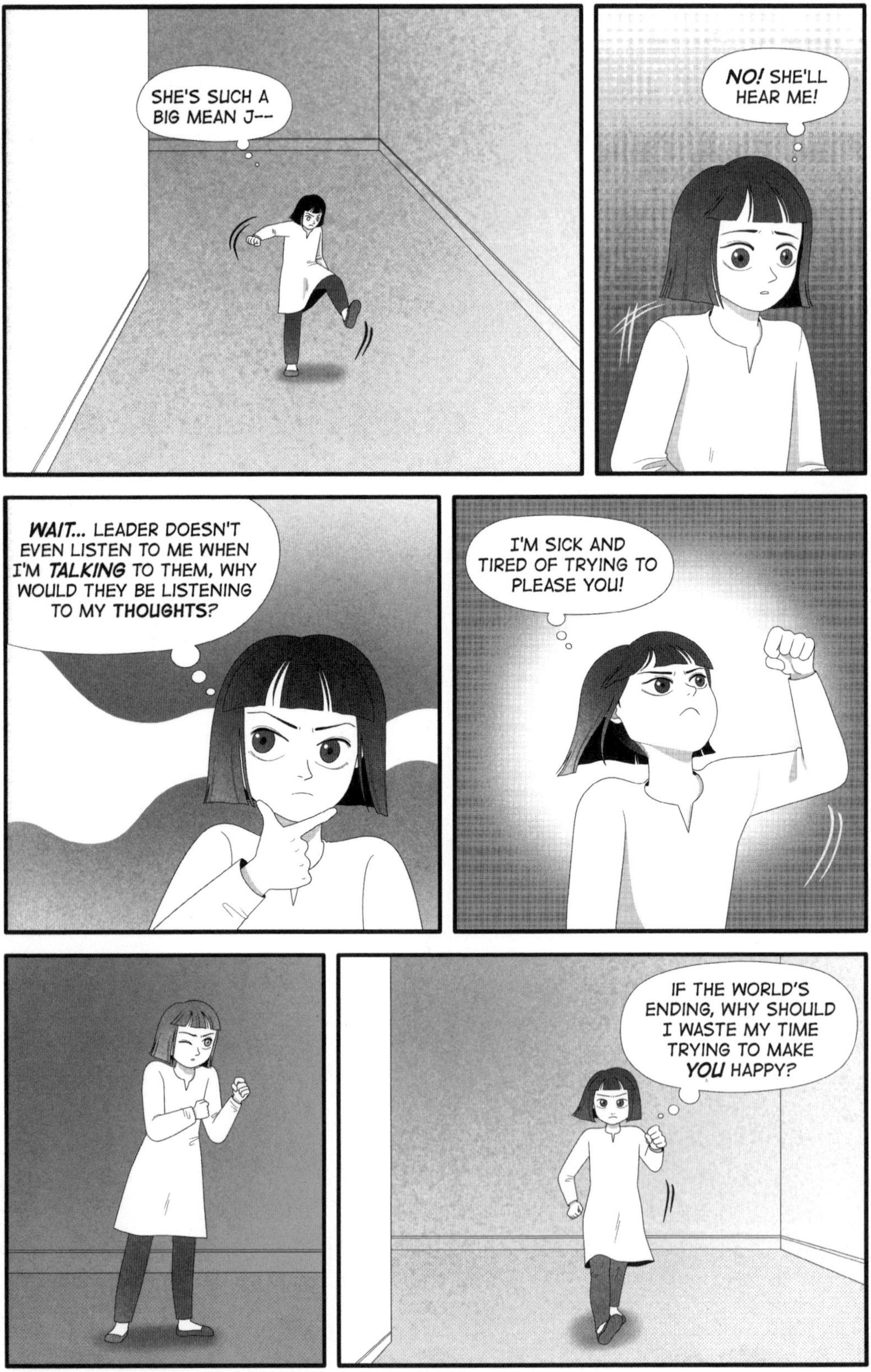
SHE'S SUCH A BIG MEAN J--
NO! SHE'LL HEAR ME!
WAIT... LEADER DOESN'T EVEN LISTEN TO ME WHEN I'M TALKING TO THEM, WHY WOULD THEY BE LISTENING TO MY THOUGHTS?
I'M SICK AND TIRED OF TRYING TO PLEASE YOU!
IF THE WORLD'S ENDING, WHY SHOULD I WASTE MY TIME TRYING TO MAKE YOU HAPPY?

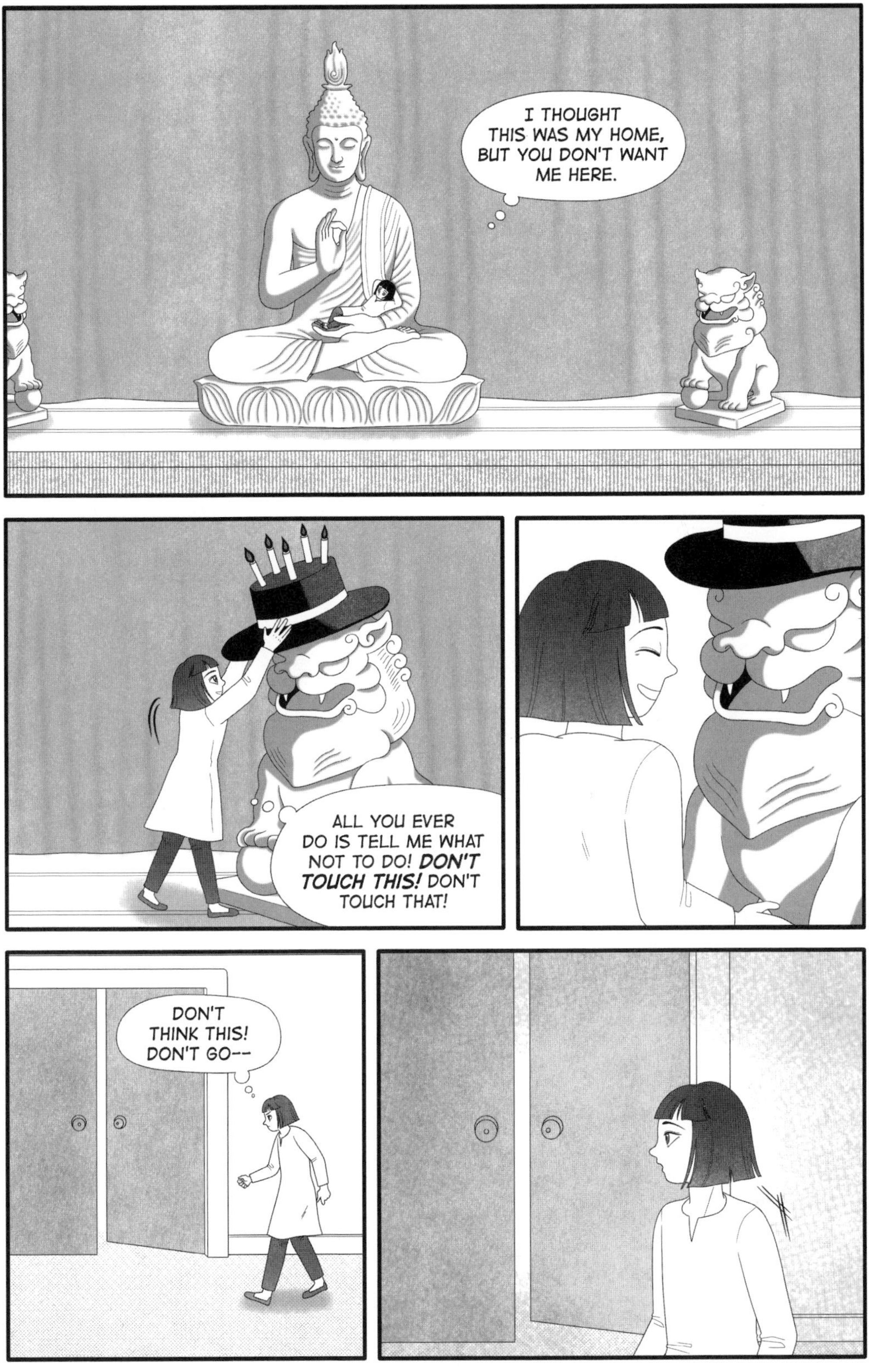
I THOUGHT THIS WAS MY HOME, BUT YOU DON'T WANT ME HERE.
ALL YOU EVER DO IS TELL ME WHAT NOT TO DO! ***DON'T TOUCH THIS!*** DON'T TOUCH THAT!
DON'T THINK THIS! DON'T GO--

CHAPTER FOUR: THE LIBRARY

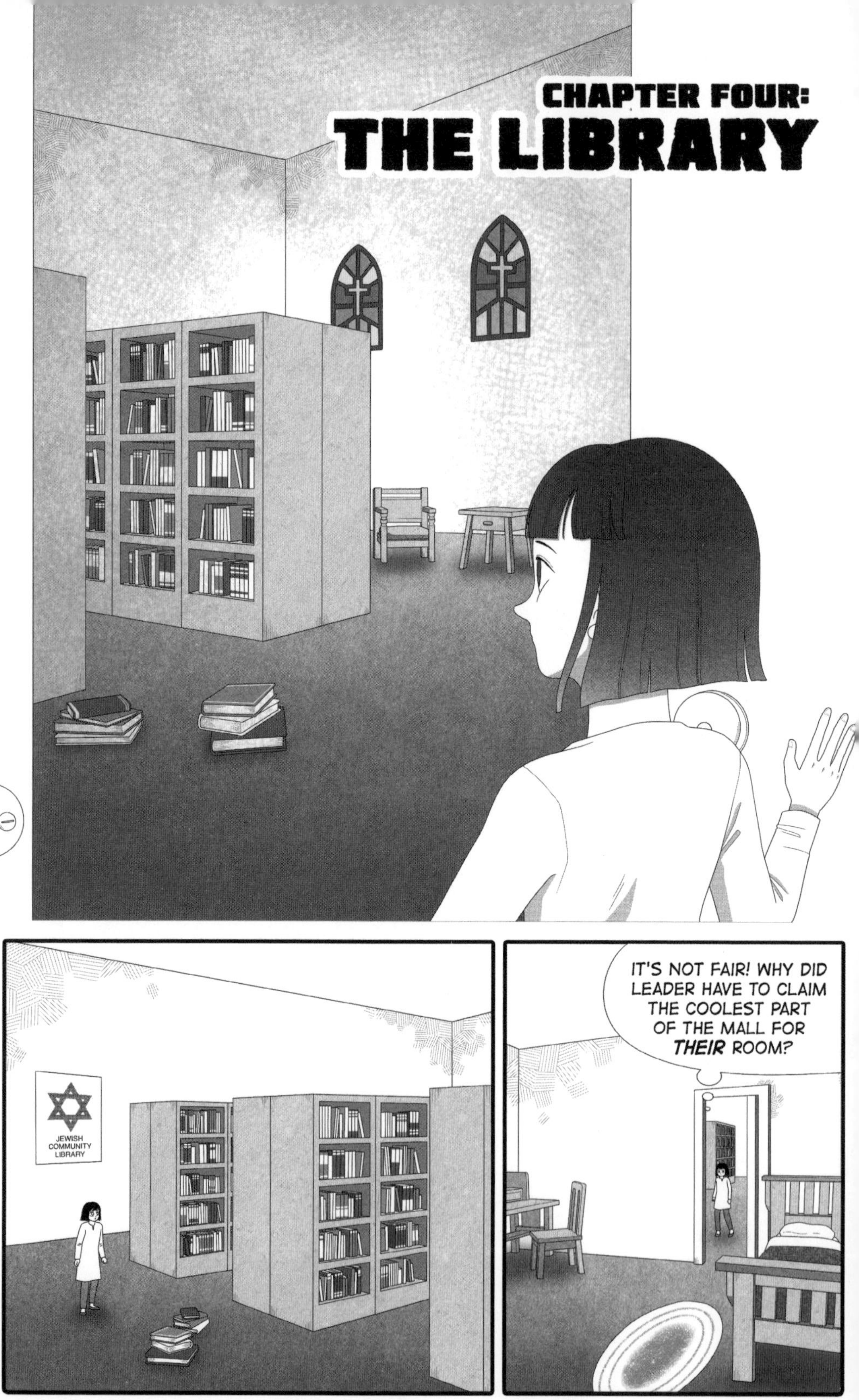
JEWISH COMMUNITY LIBRARY
IT'S NOT FAIR! WHY DID LEADER HAVE TO CLAIM THE COOLEST PART OF THE MALL FOR *THEIR* ROOM?

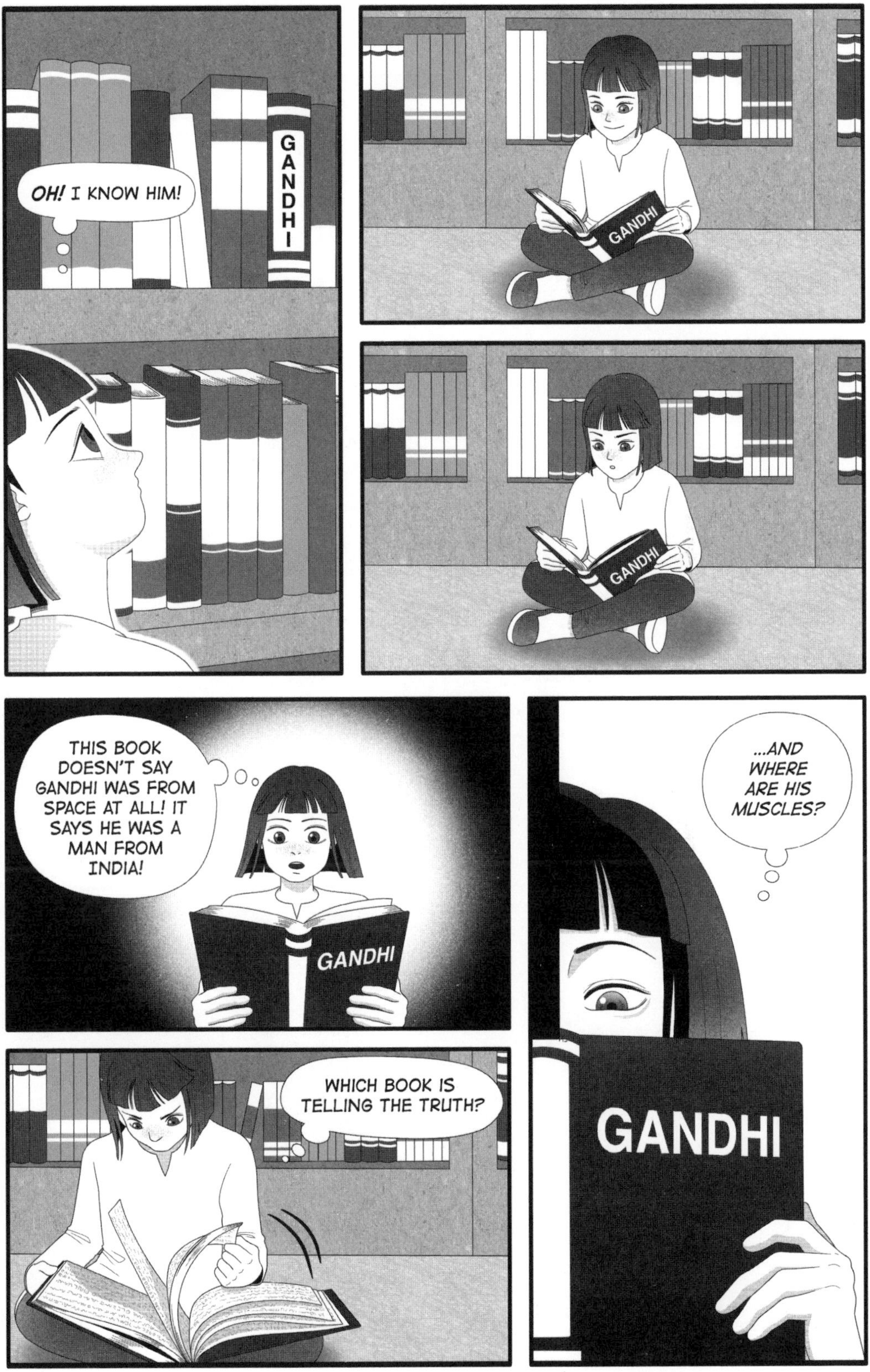
GANDHI
OH! I KNOW HIM!
GANDHI
GANDHI
THIS BOOK DOESN'T SAY GANDHI WAS FROM SPACE AT ALL! IT SAYS HE WAS A MAN FROM INDIA!
GANDHI
...AND WHERE ARE HIS MUSCLES?
WHICH BOOK IS TELLING THE TRUTH?
GANDHI

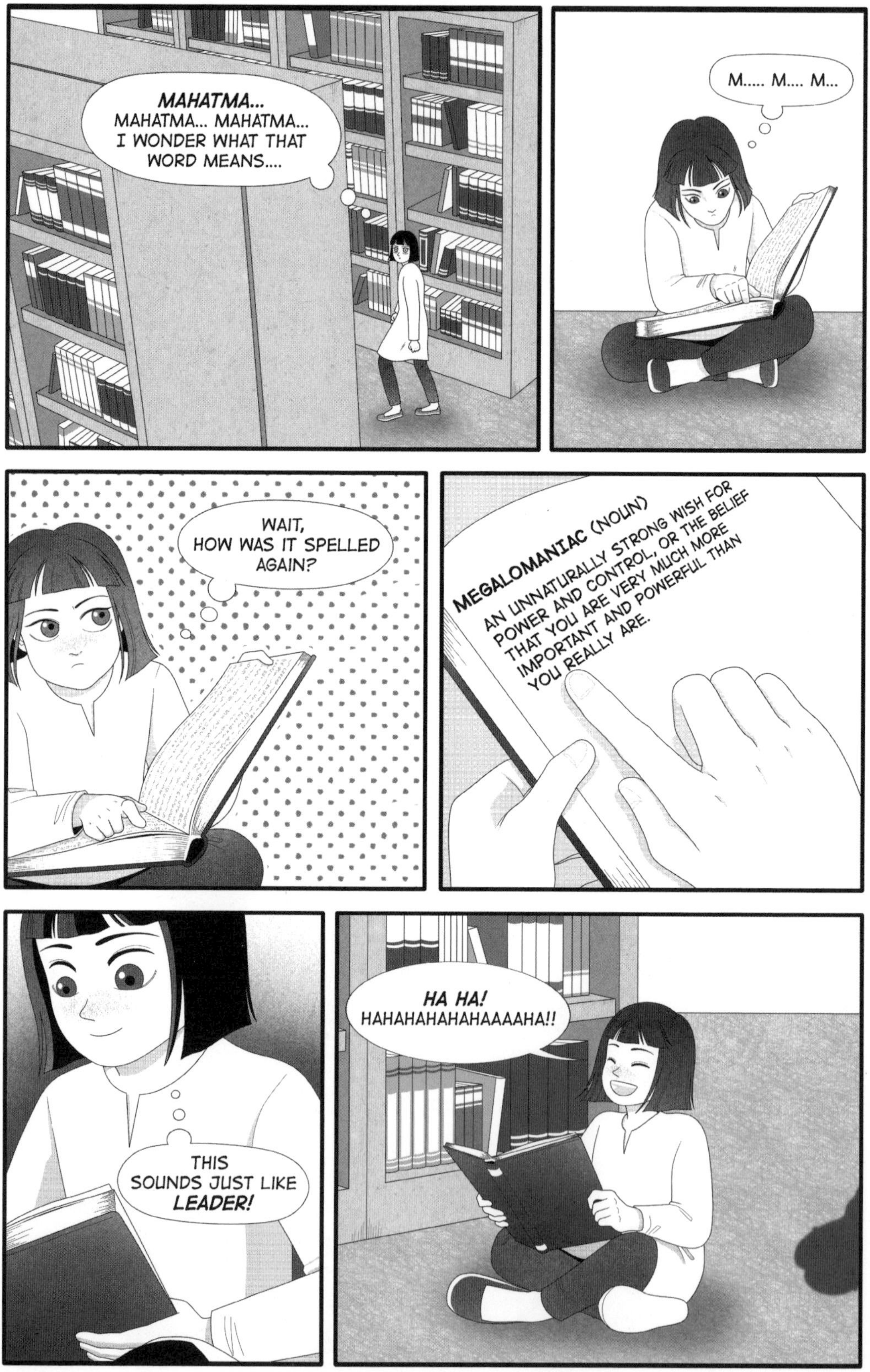
MAHATMA... MAHATMA... MAHATMA... I WONDER WHAT THAT WORD MEANS....
M..... M.... M...
WAIT, HOW WAS IT SPELLED AGAIN?
MEGALOMANIAC (NOUN)
AN UNNATURALLY STRONG WISH FOR POWER AND CONTROL, OR THE BELIEF THAT YOU ARE VERY MUCH MORE IMPORTANT AND POWERFUL THAN YOU REALLY ARE.
THIS SOUNDS JUST LIKE LEADER!
HA HA! HAHAHAHAHAHAAAAHA!!

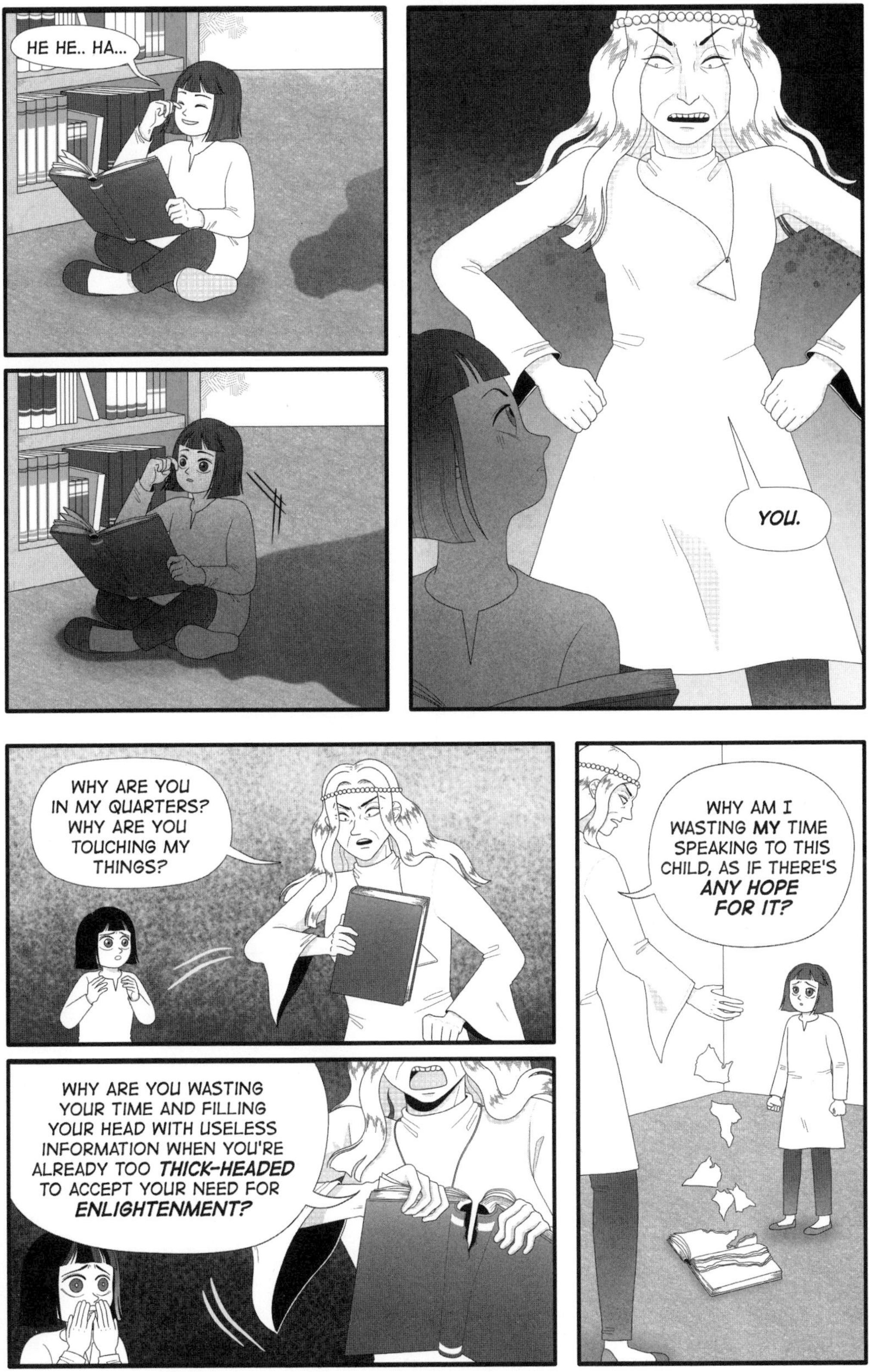
HE HE.. HA...
YOU.
WHY ARE YOU IN MY QUARTERS? WHY ARE YOU TOUCHING MY THINGS?
WHY ARE YOU WASTING YOUR TIME AND FILLING YOUR HEAD WITH USELESS INFORMATION WHEN YOU'RE ALREADY TOO *THICK-HEADED* TO ACCEPT YOUR NEED FOR *ENLIGHTENMENT?*
WHY AM I WASTING **MY** TIME SPEAKING TO THIS CHILD, AS IF THERE'S *ANY HOPE FOR IT?*

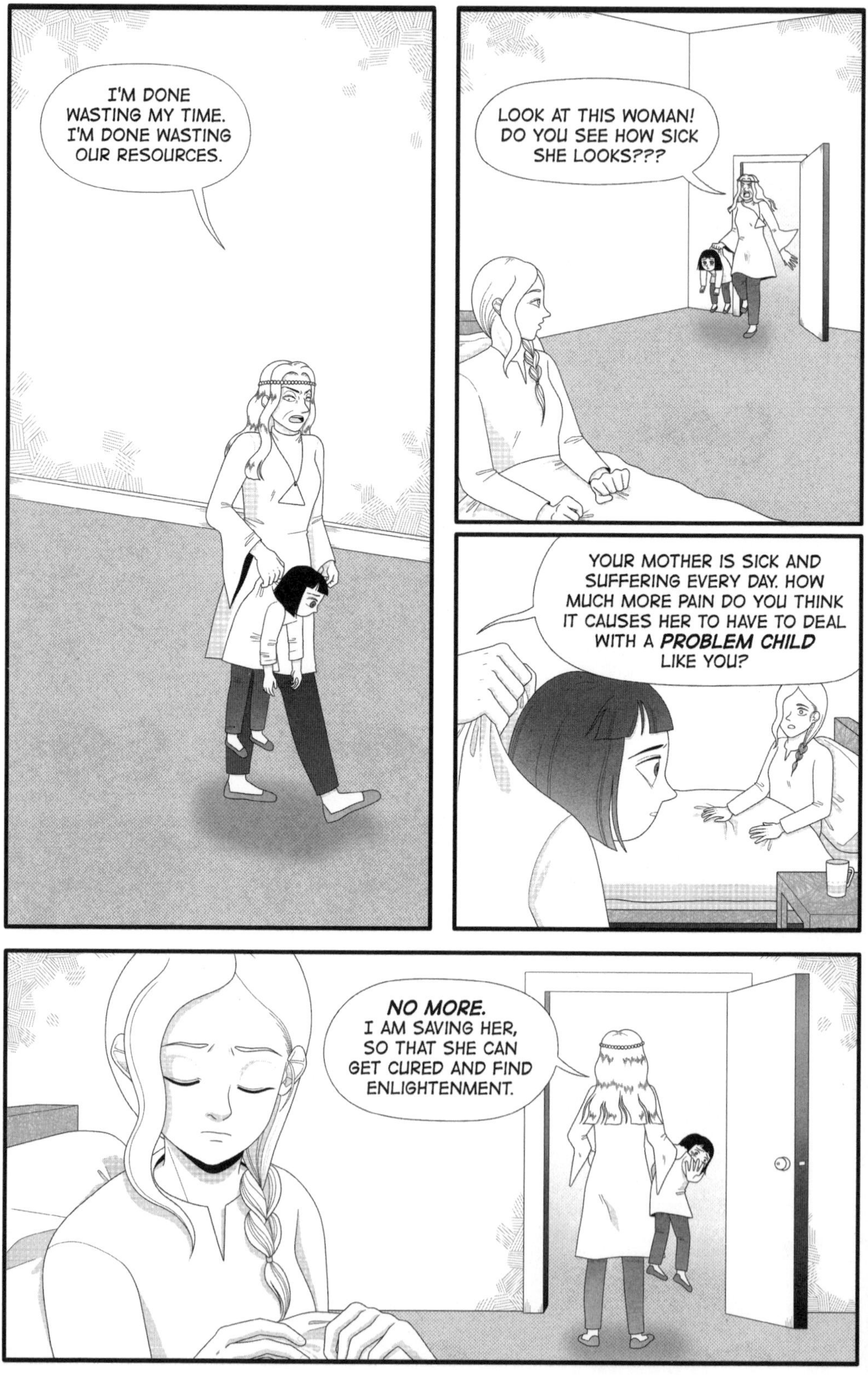
I'M DONE WASTING MY TIME. I'M DONE WASTING OUR RESOURCES.
LOOK AT THIS WOMAN! DO YOU SEE HOW SICK SHE LOOKS???
YOUR MOTHER IS SICK AND SUFFERING EVERY DAY. HOW MUCH MORE PAIN DO YOU THINK IT CAUSES HER TO HAVE TO DEAL WITH A PROBLEM CHILD LIKE YOU?
NO MORE. I AM SAVING HER, SO THAT SHE CAN GET CURED AND FIND ENLIGHTENMENT.

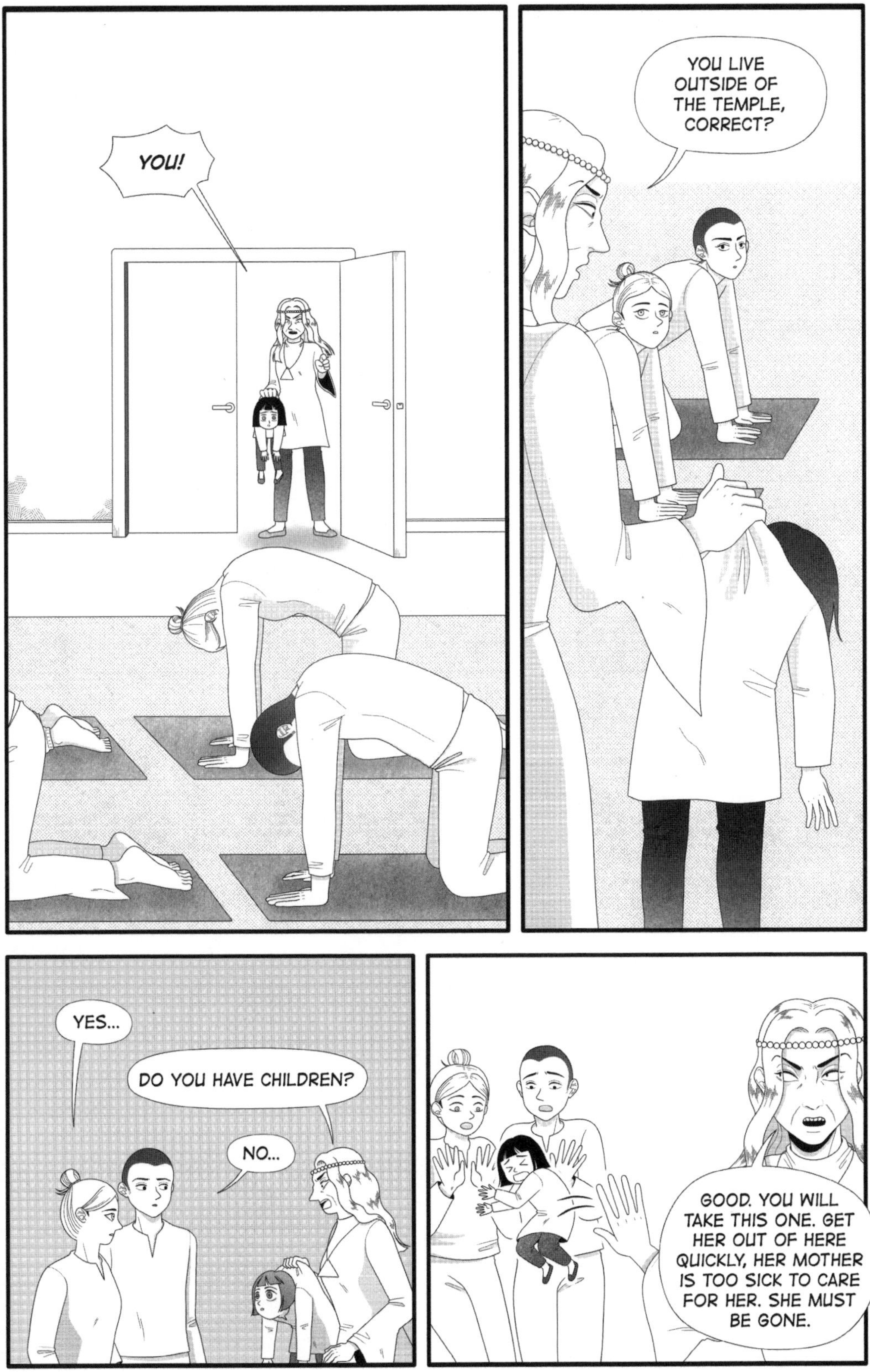
YOU!
YOU LIVE OUTSIDE OF THE TEMPLE, CORRECT?
YES...
DO YOU HAVE CHILDREN?
NO...
GOOD. YOU WILL TAKE THIS ONE. GET HER OUT OF HERE QUICKLY, HER MOTHER IS TOO SICK TO CARE FOR HER. SHE MUST BE GONE.

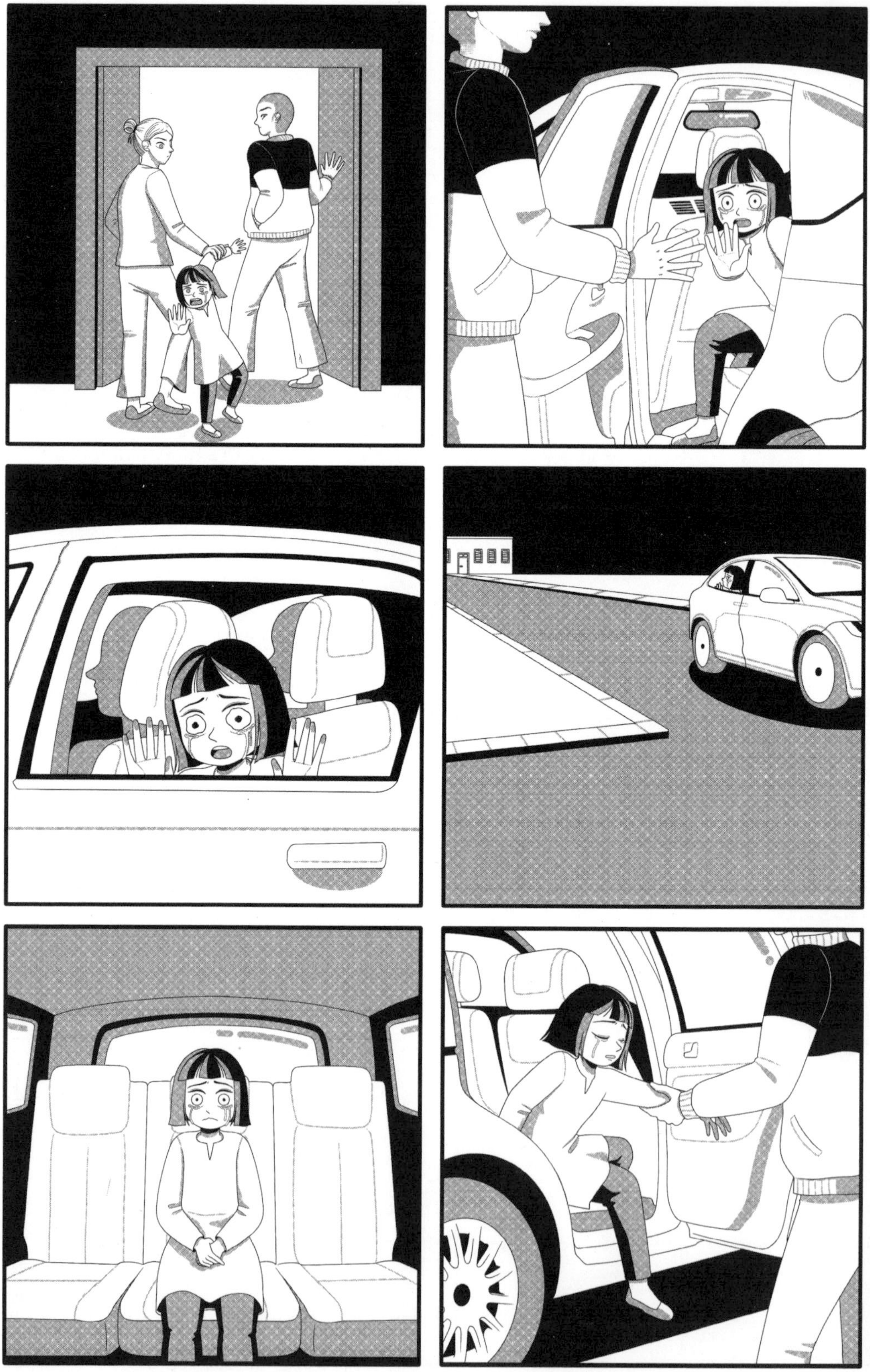

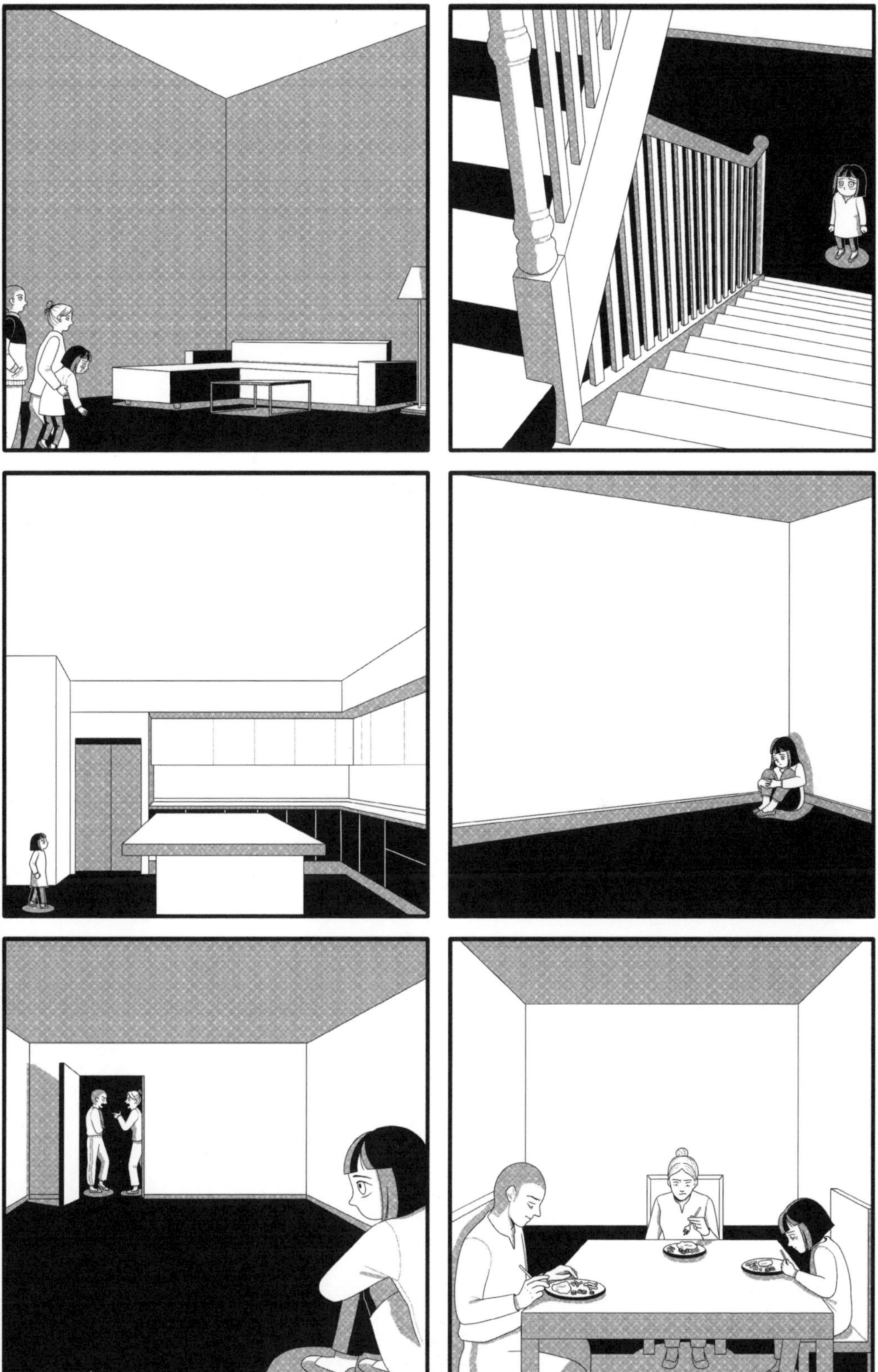

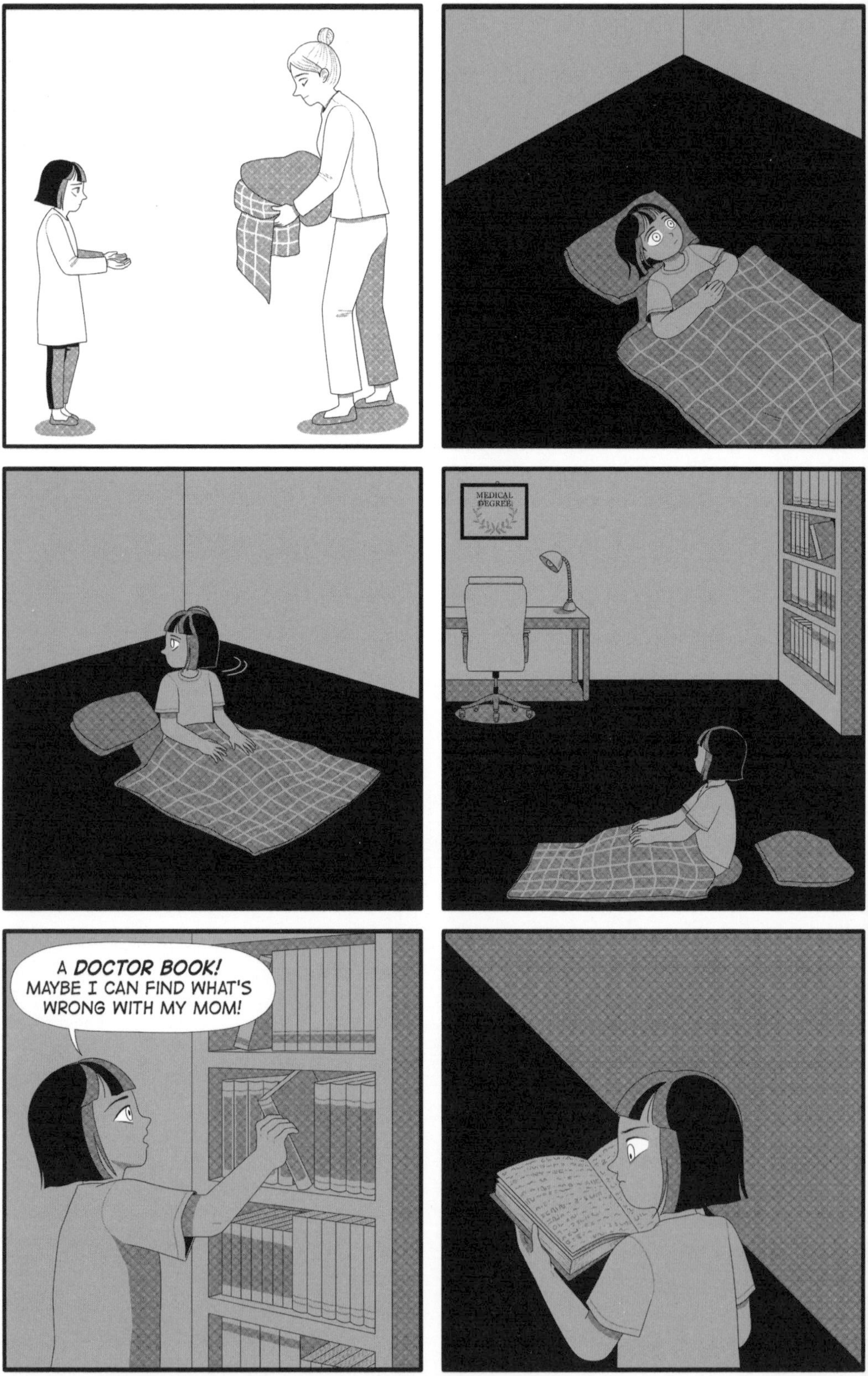
MEDICAL DEGREE
A DOCTOR BOOK! MAYBE I CAN FIND WHAT'S WRONG WITH MY MOM!

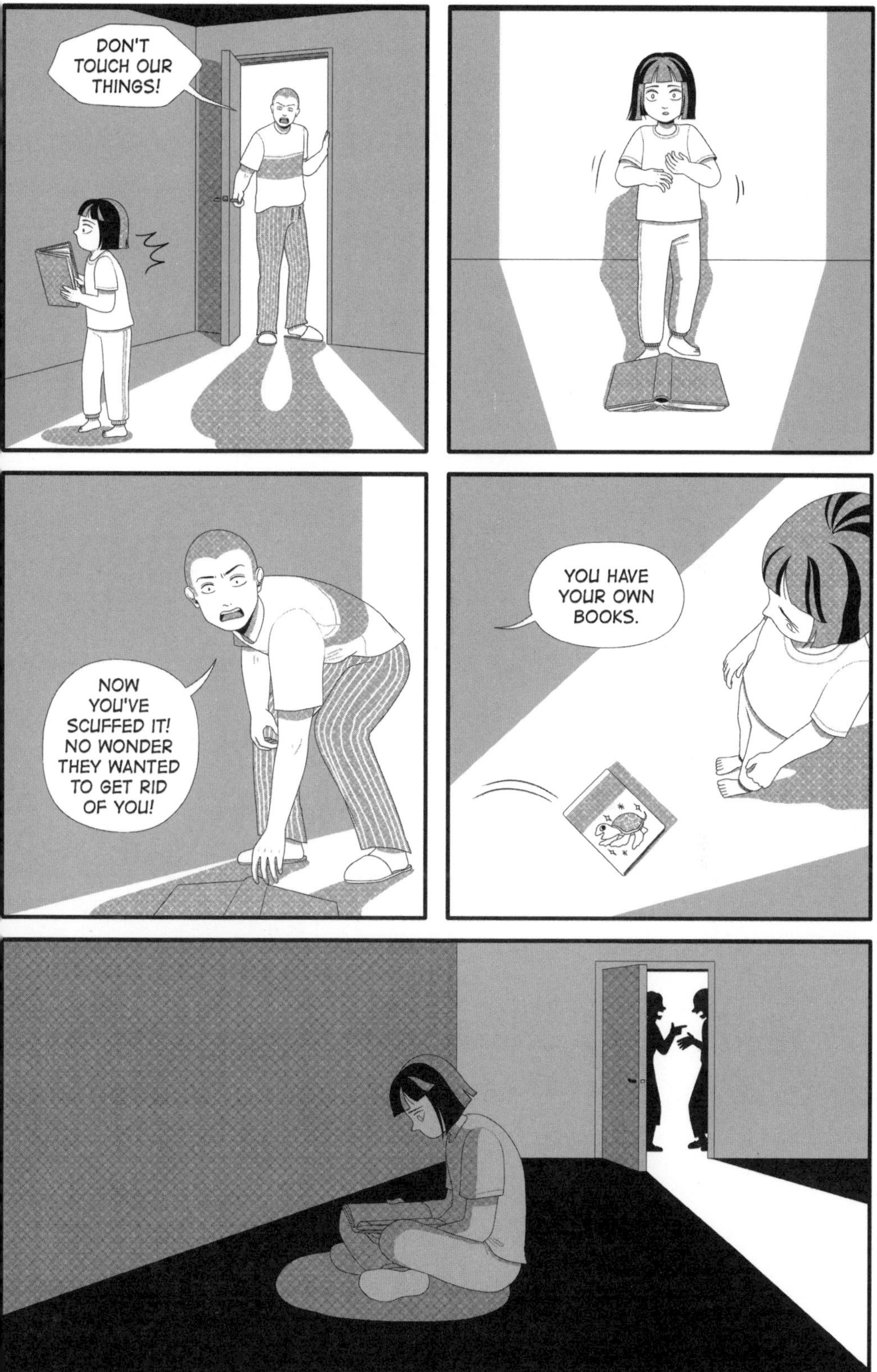
DON'T TOUCH OUR THINGS!
NOW YOU'VE SCUFFED IT! NO WONDER THEY WANTED TO GET RID OF YOU!
YOU HAVE YOUR OWN BOOKS.

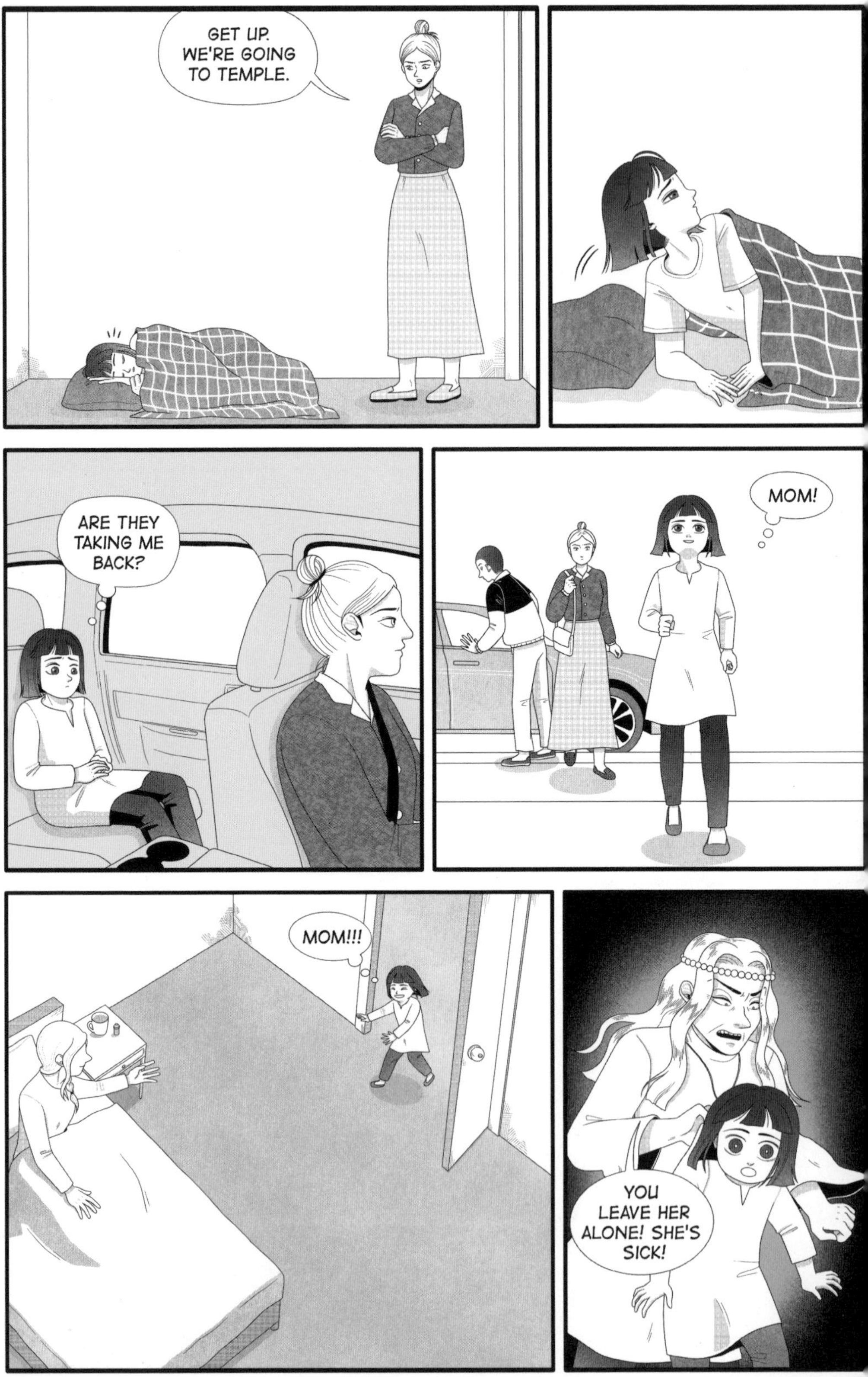
GET UP. WE'RE GOING TO TEMPLE.
ARE THEY TAKING ME BACK?
MOM!
MOM!!!
YOU LEAVE HER ALONE! SHE'S SICK!

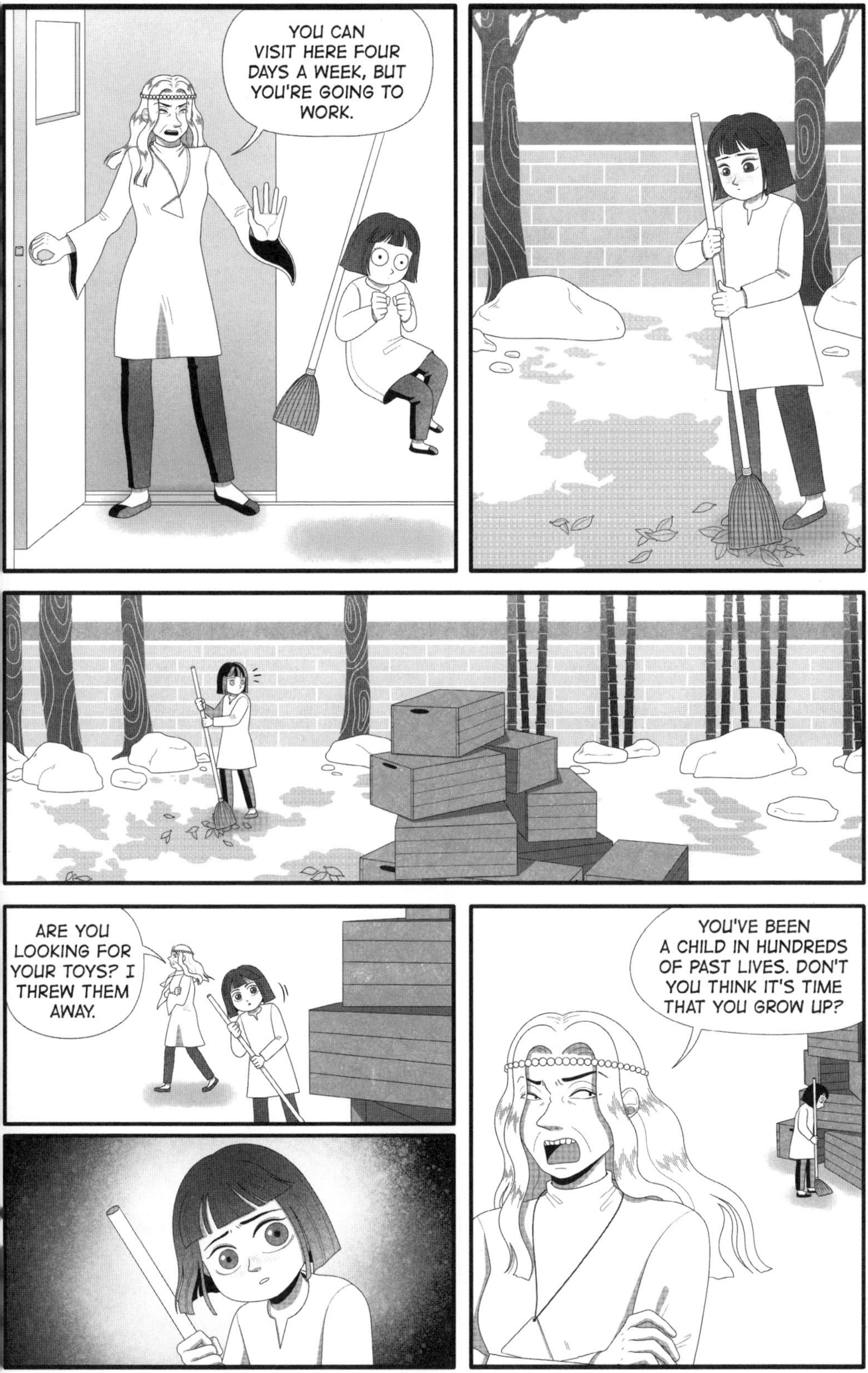
YOU CAN VISIT HERE FOUR DAYS A WEEK, BUT YOU'RE GOING TO WORK.
ARE YOU LOOKING FOR YOUR TOYS? I THREW THEM AWAY.
YOU'VE BEEN A CHILD IN HUNDREDS OF PAST LIVES. DON'T YOU THINK IT'S TIME THAT YOU GROW UP?

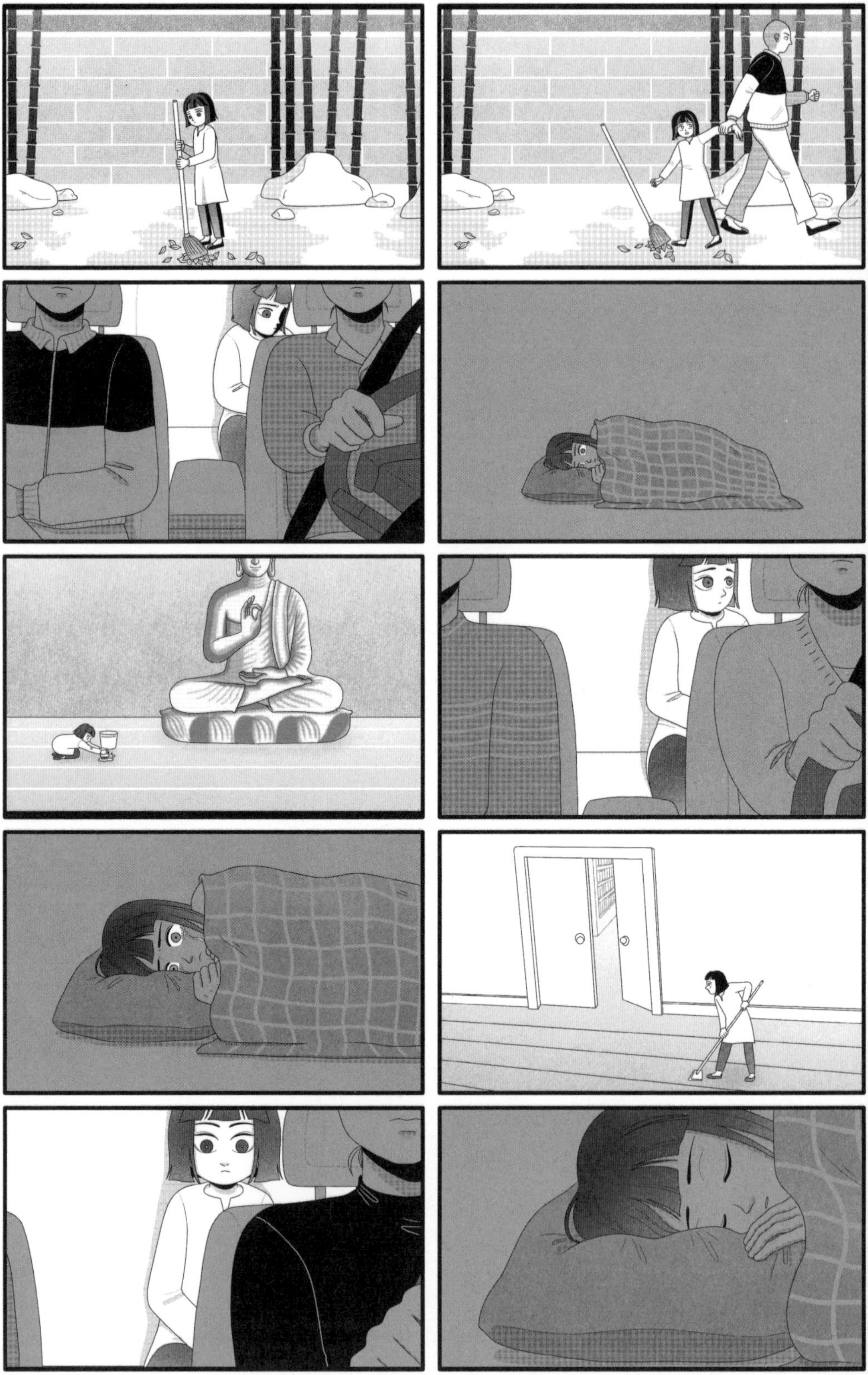

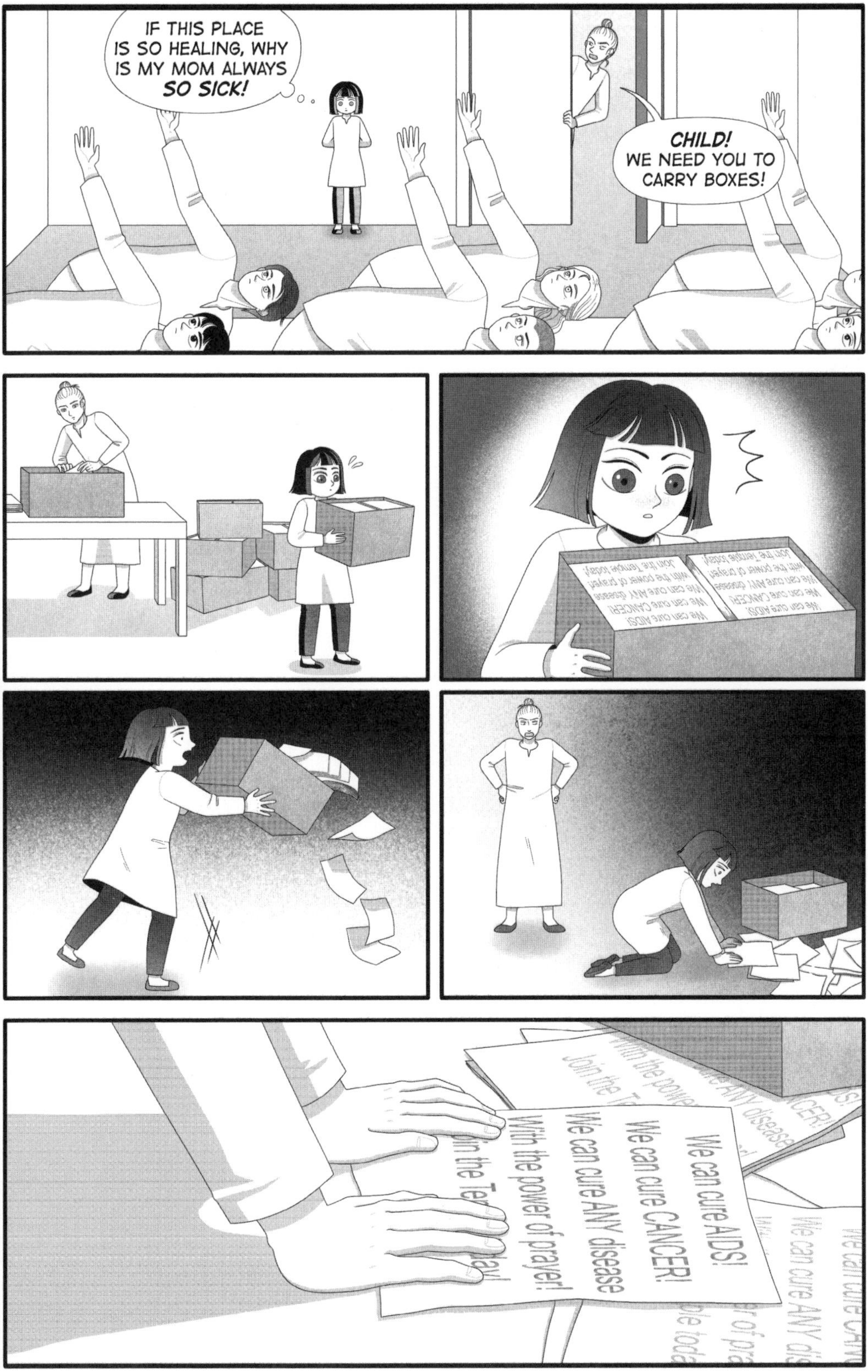
IF THIS PLACE IS SO HEALING, WHY IS MY MOM ALWAYS SO SICK!
CHILD! WE NEED YOU TO CARRY BOXES!
We can cure AIDS!
We can cure CANCER!
We can cure ANY disease
With the power of prayer!

CHAPTER FIVE

THE CURE

We can cure AIDS!
We can cure CANCER!
We can cure ANY disease
with the power of prayer!
Join the Temple today!

WE'VE TRIED. LEADER HAS DONE SO MUCH TO HELP ME. BUT IT DOESN'T WORK...

...IT'S *MY FAULT.*

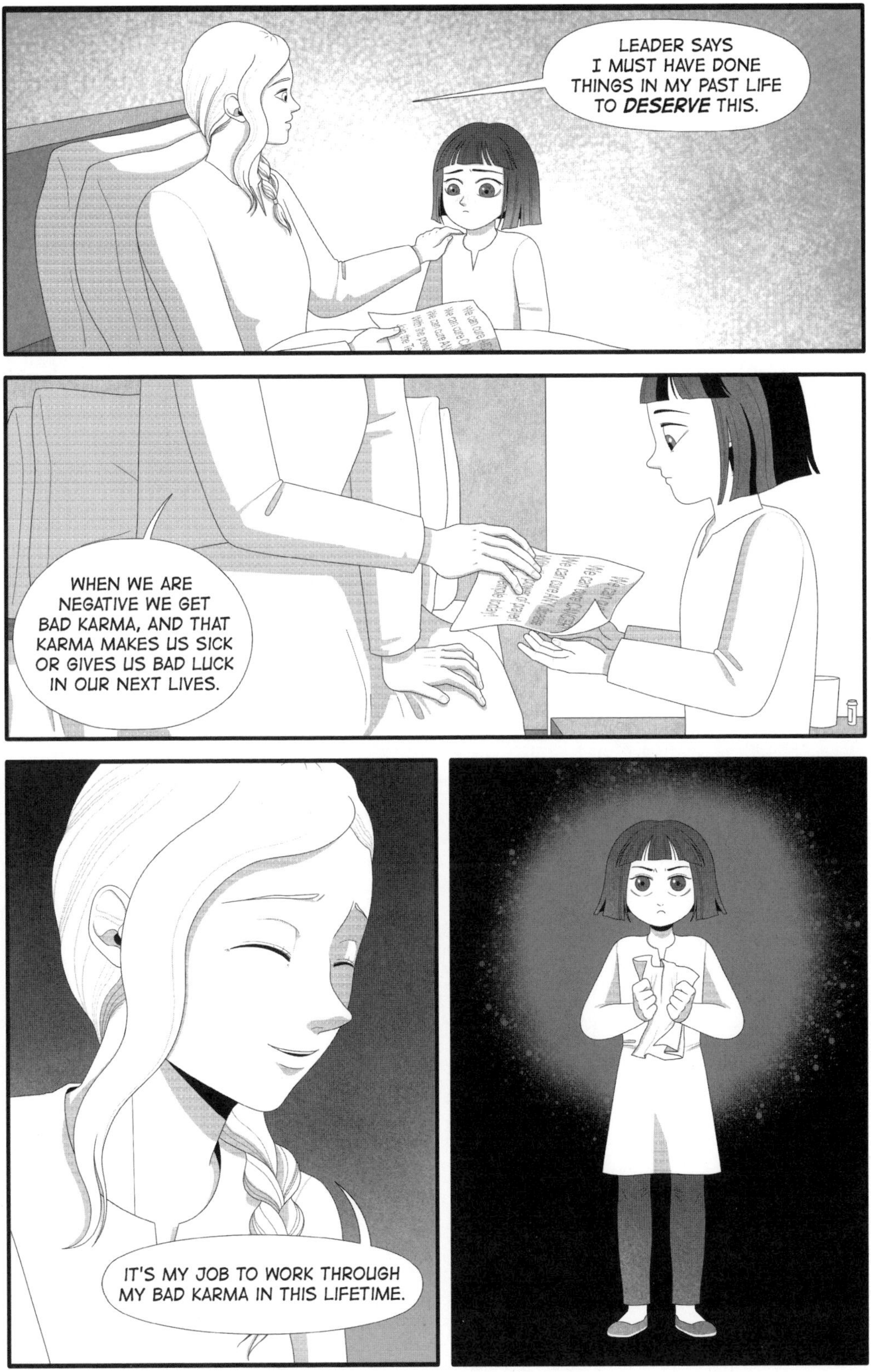
LEADER SAYS I MUST HAVE DONE THINGS IN MY PAST LIFE TO *DESERVE* THIS.
WHEN WE ARE NEGATIVE WE GET BAD KARMA, AND THAT KARMA MAKES US SICK OR GIVES US BAD LUCK IN OUR NEXT LIVES.
IT'S MY JOB TO WORK THROUGH MY BAD KARMA IN THIS LIFETIME.

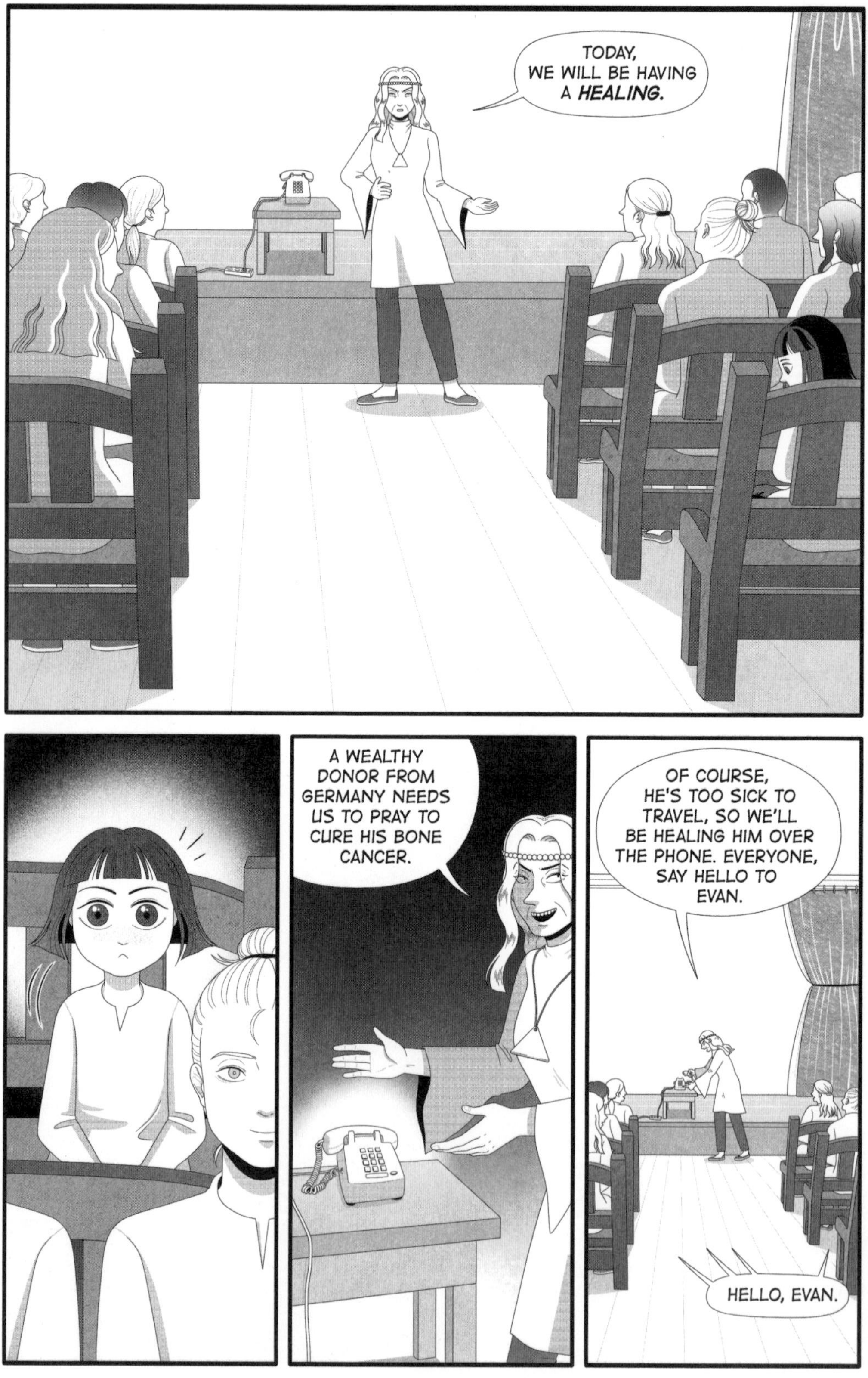
TODAY, WE WILL BE HAVING A *HEALING.*
A WEALTHY DONOR FROM GERMANY NEEDS US TO PRAY TO CURE HIS BONE CANCER.
OF COURSE, HE'S TOO SICK TO TRAVEL, SO WE'LL BE HEALING HIM OVER THE PHONE. EVERYONE, SAY HELLO TO EVAN.
HELLO, EVAN.

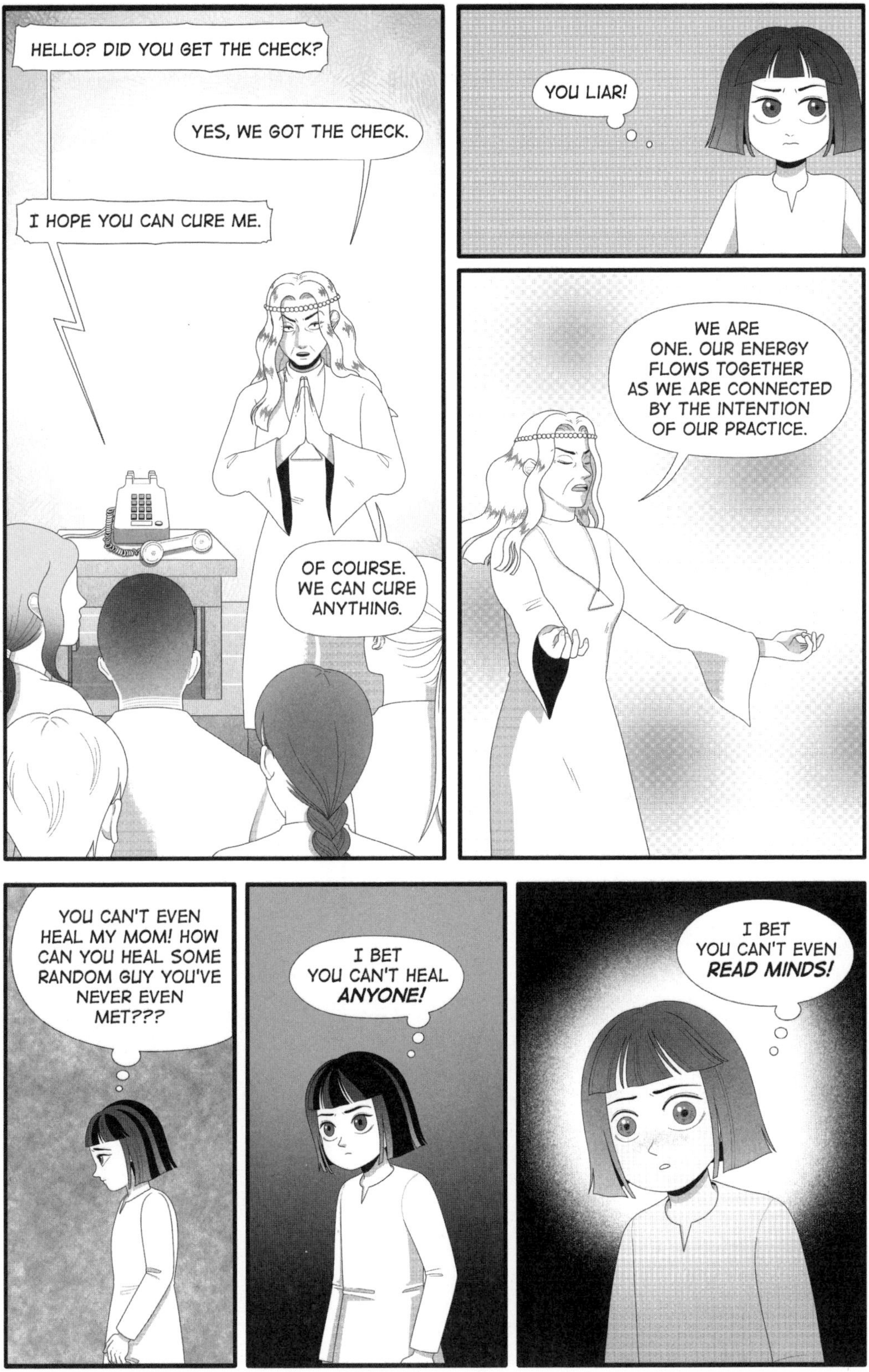
HELLO? DID YOU GET THE CHECK?
YES, WE GOT THE CHECK.
I HOPE YOU CAN CURE ME.
OF COURSE. WE CAN CURE ANYTHING.
YOU LIAR!
WE ARE ONE. OUR ENERGY FLOWS TOGETHER AS WE ARE CONNECTED BY THE INTENTION OF OUR PRACTICE.
YOU CAN'T EVEN HEAL MY MOM! HOW CAN YOU HEAL SOME RANDOM GUY YOU'VE NEVER EVEN MET???
I BET YOU CAN'T HEAL ***ANYONE!***
I BET YOU CAN'T EVEN ***READ MINDS!***

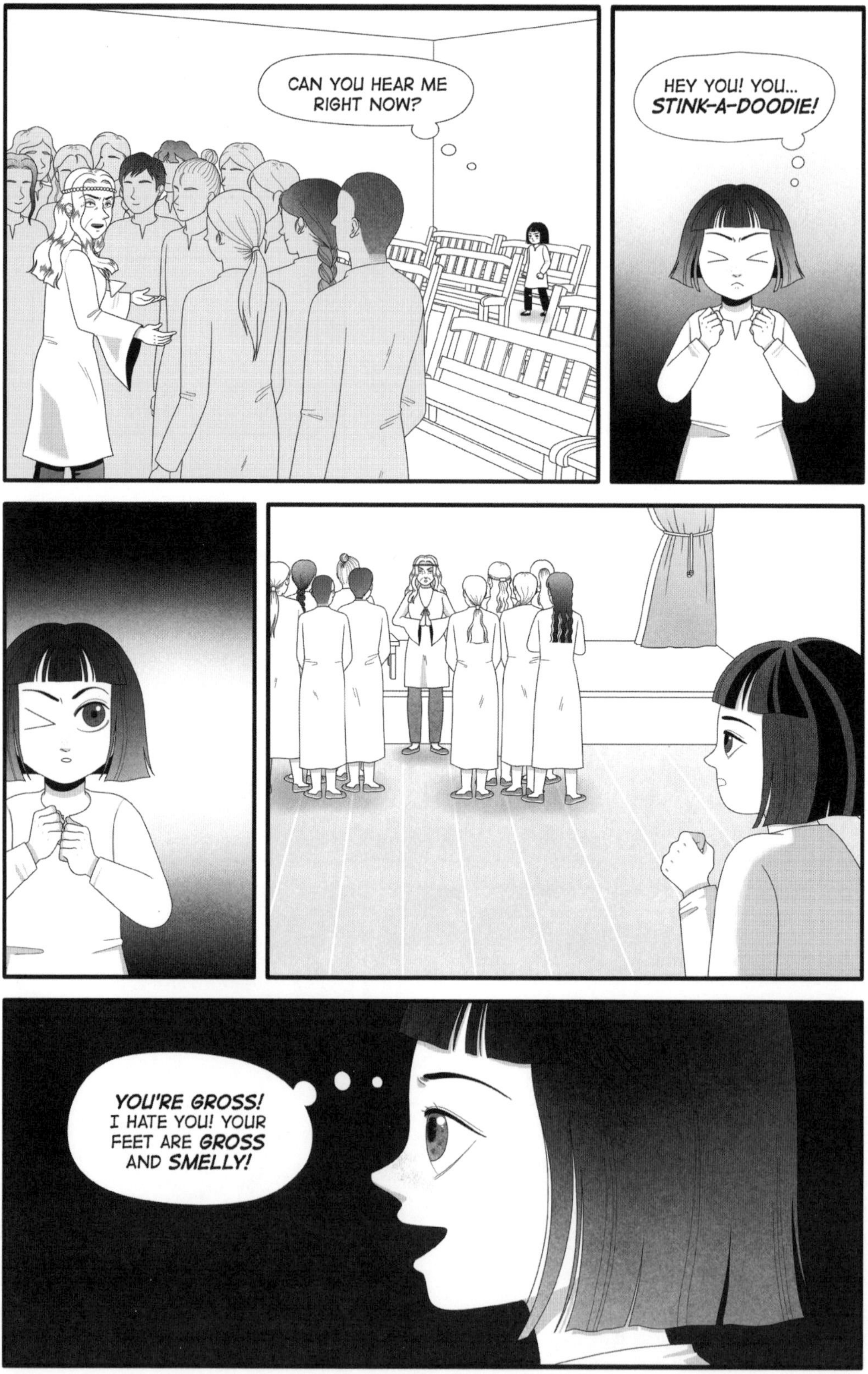
CAN YOU HEAR ME RIGHT NOW?
HEY YOU! YOU... STINK-A-DOODIE!
YOU'RE GROSS! I HATE YOU! YOUR FEET ARE GROSS AND SMELLY!

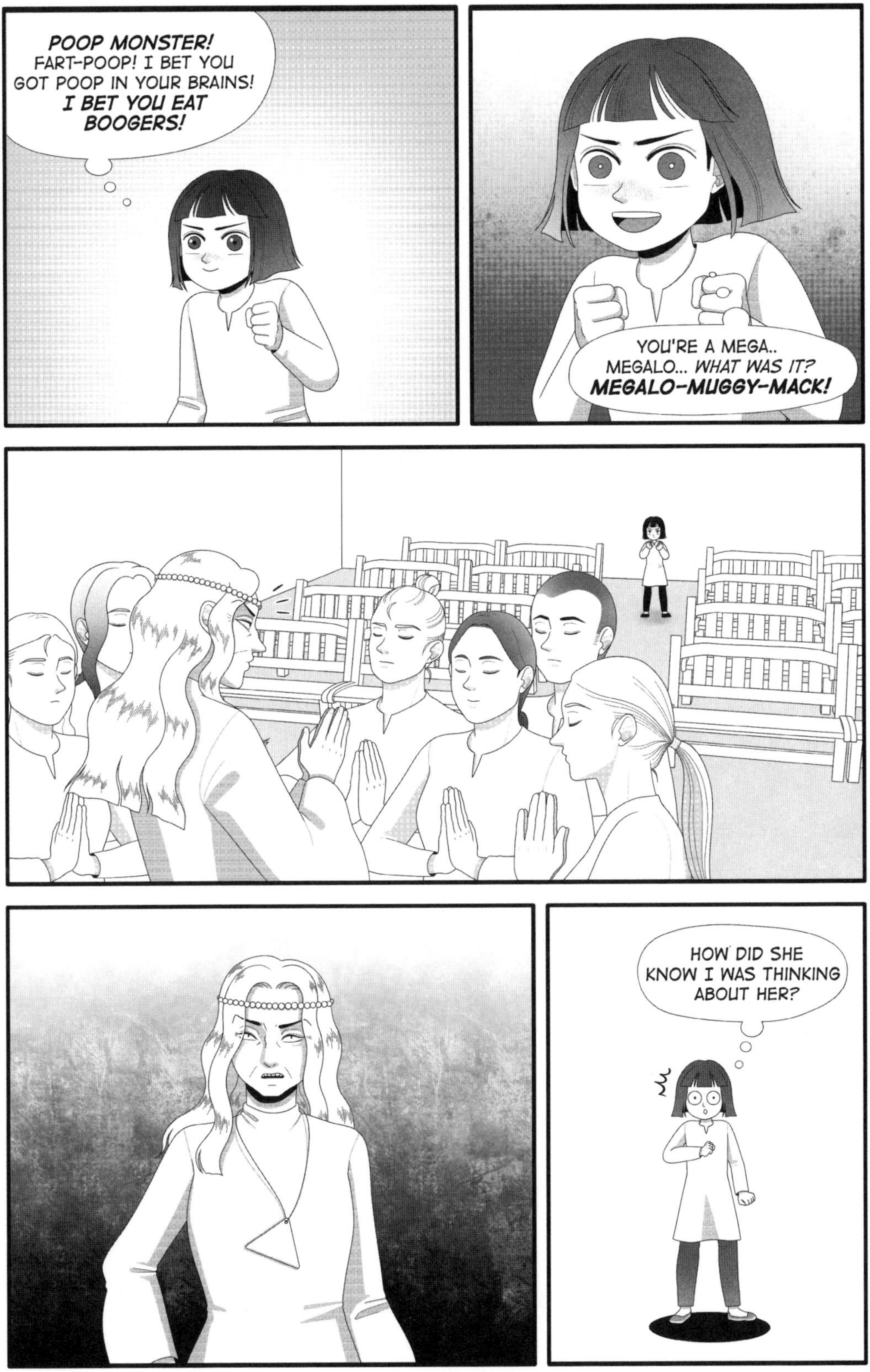
POOP MONSTER! FART-POOP! I BET YOU GOT POOP IN YOUR BRAINS! I BET YOU EAT BOOGERS!
YOU'RE A MEGA.. MEGALO... WHAT WAS IT? MEGALO-MUGGY-MACK!
HOW DID SHE KNOW I WAS THINKING ABOUT HER?

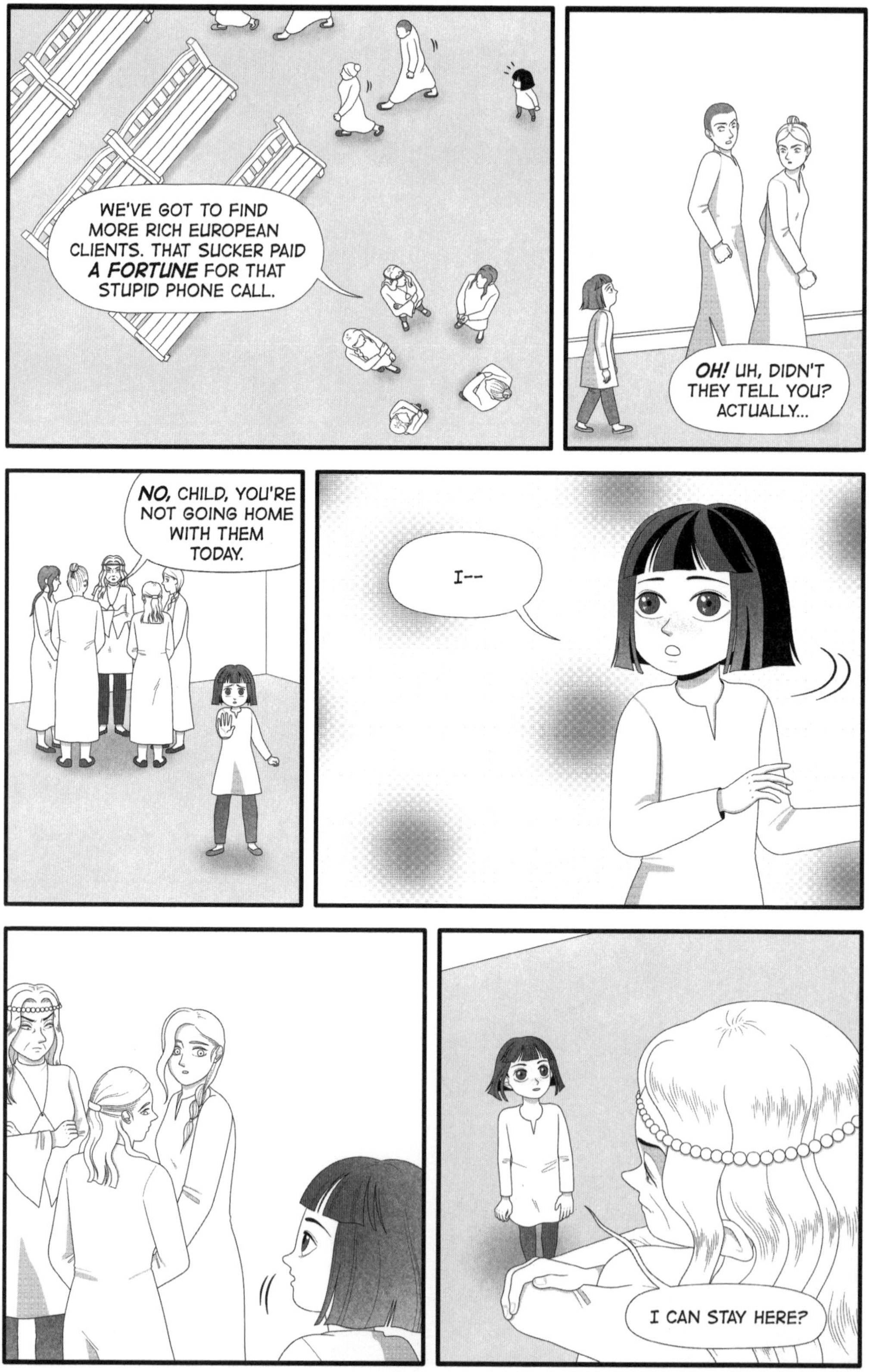
WE'VE GOT TO FIND MORE RICH EUROPEAN CLIENTS. THAT SUCKER PAID A FORTUNE FOR THAT STUPID PHONE CALL.
OH! UH, DIDN'T THEY TELL YOU? ACTUALLY...
NO, CHILD, YOU'RE NOT GOING HOME WITH THEM TODAY.
I--
I CAN STAY HERE?

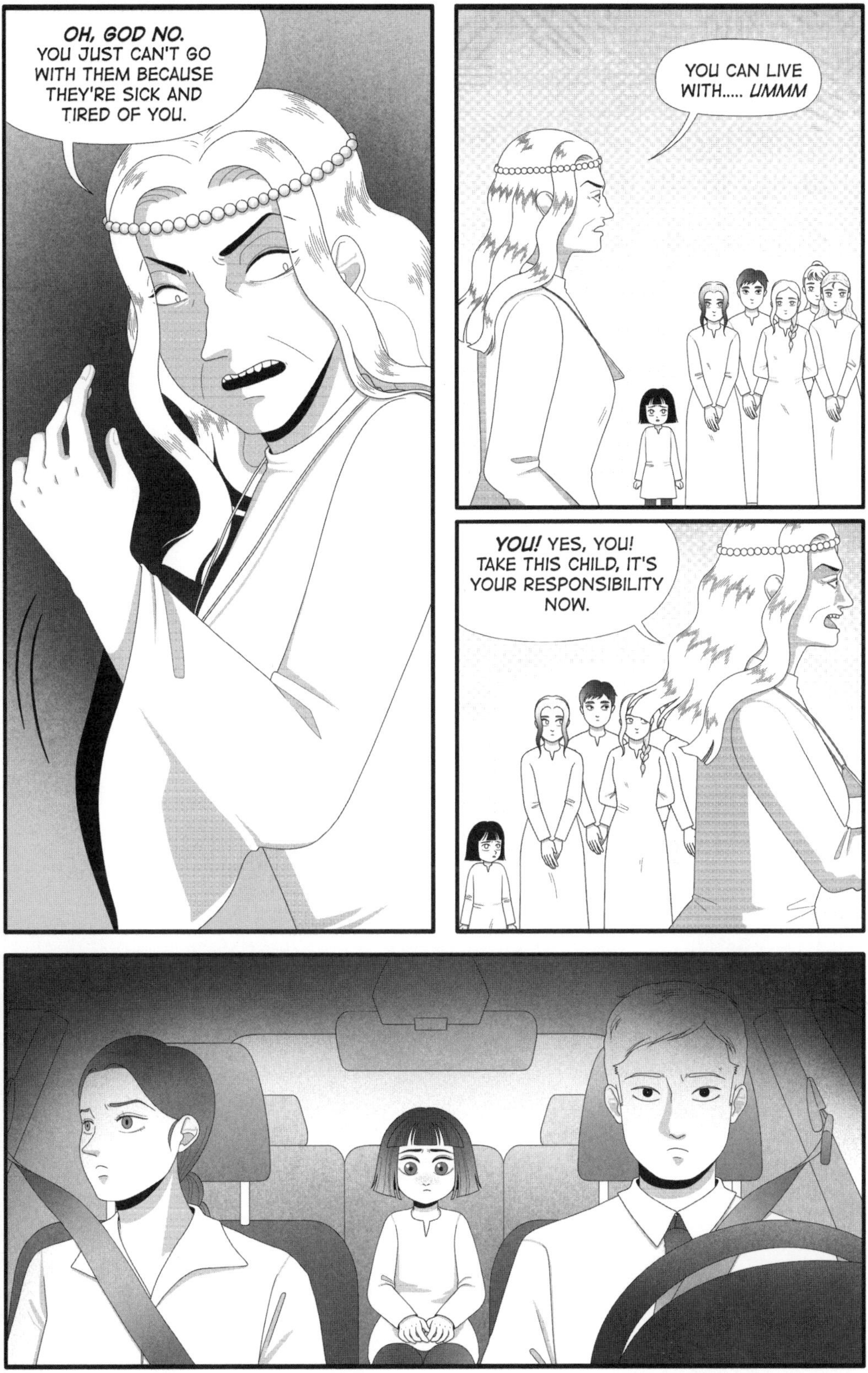
OH, GOD NO. YOU JUST CAN'T GO WITH THEM BECAUSE THEY'RE SICK AND TIRED OF YOU.
YOU CAN LIVE WITH..... UMMM
YOU! YES, YOU! TAKE THIS CHILD, IT'S YOUR RESPONSIBILITY NOW.

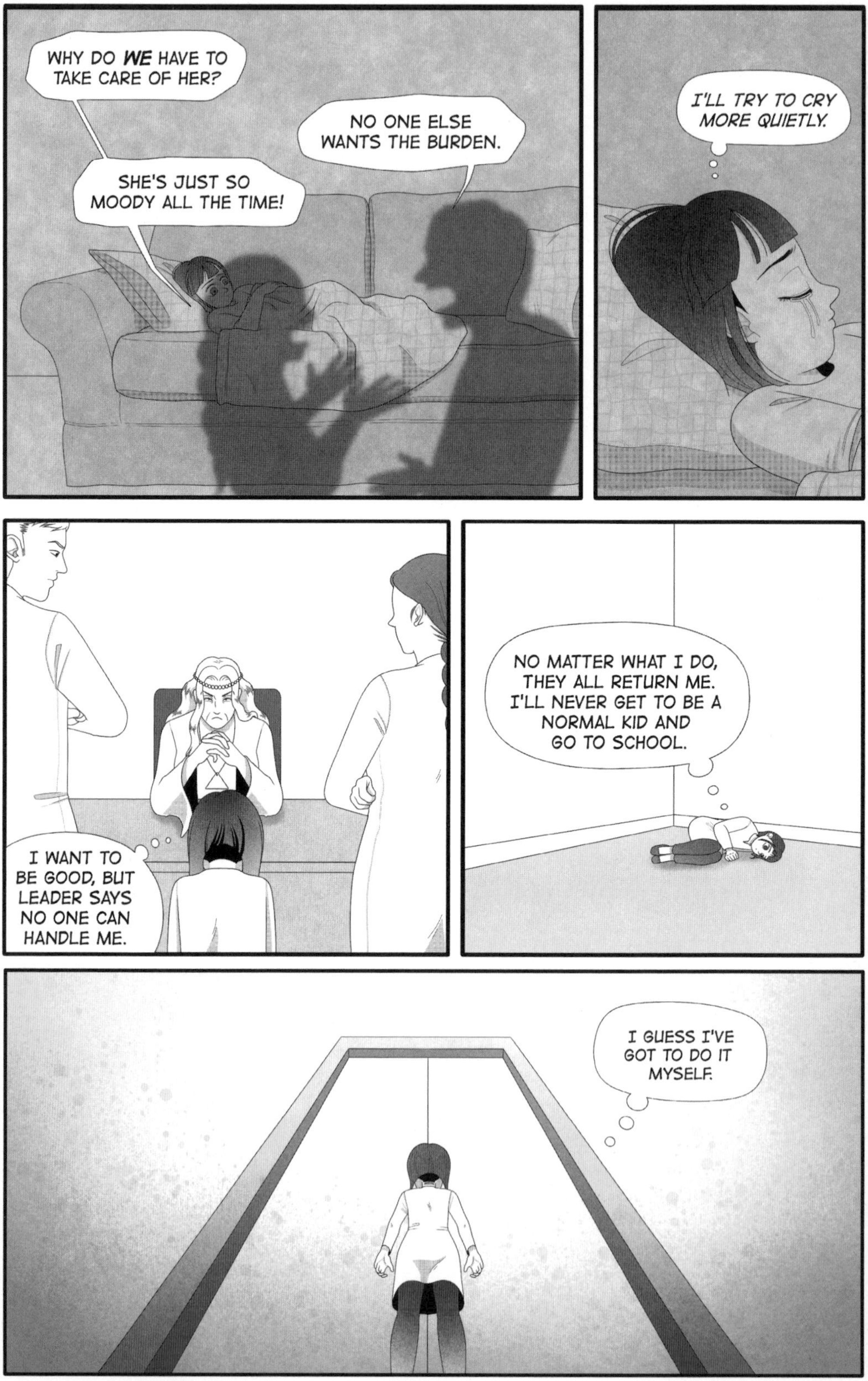
WHY DO **WE** HAVE TO TAKE CARE OF HER?
SHE'S JUST SO MOODY ALL THE TIME!
NO ONE ELSE WANTS THE BURDEN.
I'LL TRY TO CRY MORE QUIETLY.
I WANT TO BE GOOD, BUT LEADER SAYS NO ONE CAN HANDLE ME.
NO MATTER WHAT I DO, THEY ALL RETURN ME. I'LL NEVER GET TO BE A NORMAL KID AND GO TO SCHOOL.
I GUESS I'VE GOT TO DO IT MYSELF.

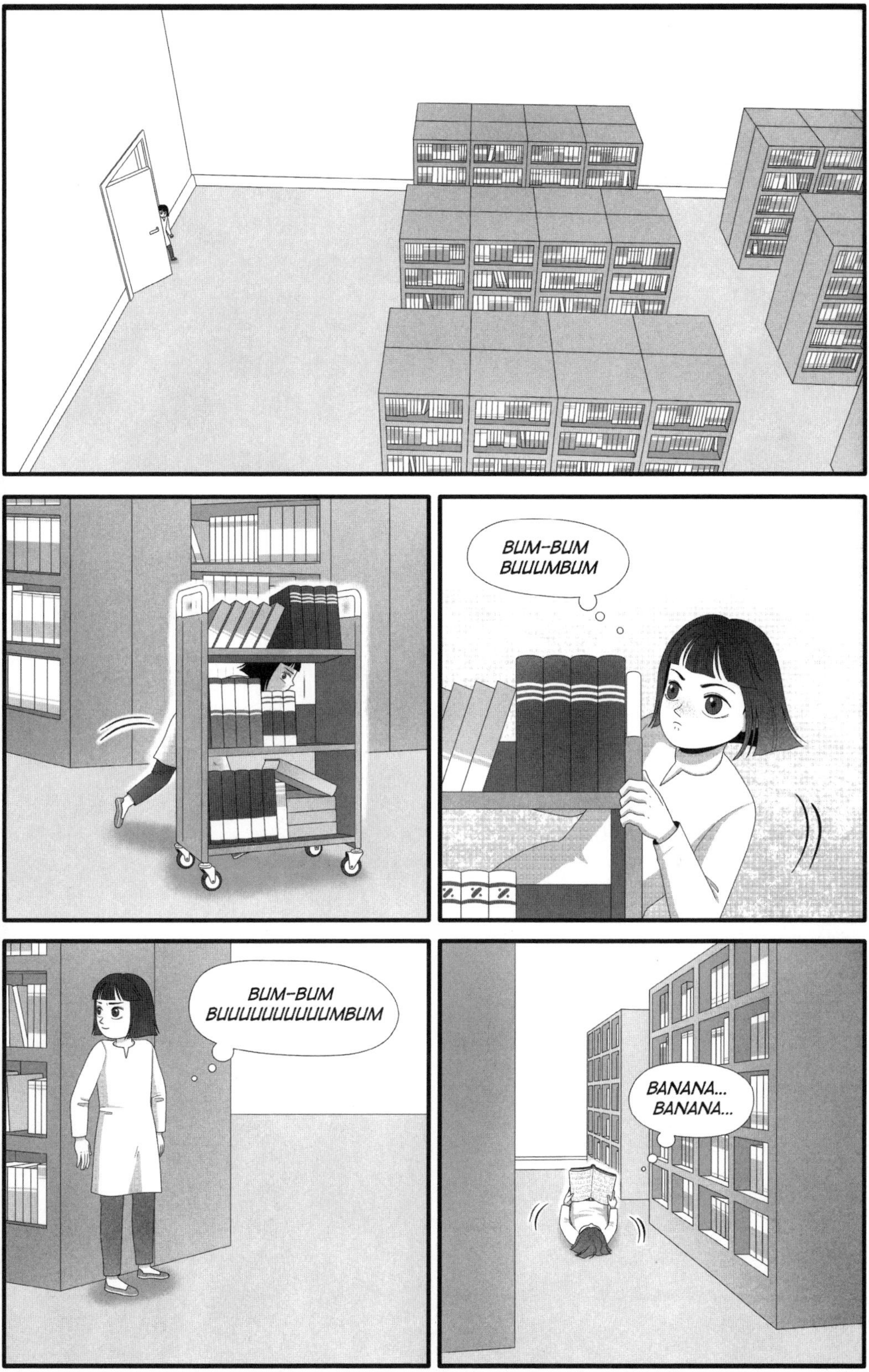
BUM-BUM
BUUUMBUM
BUM-BUM
BUUUUUUUUUUMBUM
BANANA...
BANANA...

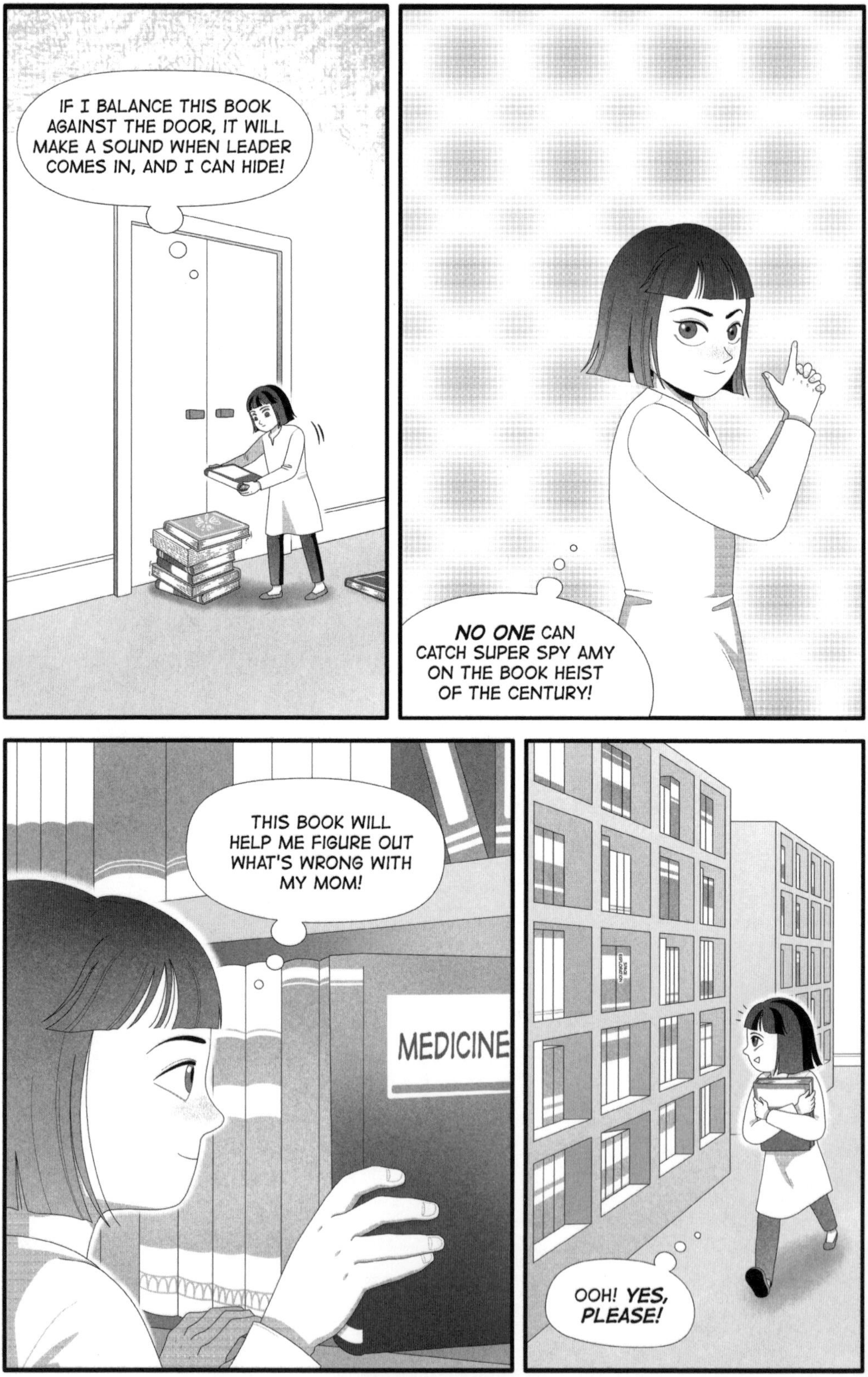
IF I BALANCE THIS BOOK AGAINST THE DOOR, IT WILL MAKE A SOUND WHEN LEADER COMES IN, AND I CAN HIDE!
NO ONE CAN CATCH SUPER SPY AMY ON THE BOOK HEIST OF THE CENTURY!
THIS BOOK WILL HELP ME FIGURE OUT WHAT'S WRONG WITH MY MOM!
MEDICINE
OOH! YES, PLEASE!

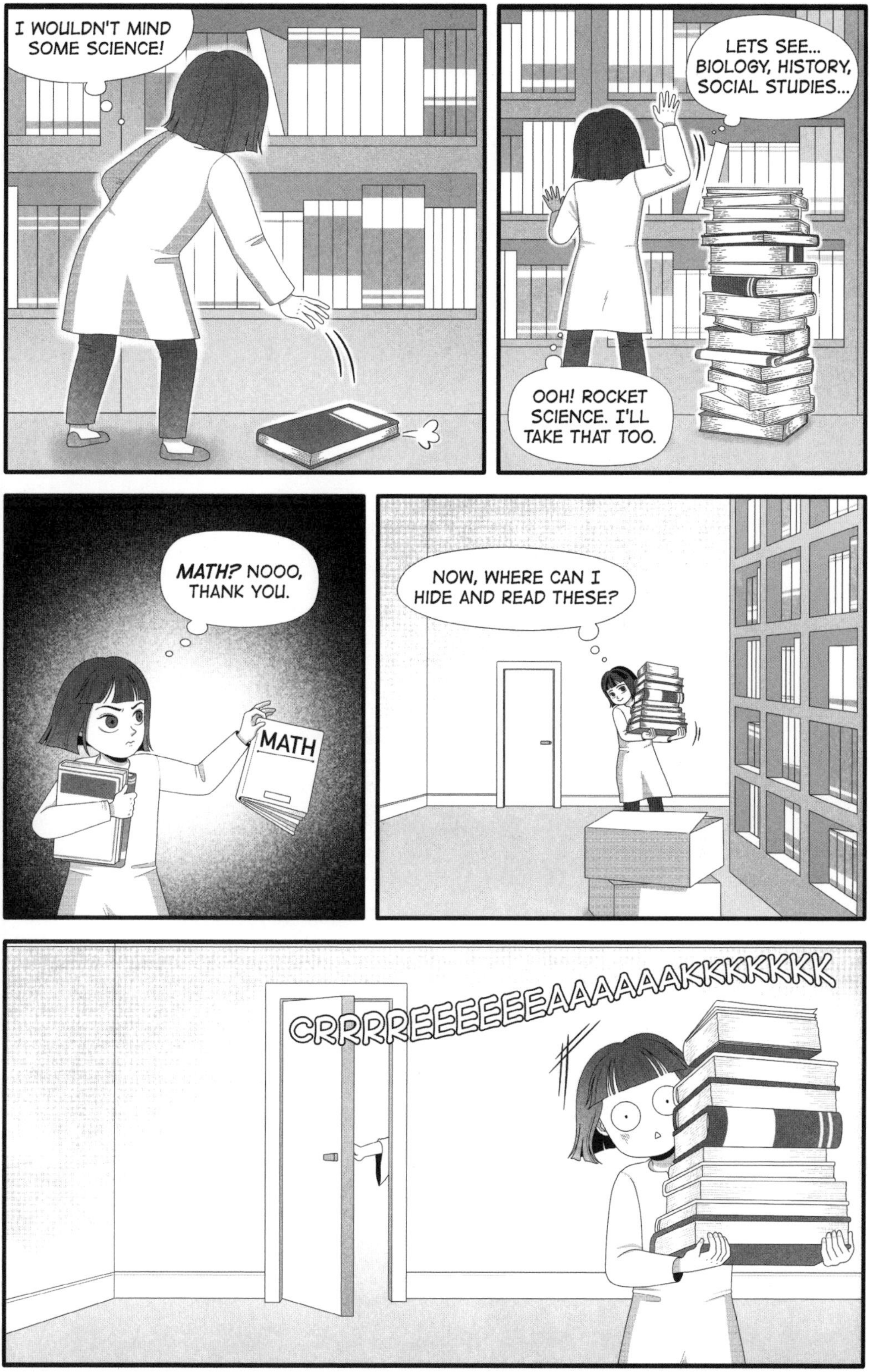
I WOULDN'T MIND SOME SCIENCE!
LETS SEE... BIOLOGY, HISTORY, SOCIAL STUDIES...
OOH! ROCKET SCIENCE. I'LL TAKE THAT TOO.
MATH? NOOO, THANK YOU.
MATH
NOW, WHERE CAN I HIDE AND READ THESE?
CRRRREEEEEEEAAAAAAKKKKKK

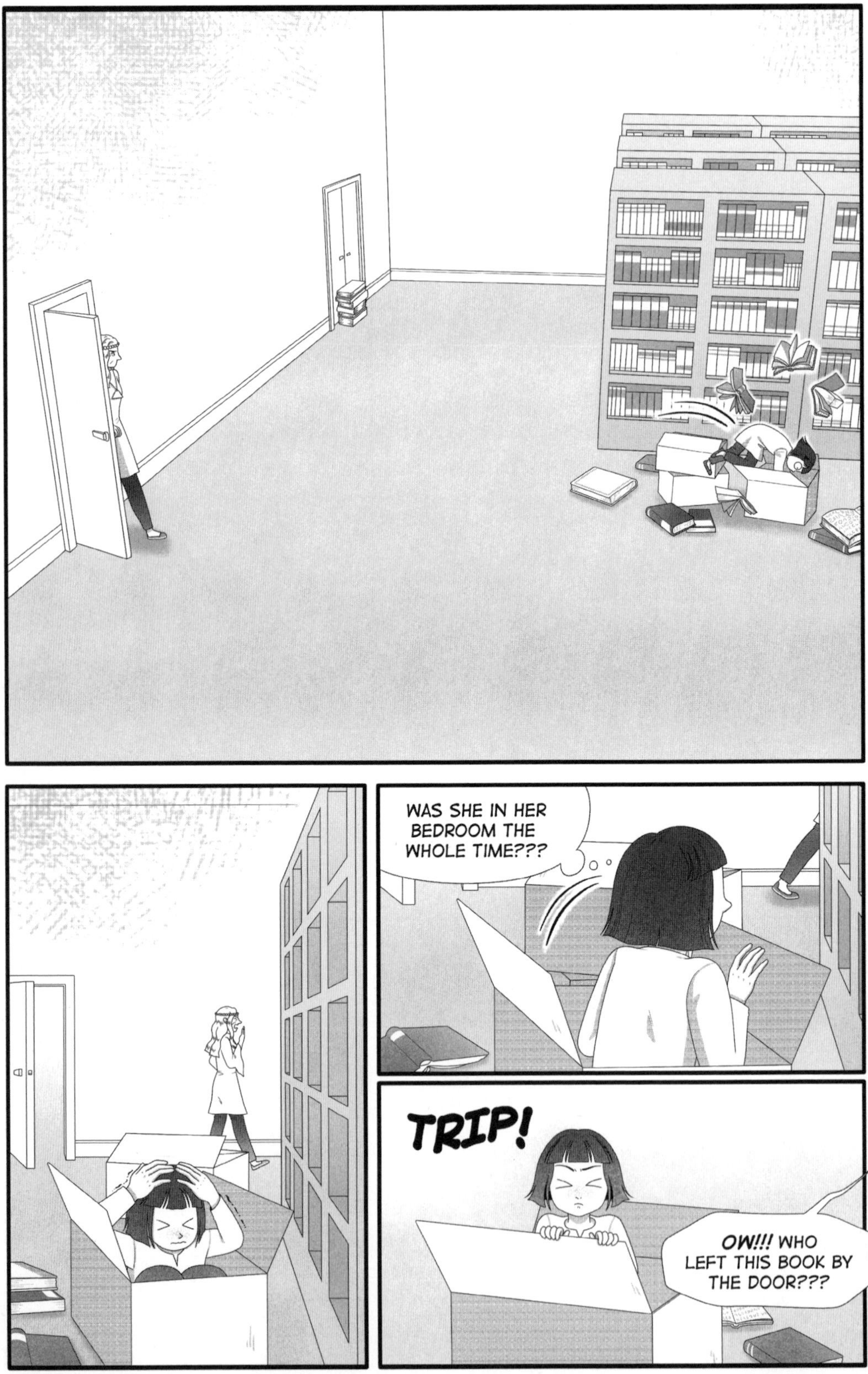
WAS SHE IN HER BEDROOM THE WHOLE TIME???
TRIP!
OW!!! WHO LEFT THIS BOOK BY THE DOOR???

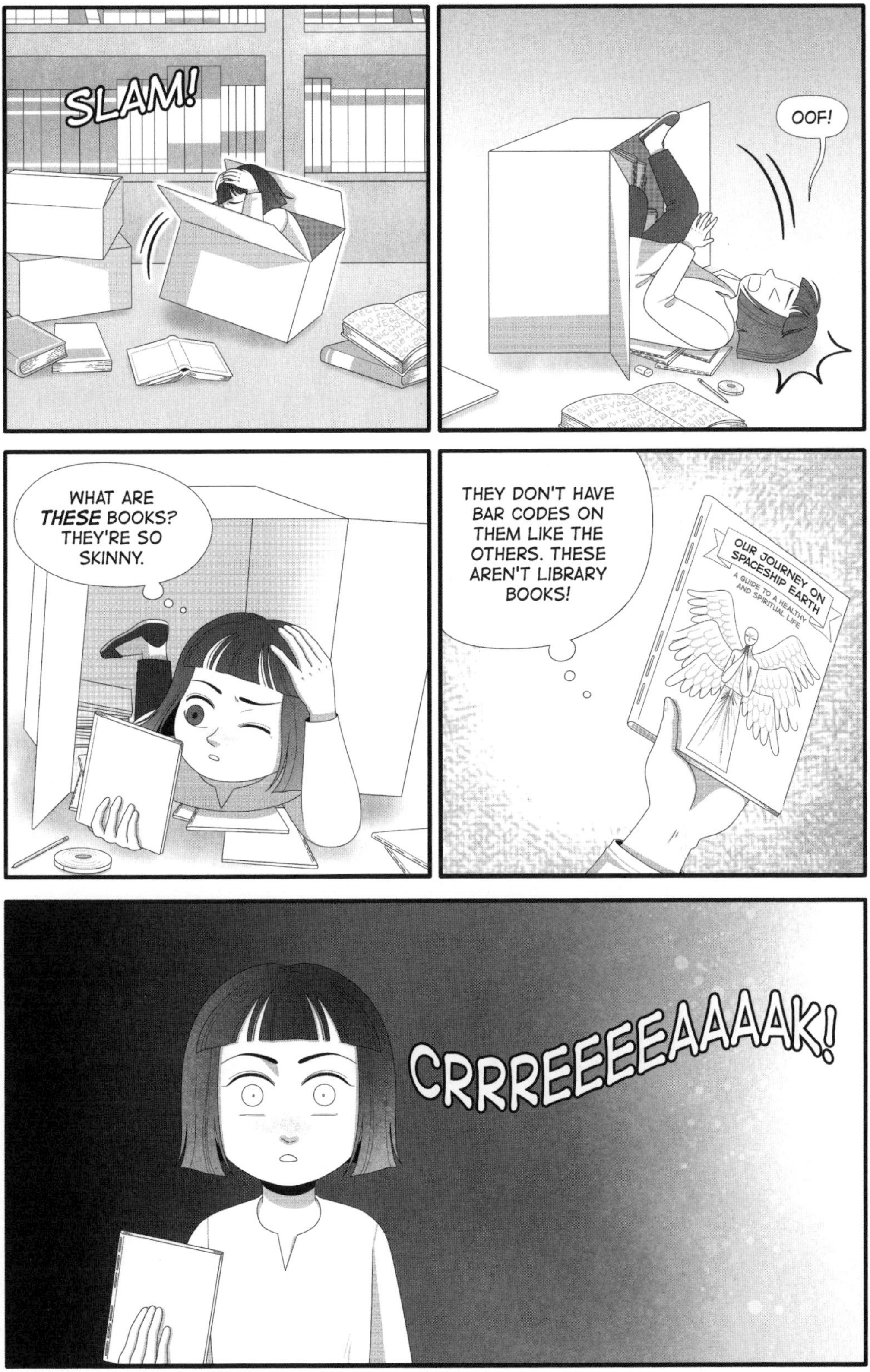
SLAM!
OOF!
WHAT ARE THESE BOOKS? THEY'RE SO SKINNY.
THEY DON'T HAVE BAR CODES ON THEM LIKE THE OTHERS. THESE AREN'T LIBRARY BOOKS!
OUR JOURNEY ON SPACESHIP EARTH
A GUIDE TO A HEALTHY AND SPIRITUAL LIFE
CRRREEEEEAAAAK!

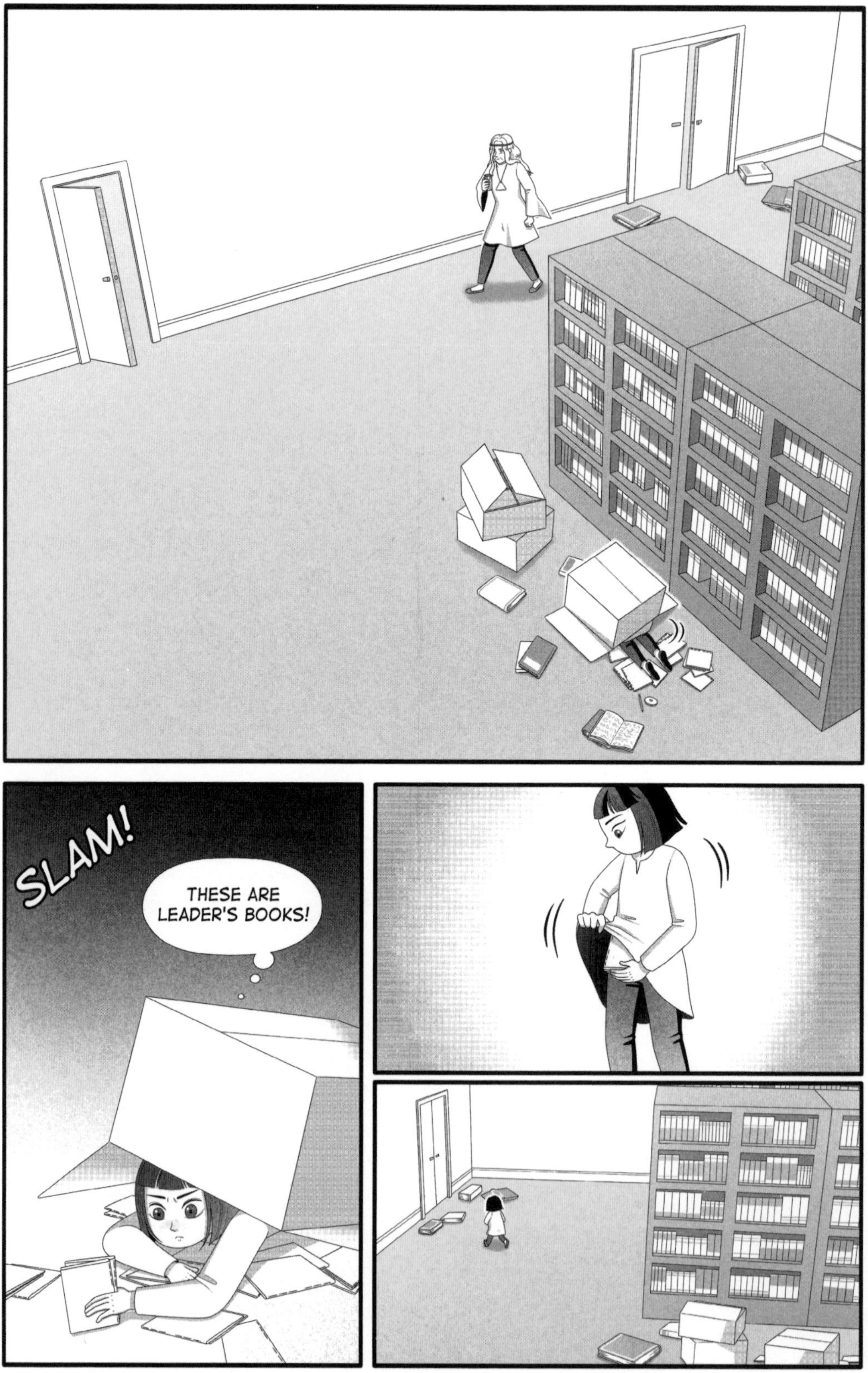
SLAM!
THESE ARE LEADER'S BOOKS!

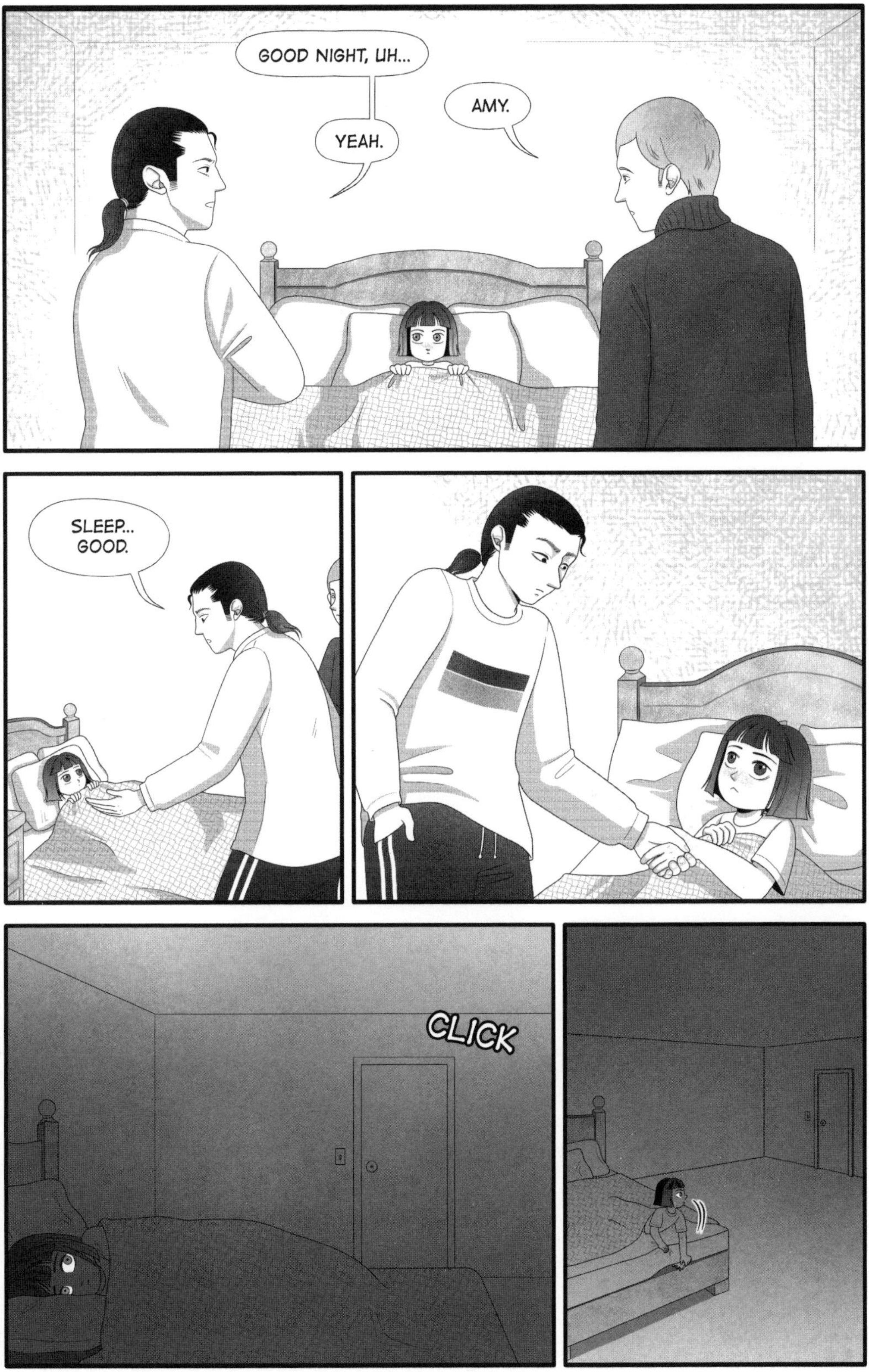
GOOD NIGHT, UH...
YEAH.
AMY.
SLEEP... GOOD.
CLICK

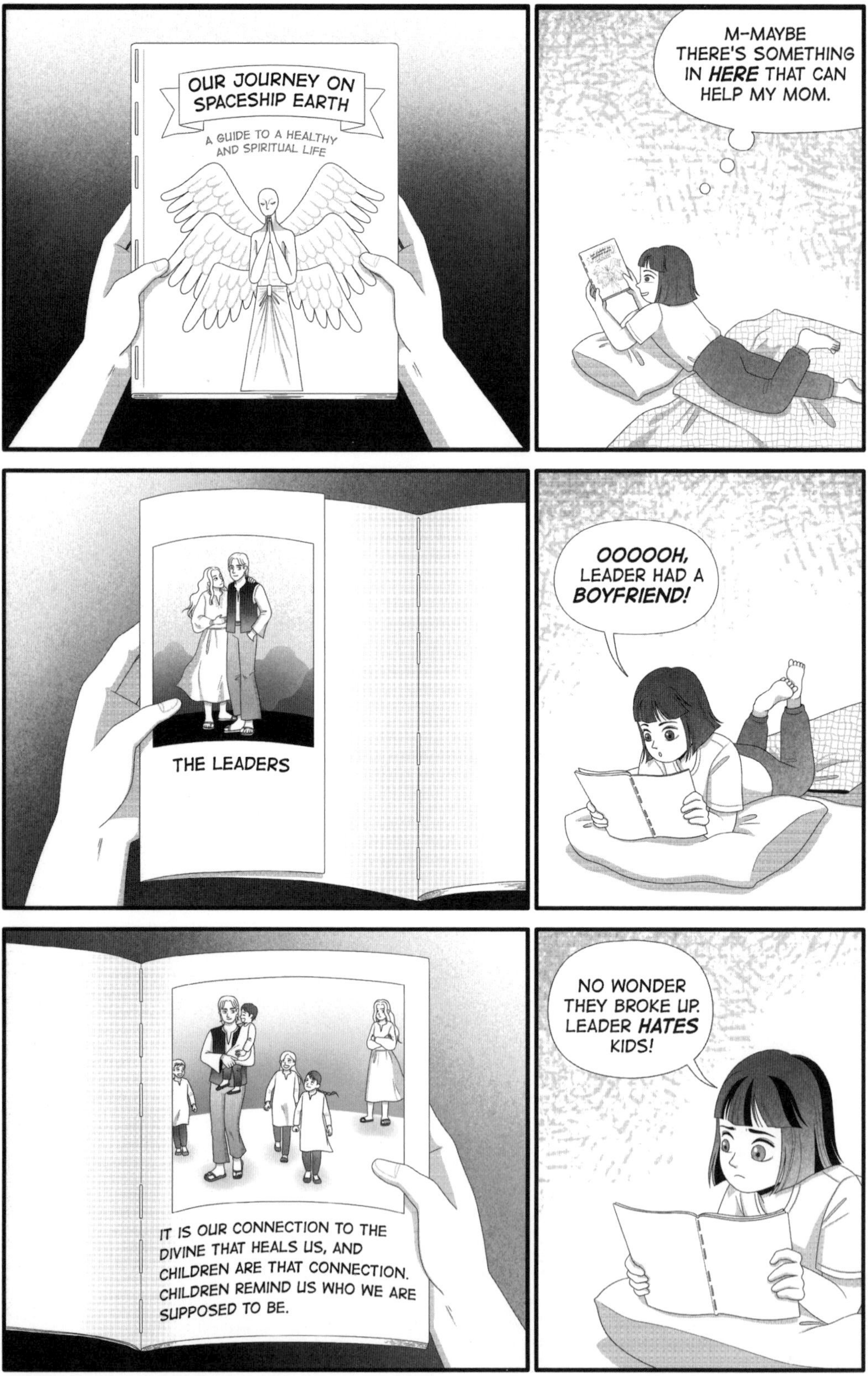
OUR JOURNEY ON SPACESHIP EARTH
A GUIDE TO A HEALTHY AND SPIRITUAL LIFE
M–MAYBE THERE'S SOMETHING IN *HERE* THAT CAN HELP MY MOM.
THE LEADERS
OOOOOH, LEADER HAD A *BOYFRIEND!*
IT IS OUR CONNECTION TO THE DIVINE THAT HEALS US, AND CHILDREN ARE THAT CONNECTION. CHILDREN REMIND US WHO WE ARE SUPPOSED TO BE.
NO WONDER THEY BROKE UP. LEADER *HATES* KIDS!

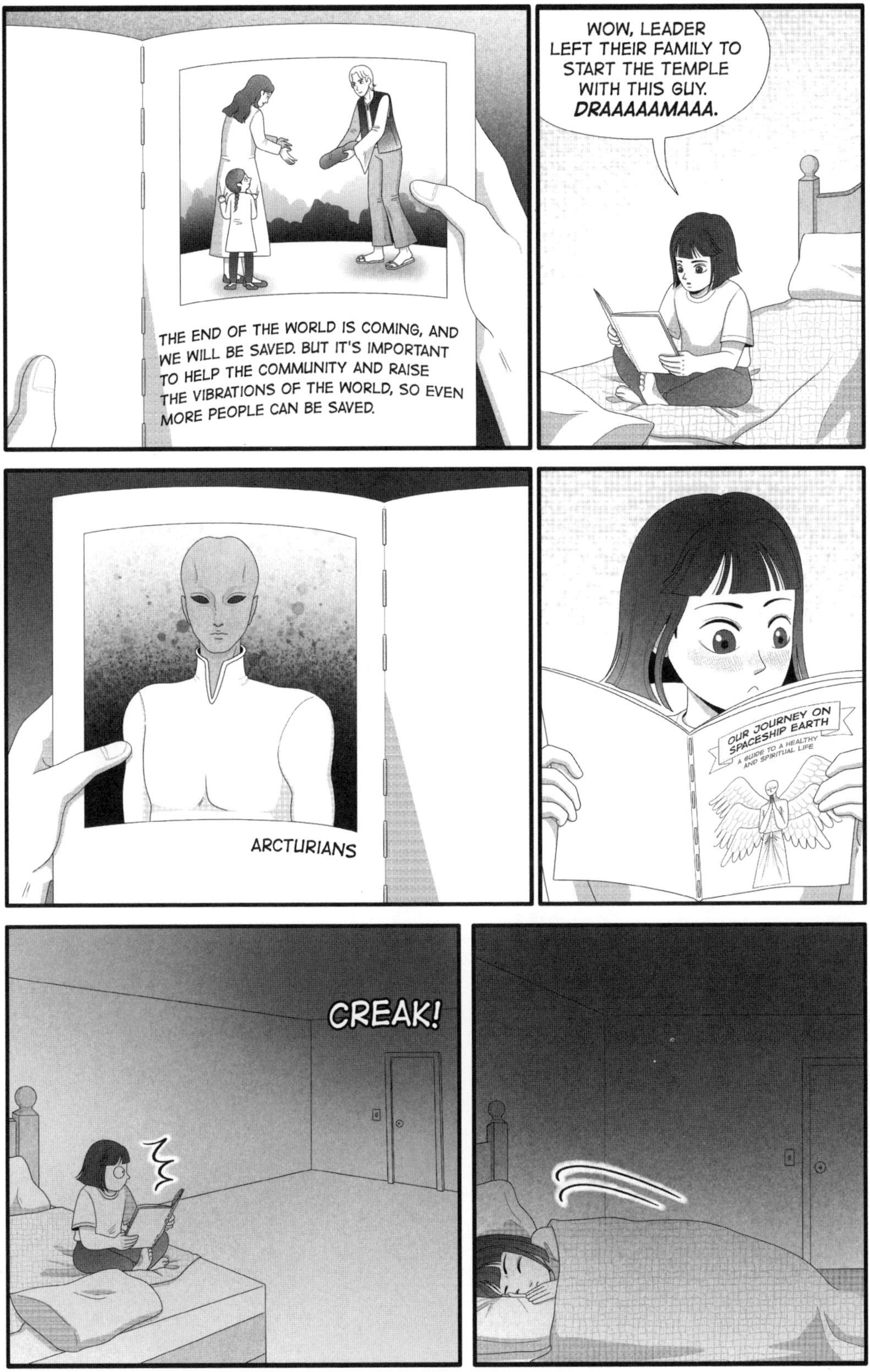
THE END OF THE WORLD IS COMING, AND WE WILL BE SAVED. BUT IT'S IMPORTANT TO HELP THE COMMUNITY AND RAISE THE VIBRATIONS OF THE WORLD, SO EVEN MORE PEOPLE CAN BE SAVED.
WOW, LEADER LEFT THEIR FAMILY TO START THE TEMPLE WITH THIS GUY. *DRAAAAAMAAA.*
ARCTURIANS
OUR JOURNEY ON SPACESHIP EARTH
A GUIDE TO A HEALTHY AND SPIRITUAL LIFE
CREAK!

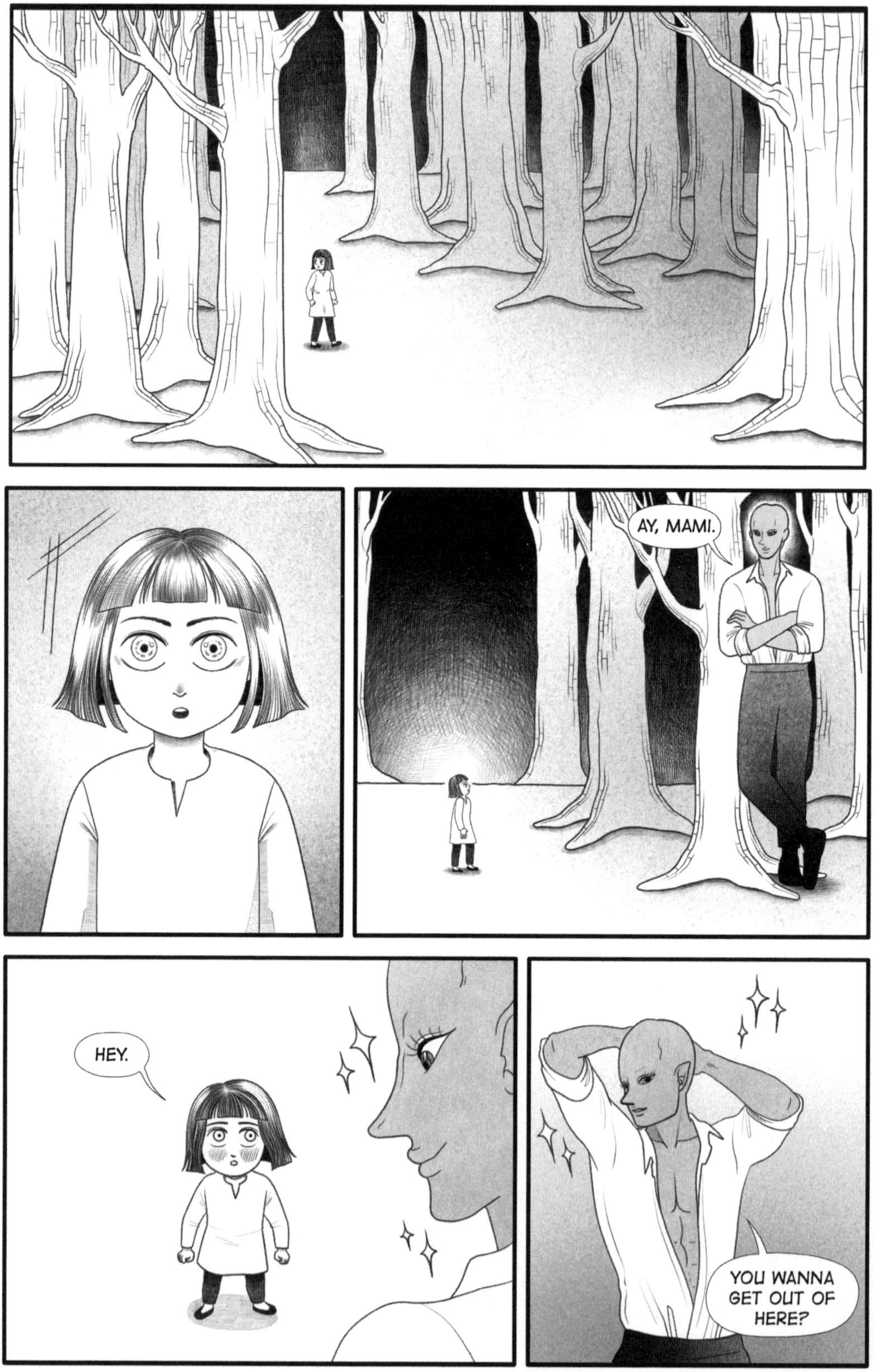
AY, MAMI.
HEY.
YOU WANNA GET OUT OF HERE?

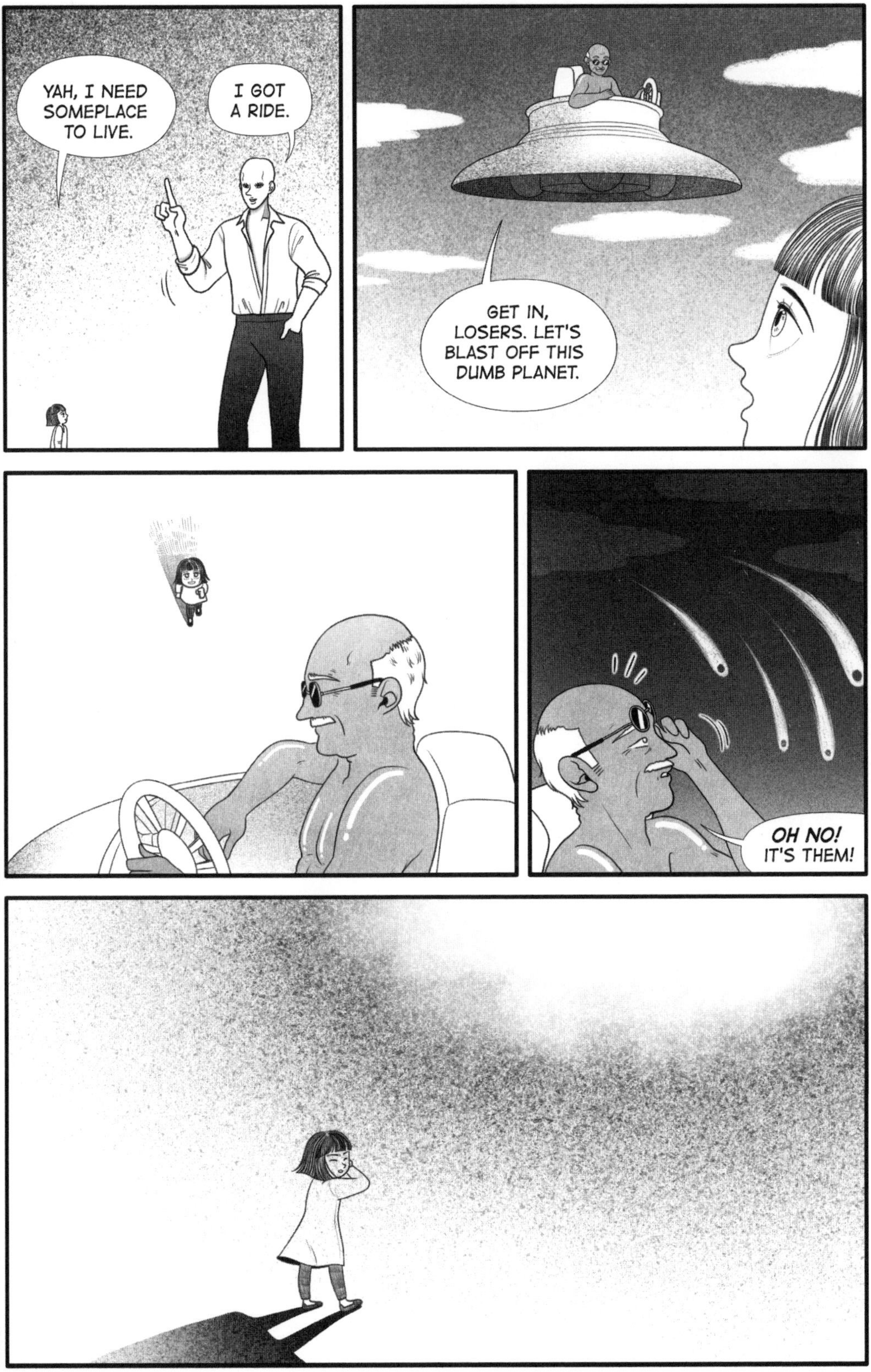

YAH, I NEED SOMEPLACE TO LIVE.
I GOT A RIDE.
GET IN, LOSERS. LET'S BLAST OFF THIS DUMB PLANET.
OH NO! IT'S THEM!

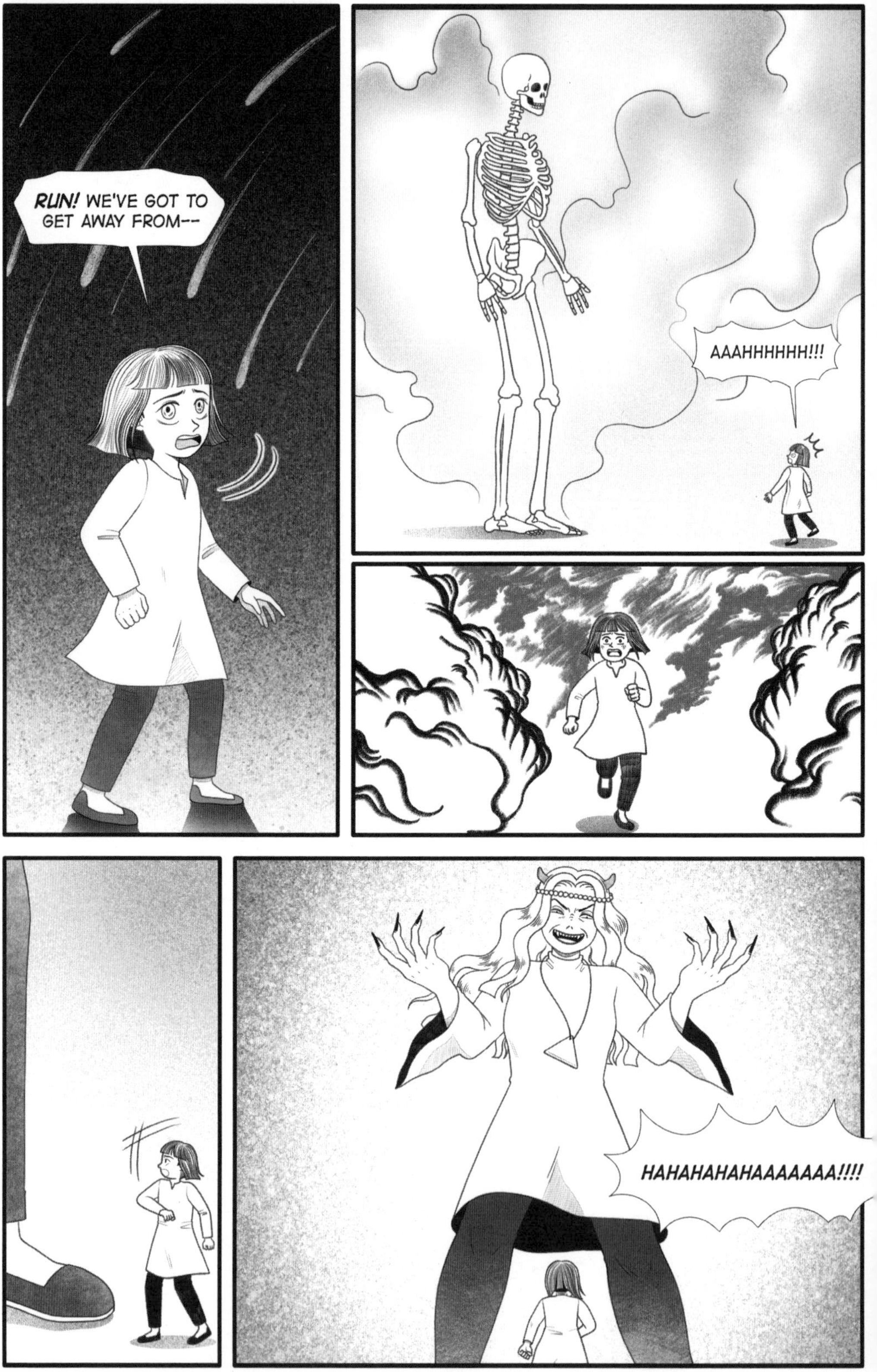
RUN! WE'VE GOT TO GET AWAY FROM--
AAAHHHHHH!!!
HAHAHAHAHAAAAAAA!!!!

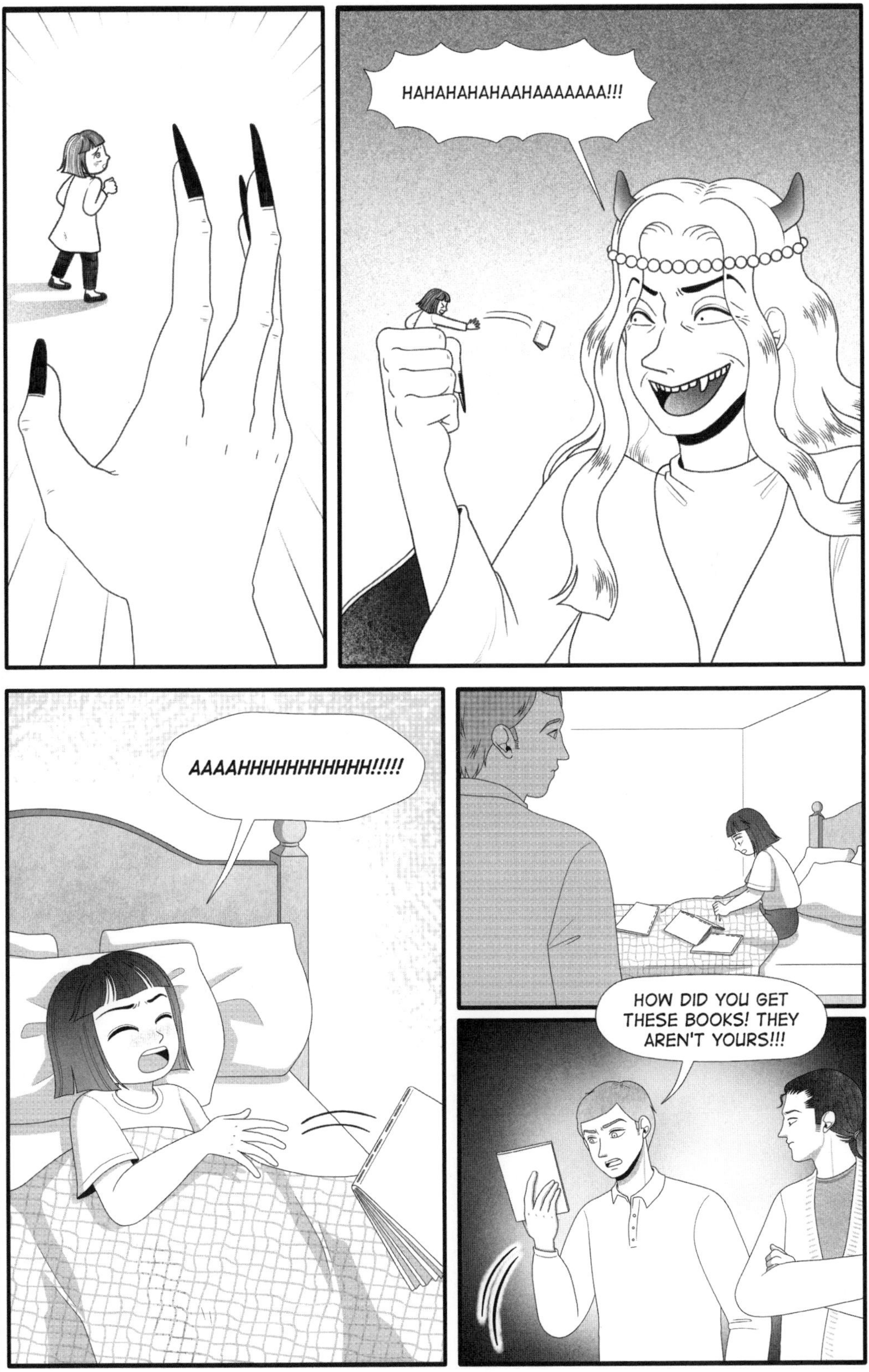
HAHAHAHAHAAHAAAAAAA!!!
AAAAHHHHHHHHHHH!!!!!
HOW DID YOU GET THESE BOOKS! THEY AREN'T YOURS!!!

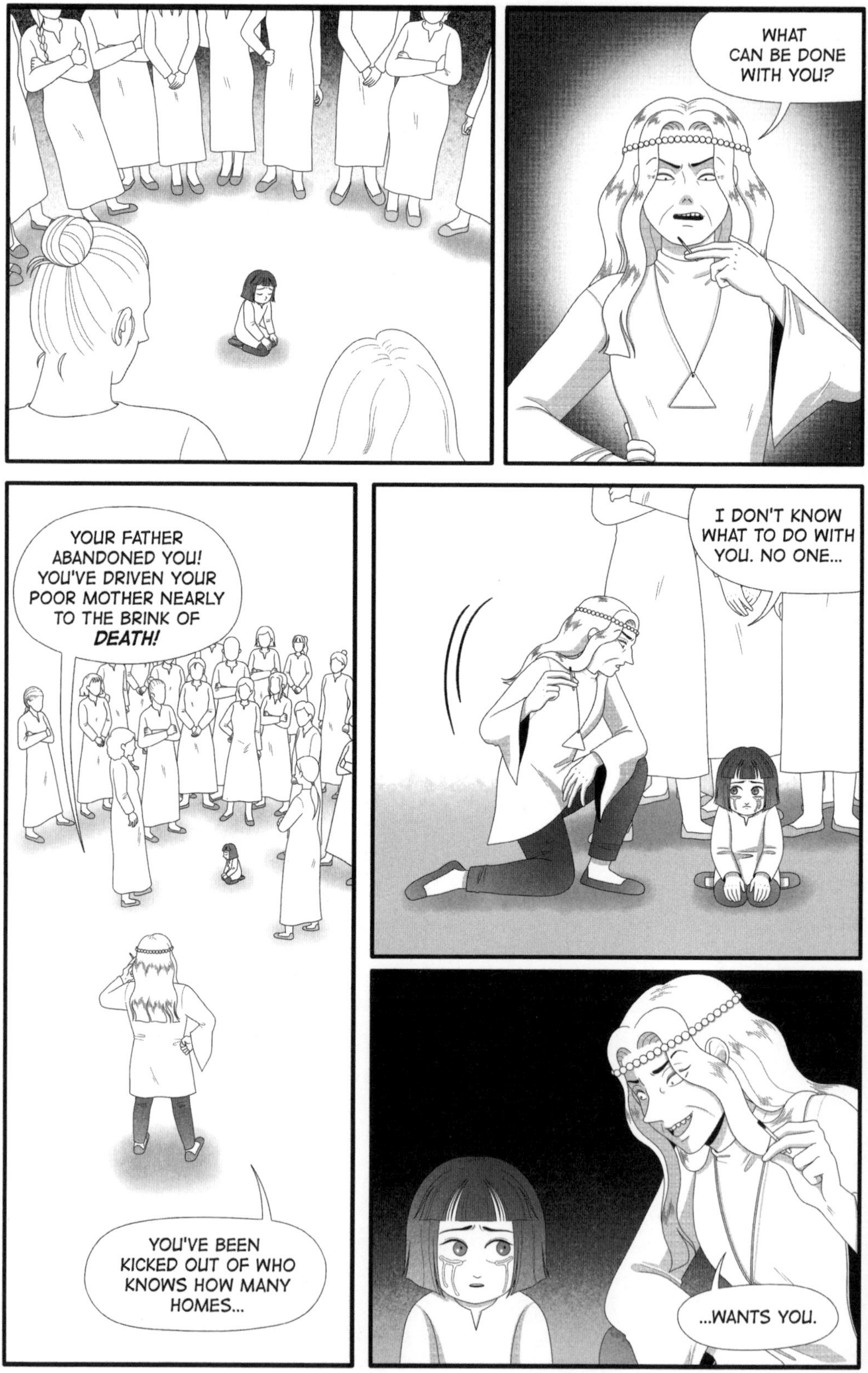
WHAT CAN BE DONE WITH YOU?
YOUR FATHER ABANDONED YOU! YOU'VE DRIVEN YOUR POOR MOTHER NEARLY TO THE BRINK OF *DEATH!*
YOU'VE BEEN KICKED OUT OF WHO KNOWS HOW MANY HOMES...
I DON'T KNOW WHAT TO DO WITH YOU. NO ONE...
...WANTS YOU.

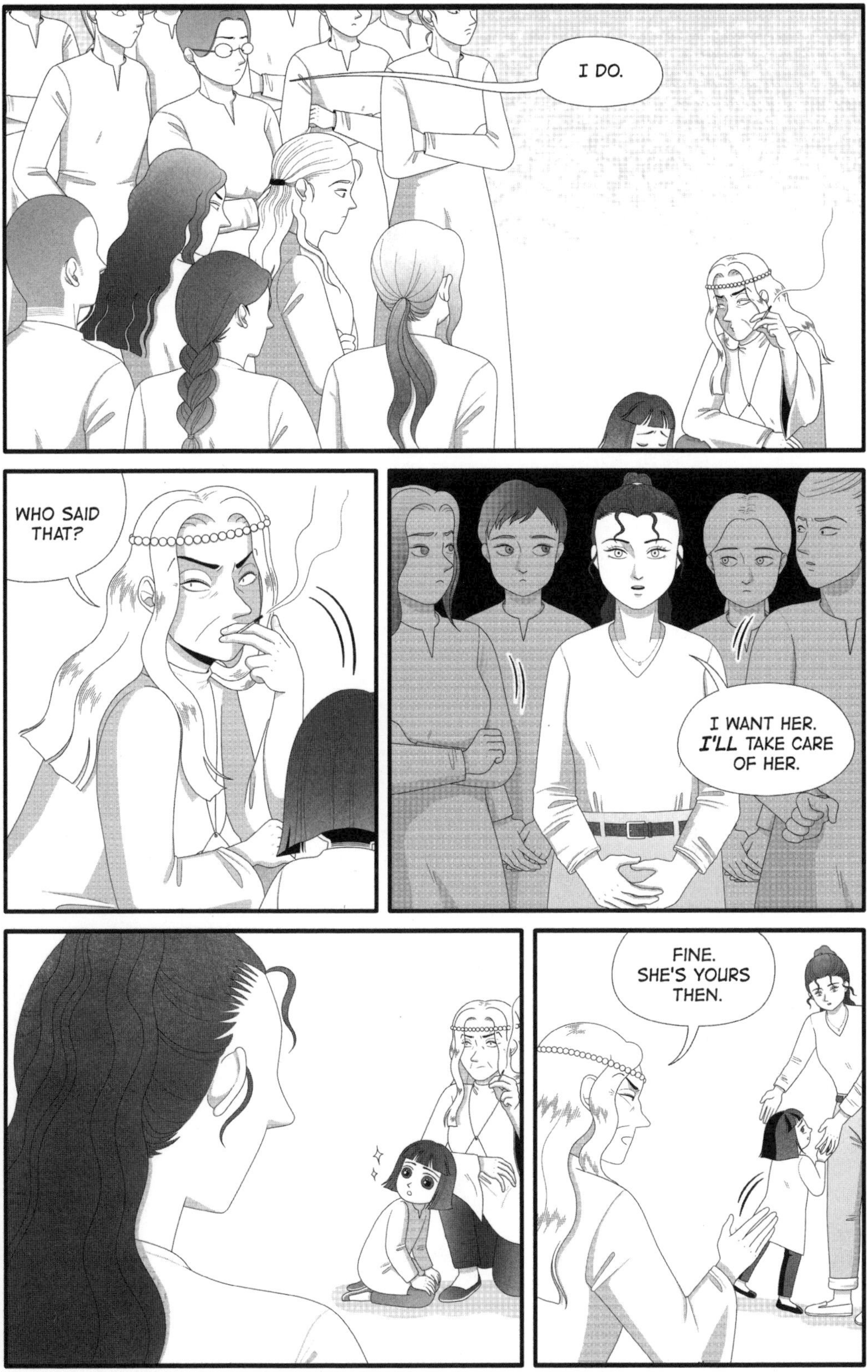
I DO.
WHO SAID THAT?
I WANT HER. I'LL TAKE CARE OF HER.
FINE. SHE'S YOURS THEN.

CHAPTER SIX: THE HOME

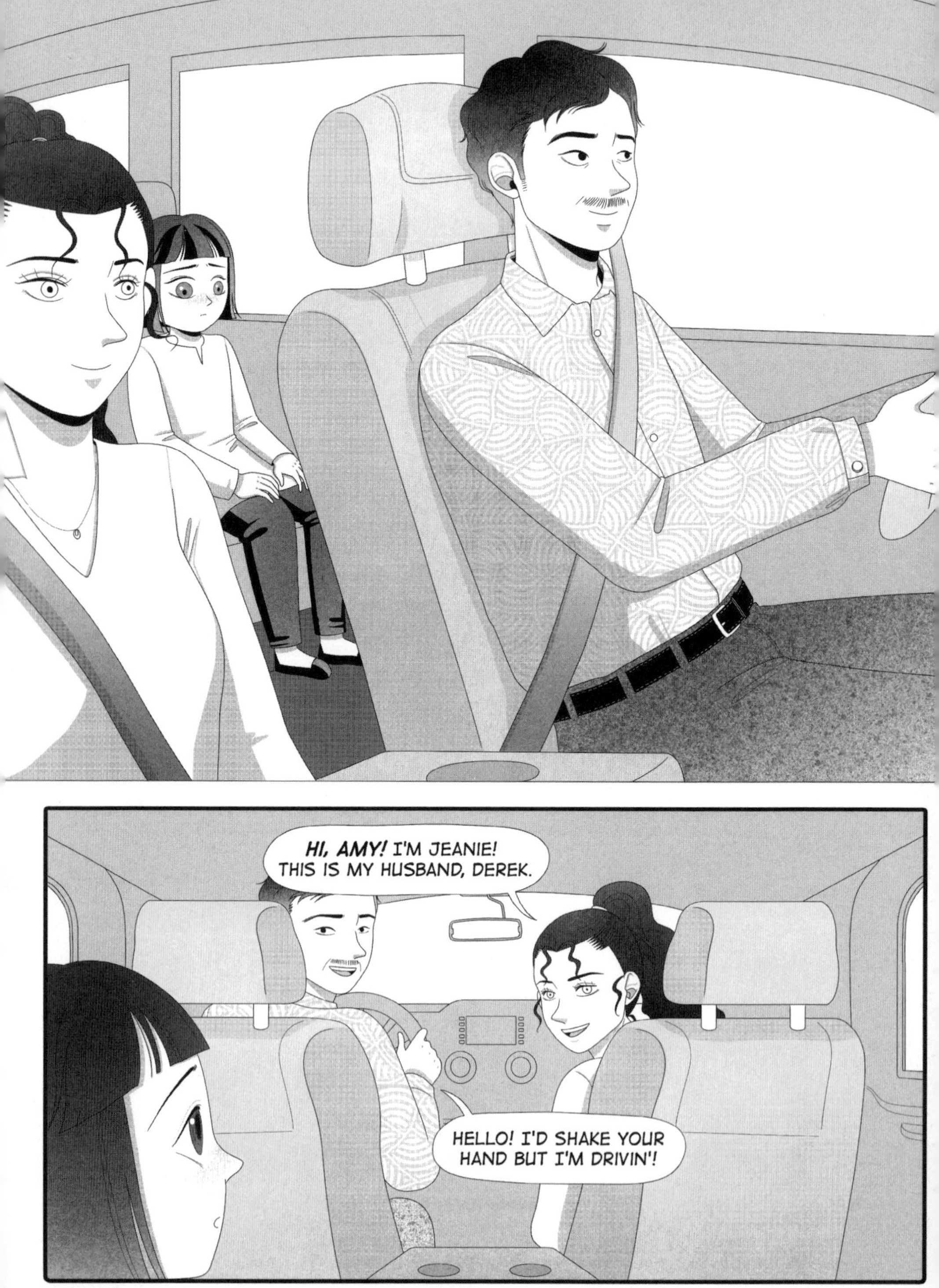
HI, AMY! I'M JEANIE! THIS IS MY HUSBAND, DEREK.
HELLO! I'D SHAKE YOUR HAND BUT I'M DRIVIN'!

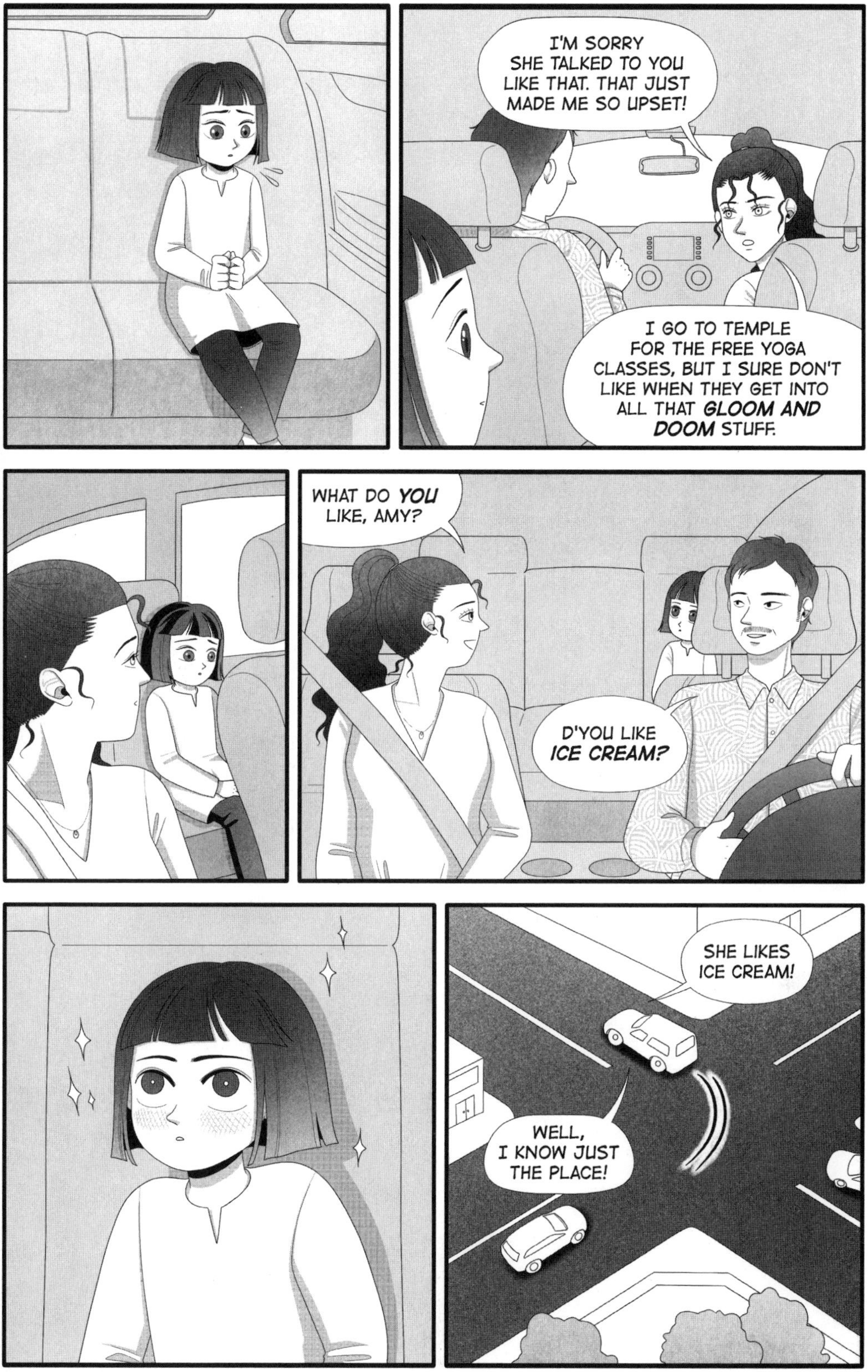
I'M SORRY SHE TALKED TO YOU LIKE THAT. THAT JUST MADE ME SO UPSET!
I GO TO TEMPLE FOR THE FREE YOGA CLASSES, BUT I SURE DON'T LIKE WHEN THEY GET INTO ALL THAT GLOOM AND DOOM STUFF.
WHAT DO YOU LIKE, AMY?
D'YOU LIKE ICE CREAM?
SHE LIKES ICE CREAM!
WELL, I KNOW JUST THE PLACE!

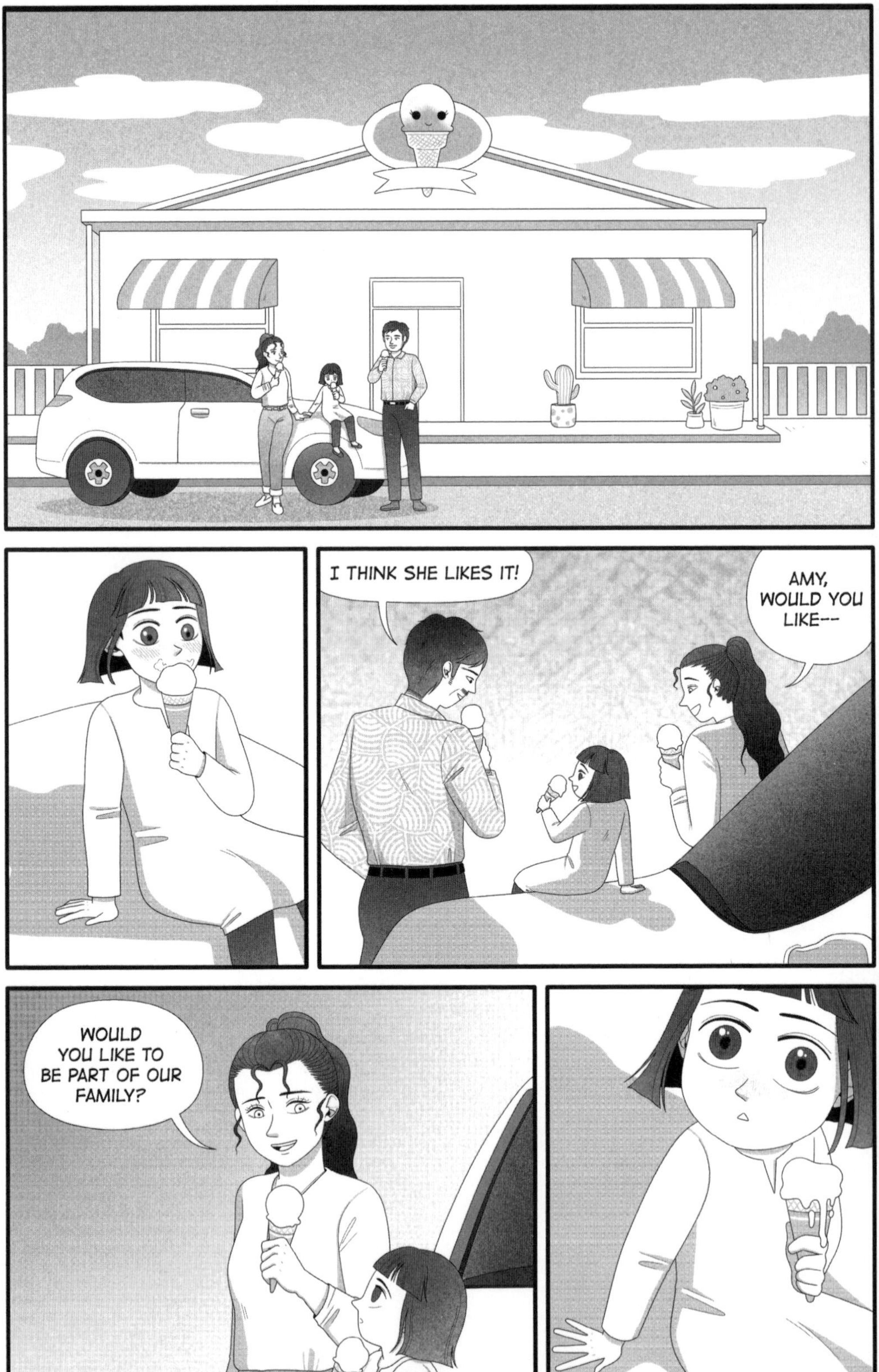
I THINK SHE LIKES IT!
AMY, WOULD YOU LIKE--
WOULD YOU LIKE TO BE PART OF OUR FAMILY?

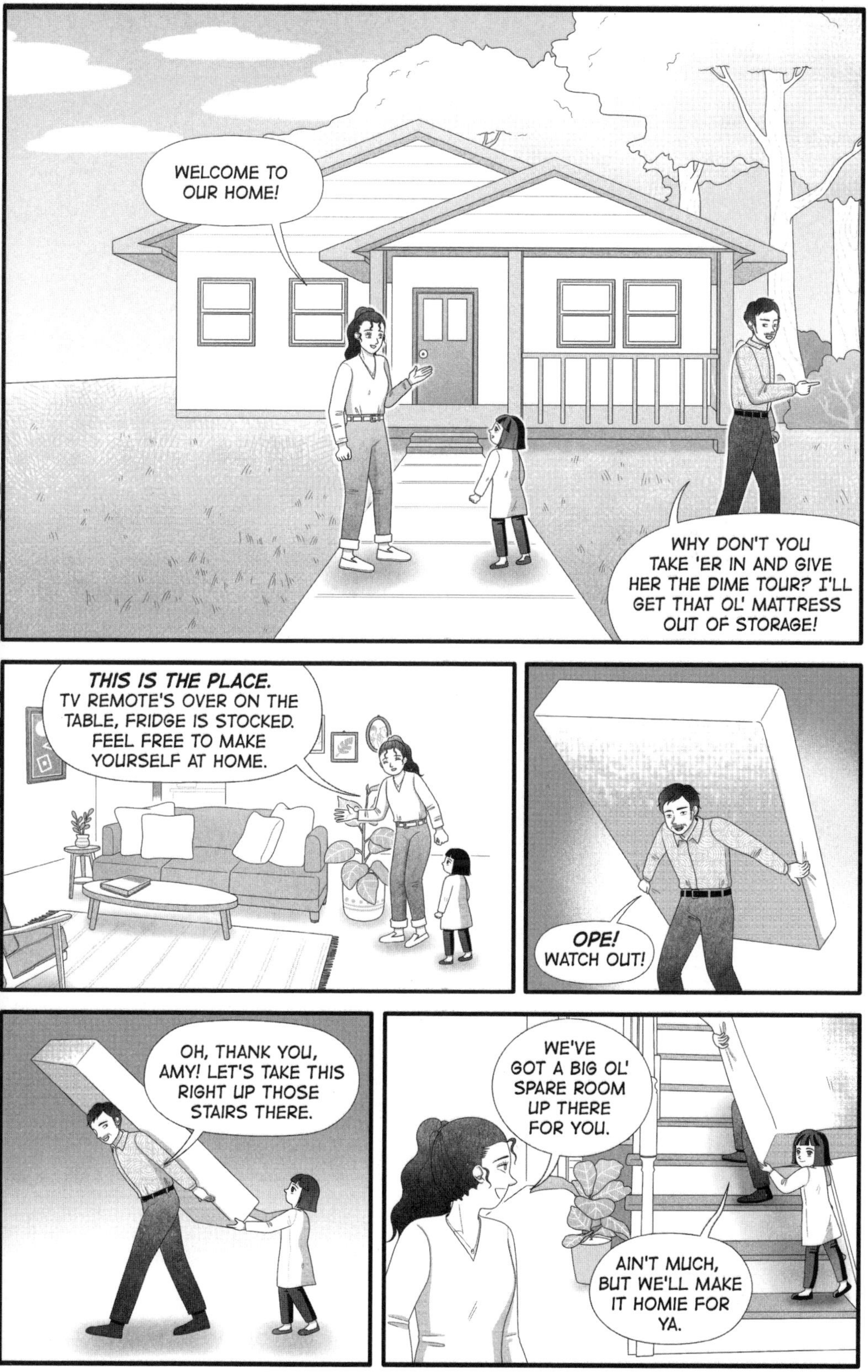
WELCOME TO OUR HOME!
WHY DON'T YOU TAKE 'ER IN AND GIVE HER THE DIME TOUR? I'LL GET THAT OL' MATTRESS OUT OF STORAGE!
THIS IS THE PLACE. TV REMOTE'S OVER ON THE TABLE, FRIDGE IS STOCKED. FEEL FREE TO MAKE YOURSELF AT HOME.
OPE! WATCH OUT!
OH, THANK YOU, AMY! LET'S TAKE THIS RIGHT UP THOSE STAIRS THERE.
WE'VE GOT A BIG OL' SPARE ROOM UP THERE FOR YOU.
AIN'T MUCH, BUT WE'LL MAKE IT HOMIE FOR YA.

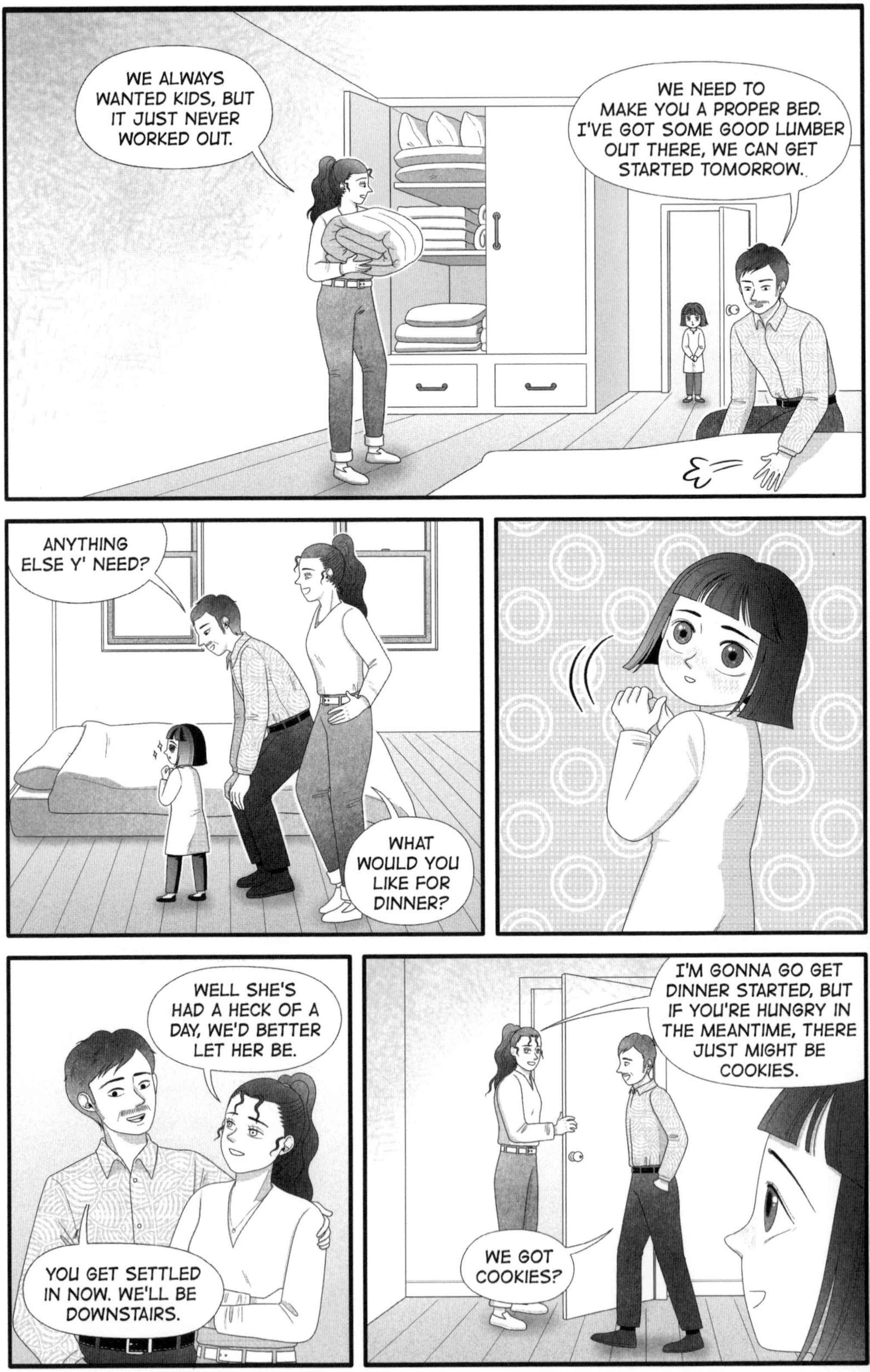
WE ALWAYS WANTED KIDS, BUT IT JUST NEVER WORKED OUT.
WE NEED TO MAKE YOU A PROPER BED. I'VE GOT SOME GOOD LUMBER OUT THERE, WE CAN GET STARTED TOMORROW.
ANYTHING ELSE Y' NEED?
WHAT WOULD YOU LIKE FOR DINNER?
WELL SHE'S HAD A HECK OF A DAY, WE'D BETTER LET HER BE.
YOU GET SETTLED IN NOW. WE'LL BE DOWNSTAIRS.
I'M GONNA GO GET DINNER STARTED, BUT IF YOU'RE HUNGRY IN THE MEANTIME, THERE JUST MIGHT BE COOKIES.
WE GOT COOKIES?

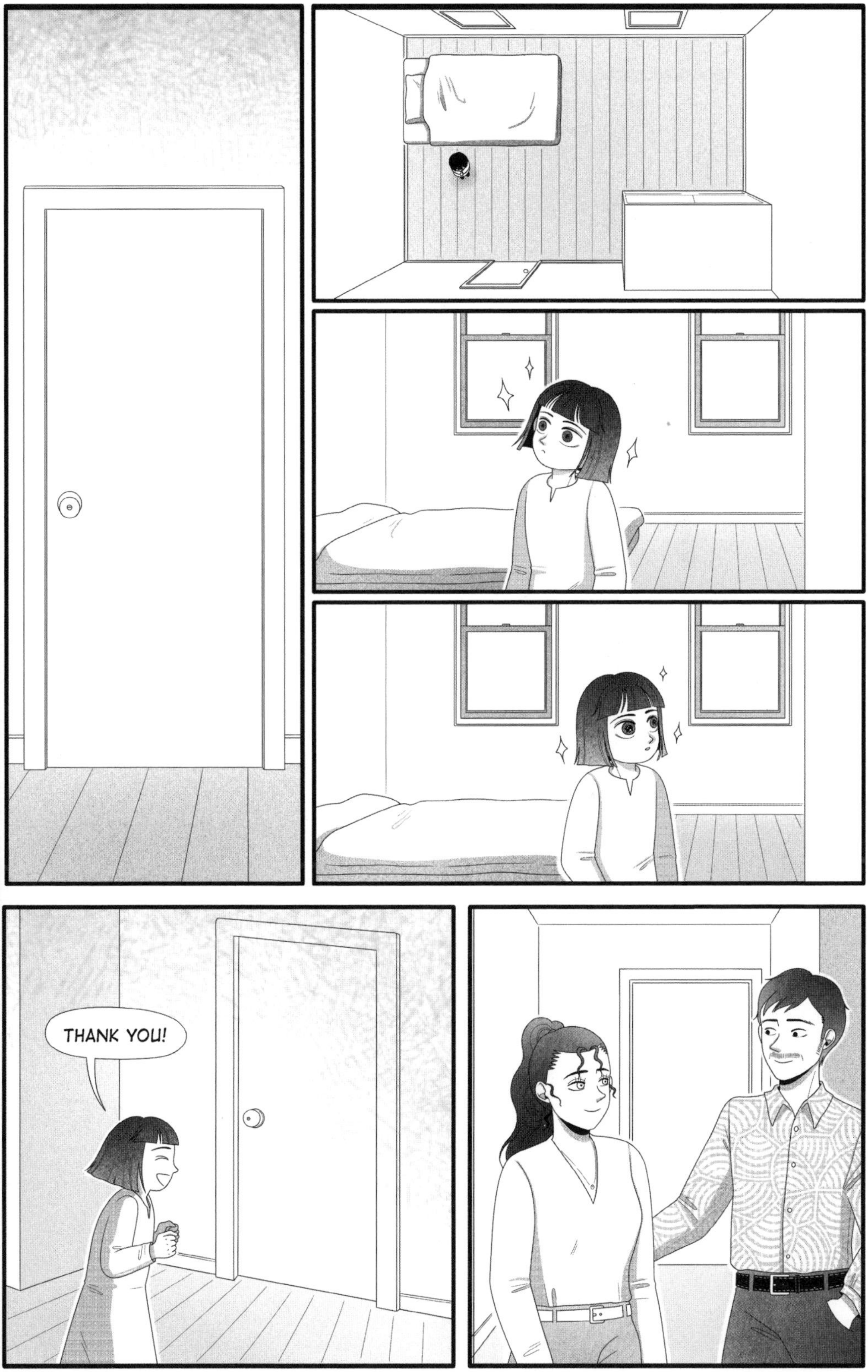
THANK YOU!

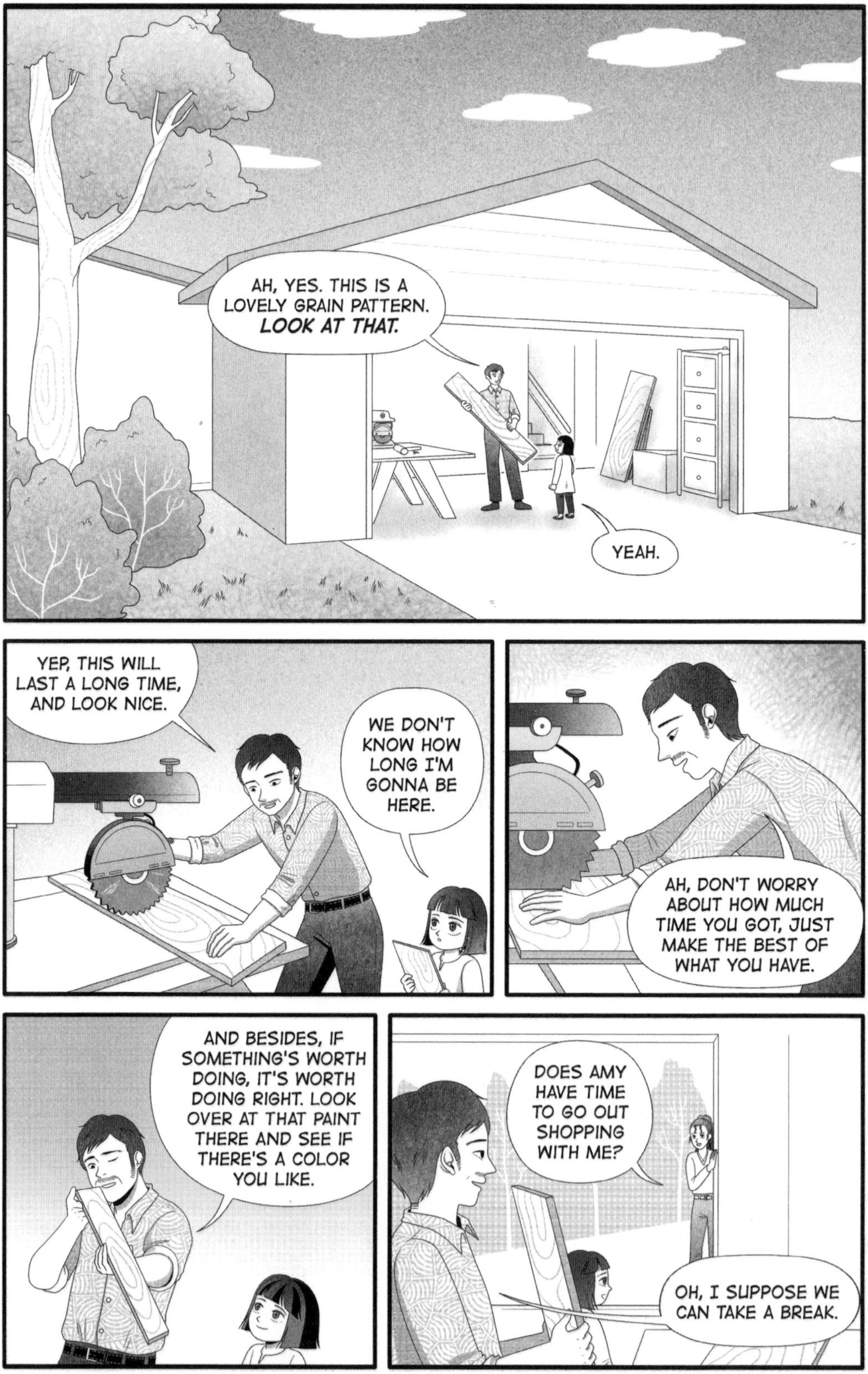
AH, YES. THIS IS A LOVELY GRAIN PATTERN. *LOOK AT THAT.*
YEAH.
YEP, THIS WILL LAST A LONG TIME, AND LOOK NICE.
WE DON'T KNOW HOW LONG I'M GONNA BE HERE.
AH, DON'T WORRY ABOUT HOW MUCH TIME YOU GOT, JUST MAKE THE BEST OF WHAT YOU HAVE.
AND BESIDES, IF SOMETHING'S WORTH DOING, IT'S WORTH DOING RIGHT. LOOK OVER AT THAT PAINT THERE AND SEE IF THERE'S A COLOR YOU LIKE.
DOES AMY HAVE TIME TO GO OUT SHOPPING WITH ME?
OH, I SUPPOSE WE CAN TAKE A BREAK.

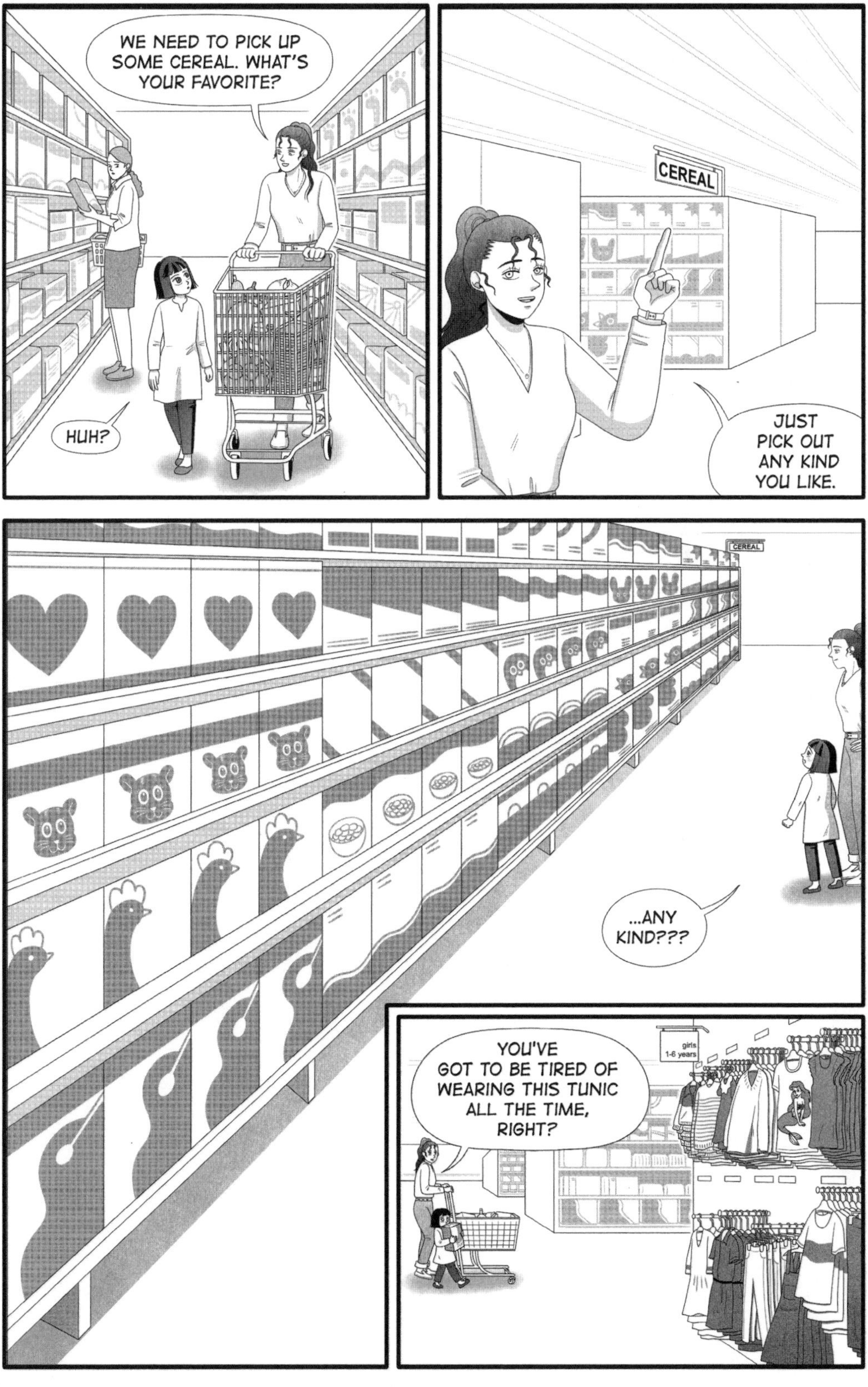
WE NEED TO PICK UP SOME CEREAL. WHAT'S YOUR FAVORITE?
HUH?
CEREAL
JUST PICK OUT ANY KIND YOU LIKE.
CEREAL
...ANY KIND???
YOU'VE GOT TO BE TIRED OF WEARING THIS TUNIC ALL THE TIME, RIGHT?
girls 1-6 years

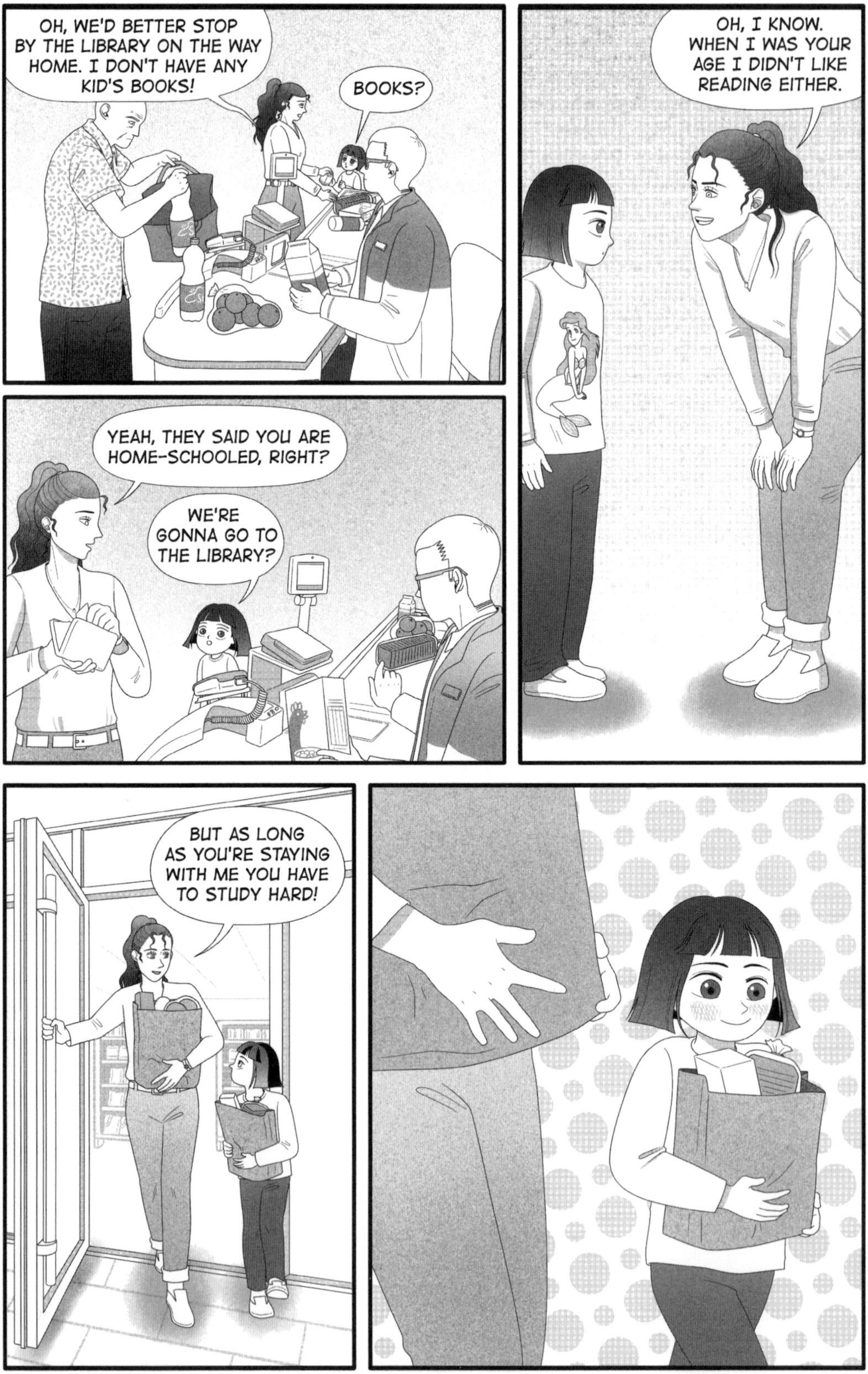
OH, WE'D BETTER STOP BY THE LIBRARY ON THE WAY HOME. I DON'T HAVE ANY KID'S BOOKS!
BOOKS?
OH, I KNOW. WHEN I WAS YOUR AGE I DIDN'T LIKE READING EITHER.
YEAH, THEY SAID YOU ARE HOME-SCHOOLED, RIGHT?
WE'RE GONNA GO TO THE LIBRARY?
BUT AS LONG AS YOU'RE STAYING WITH ME YOU HAVE TO STUDY HARD!

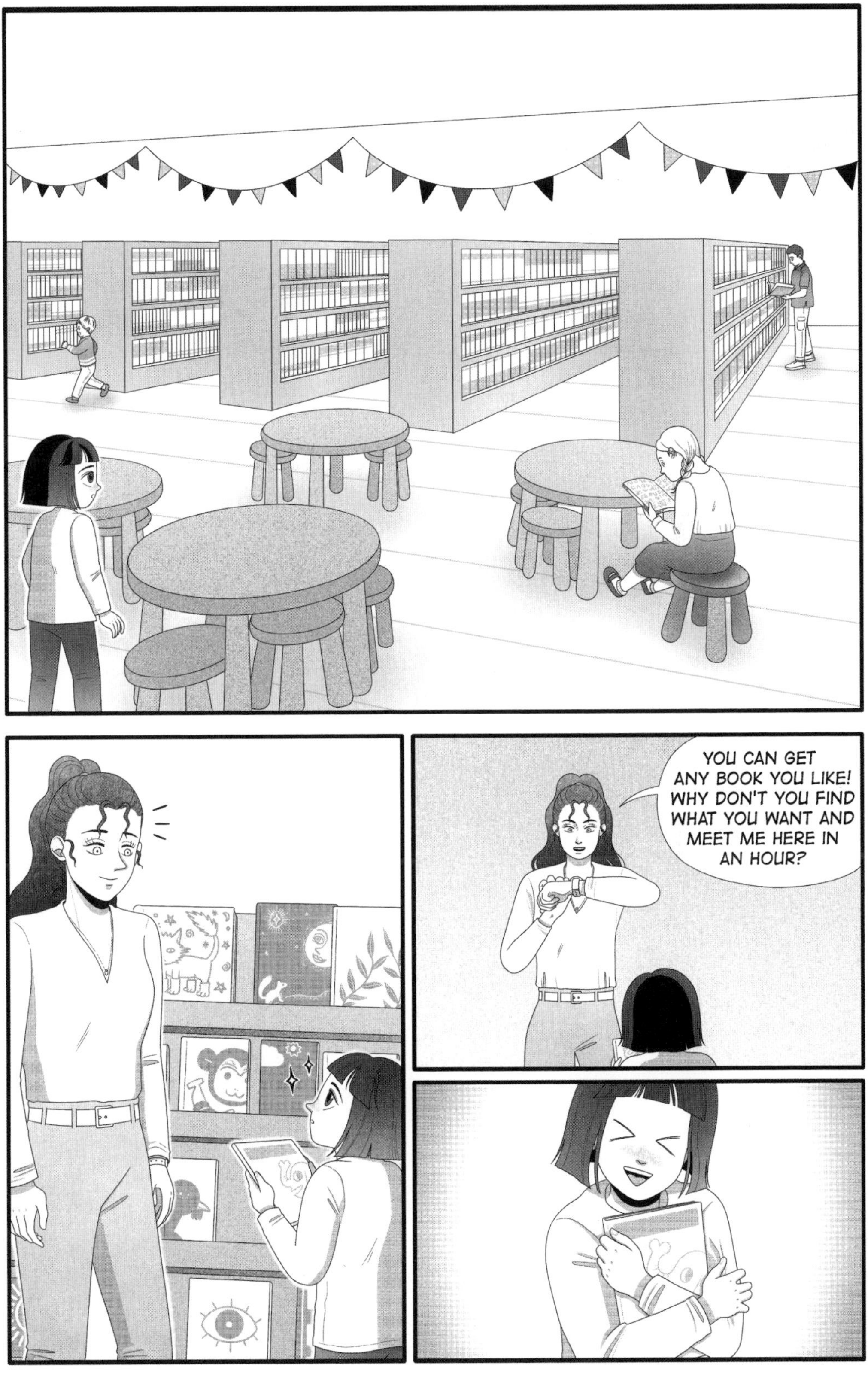
YOU CAN GET ANY BOOK YOU LIKE! WHY DON'T YOU FIND WHAT YOU WANT AND MEET ME HERE IN AN HOUR?

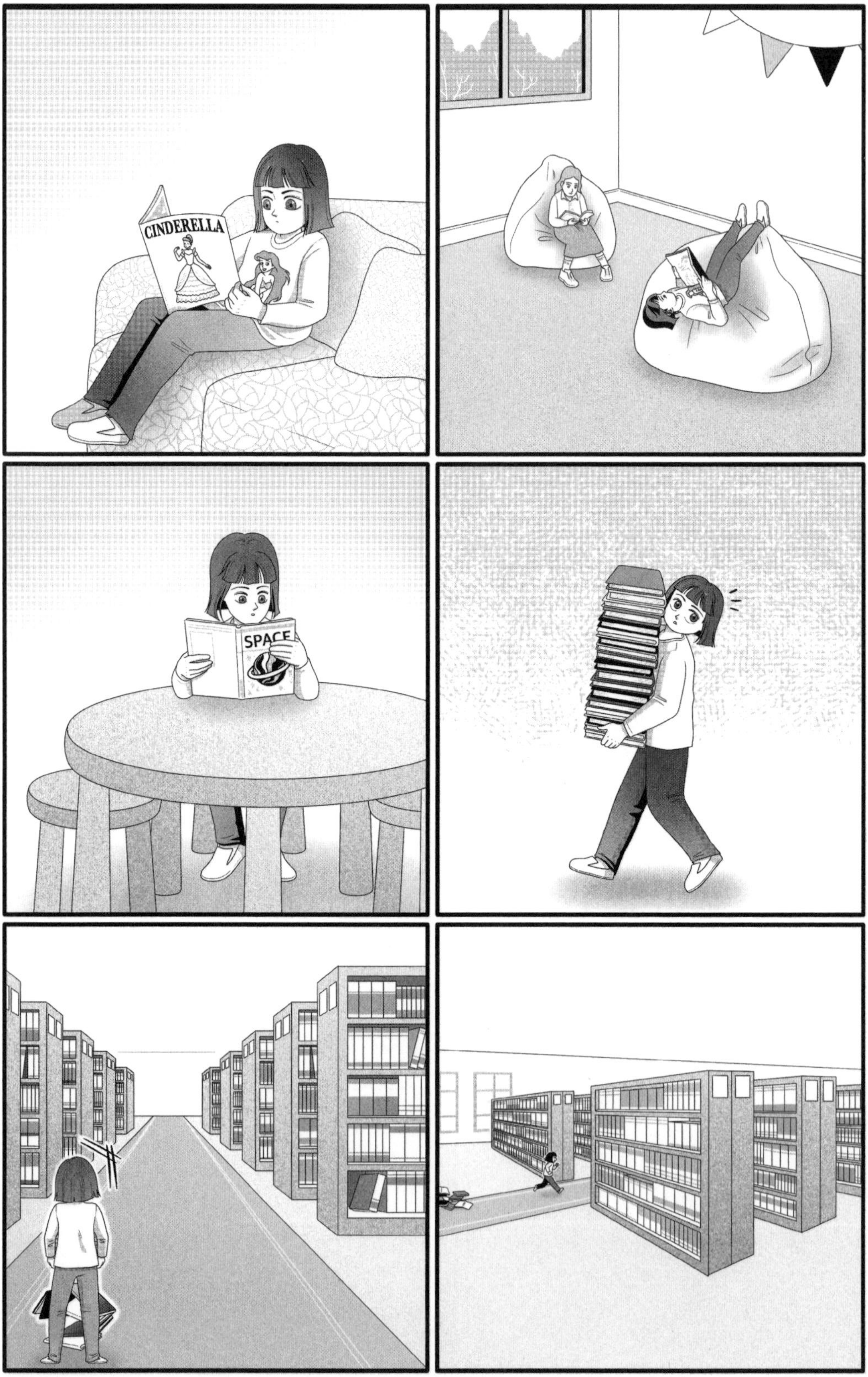
CINDERELLA
SPACE

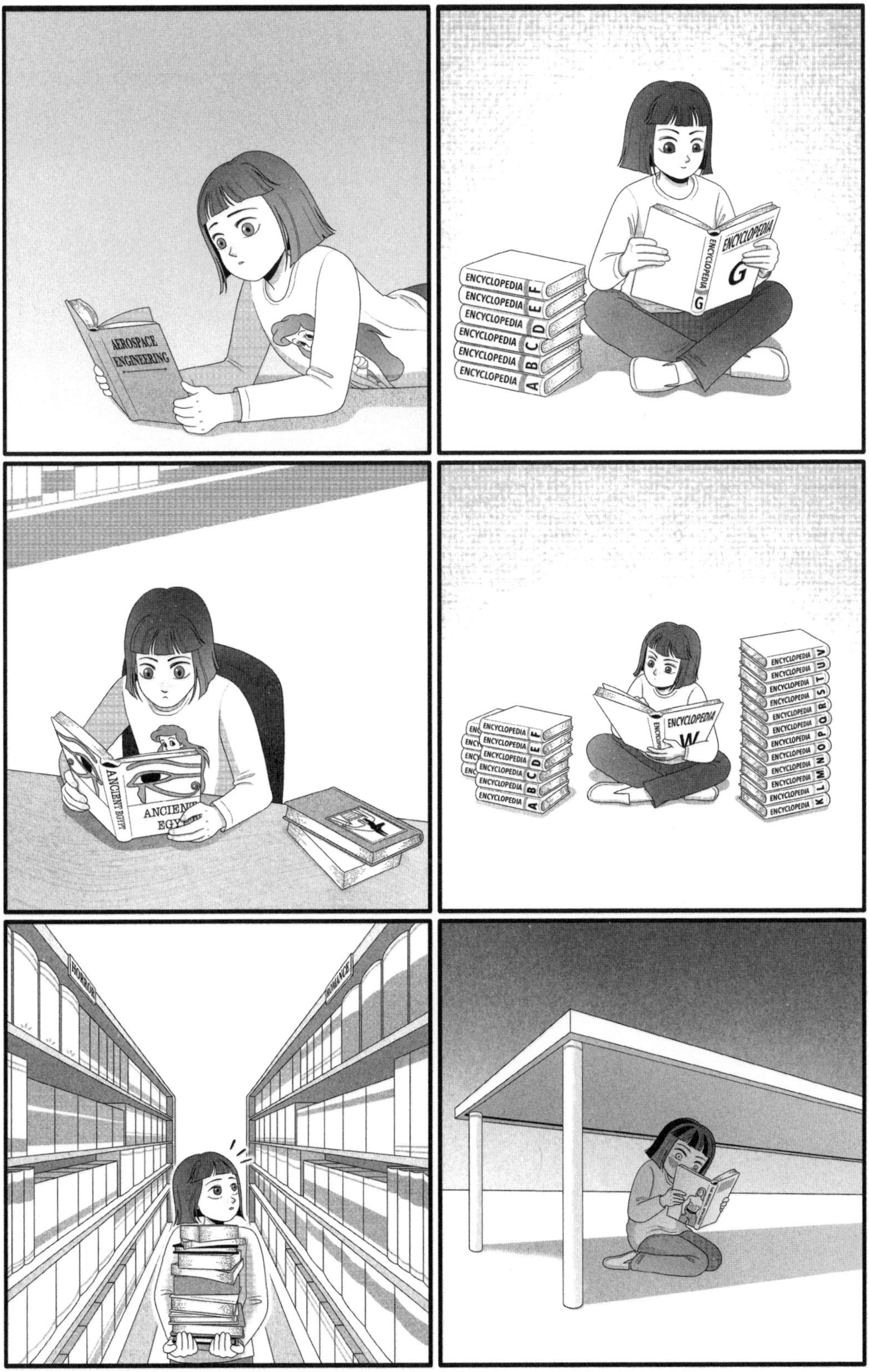
AEROSPACE ENGINEERING
ENCYCLOPEDIA G
ENCYCLOPEDIA A
ENCYCLOPEDIA B
ENCYCLOPEDIA C
ENCYCLOPEDIA D
ENCYCLOPEDIA E
ENCYCLOPEDIA F
ANCIENT EGYPT
ENCYCLOPEDIA W
HORROR
ROMANCE

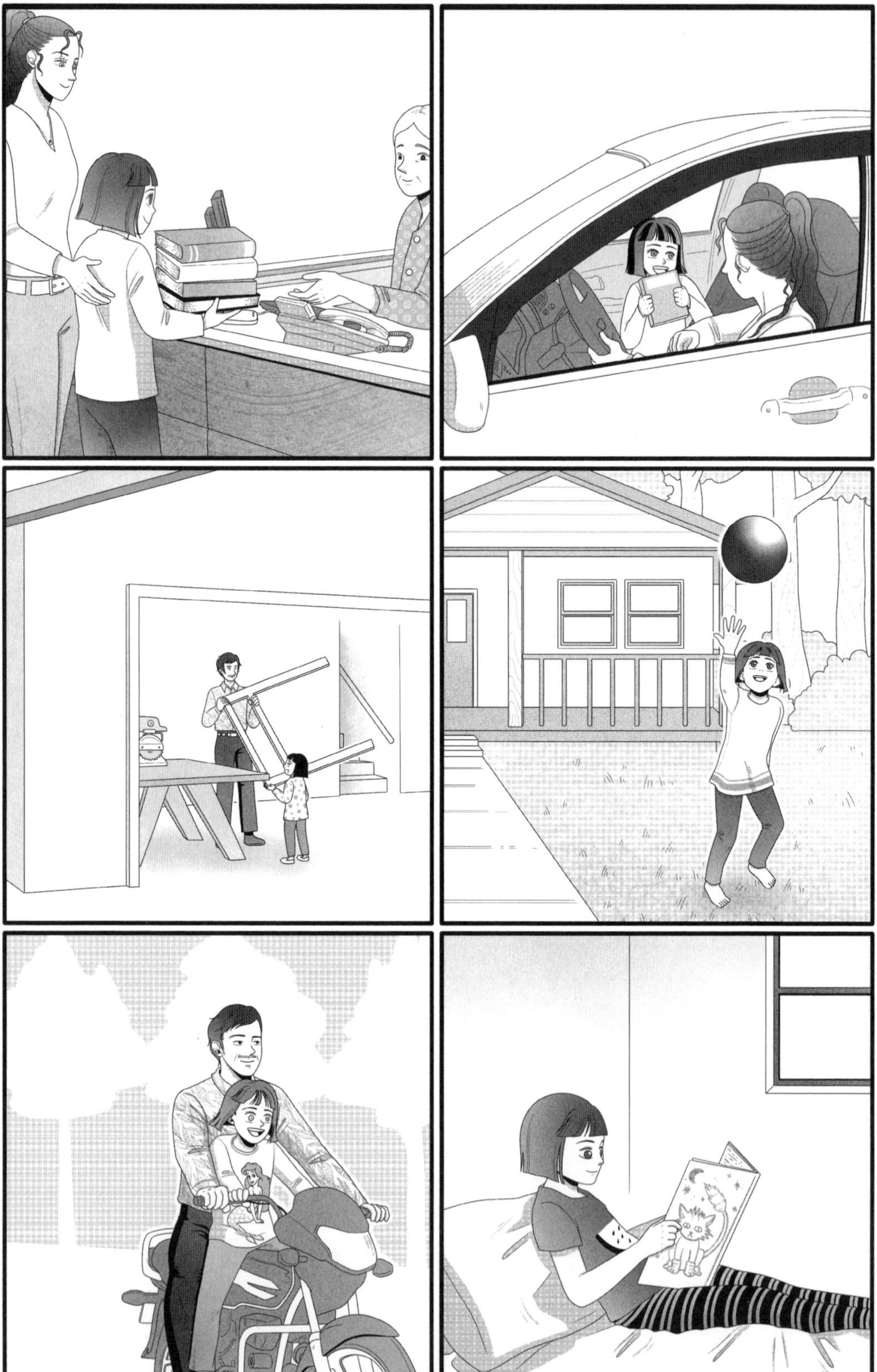

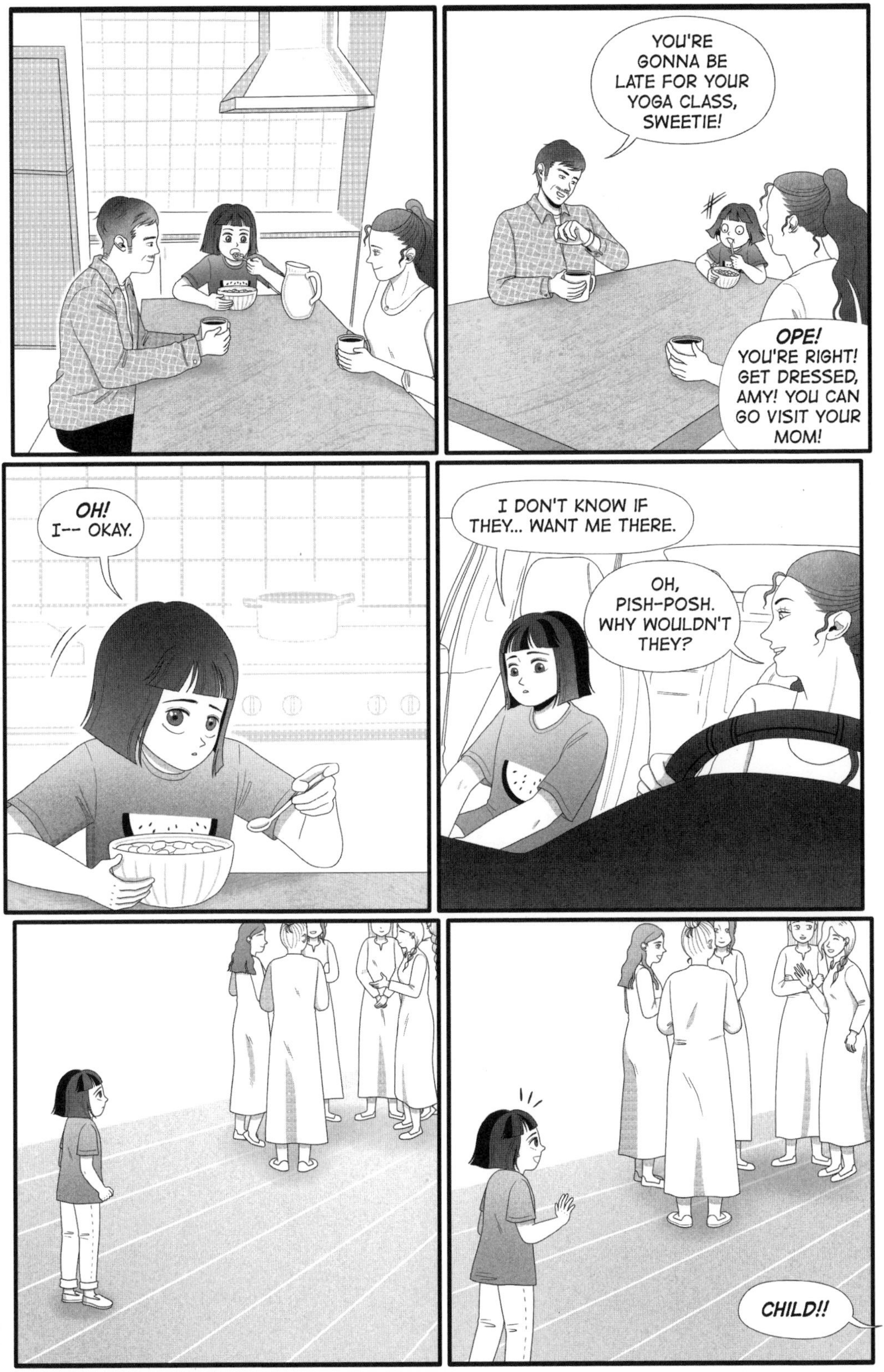
YOU'RE GONNA BE LATE FOR YOUR YOGA CLASS, SWEETIE!
OPE! YOU'RE RIGHT! GET DRESSED, AMY! YOU CAN GO VISIT YOUR MOM!
OH! I-- OKAY.
I DON'T KNOW IF THEY... WANT ME THERE.
OH, PISH-POSH. WHY WOULDN'T THEY?
CHILD!!

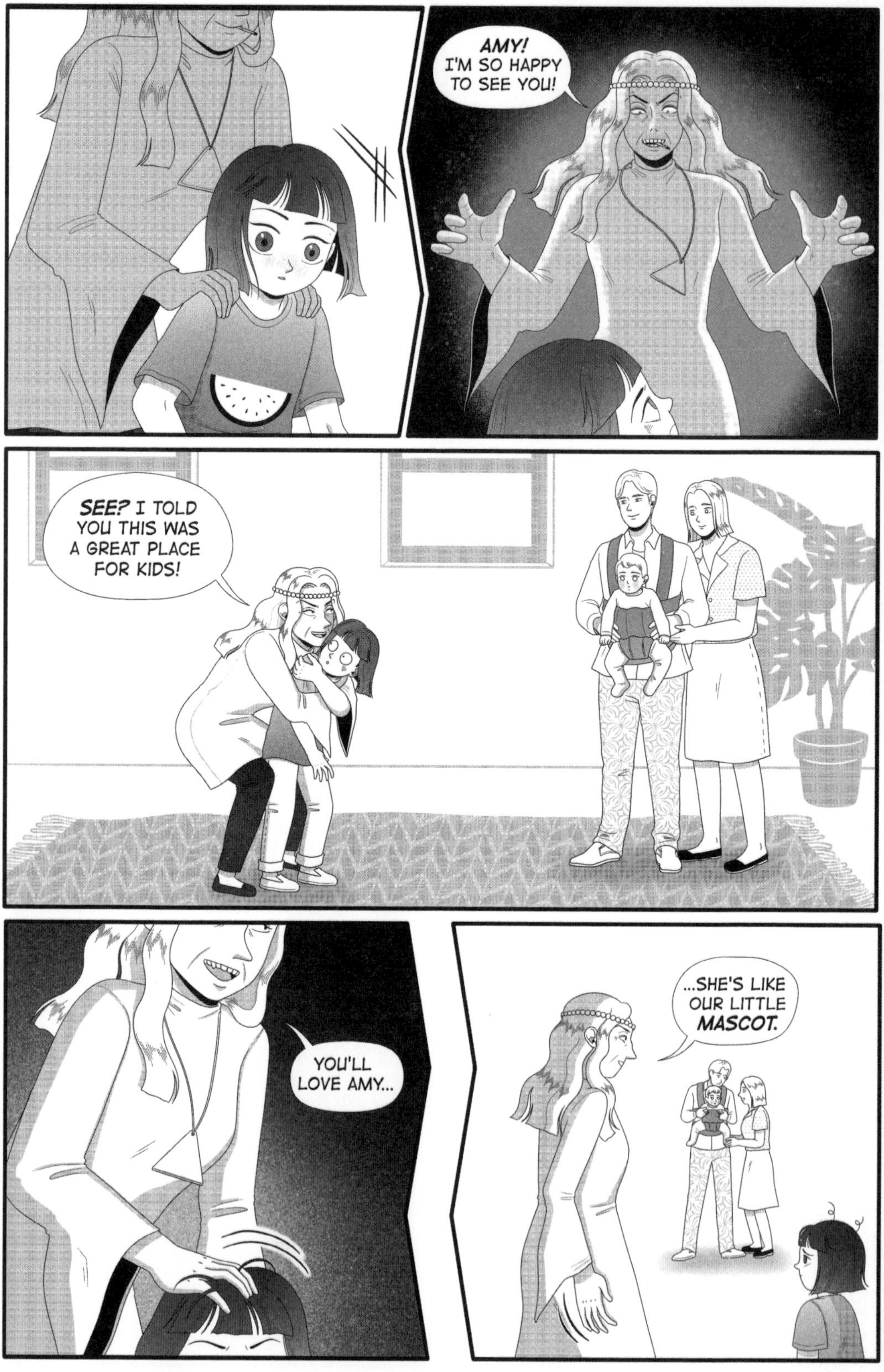
AMY!
I'M SO HAPPY TO SEE YOU!
SEE? I TOLD YOU THIS WAS A GREAT PLACE FOR KIDS!
YOU'LL LOVE AMY...
...SHE'S LIKE OUR LITTLE MASCOT.

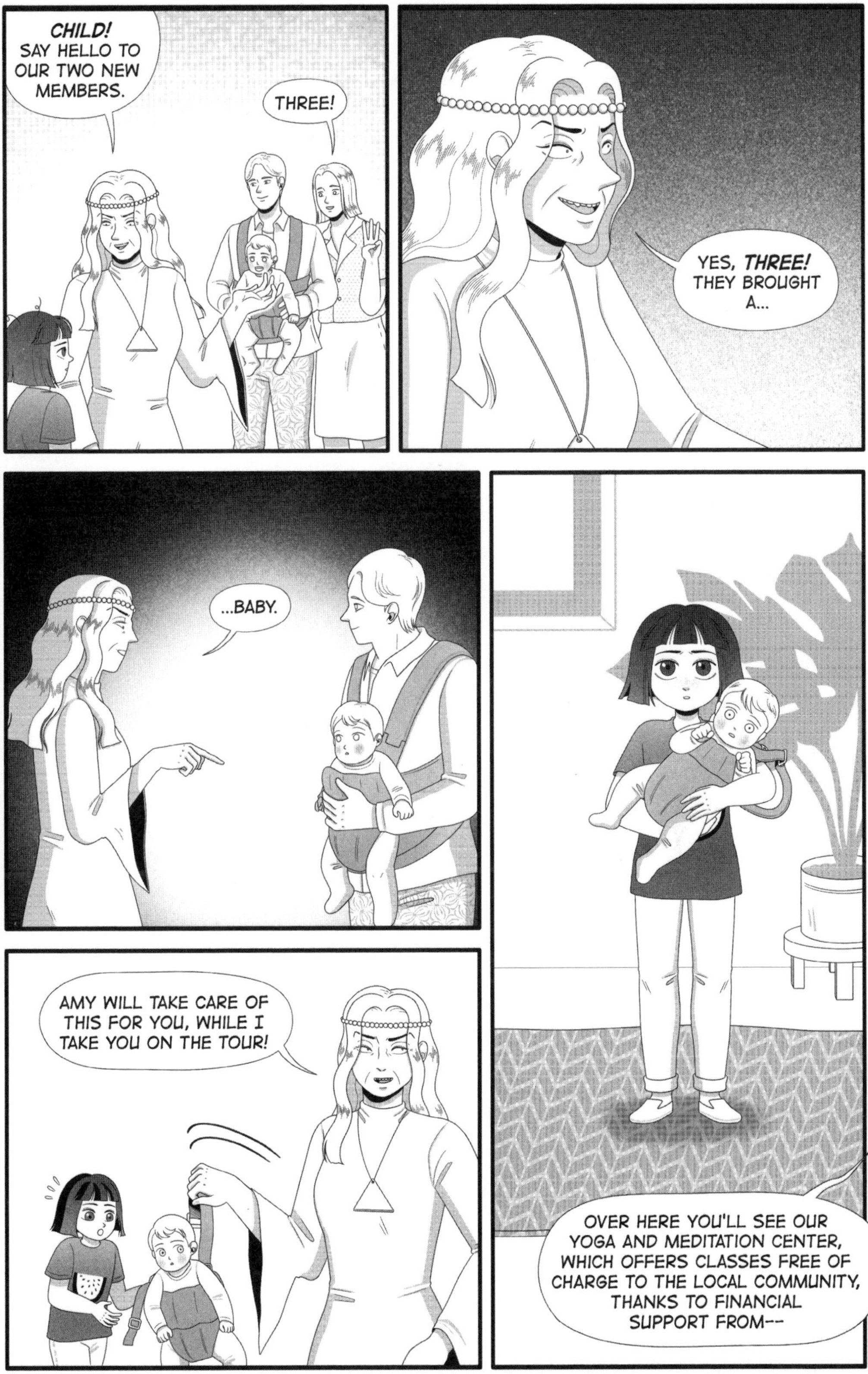
CHILD! SAY HELLO TO OUR TWO NEW MEMBERS.
THREE!
YES, THREE! THEY BROUGHT A...
...BABY.
AMY WILL TAKE CARE OF THIS FOR YOU, WHILE I TAKE YOU ON THE TOUR!
OVER HERE YOU'LL SEE OUR YOGA AND MEDITATION CENTER, WHICH OFFERS CLASSES FREE OF CHARGE TO THE LOCAL COMMUNITY, THANKS TO FINANCIAL SUPPORT FROM--

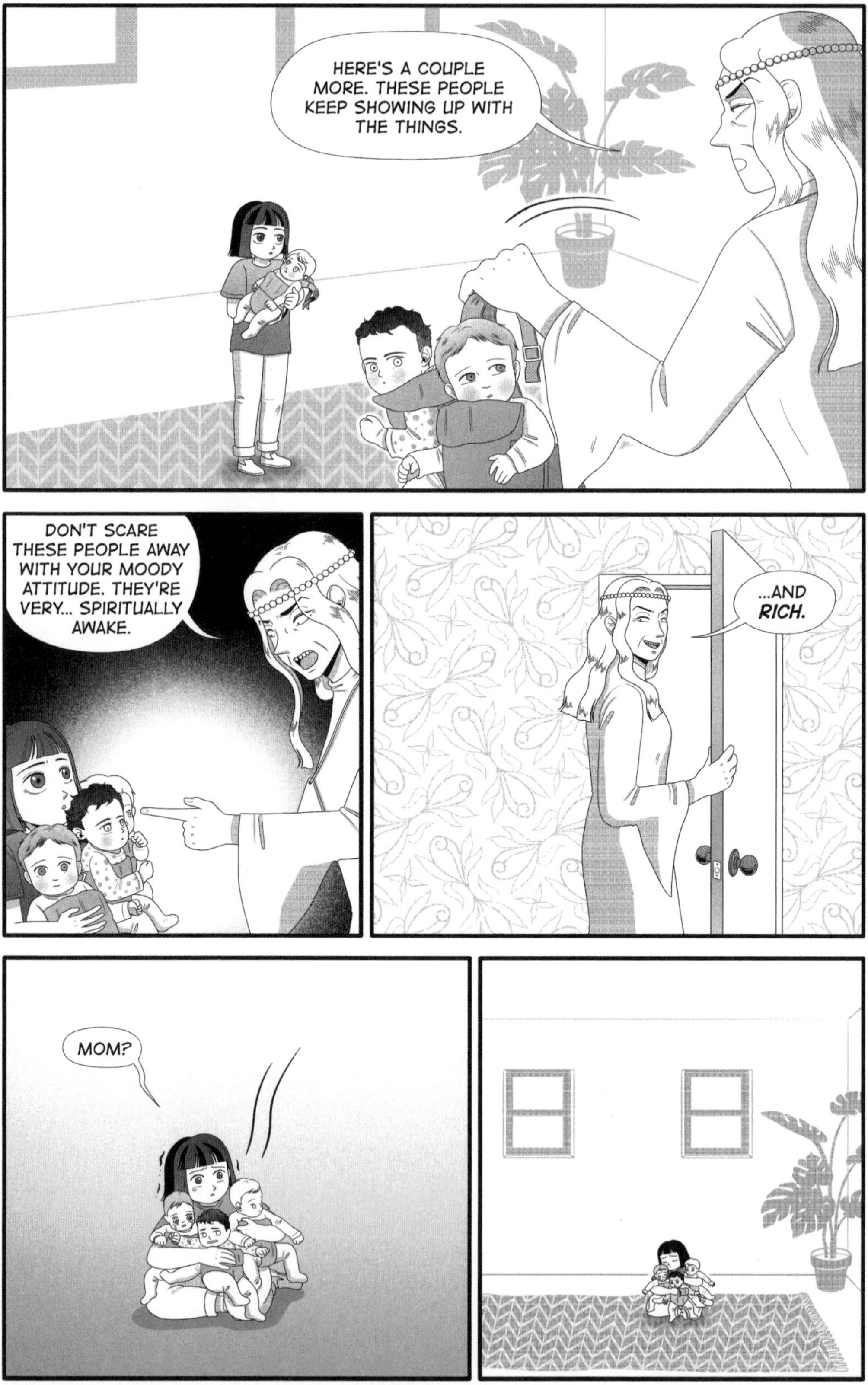
HERE'S A COUPLE MORE. THESE PEOPLE KEEP SHOWING UP WITH THE THINGS.
DON'T SCARE THESE PEOPLE AWAY WITH YOUR MOODY ATTITUDE. THEY'RE VERY... SPIRITUALLY AWAKE.
...AND *RICH.*
MOM?

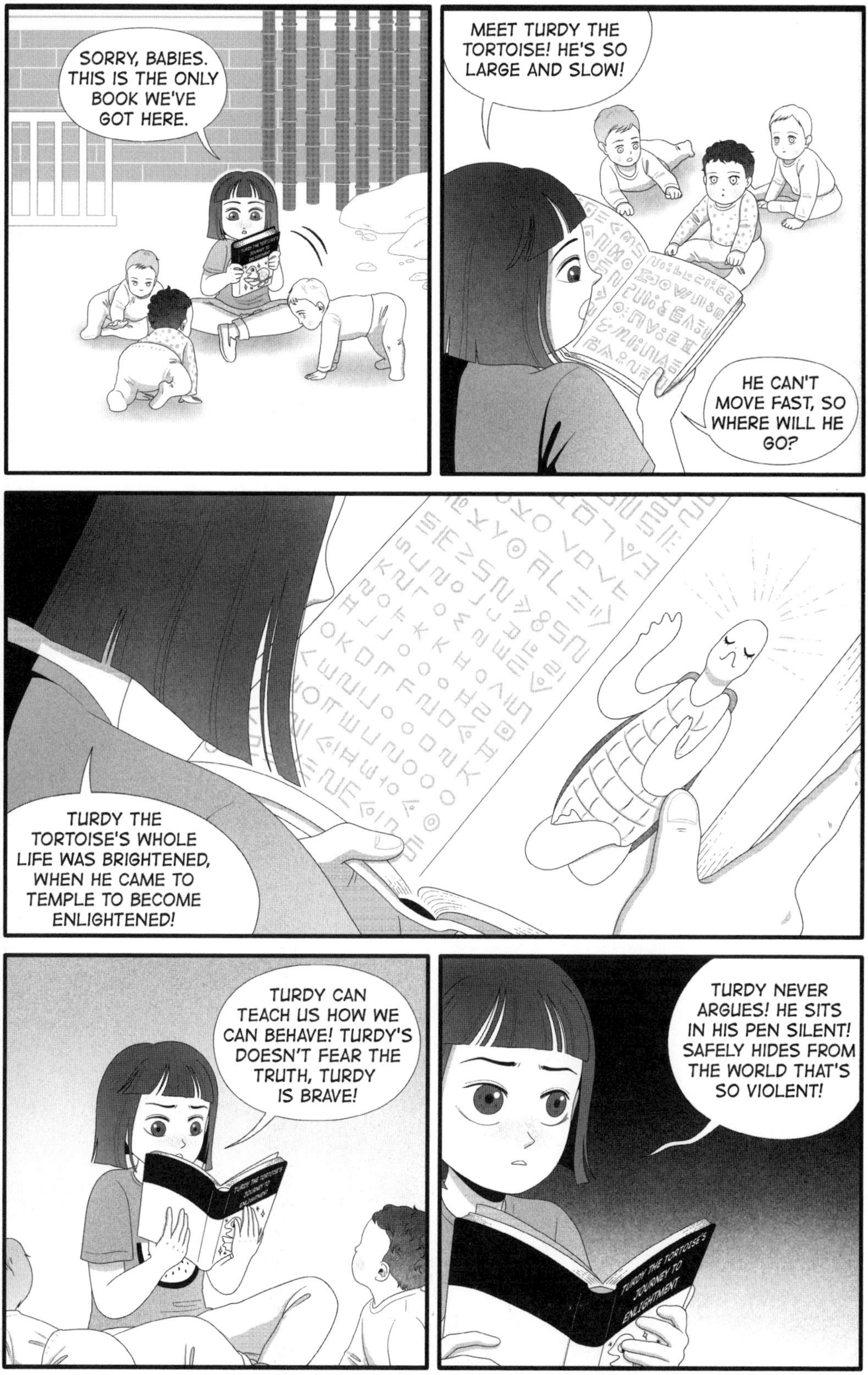
SORRY, BABIES. THIS IS THE ONLY BOOK WE'VE GOT HERE.
MEET TURDY THE TORTOISE! HE'S SO LARGE AND SLOW!
HE CAN'T MOVE FAST, SO WHERE WILL HE GO?
TURDY THE TORTOISE'S WHOLE LIFE WAS BRIGHTENED, WHEN HE CAME TO TEMPLE TO BECOME ENLIGHTENED!
TURDY CAN TEACH US HOW WE CAN BEHAVE! TURDY'S DOESN'T FEAR THE TRUTH, TURDY IS BRAVE!
TURDY NEVER ARGUES! HE SITS IN HIS PEN SILENT! SAFELY HIDES FROM THE WORLD THAT'S SO VIOLENT!
TURDY THE TORTOISE'S JOURNEY TO ENLIGHTMENT

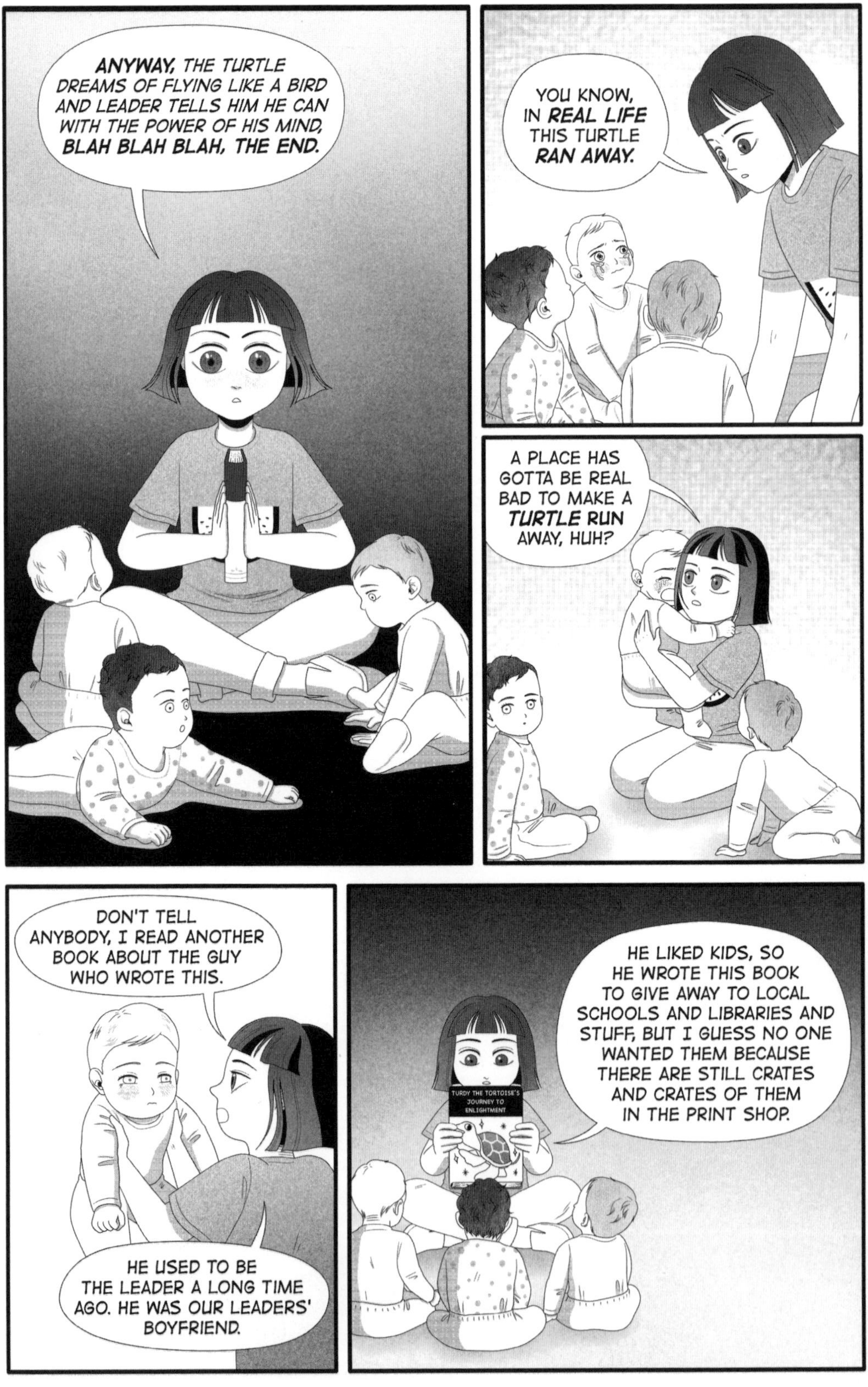
ANYWAY, THE TURTLE DREAMS OF FLYING LIKE A BIRD AND LEADER TELLS HIM HE CAN WITH THE POWER OF HIS MIND, BLAH BLAH BLAH, THE END.
YOU KNOW, IN REAL LIFE THIS TURTLE RAN AWAY.
A PLACE HAS GOTTA BE REAL BAD TO MAKE A TURTLE RUN AWAY, HUH?
DON'T TELL ANYBODY, I READ ANOTHER BOOK ABOUT THE GUY WHO WROTE THIS.
HE USED TO BE THE LEADER A LONG TIME AGO. HE WAS OUR LEADERS' BOYFRIEND.
HE LIKED KIDS, SO HE WROTE THIS BOOK TO GIVE AWAY TO LOCAL SCHOOLS AND LIBRARIES AND STUFF, BUT I GUESS NO ONE WANTED THEM BECAUSE THERE ARE STILL CRATES AND CRATES OF THEM IN THE PRINT SHOP.
TURDY THE TORTOISE'S JOURNEY TO ENLIGHTMENT

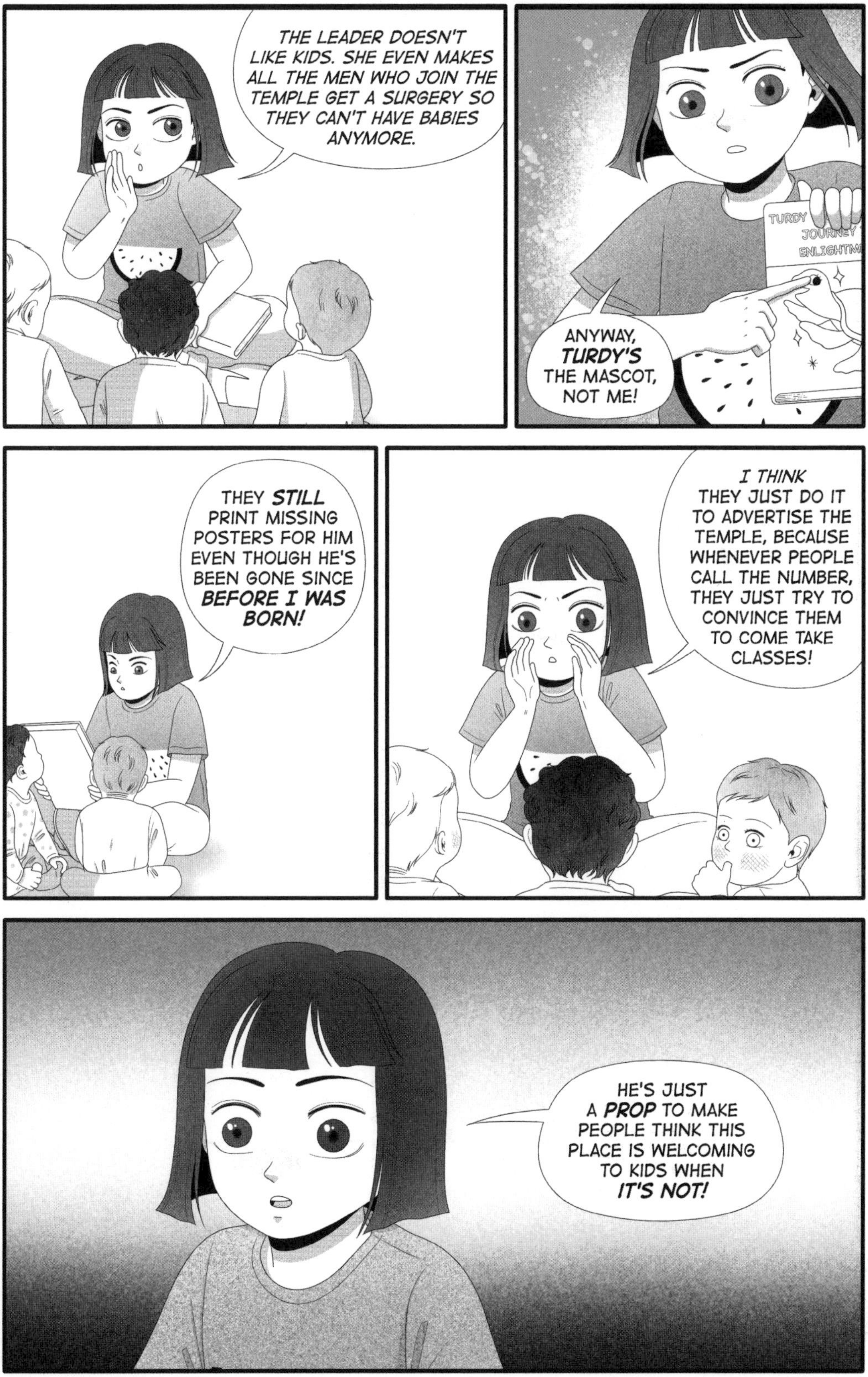
THE LEADER DOESN'T LIKE KIDS. SHE EVEN MAKES ALL THE MEN WHO JOIN THE TEMPLE GET A SURGERY SO THEY CAN'T HAVE BABIES ANYMORE.
TURDY JOURNEY ENLIGHTM
ANYWAY, TURDY'S THE MASCOT, NOT ME!
THEY STILL PRINT MISSING POSTERS FOR HIM EVEN THOUGH HE'S BEEN GONE SINCE BEFORE I WAS BORN!
I THINK THEY JUST DO IT TO ADVERTISE THE TEMPLE, BECAUSE WHENEVER PEOPLE CALL THE NUMBER, THEY JUST TRY TO CONVINCE THEM TO COME TAKE CLASSES!
HE'S JUST A PROP TO MAKE PEOPLE THINK THIS PLACE IS WELCOMING TO KIDS WHEN IT'S NOT!

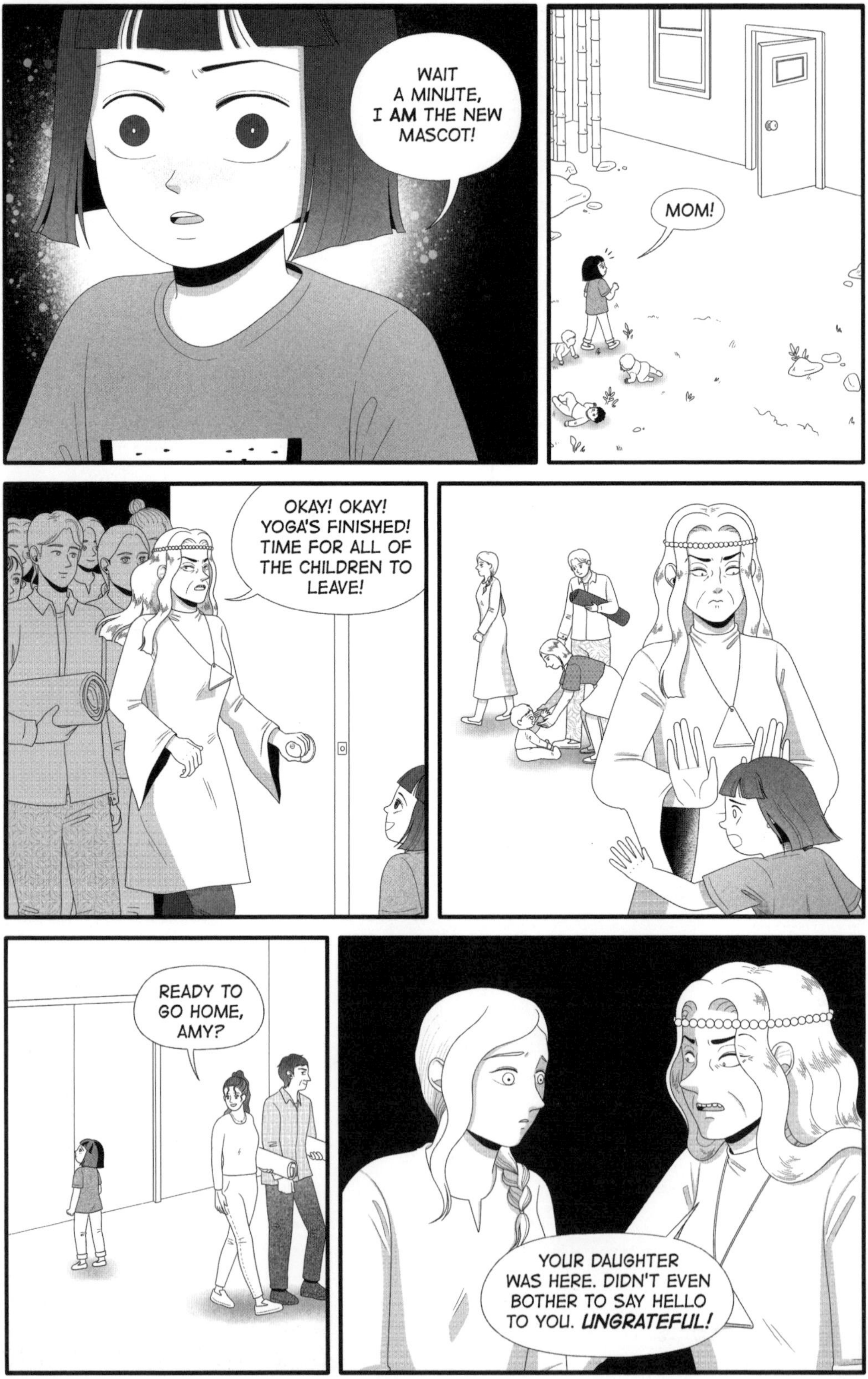
WAIT A MINUTE, I AM THE NEW MASCOT!
MOM!
OKAY! OKAY! YOGA'S FINISHED! TIME FOR ALL OF THE CHILDREN TO LEAVE!
READY TO GO HOME, AMY?
YOUR DAUGHTER WAS HERE. DIDN'T EVEN BOTHER TO SAY HELLO TO YOU. *UNGRATEFUL!*

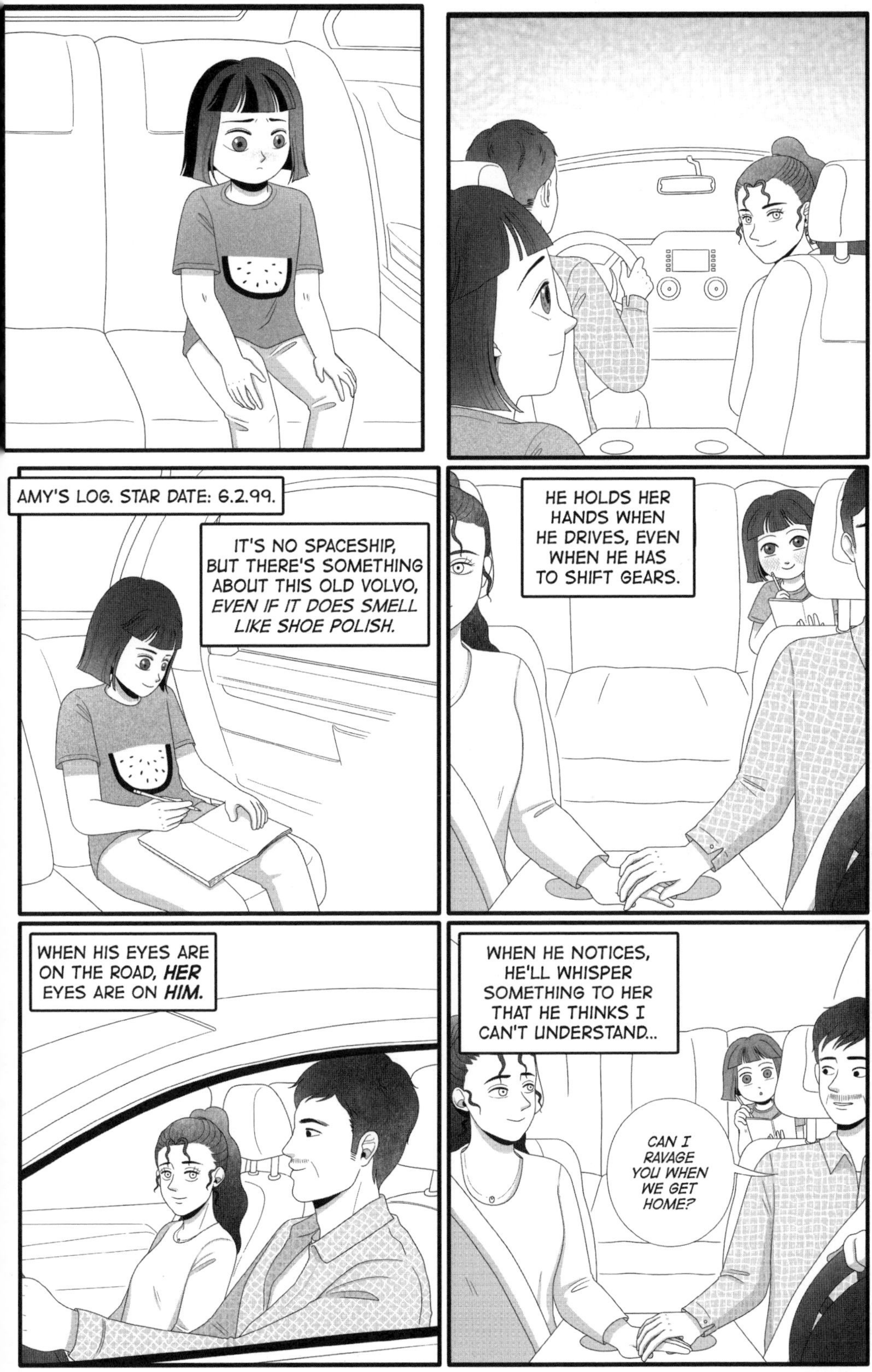

AMY'S LOG. STAR DATE: 6.2.99.
IT'S NO SPACESHIP, BUT THERE'S SOMETHING ABOUT THIS OLD VOLVO, *EVEN IF IT DOES SMELL LIKE SHOE POLISH.*
HE HOLDS HER HANDS WHEN HE DRIVES, EVEN WHEN HE HAS TO SHIFT GEARS.
WHEN HIS EYES ARE ON THE ROAD, ***HER*** EYES ARE ON ***HIM.***
WHEN HE NOTICES, HE'LL WHISPER SOMETHING TO HER THAT HE THINKS I CAN'T UNDERSTAND...
CAN I RAVAGE YOU WHEN WE GET HOME?

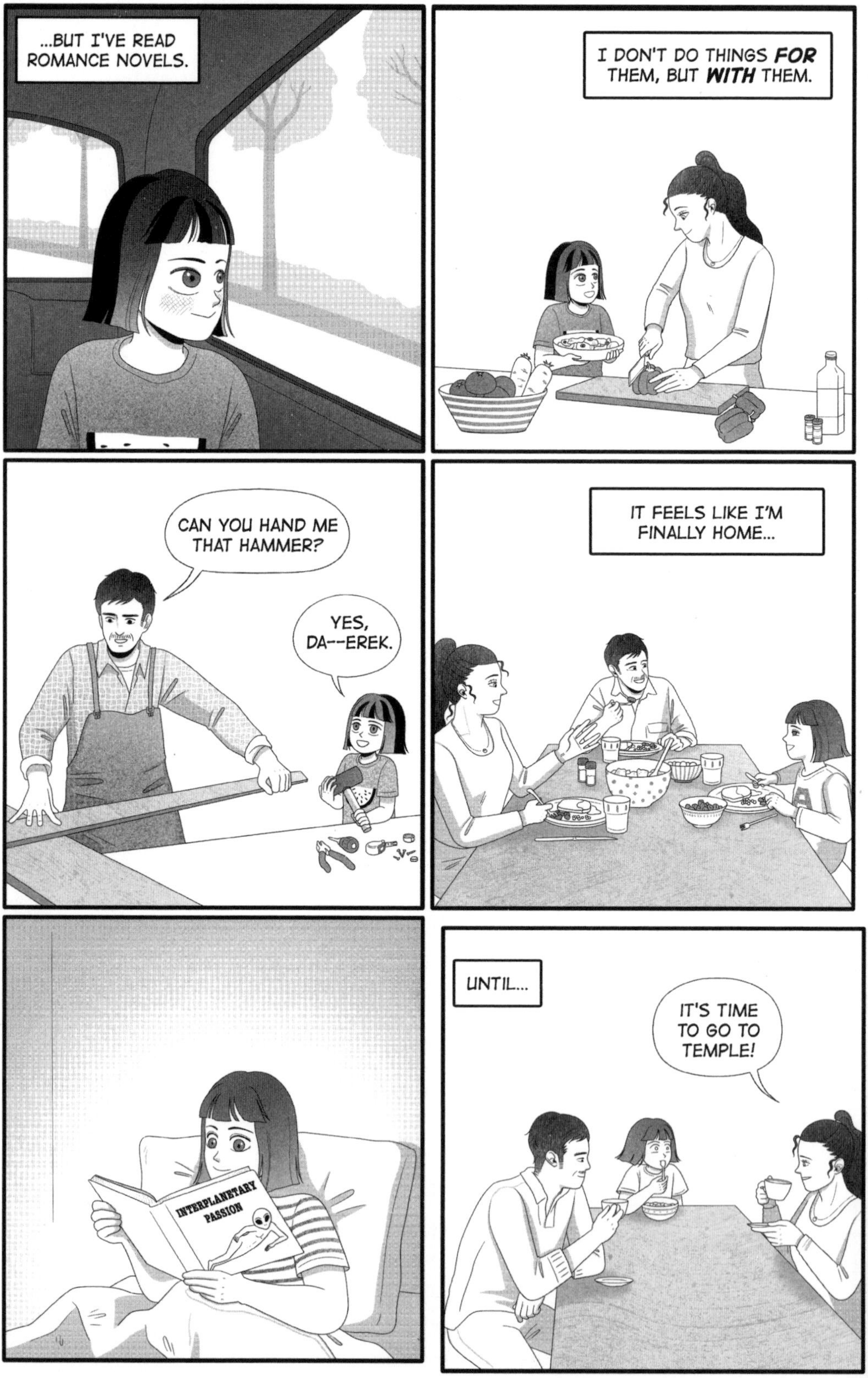
...BUT I'VE READ ROMANCE NOVELS.
I DON'T DO THINGS **FOR** THEM, BUT **WITH** THEM.
CAN YOU HAND ME THAT HAMMER?
YES, DA--EREK.
IT FEELS LIKE I'M FINALLY HOME...
INTERPLANETARY PASSION
UNTIL...
IT'S TIME TO GO TO TEMPLE!

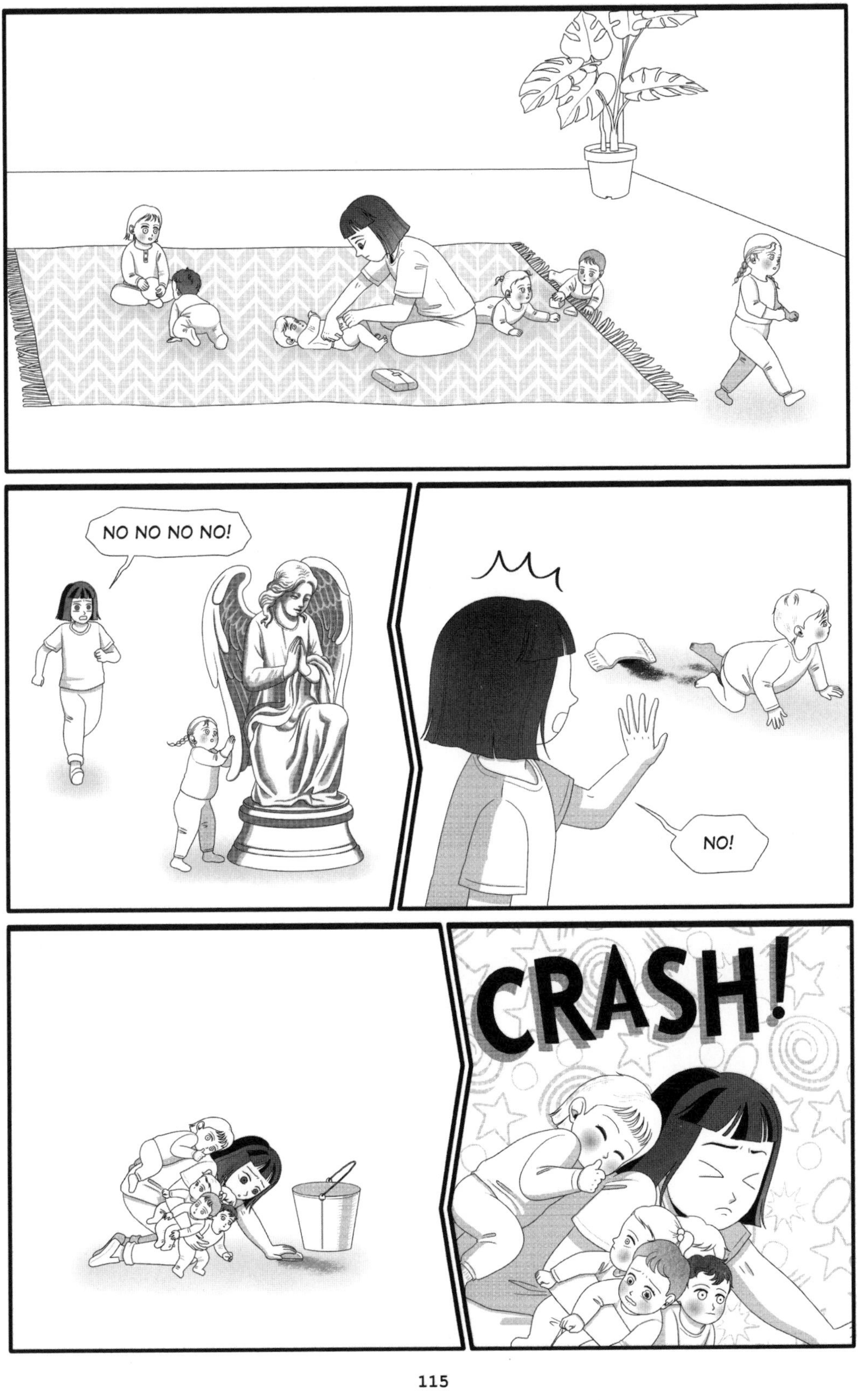
NO NO NO NO!
NO!
CRASH!

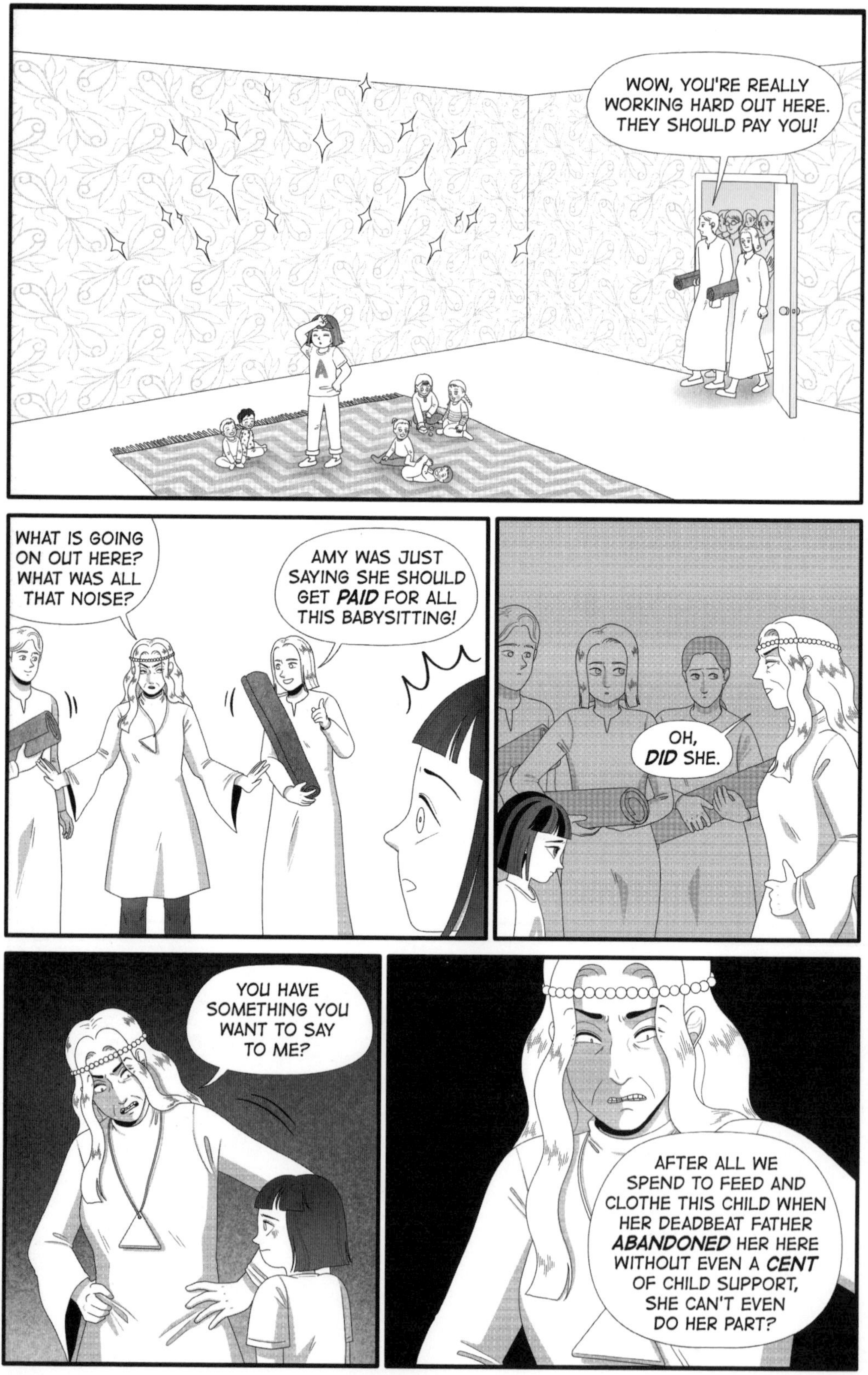
WOW, YOU'RE REALLY WORKING HARD OUT HERE. THEY SHOULD PAY YOU!
WHAT IS GOING ON OUT HERE? WHAT WAS ALL THAT NOISE?
AMY WAS JUST SAYING SHE SHOULD GET **PAID** FOR ALL THIS BABYSITTING!
OH, **DID** SHE.
YOU HAVE SOMETHING YOU WANT TO SAY TO ME?
AFTER ALL WE SPEND TO FEED AND CLOTHE THIS CHILD WHEN HER DEADBEAT FATHER **ABANDONED** HER HERE WITHOUT EVEN A **CENT** OF CHILD SUPPORT, SHE CAN'T EVEN DO HER PART?

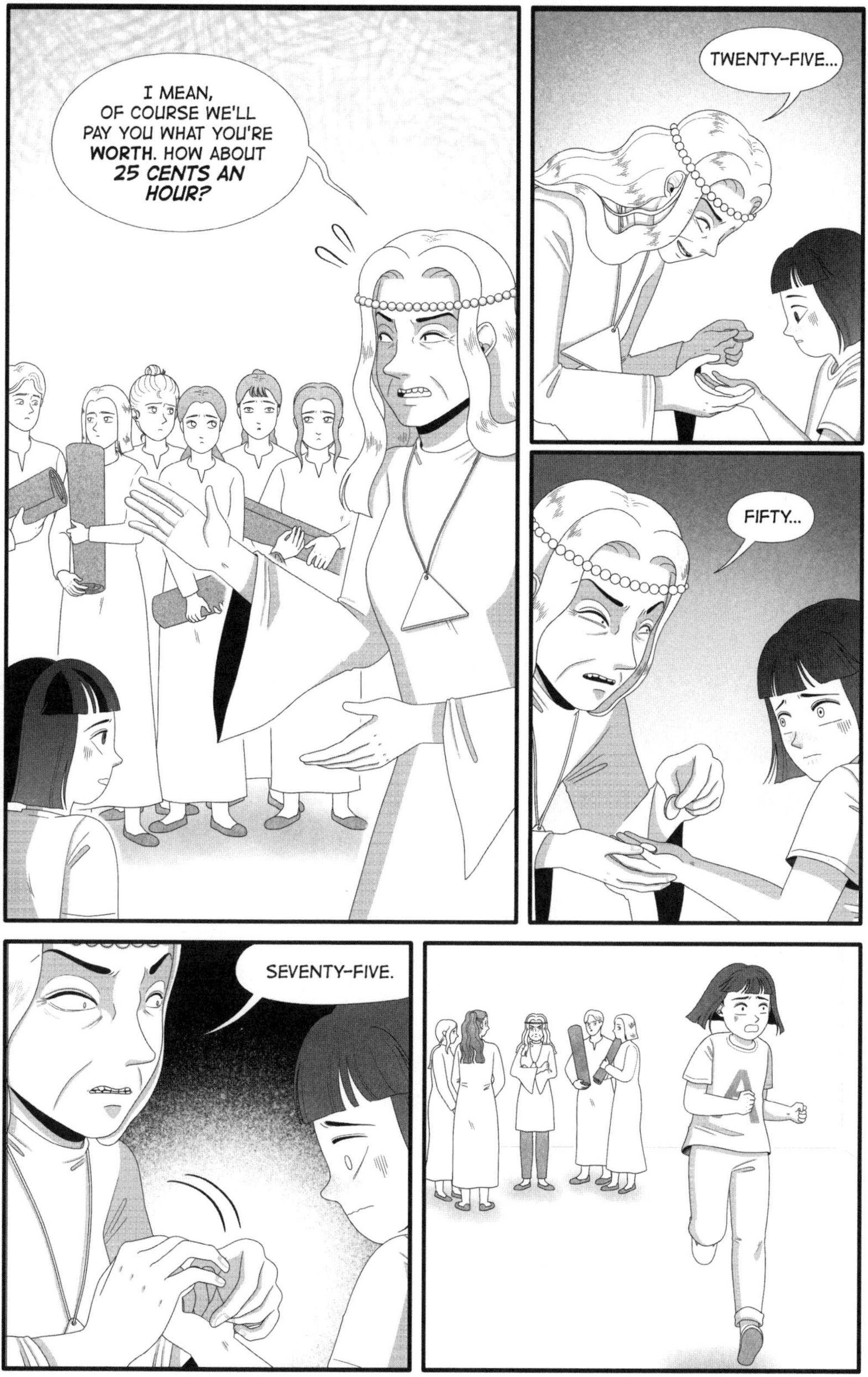
I MEAN, OF COURSE WE'LL PAY YOU WHAT YOU'RE **WORTH**. HOW ABOUT ***25 CENTS AN HOUR?***
TWENTY-FIVE...
FIFTY...
SEVENTY-FIVE.

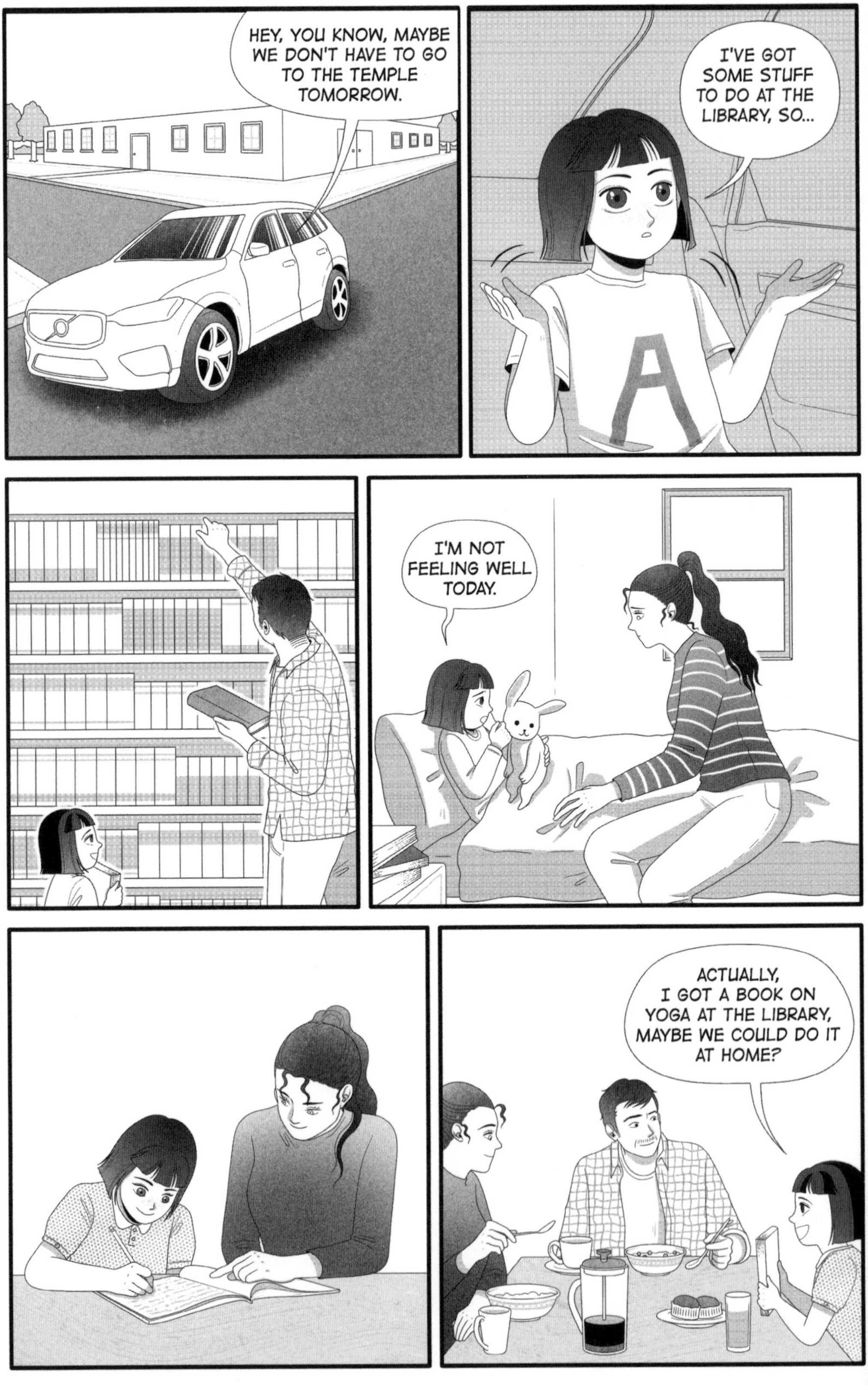
HEY, YOU KNOW, MAYBE WE DON'T HAVE TO GO TO THE TEMPLE TOMORROW.
I'VE GOT SOME STUFF TO DO AT THE LIBRARY, SO...
I'M NOT FEELING WELL TODAY.
ACTUALLY, I GOT A BOOK ON YOGA AT THE LIBRARY, MAYBE WE COULD DO IT AT HOME?

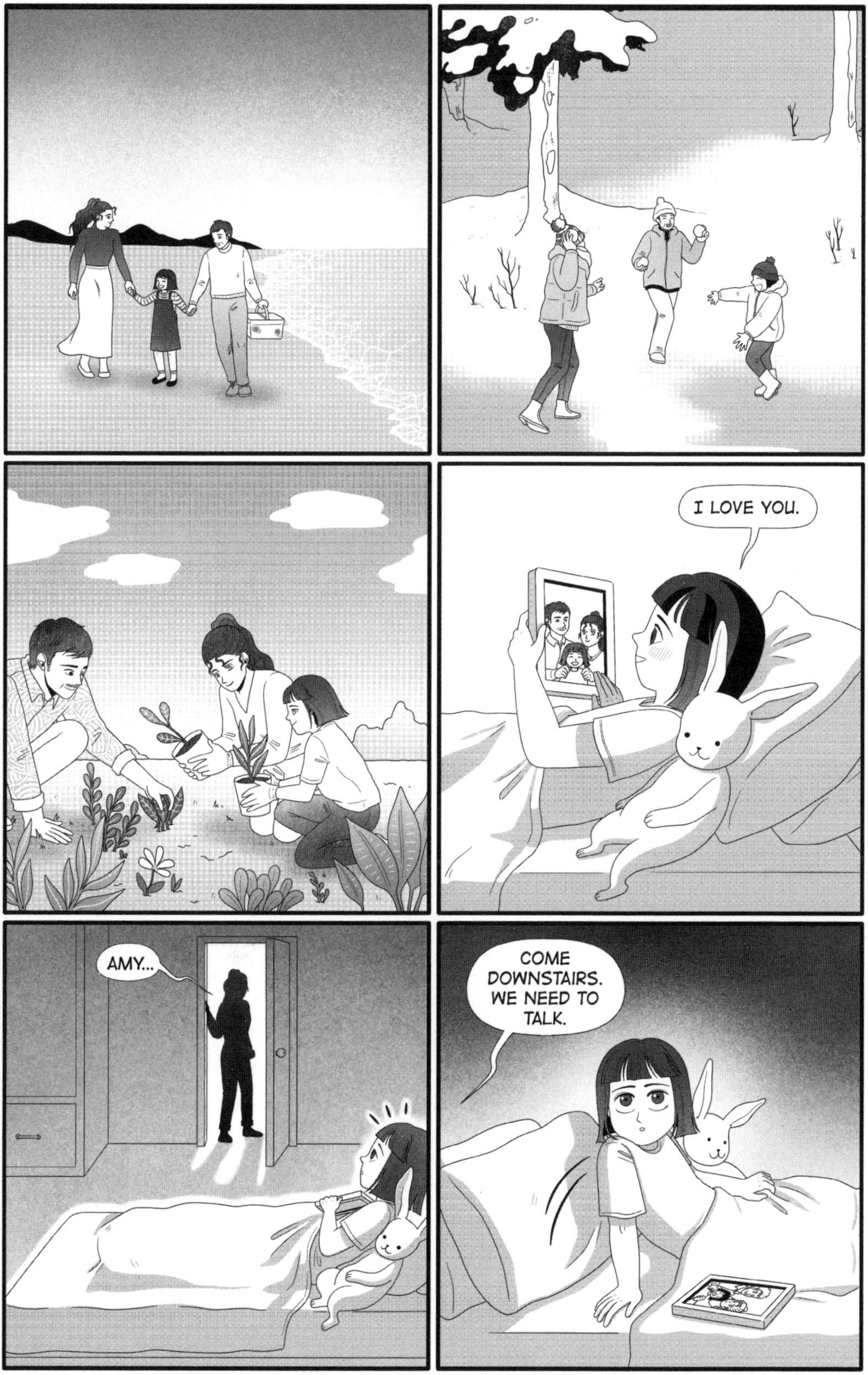
I LOVE YOU.
AMY...
COME DOWNSTAIRS. WE NEED TO TALK.

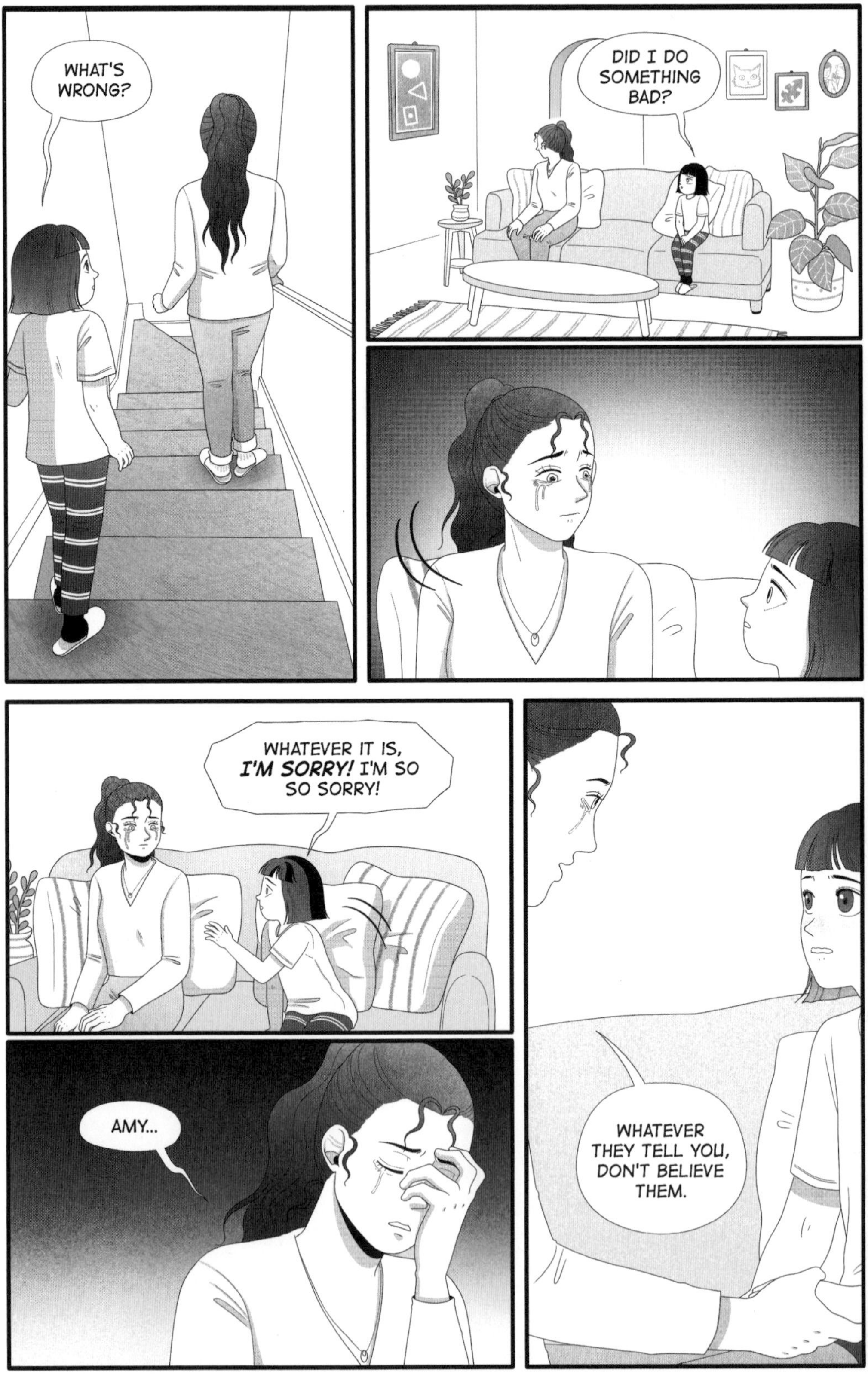
WHAT'S WRONG?
DID I DO SOMETHING BAD?
WHATEVER IT IS, **I'M SORRY!** I'M SO SO SORRY!
AMY...
WHATEVER THEY TELL YOU, DON'T BELIEVE THEM.

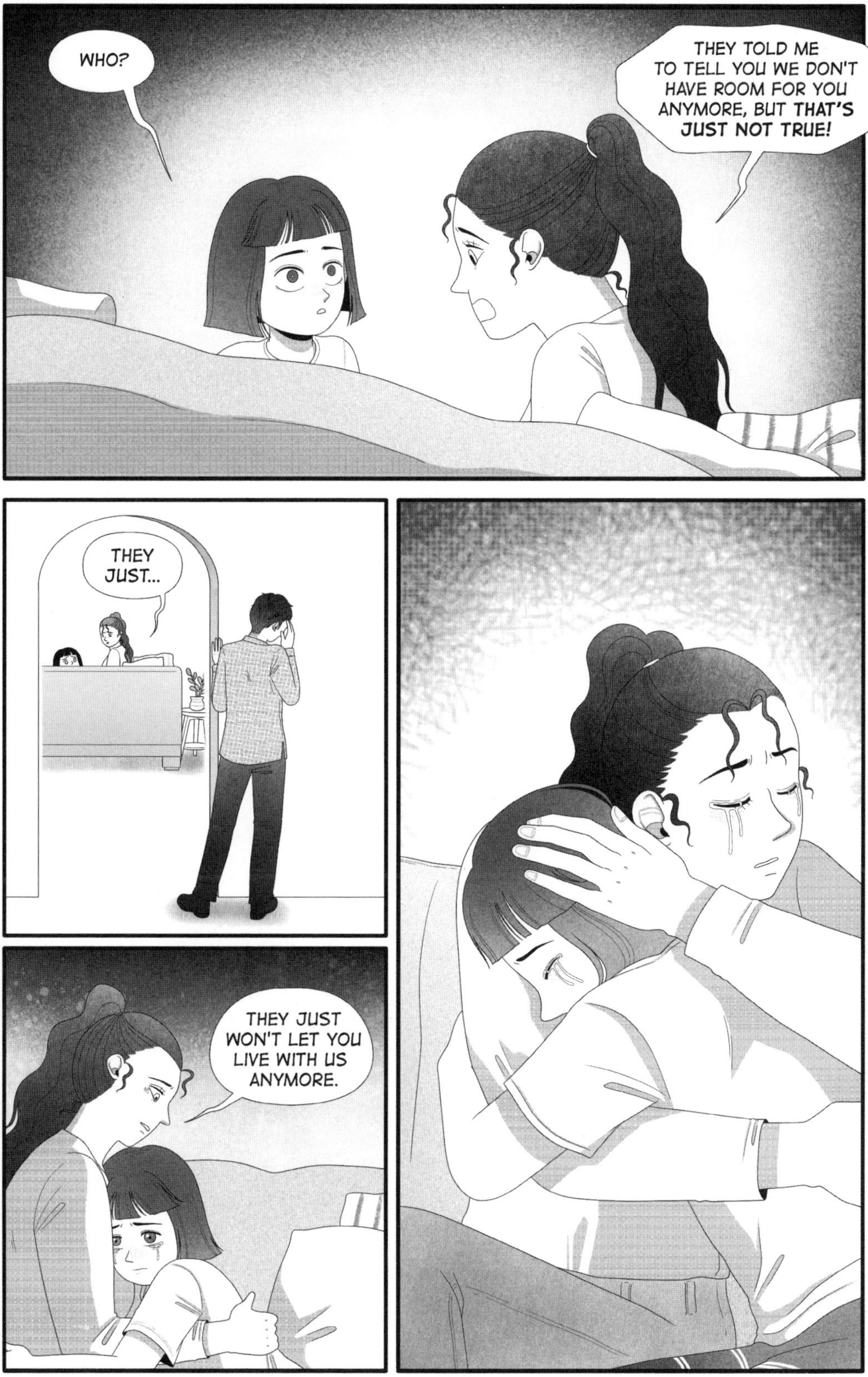
WHO?
THEY TOLD ME TO TELL YOU WE DON'T HAVE ROOM FOR YOU ANYMORE, BUT THAT'S JUST NOT TRUE!
THEY JUST...
THEY JUST WON'T LET YOU LIVE WITH US ANYMORE.

CHAPTER SEVEN:
THE RETURN

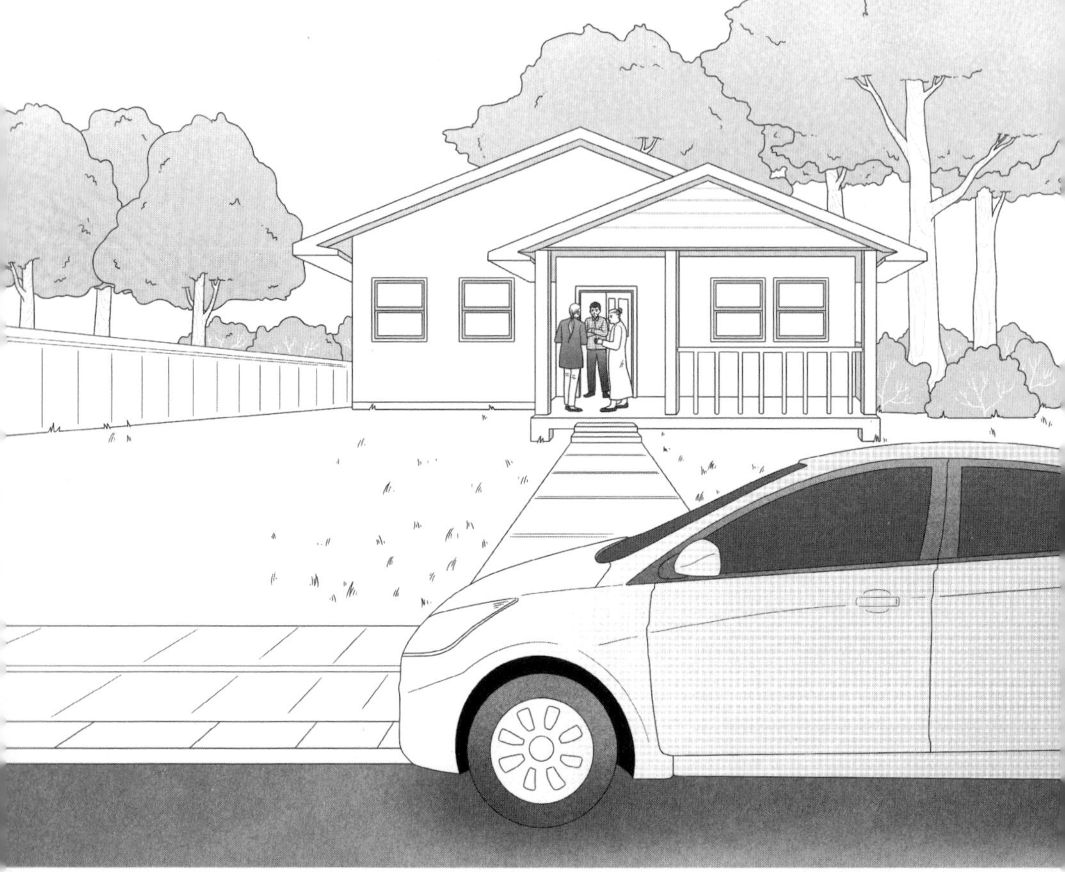

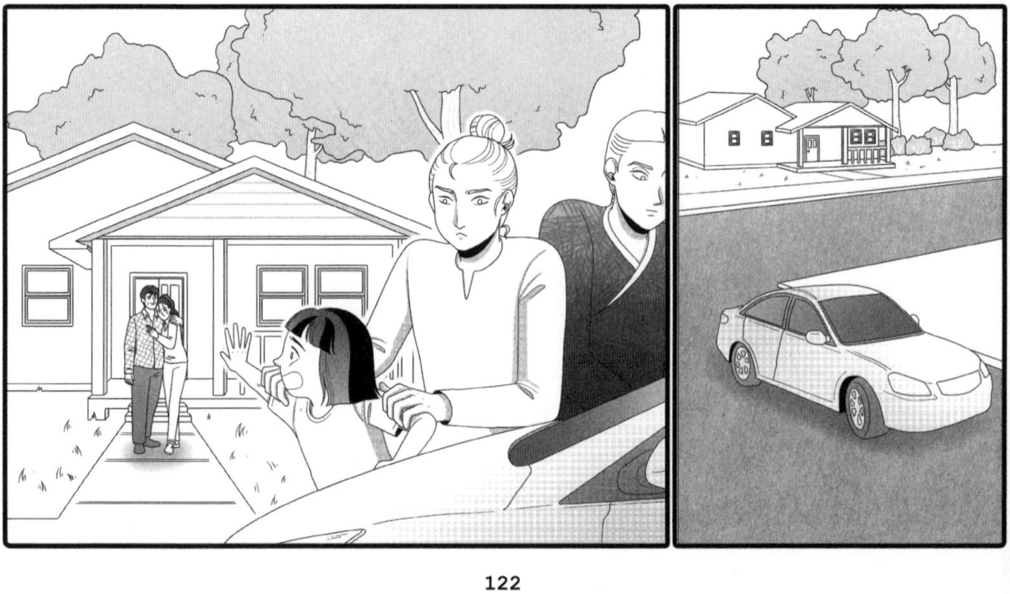

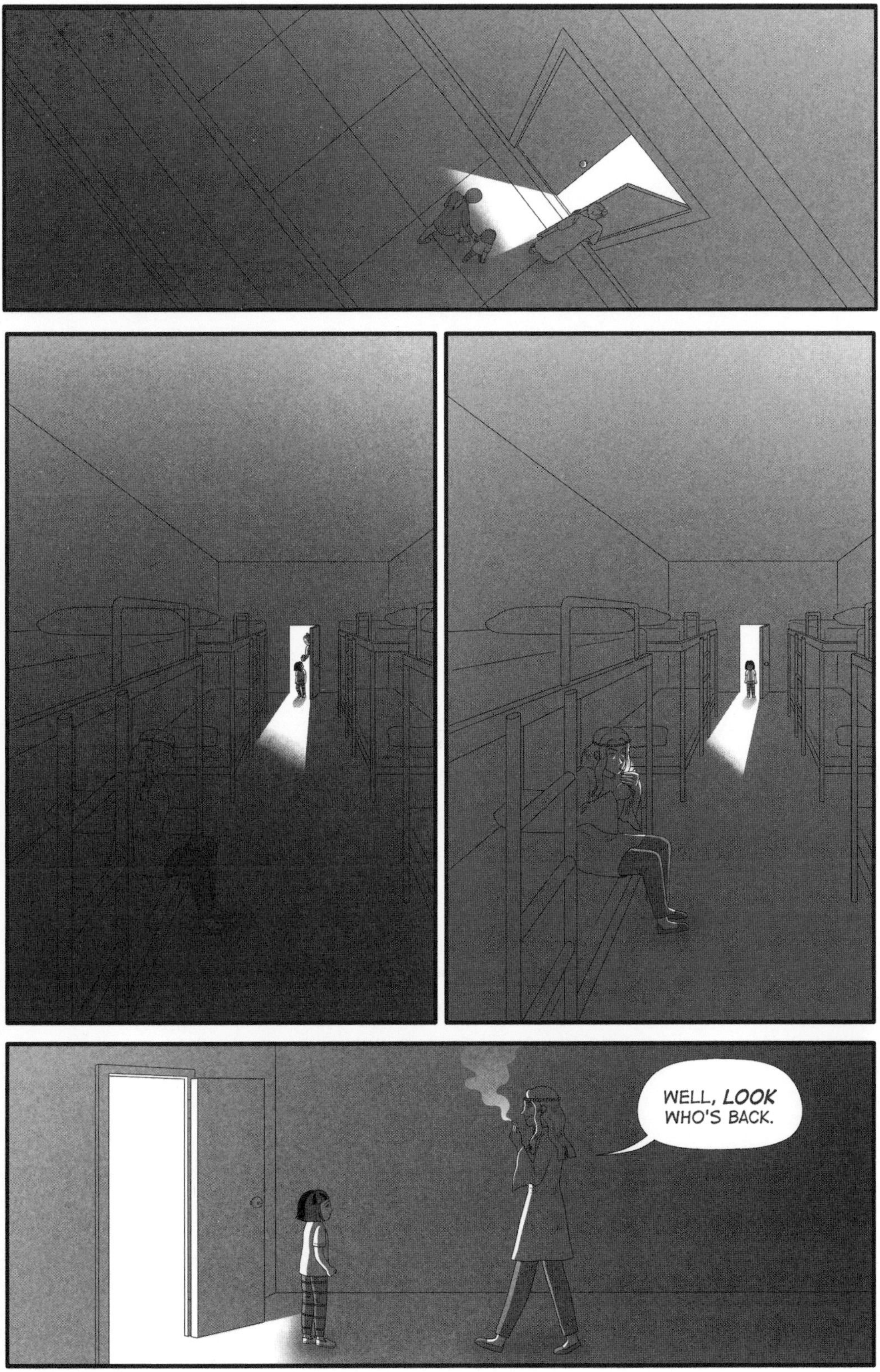
WELL, LOOK WHO'S BACK.

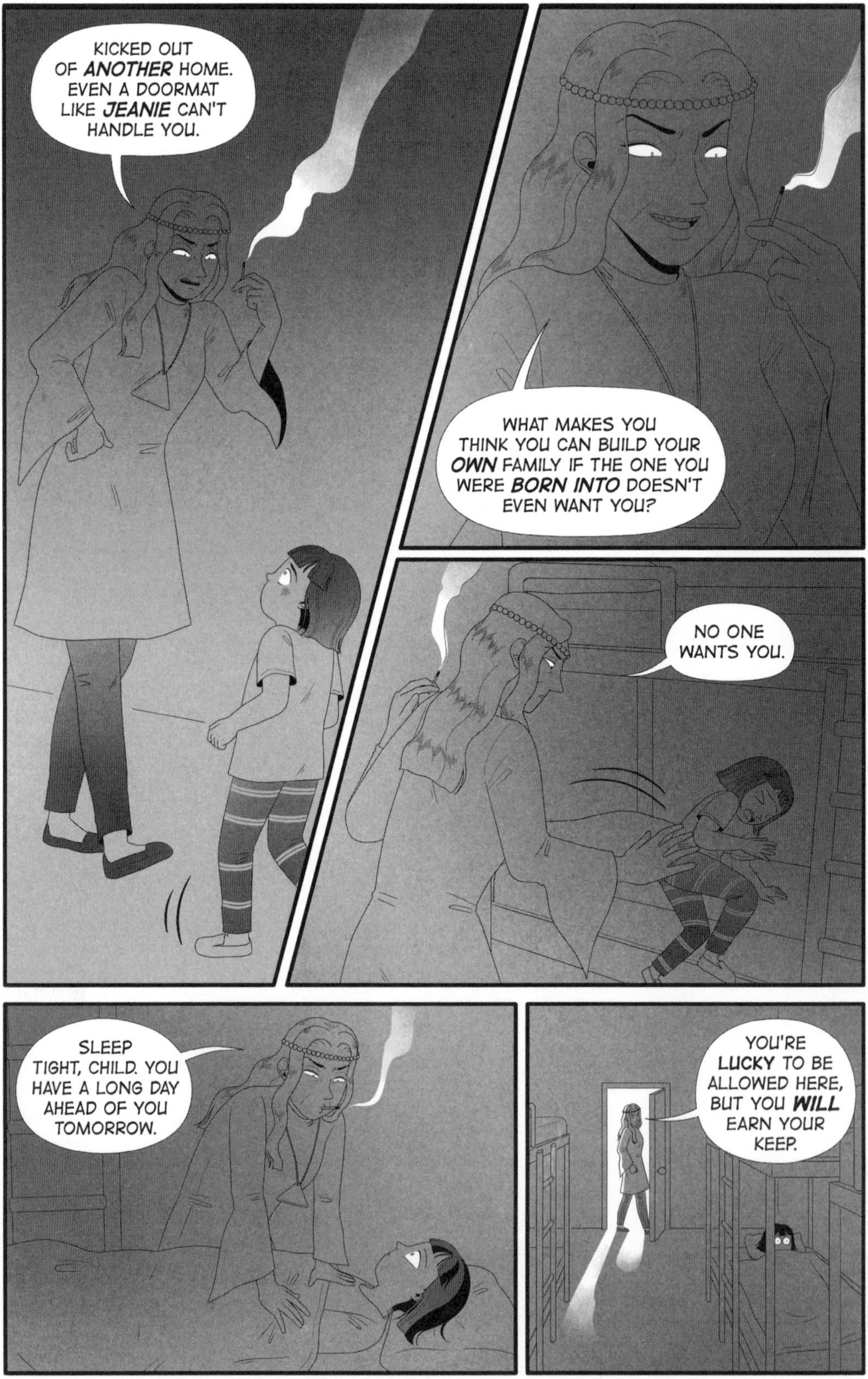
KICKED OUT OF ANOTHER HOME. EVEN A DOORMAT LIKE JEANIE CAN'T HANDLE YOU.
WHAT MAKES YOU THINK YOU CAN BUILD YOUR OWN FAMILY IF THE ONE YOU WERE BORN INTO DOESN'T EVEN WANT YOU?
NO ONE WANTS YOU.
SLEEP TIGHT, CHILD. YOU HAVE A LONG DAY AHEAD OF YOU TOMORROW.
YOU'RE LUCKY TO BE ALLOWED HERE, BUT YOU WILL EARN YOUR KEEP.

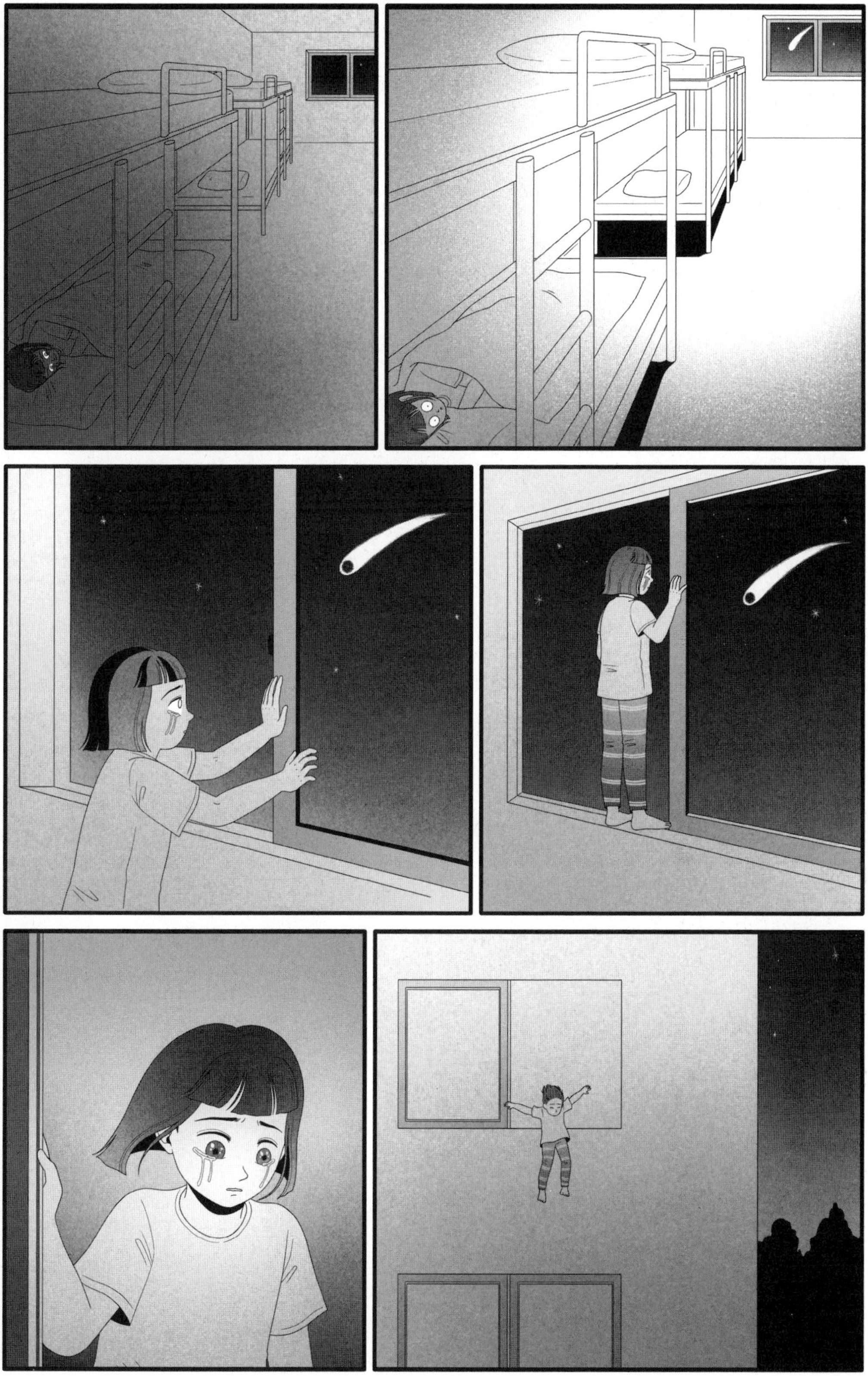

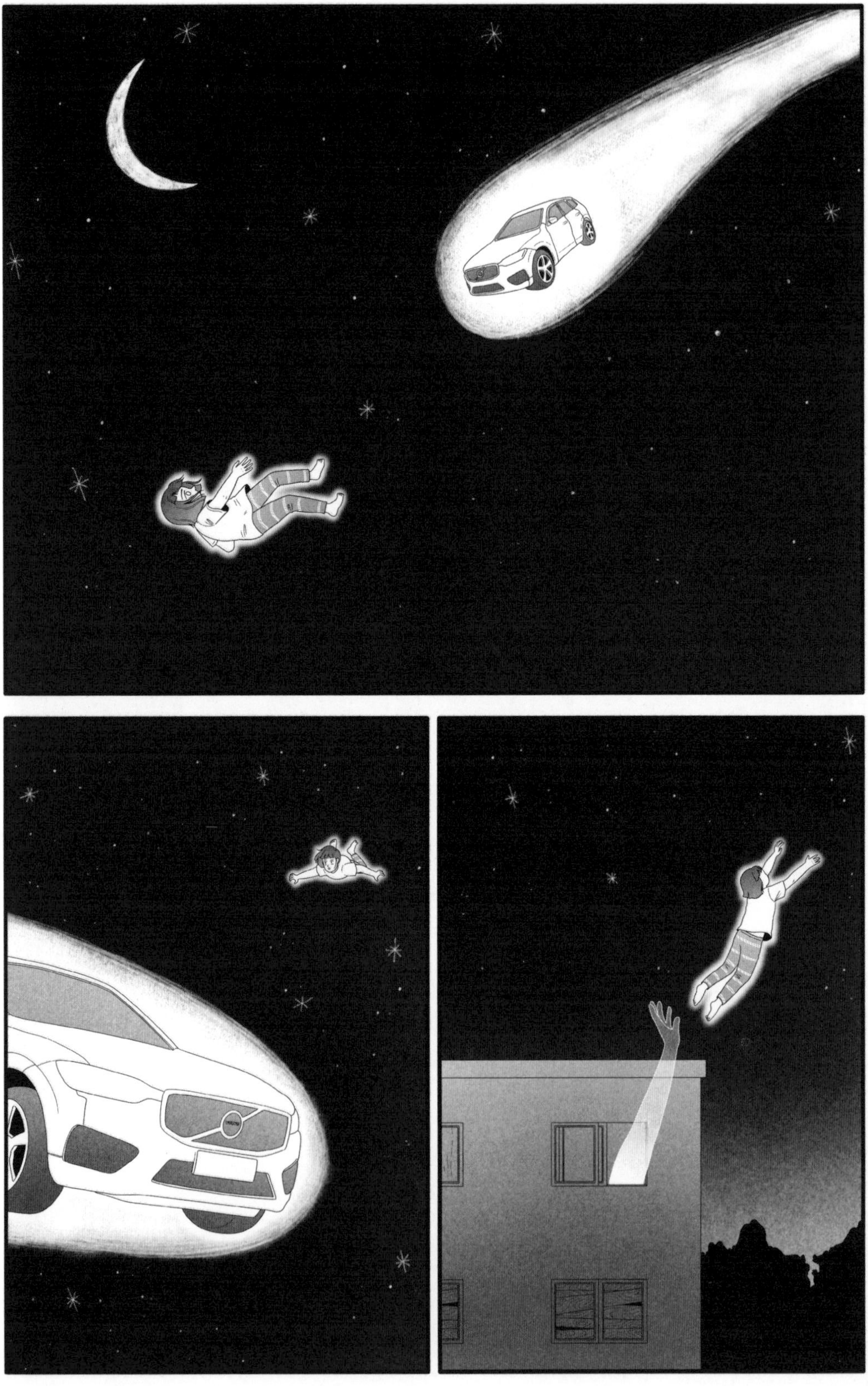

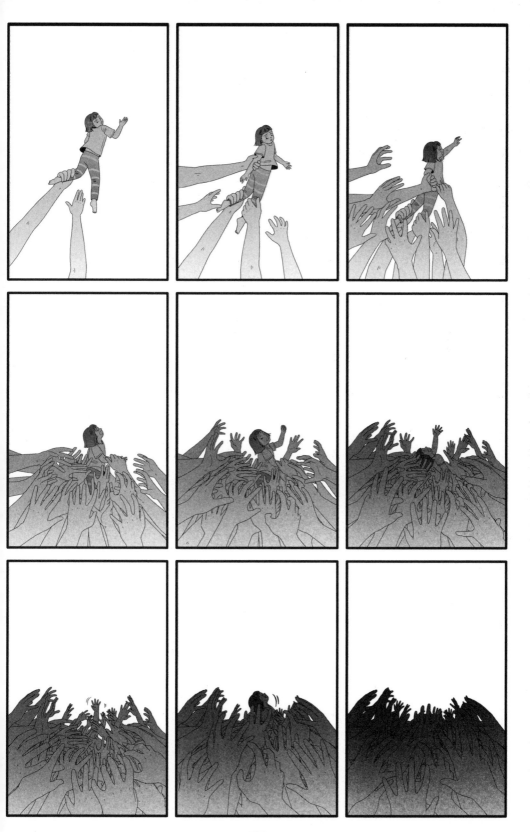

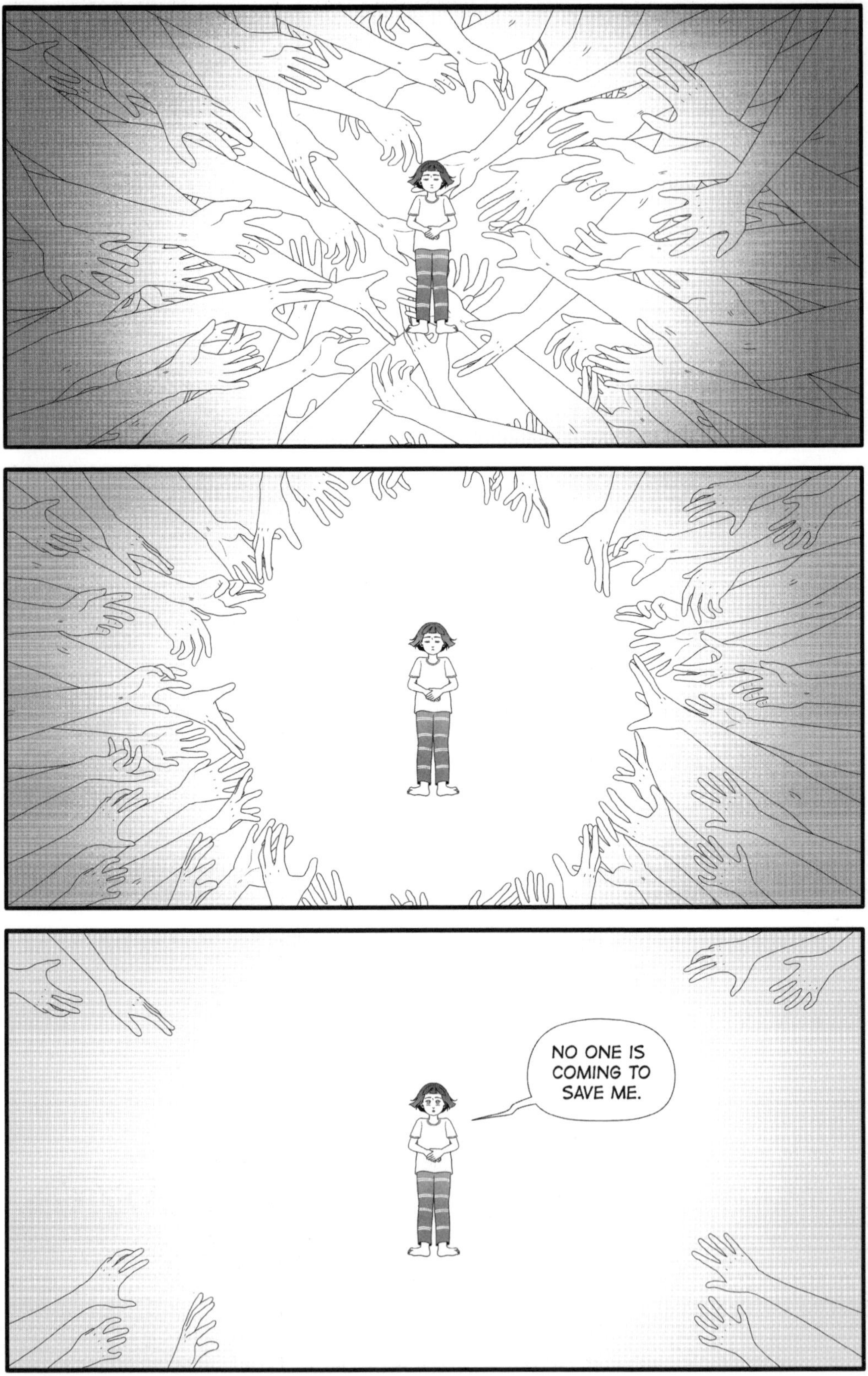
NO ONE IS
COMING TO
SAVE ME.

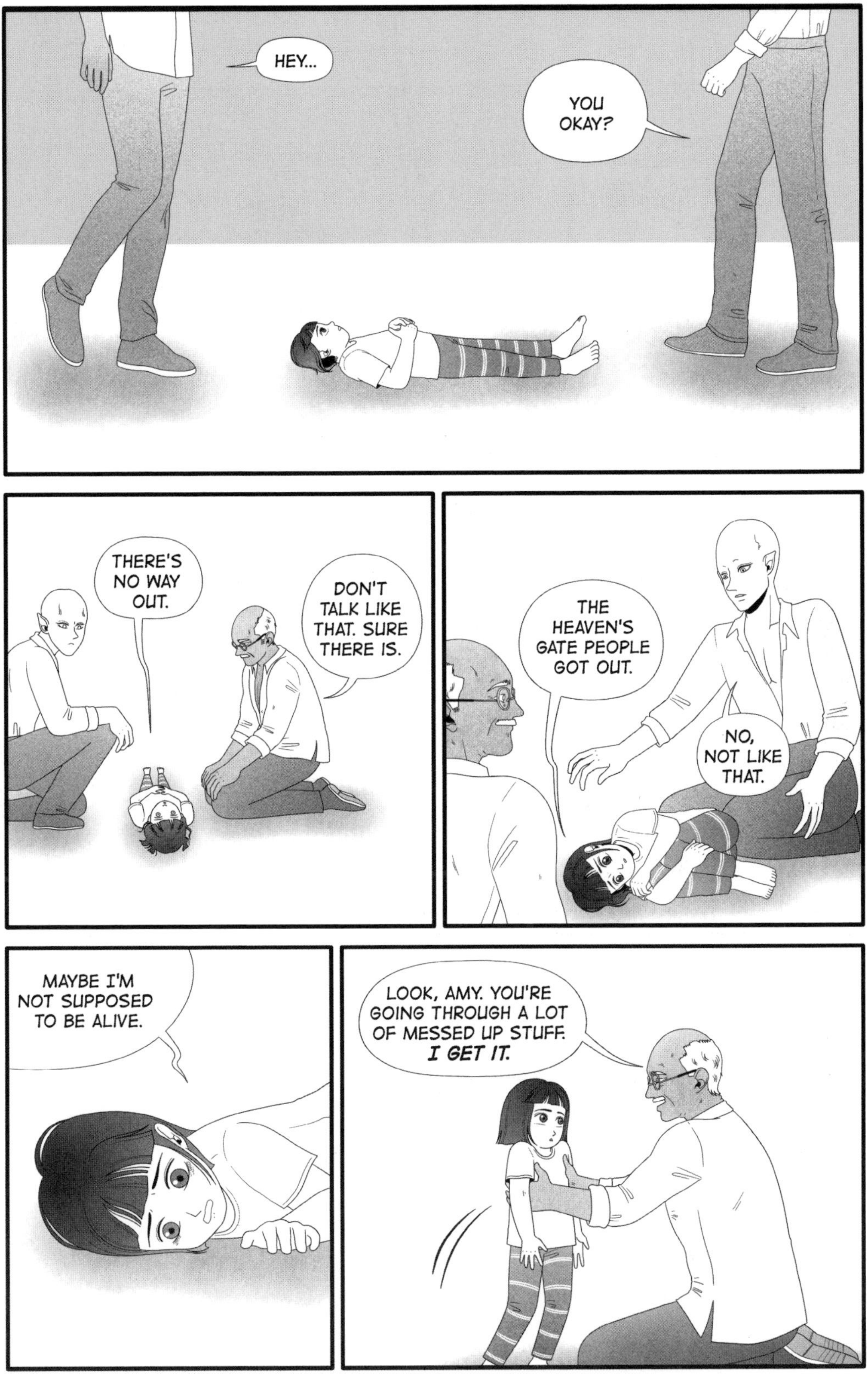
HEY...
YOU OKAY?
THERE'S NO WAY OUT.
DON'T TALK LIKE THAT. SURE THERE IS.
THE HEAVEN'S GATE PEOPLE GOT OUT.
NO, NOT LIKE THAT.
MAYBE I'M NOT SUPPOSED TO BE ALIVE.
LOOK, AMY. YOU'RE GOING THROUGH A LOT OF MESSED UP STUFF. *I GET IT.*

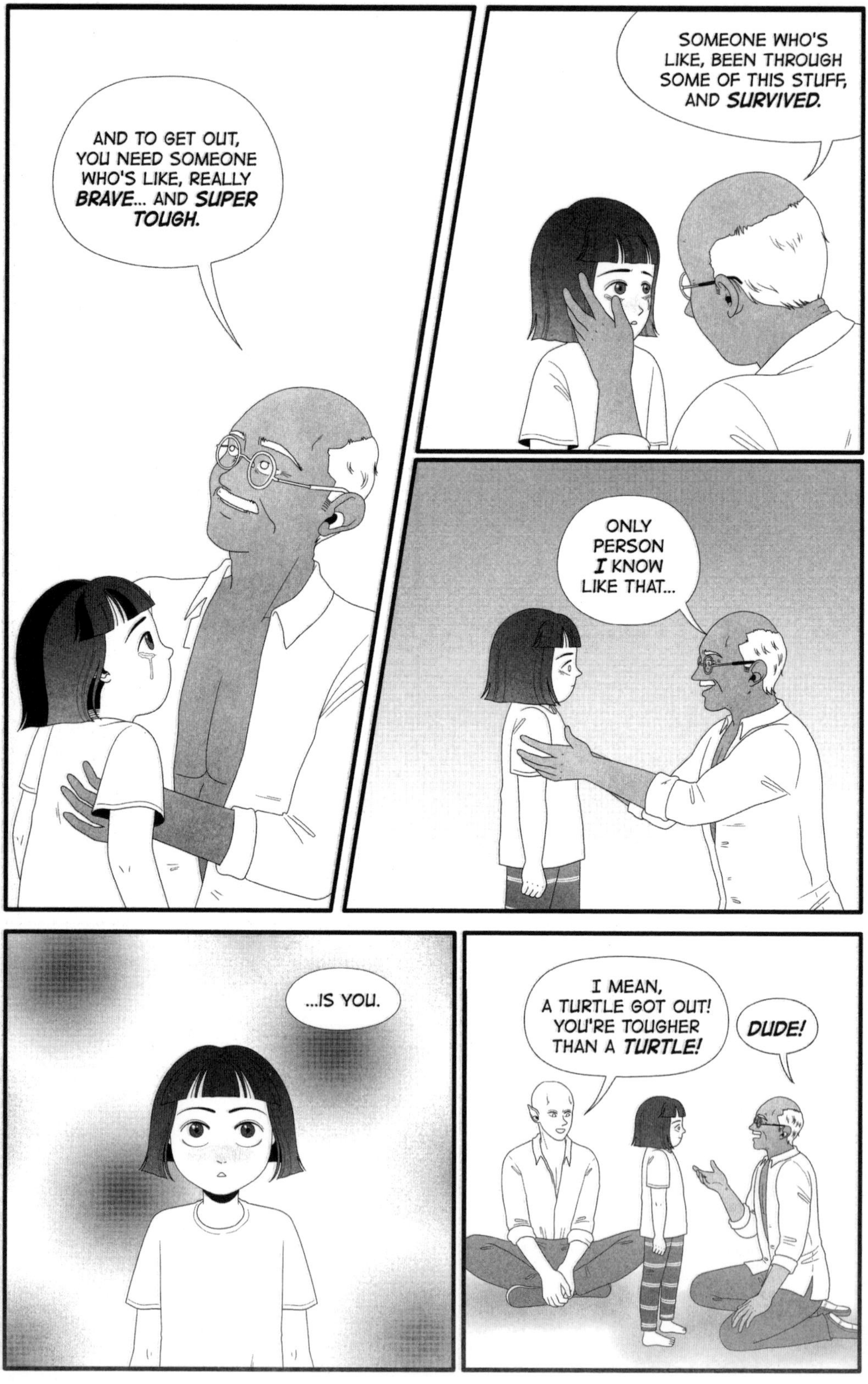
AND TO GET OUT, YOU NEED SOMEONE WHO'S LIKE, REALLY BRAVE... AND SUPER TOUGH.
SOMEONE WHO'S LIKE, BEEN THROUGH SOME OF THIS STUFF, AND SURVIVED.
ONLY PERSON I KNOW LIKE THAT...
...IS YOU.
I MEAN, A TURTLE GOT OUT! YOU'RE TOUGHER THAN A TURTLE!
DUDE!

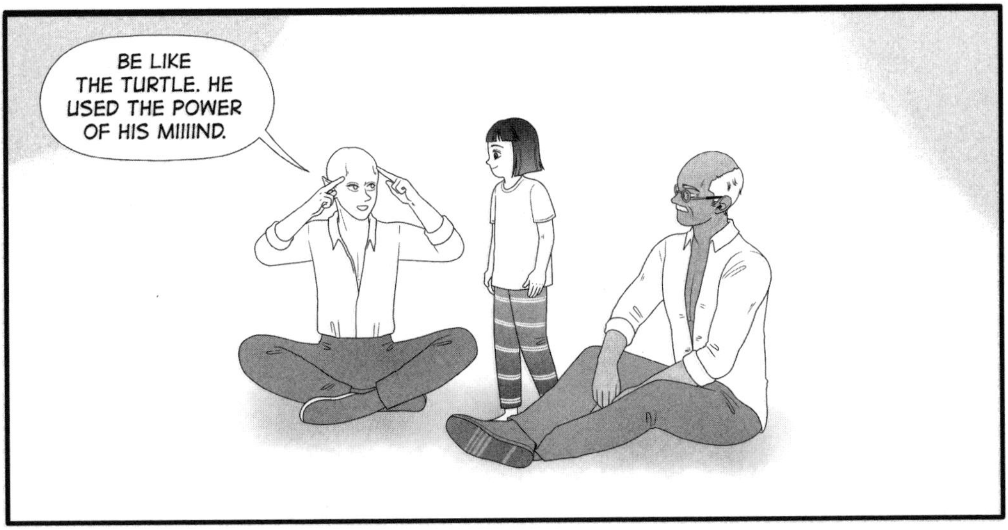
BE LIKE THE TURTLE. HE USED THE POWER OF HIS MIIIIND.

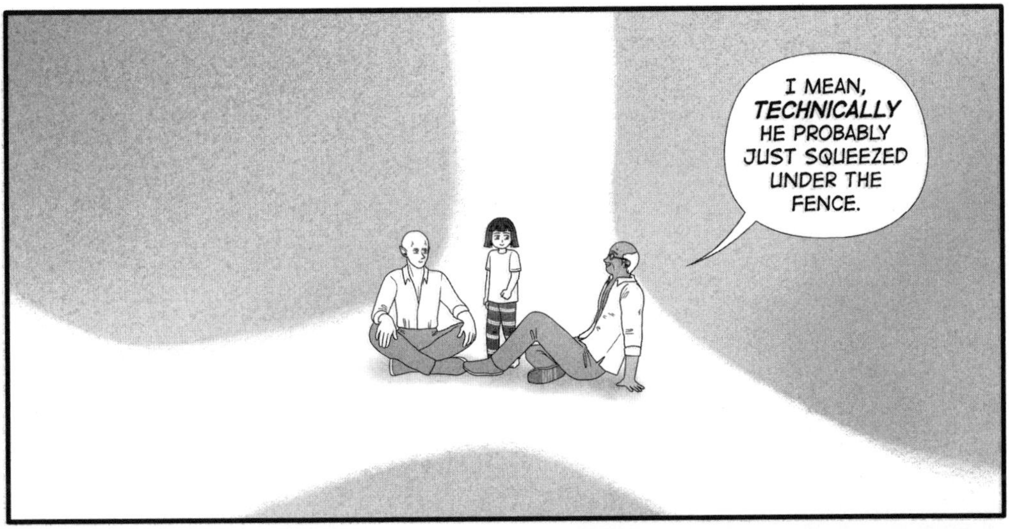
I MEAN, TECHNICALLY HE PROBABLY JUST SQUEEZED UNDER THE FENCE.

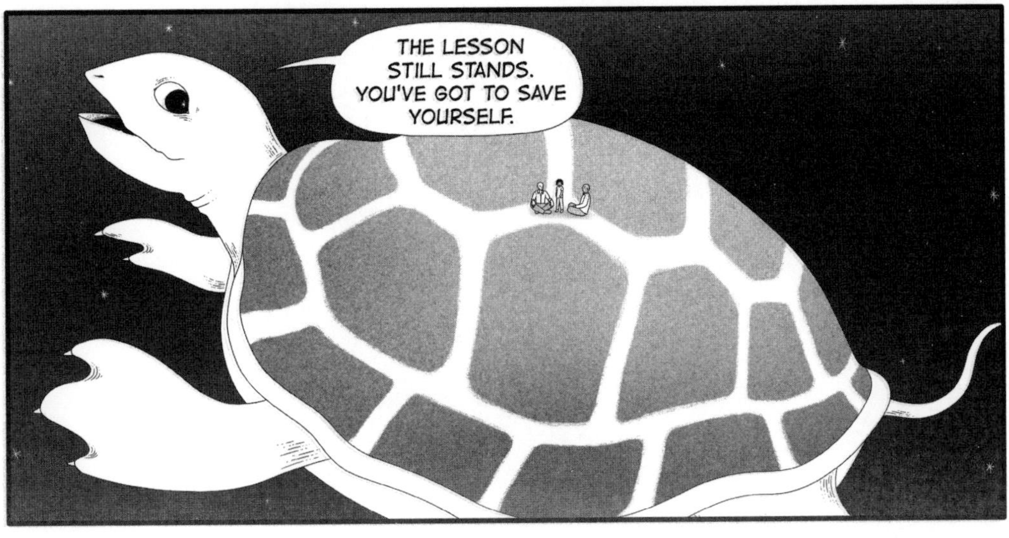
THE LESSON STILL STANDS. YOU'VE GOT TO SAVE YOURSELF.

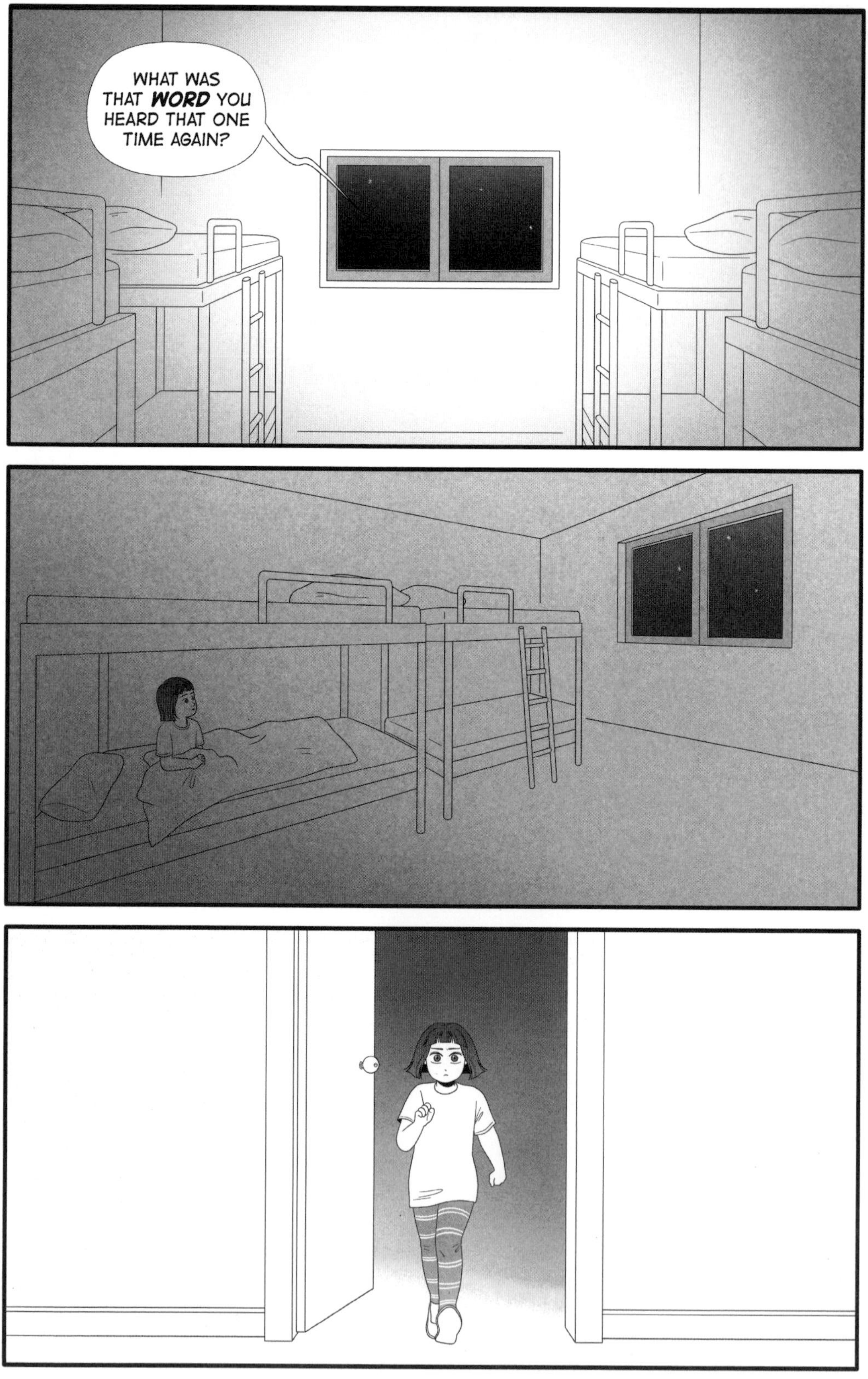
WHAT WAS THAT WORD YOU HEARD THAT ONE TIME AGAIN?

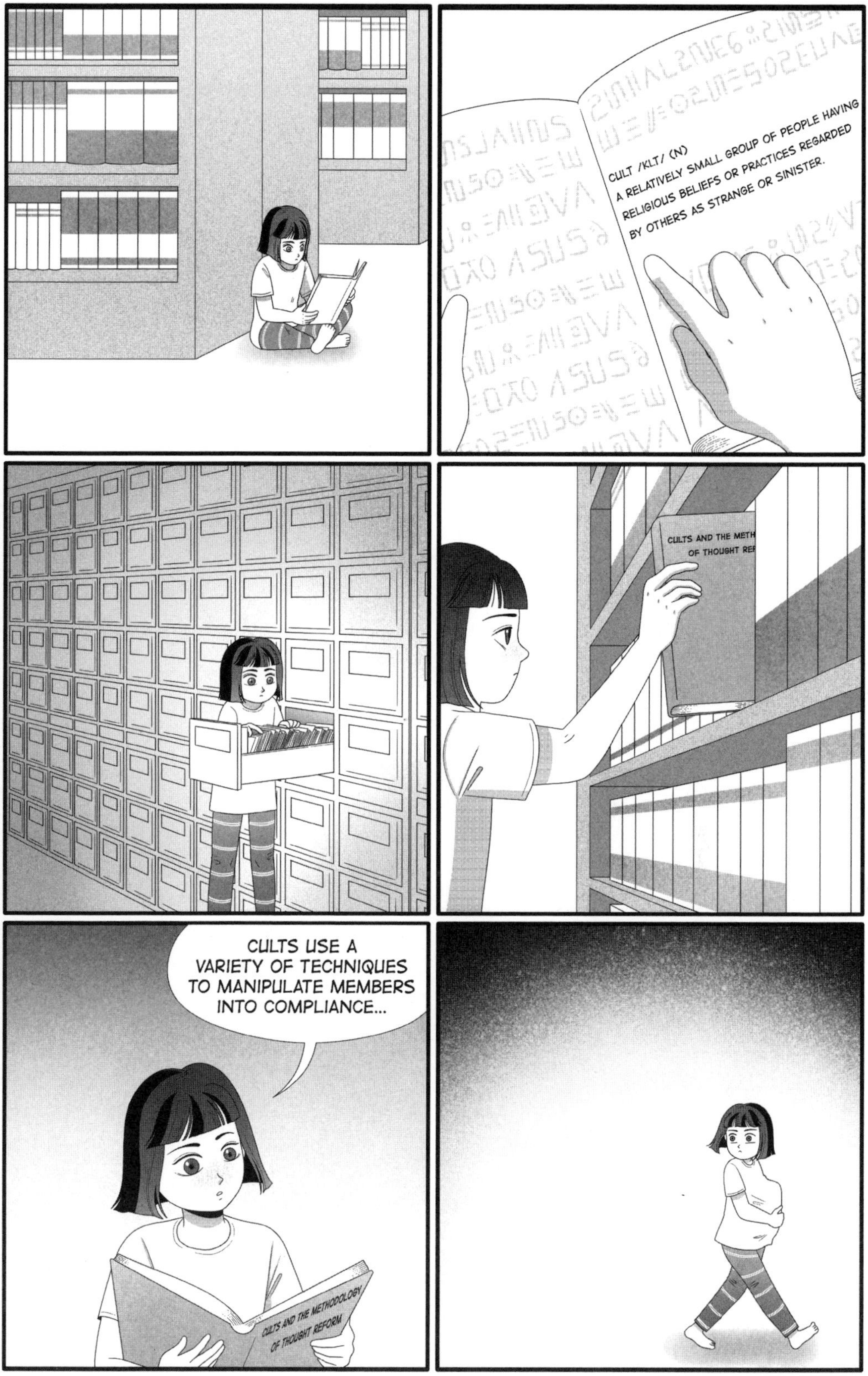
CULT /KLT/ (N)
A RELATIVELY SMALL GROUP OF PEOPLE HAVING RELIGIOUS BELIEFS OR PRACTICES REGARDED BY OTHERS AS STRANGE OR SINISTER.
CULTS AND THE METH
OF THOUGHT REF
CULTS USE A VARIETY OF TECHNIQUES TO MANIPULATE MEMBERS INTO COMPLIANCE...
CULTS AND THE METHODOLOGY OF THOUGHT REFORM

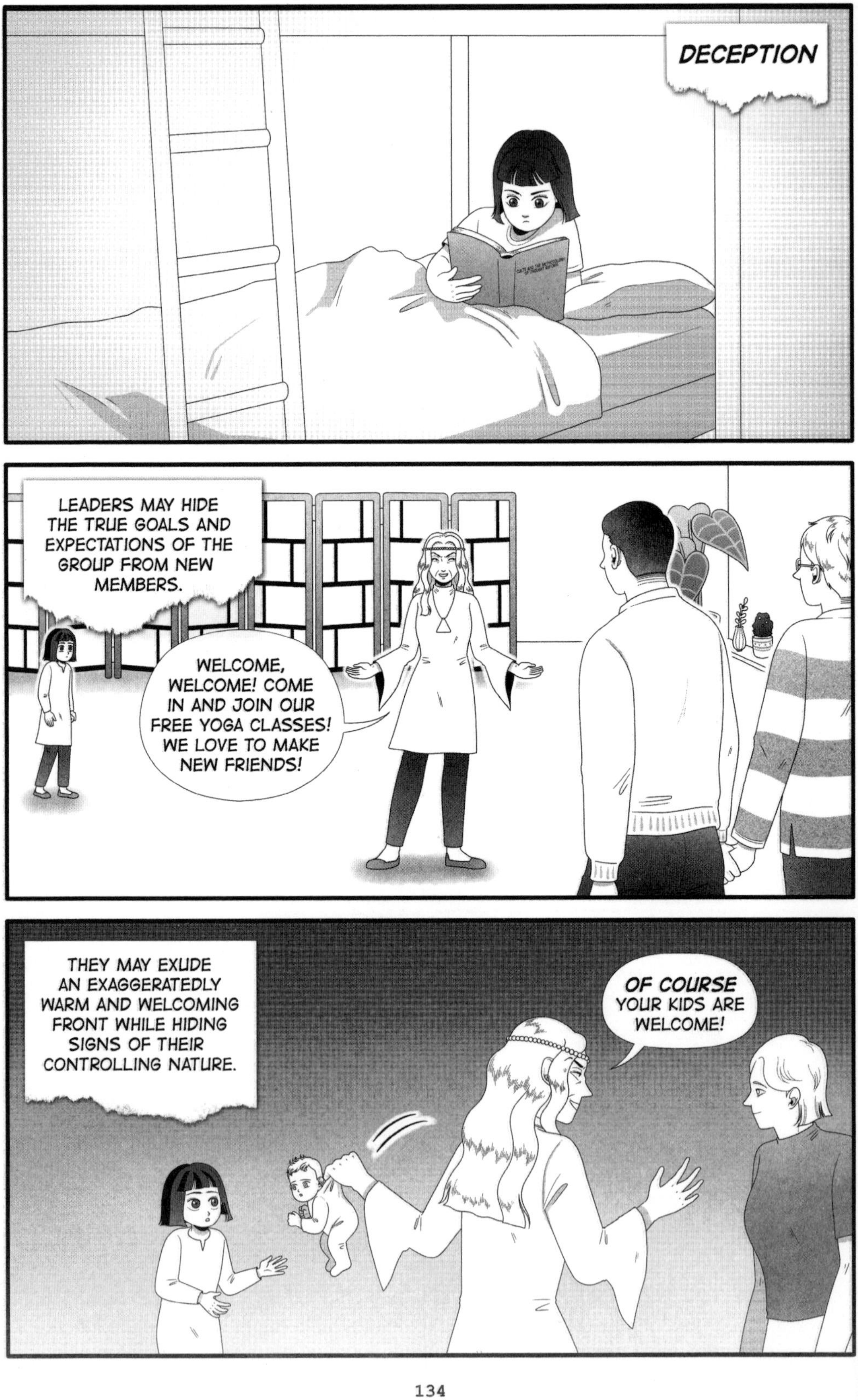
DECEPTION
LEADERS MAY HIDE THE TRUE GOALS AND EXPECTATIONS OF THE GROUP FROM NEW MEMBERS.
WELCOME, WELCOME! COME IN AND JOIN OUR FREE YOGA CLASSES! WE LOVE TO MAKE NEW FRIENDS!
THEY MAY EXUDE AN EXAGGERATEDLY WARM AND WELCOMING FRONT WHILE HIDING SIGNS OF THEIR CONTROLLING NATURE.
OF COURSE YOUR KIDS ARE WELCOME!

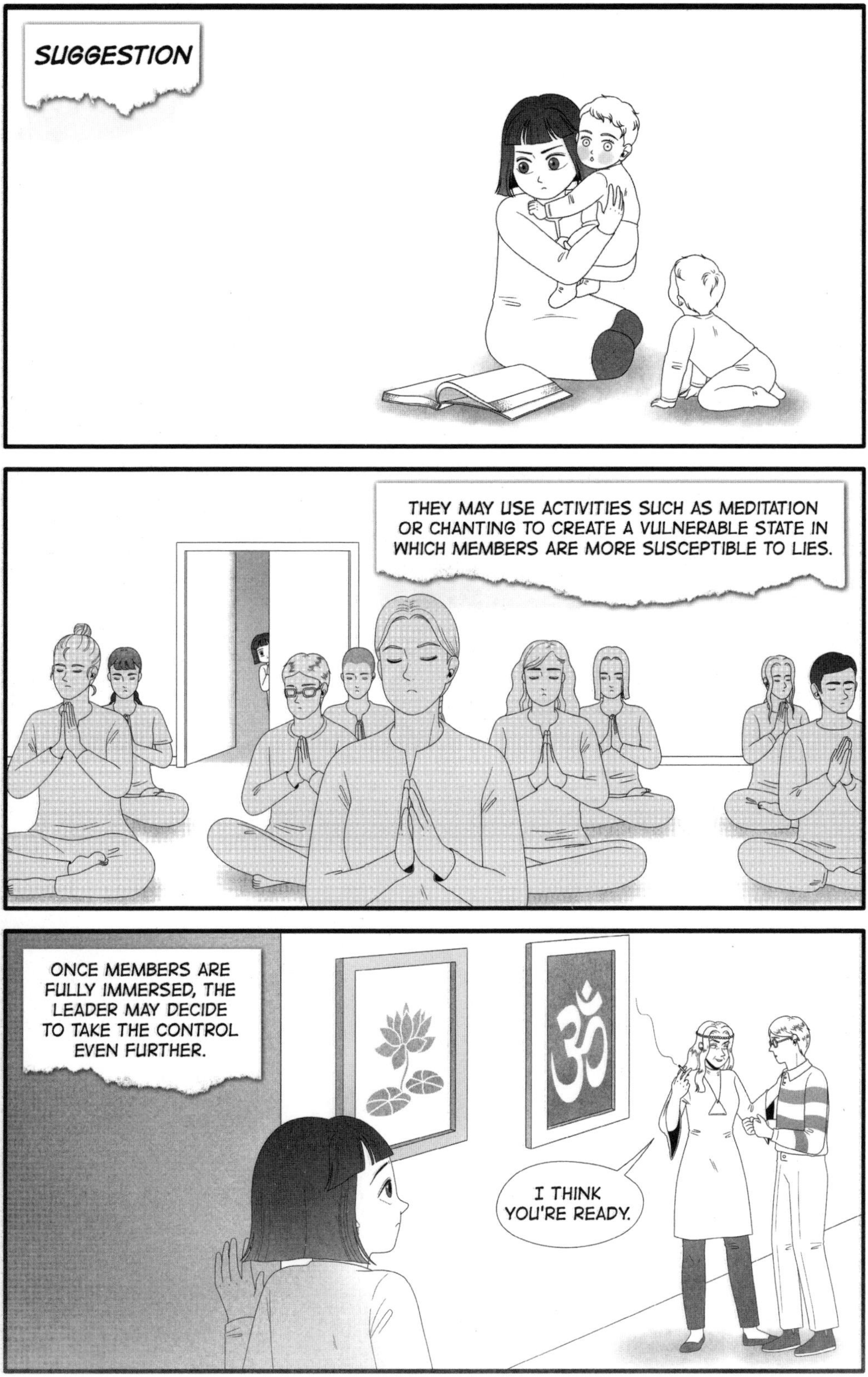
SUGGESTION
THEY MAY USE ACTIVITIES SUCH AS MEDITATION OR CHANTING TO CREATE A VULNERABLE STATE IN WHICH MEMBERS ARE MORE SUSCEPTIBLE TO LIES.
ONCE MEMBERS ARE FULLY IMMERSED, THE LEADER MAY DECIDE TO TAKE THE CONTROL EVEN FURTHER.
I THINK YOU'RE READY.

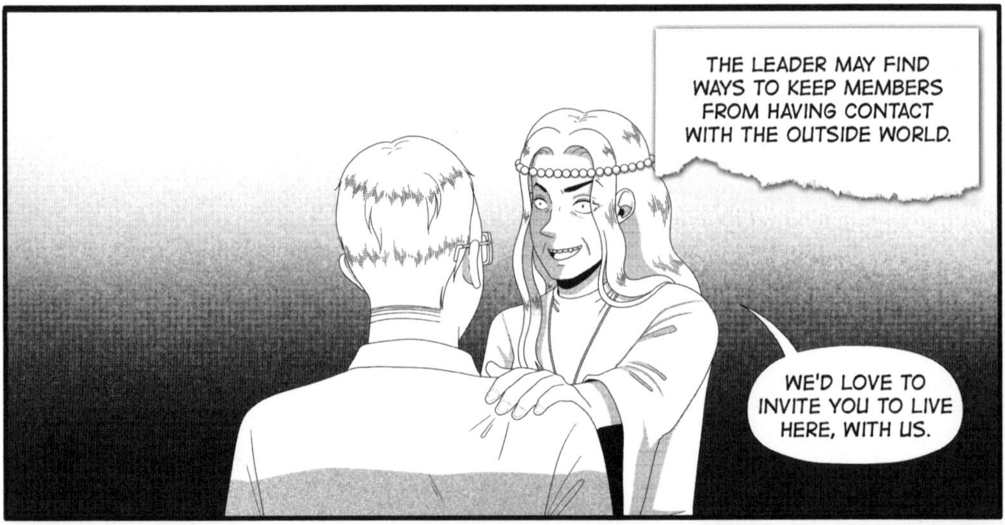
THE LEADER MAY FIND WAYS TO KEEP MEMBERS FROM HAVING CONTACT WITH THE OUTSIDE WORLD.
WE'D LOVE TO INVITE YOU TO LIVE HERE, WITH US.

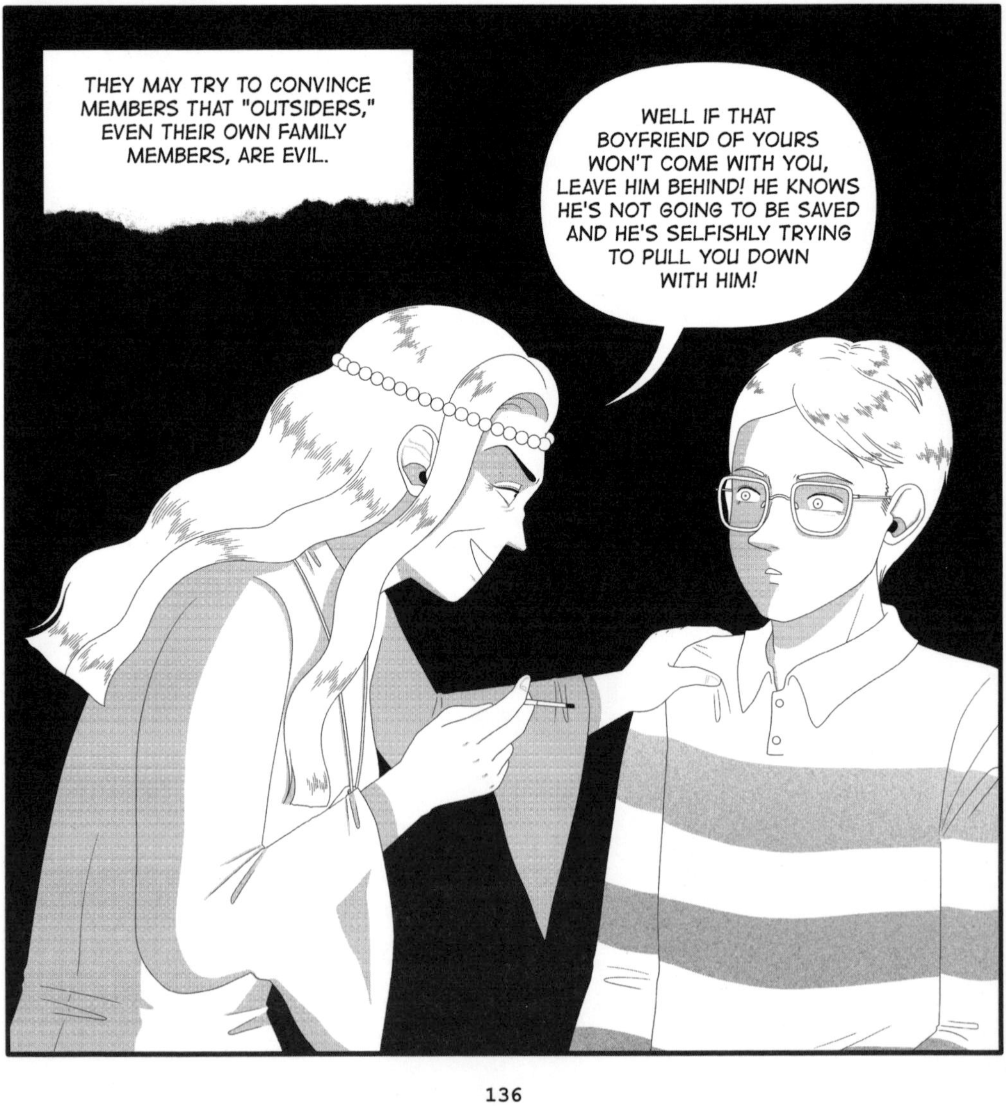
THEY MAY TRY TO CONVINCE MEMBERS THAT "OUTSIDERS," EVEN THEIR OWN FAMILY MEMBERS, ARE EVIL.
WELL IF THAT BOYFRIEND OF YOURS WON'T COME WITH YOU, LEAVE HIM BEHIND! HE KNOWS HE'S NOT GOING TO BE SAVED AND HE'S SELFISHLY TRYING TO PULL YOU DOWN WITH HIM!

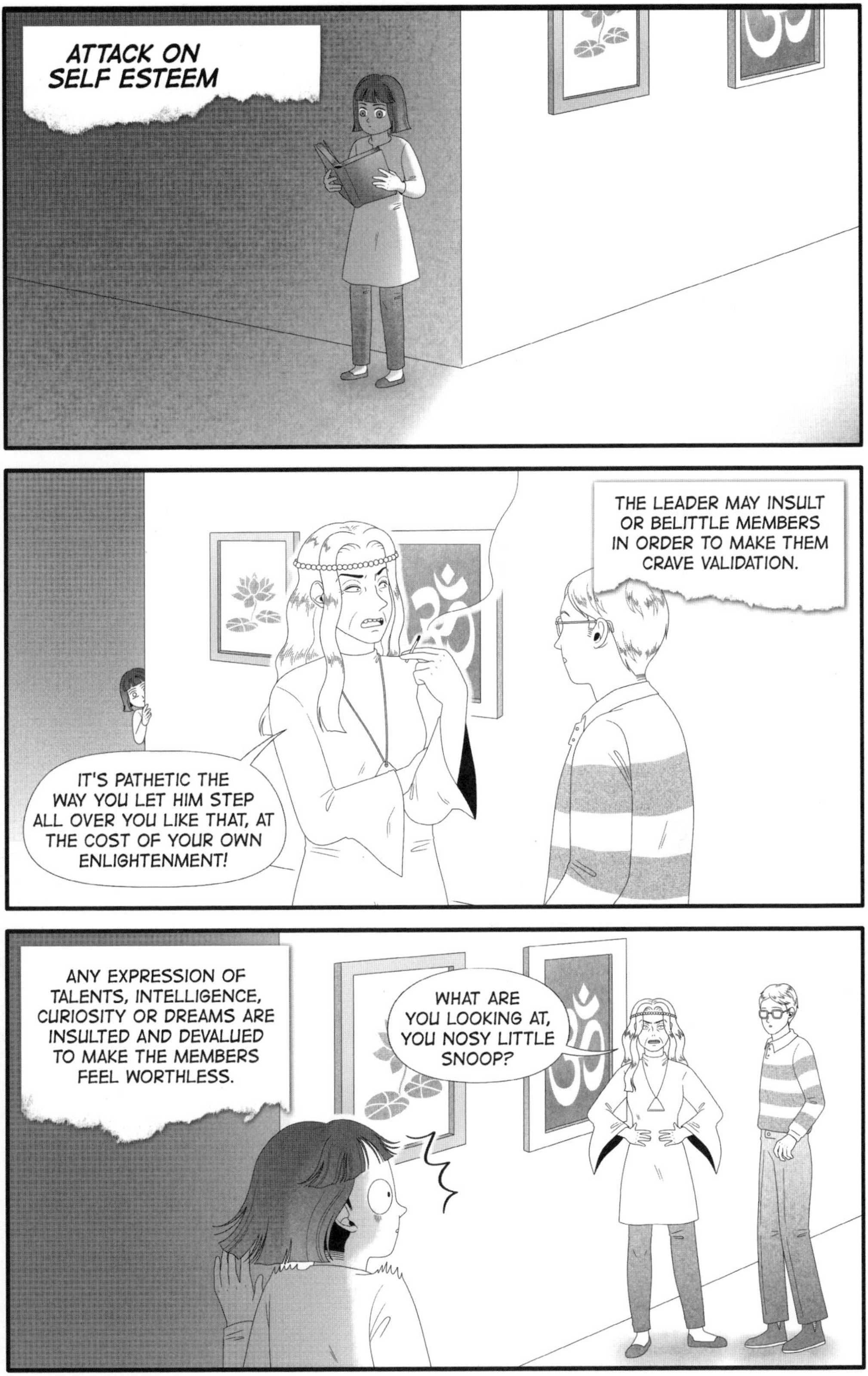
ATTACK ON SELF ESTEEM
THE LEADER MAY INSULT OR BELITTLE MEMBERS IN ORDER TO MAKE THEM CRAVE VALIDATION.
IT'S PATHETIC THE WAY YOU LET HIM STEP ALL OVER YOU LIKE THAT, AT THE COST OF YOUR OWN ENLIGHTENMENT!
ANY EXPRESSION OF TALENTS, INTELLIGENCE, CURIOSITY OR DREAMS ARE INSULTED AND DEVALUED TO MAKE THE MEMBERS FEEL WORTHLESS.
WHAT ARE YOU LOOKING AT, YOU NOSY LITTLE SNOOP?

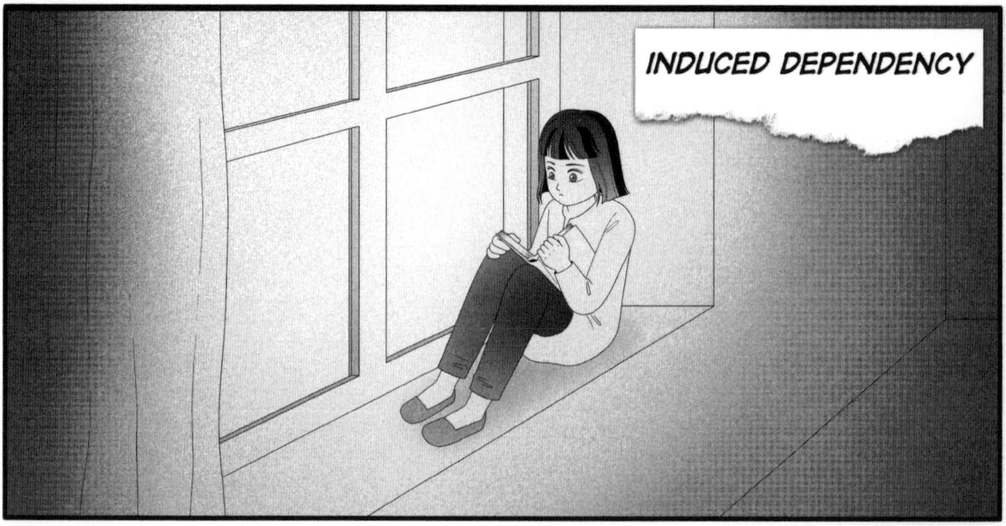
INDUCED DEPENDENCY

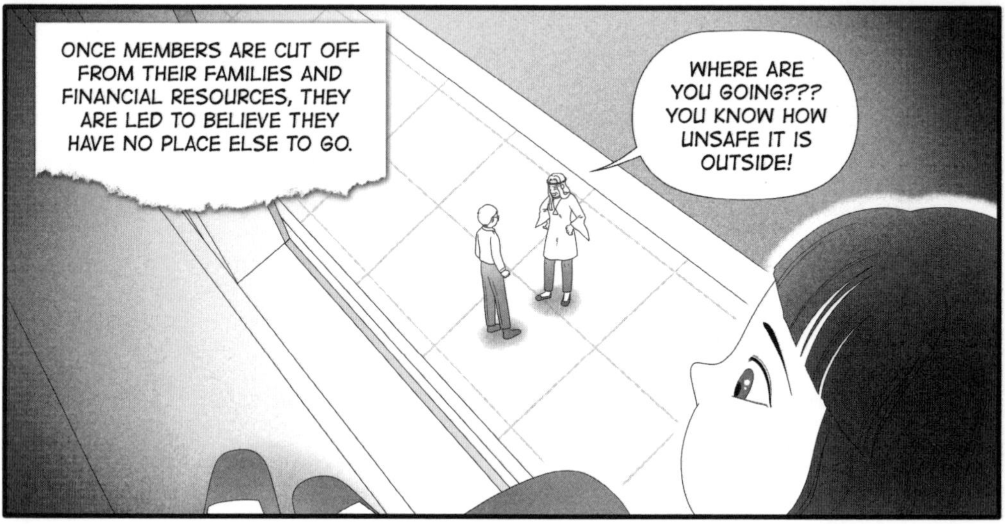
ONCE MEMBERS ARE CUT OFF FROM THEIR FAMILIES AND FINANCIAL RESOURCES, THEY ARE LED TO BELIEVE THEY HAVE NO PLACE ELSE TO GO.
WHERE ARE YOU GOING??? YOU KNOW HOW UNSAFE IT IS OUTSIDE!

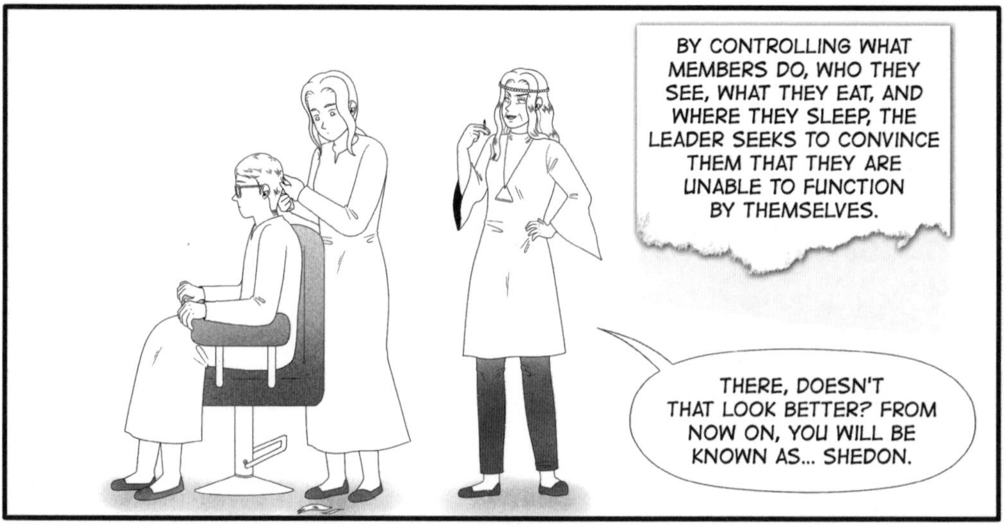
BY CONTROLLING WHAT MEMBERS DO, WHO THEY SEE, WHAT THEY EAT, AND WHERE THEY SLEEP, THE LEADER SEEKS TO CONVINCE THEM THAT THEY ARE UNABLE TO FUNCTION BY THEMSELVES.
THERE, DOESN'T THAT LOOK BETTER? FROM NOW ON, YOU WILL BE KNOWN AS... SHEDON.

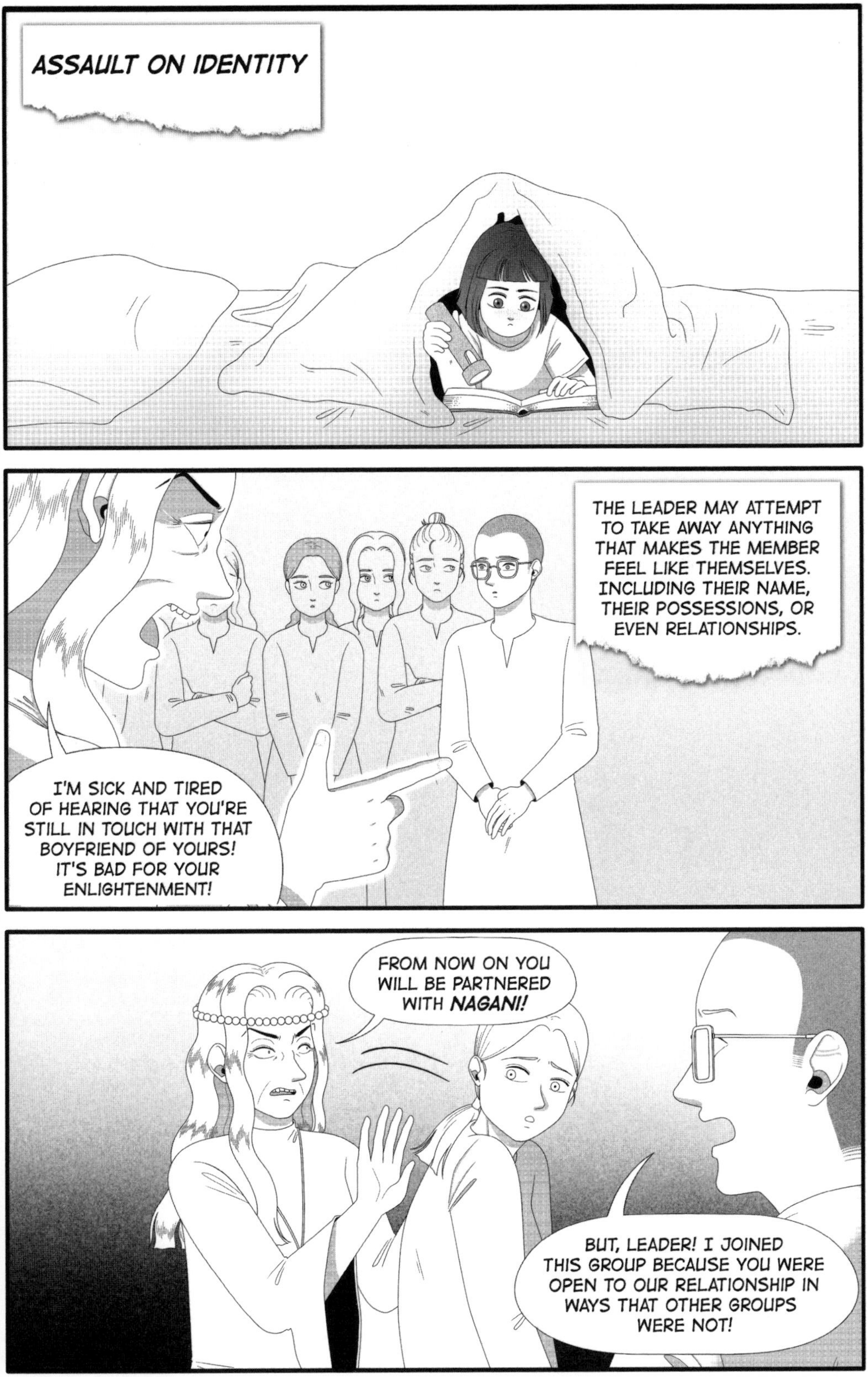
ASSAULT ON IDENTITY
THE LEADER MAY ATTEMPT TO TAKE AWAY ANYTHING THAT MAKES THE MEMBER FEEL LIKE THEMSELVES. INCLUDING THEIR NAME, THEIR POSSESSIONS, OR EVEN RELATIONSHIPS.
I'M SICK AND TIRED OF HEARING THAT YOU'RE STILL IN TOUCH WITH THAT BOYFRIEND OF YOURS! IT'S BAD FOR YOUR ENLIGHTENMENT!
FROM NOW ON YOU WILL BE PARTNERED WITH NAGANI!
BUT, LEADER! I JOINED THIS GROUP BECAUSE YOU WERE OPEN TO OUR RELATIONSHIP IN WAYS THAT OTHER GROUPS WERE NOT!

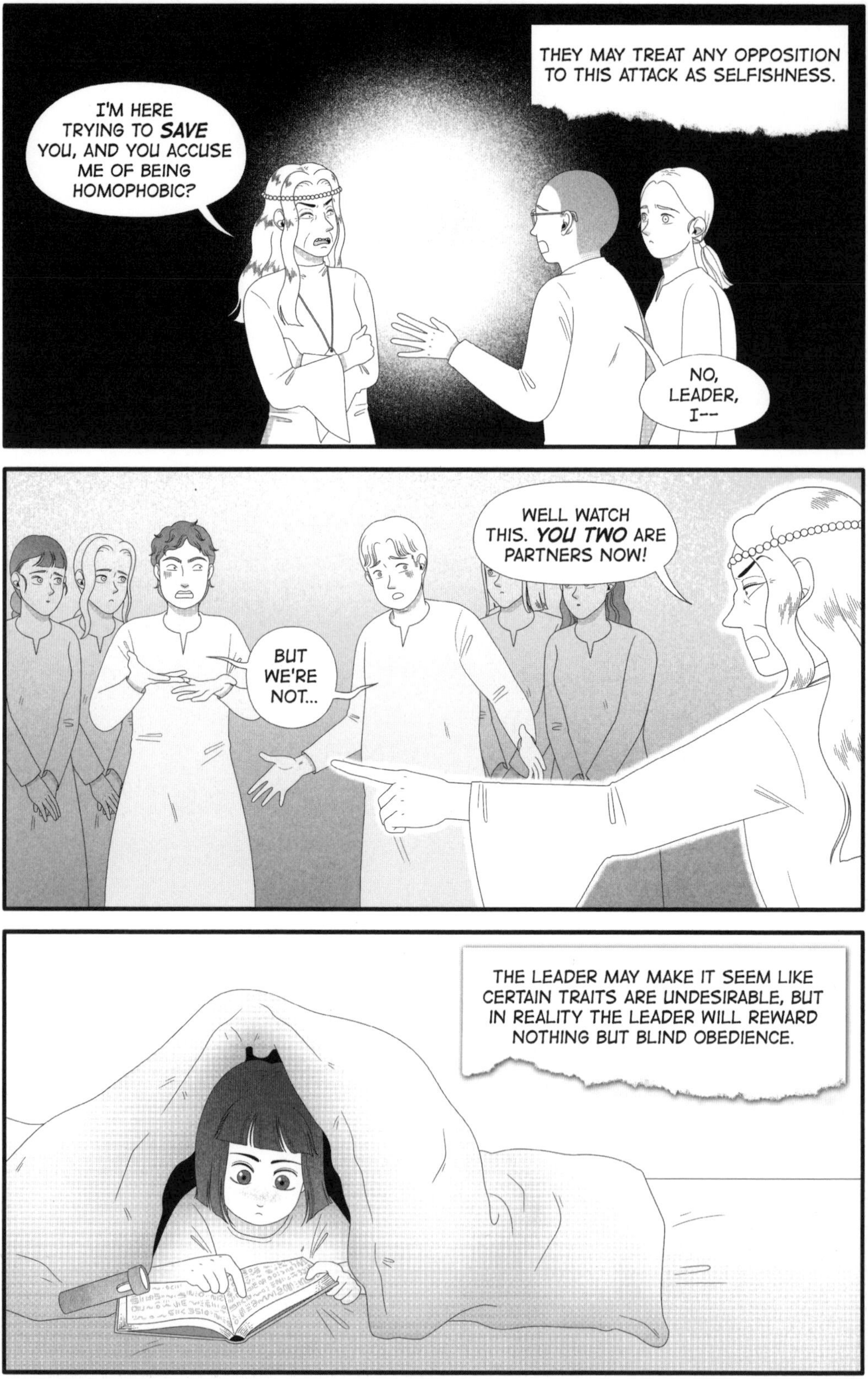
THEY MAY TREAT ANY OPPOSITION TO THIS ATTACK AS SELFISHNESS.
I'M HERE TRYING TO *SAVE* YOU, AND YOU ACCUSE ME OF BEING HOMOPHOBIC?
NO, LEADER, I--
WELL WATCH THIS. *YOU TWO* ARE PARTNERS NOW!
BUT WE'RE NOT...
THE LEADER MAY MAKE IT SEEM LIKE CERTAIN TRAITS ARE UNDESIRABLE, BUT IN REALITY THE LEADER WILL REWARD NOTHING BUT BLIND OBEDIENCE.

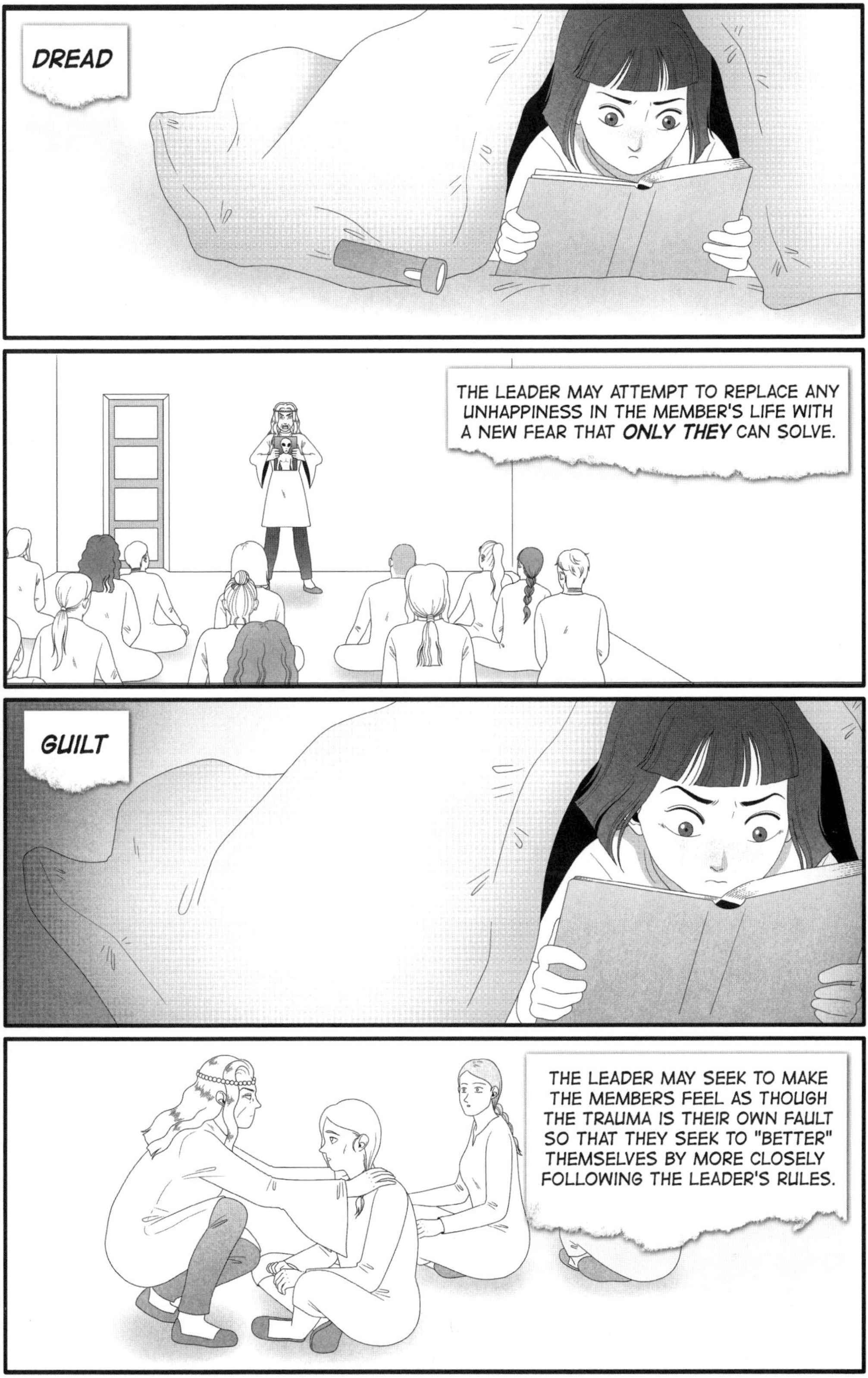
DREAD
THE LEADER MAY ATTEMPT TO REPLACE ANY UNHAPPINESS IN THE MEMBER'S LIFE WITH A NEW FEAR THAT ONLY THEY CAN SOLVE.
GUILT
THE LEADER MAY SEEK TO MAKE THE MEMBERS FEEL AS THOUGH THE TRAUMA IS THEIR OWN FAULT SO THAT THEY SEEK TO "BETTER" THEMSELVES BY MORE CLOSELY FOLLOWING THE LEADER'S RULES.

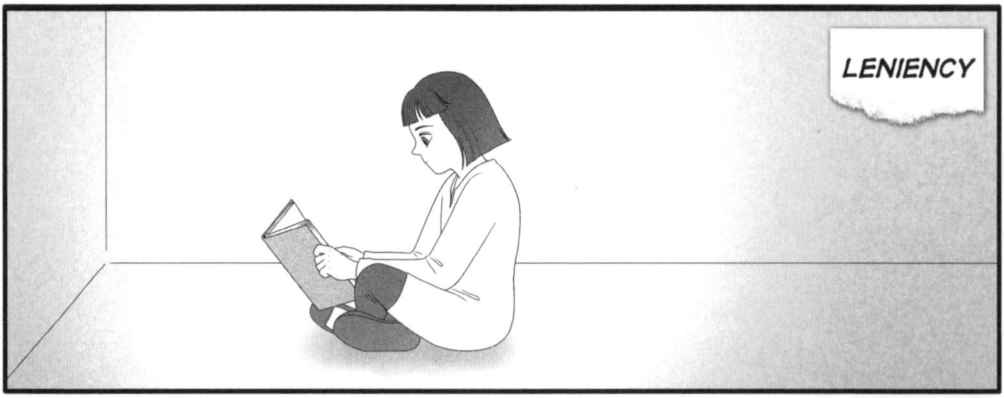
LENIENCY

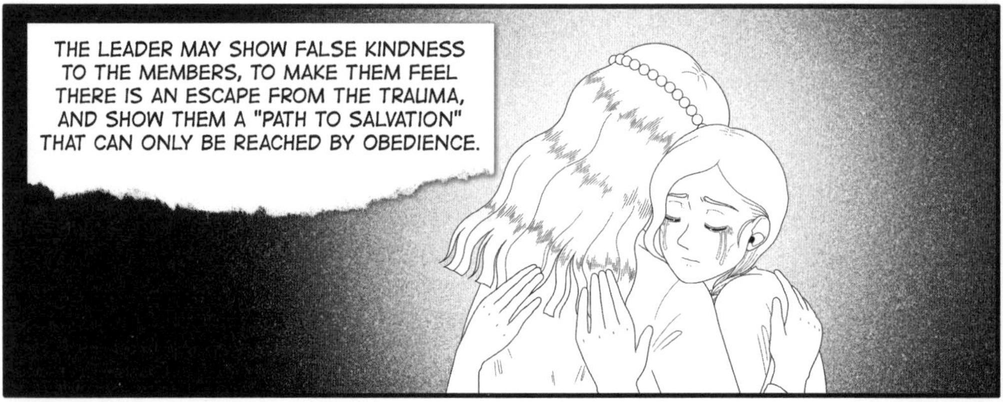
THE LEADER MAY SHOW FALSE KINDNESS TO THE MEMBERS, TO MAKE THEM FEEL THERE IS AN ESCAPE FROM THE TRAUMA, AND SHOW THEM A "PATH TO SALVATION" THAT CAN ONLY BE REACHED BY OBEDIENCE.

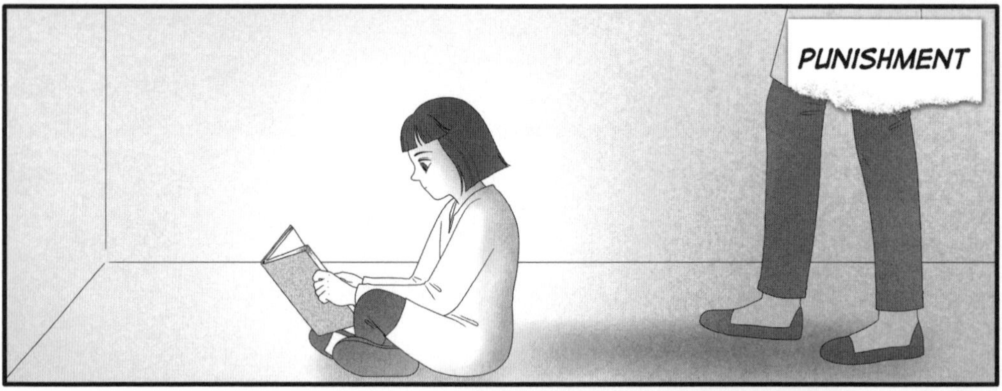
PUNISHMENT

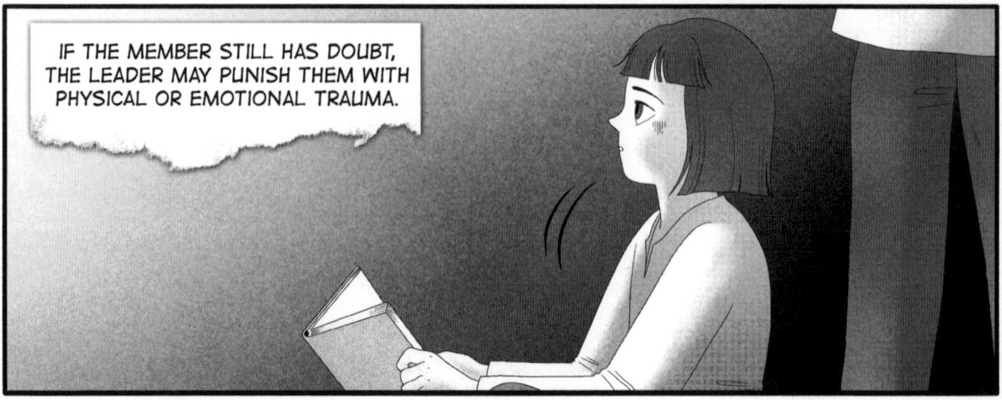
IF THE MEMBER STILL HAS DOUBT, THE LEADER MAY PUNISH THEM WITH PHYSICAL OR EMOTIONAL TRAUMA.

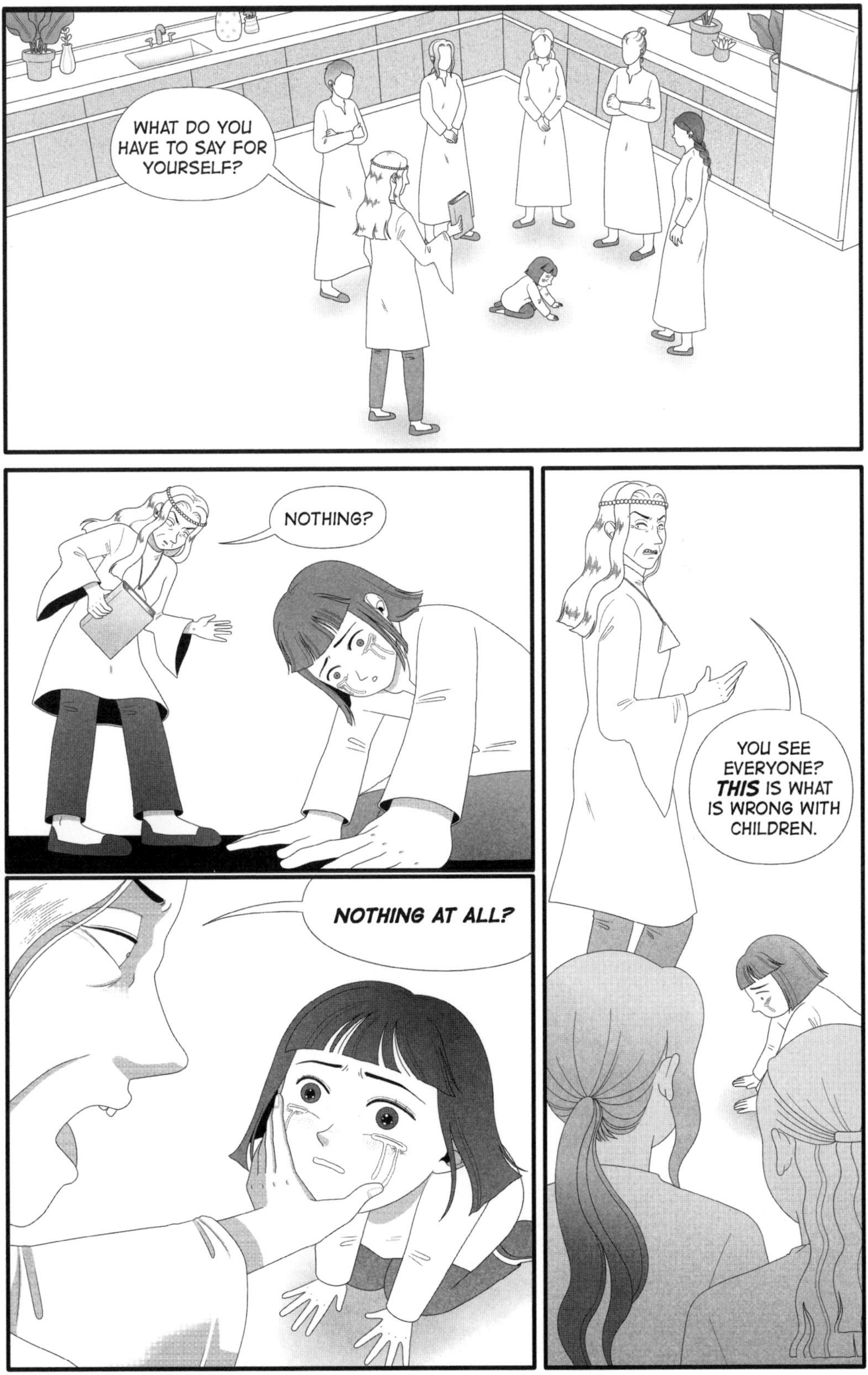

WHAT DO YOU HAVE TO SAY FOR YOURSELF?
NOTHING?
NOTHING AT ALL?
YOU SEE EVERYONE? THIS IS WHAT IS WRONG WITH CHILDREN.

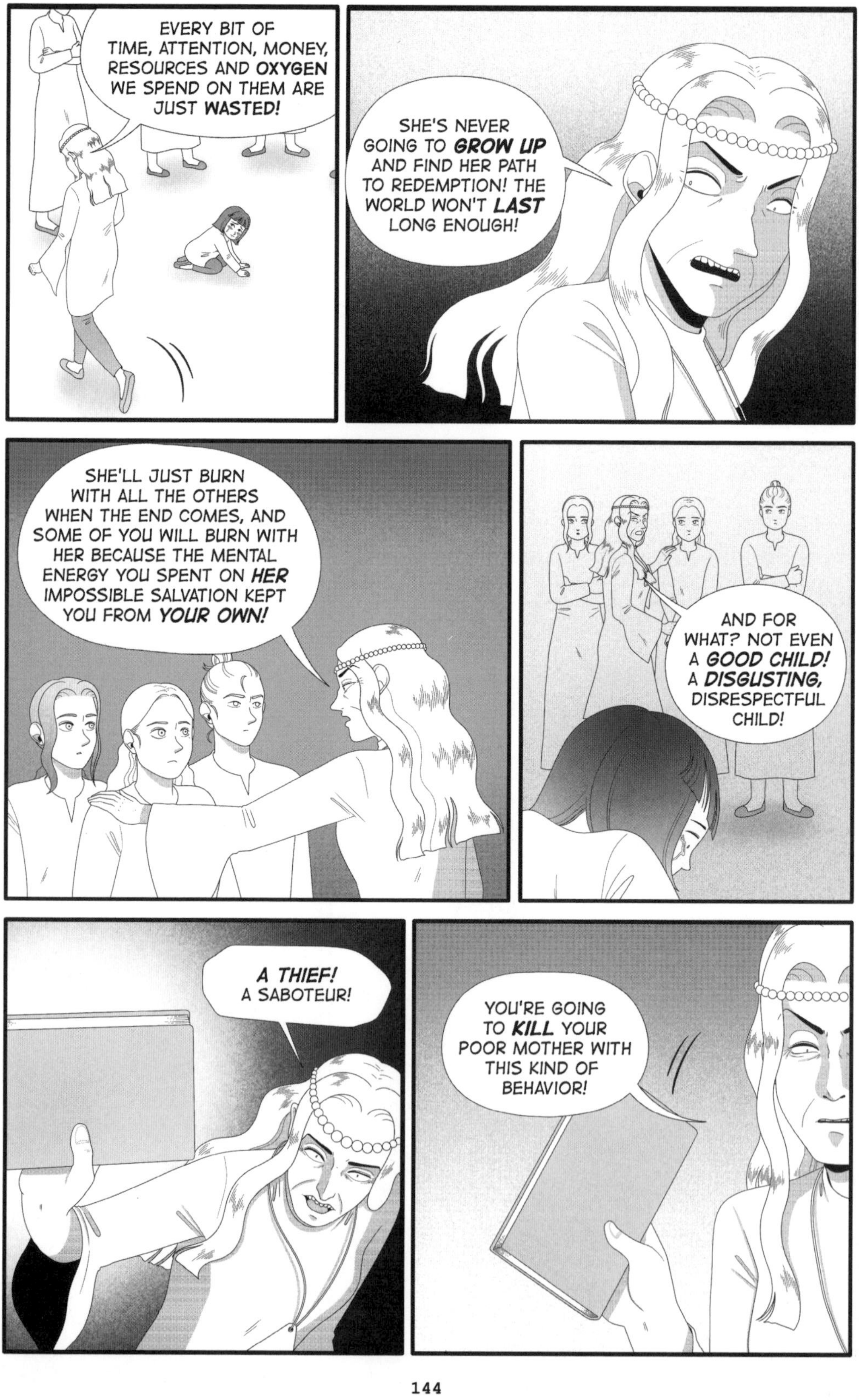
EVERY BIT OF TIME, ATTENTION, MONEY, RESOURCES AND OXYGEN WE SPEND ON THEM ARE JUST WASTED!
SHE'S NEVER GOING TO GROW UP AND FIND HER PATH TO REDEMPTION! THE WORLD WON'T LAST LONG ENOUGH!
SHE'LL JUST BURN WITH ALL THE OTHERS WHEN THE END COMES, AND SOME OF YOU WILL BURN WITH HER BECAUSE THE MENTAL ENERGY YOU SPENT ON HER IMPOSSIBLE SALVATION KEPT YOU FROM YOUR OWN!
AND FOR WHAT? NOT EVEN A GOOD CHILD! A DISGUSTING, DISRESPECTFUL CHILD!
A THIEF! A SABOTEUR!
YOU'RE GOING TO KILL YOUR POOR MOTHER WITH THIS KIND OF BEHAVIOR!

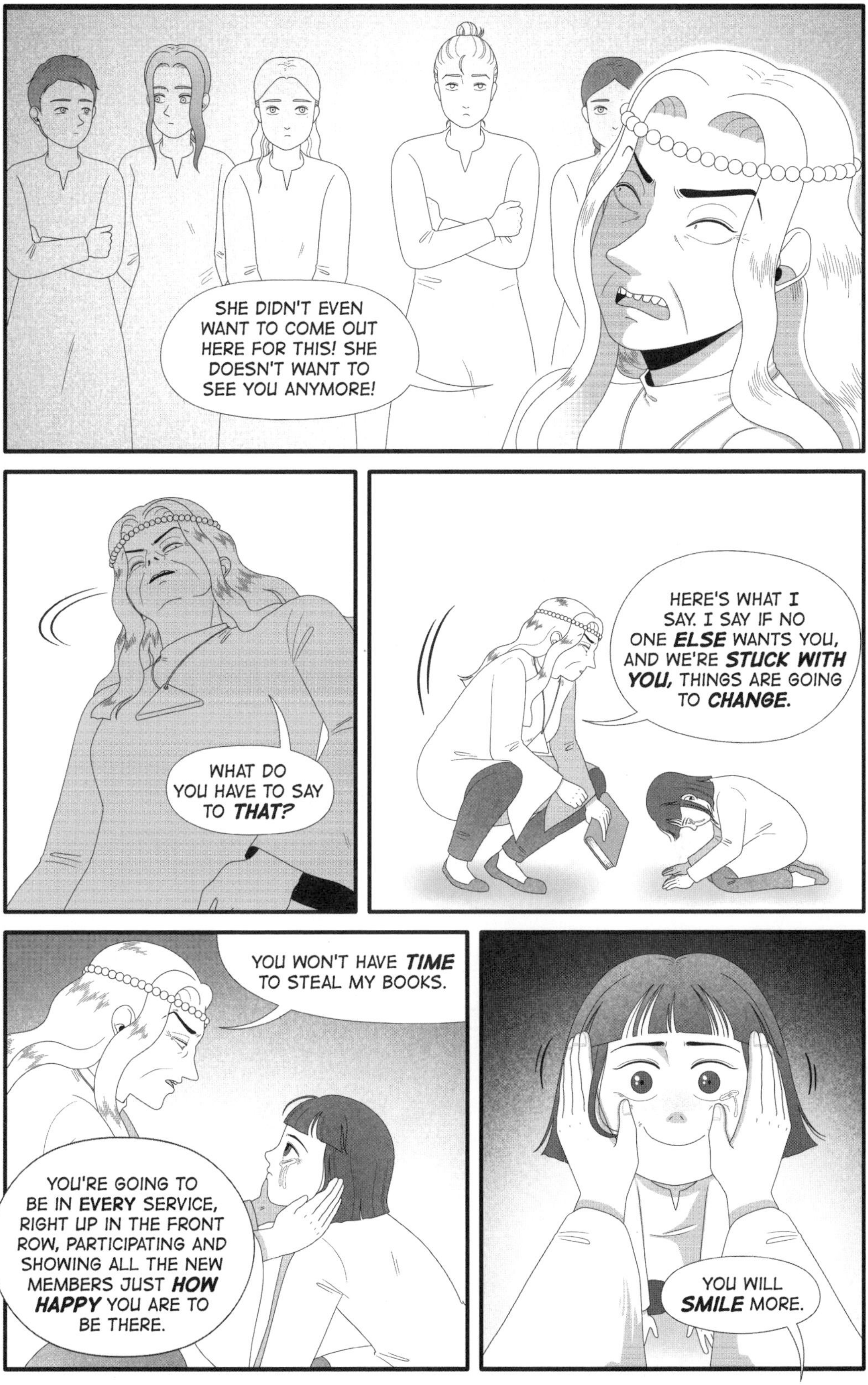
SHE DIDN'T EVEN WANT TO COME OUT HERE FOR THIS! SHE DOESN'T WANT TO SEE YOU ANYMORE!
WHAT DO YOU HAVE TO SAY TO THAT?
HERE'S WHAT I SAY. I SAY IF NO ONE ELSE WANTS YOU, AND WE'RE STUCK WITH YOU, THINGS ARE GOING TO CHANGE.
YOU WON'T HAVE TIME TO STEAL MY BOOKS.
YOU'RE GOING TO BE IN EVERY SERVICE, RIGHT UP IN THE FRONT ROW, PARTICIPATING AND SHOWING ALL THE NEW MEMBERS JUST HOW HAPPY YOU ARE TO BE THERE.
YOU WILL SMILE MORE.

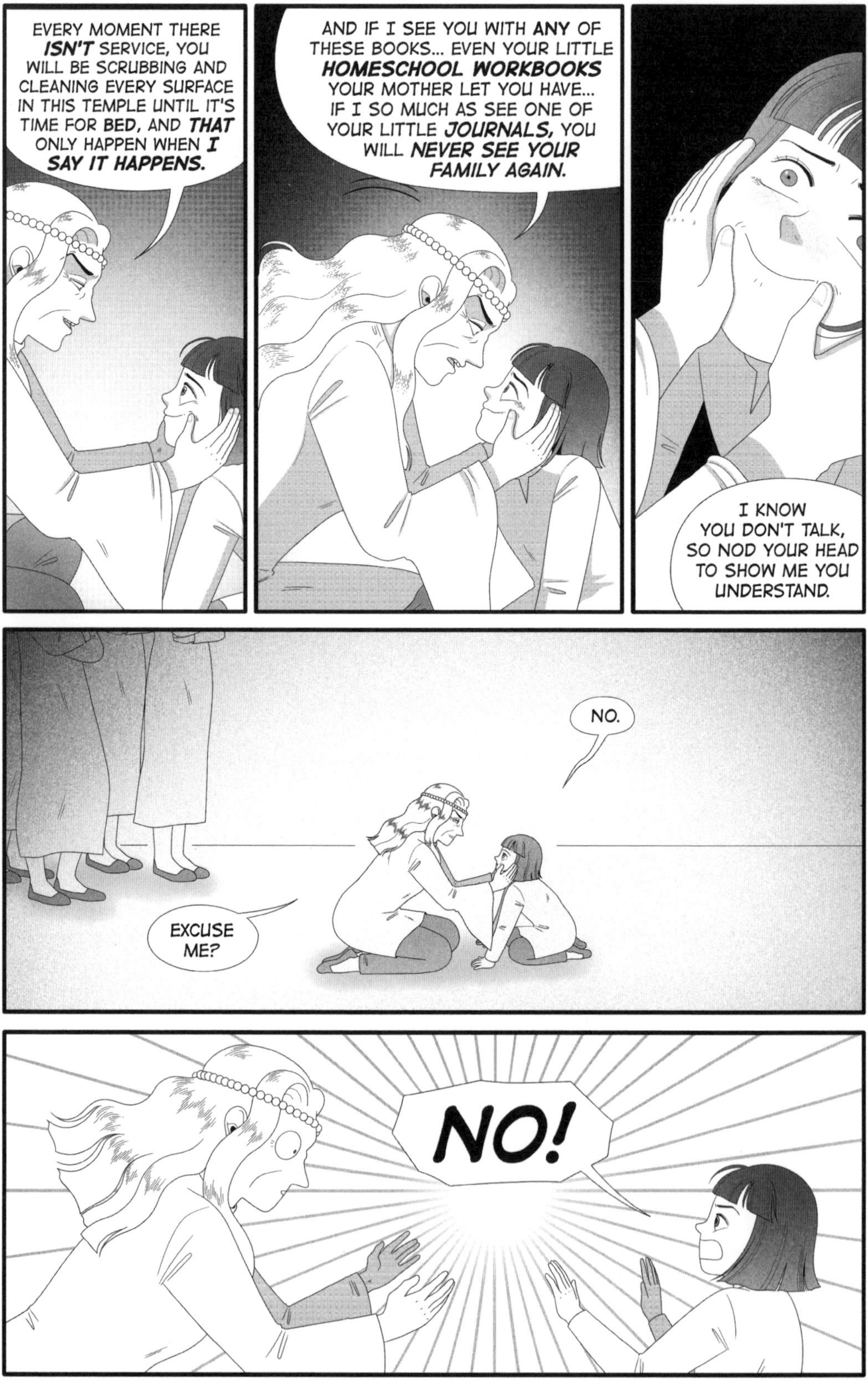
EVERY MOMENT THERE ISN'T SERVICE, YOU WILL BE SCRUBBING AND CLEANING EVERY SURFACE IN THIS TEMPLE UNTIL IT'S TIME FOR BED, AND THAT ONLY HAPPEN WHEN I SAY IT HAPPENS.
AND IF I SEE YOU WITH ANY OF THESE BOOKS... EVEN YOUR LITTLE HOMESCHOOL WORKBOOKS YOUR MOTHER LET YOU HAVE... IF I SO MUCH AS SEE ONE OF YOUR LITTLE JOURNALS, YOU WILL NEVER SEE YOUR FAMILY AGAIN.
I KNOW YOU DON'T TALK, SO NOD YOUR HEAD TO SHOW ME YOU UNDERSTAND.
NO.
EXCUSE ME?
NO!

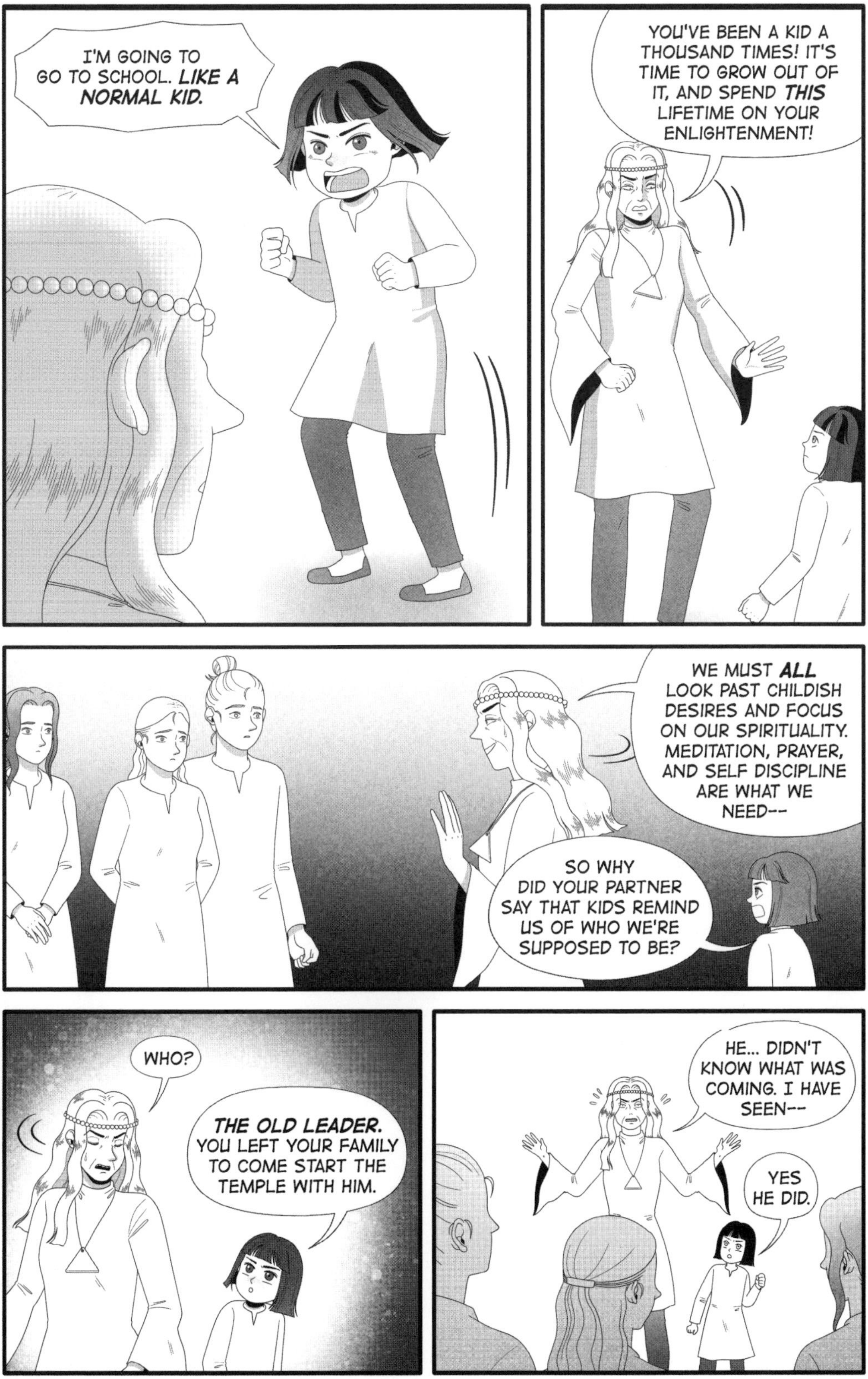
I'M GOING TO GO TO SCHOOL. ***LIKE A NORMAL KID.***
YOU'VE BEEN A KID A THOUSAND TIMES! IT'S TIME TO GROW OUT OF IT, AND SPEND ***THIS*** LIFETIME ON YOUR ENLIGHTENMENT!
WE MUST ***ALL*** LOOK PAST CHILDISH DESIRES AND FOCUS ON OUR SPIRITUALITY. MEDITATION, PRAYER, AND SELF DISCIPLINE ARE WHAT WE NEED--
SO WHY DID YOUR PARTNER SAY THAT KIDS REMIND US OF WHO WE'RE SUPPOSED TO BE?
WHO?
THE OLD LEADER. YOU LEFT YOUR FAMILY TO COME START THE TEMPLE WITH HIM.
HE... DIDN'T KNOW WHAT WAS COMING. I HAVE SEEN--
YES HE DID.

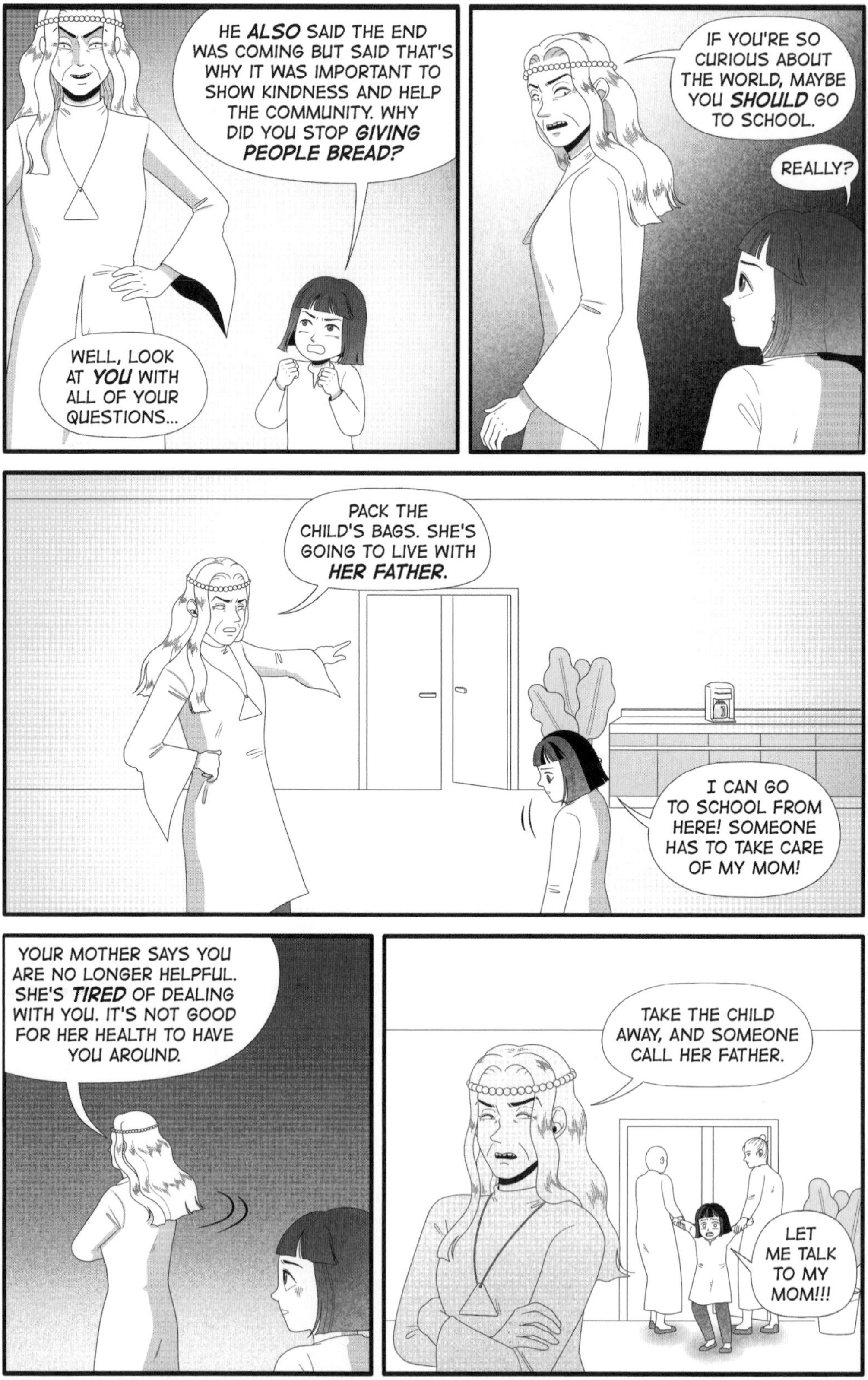
HE ALSO SAID THE END WAS COMING BUT SAID THAT'S WHY IT WAS IMPORTANT TO SHOW KINDNESS AND HELP THE COMMUNITY. WHY DID YOU STOP GIVING PEOPLE BREAD?
WELL, LOOK AT YOU WITH ALL OF YOUR QUESTIONS...
IF YOU'RE SO CURIOUS ABOUT THE WORLD, MAYBE YOU SHOULD GO TO SCHOOL.
REALLY?
PACK THE CHILD'S BAGS. SHE'S GOING TO LIVE WITH HER FATHER.
I CAN GO TO SCHOOL FROM HERE! SOMEONE HAS TO TAKE CARE OF MY MOM!
YOUR MOTHER SAYS YOU ARE NO LONGER HELPFUL. SHE'S TIRED OF DEALING WITH YOU. IT'S NOT GOOD FOR HER HEALTH TO HAVE YOU AROUND.
TAKE THE CHILD AWAY, AND SOMEONE CALL HER FATHER.
LET ME TALK TO MY MOM!!!

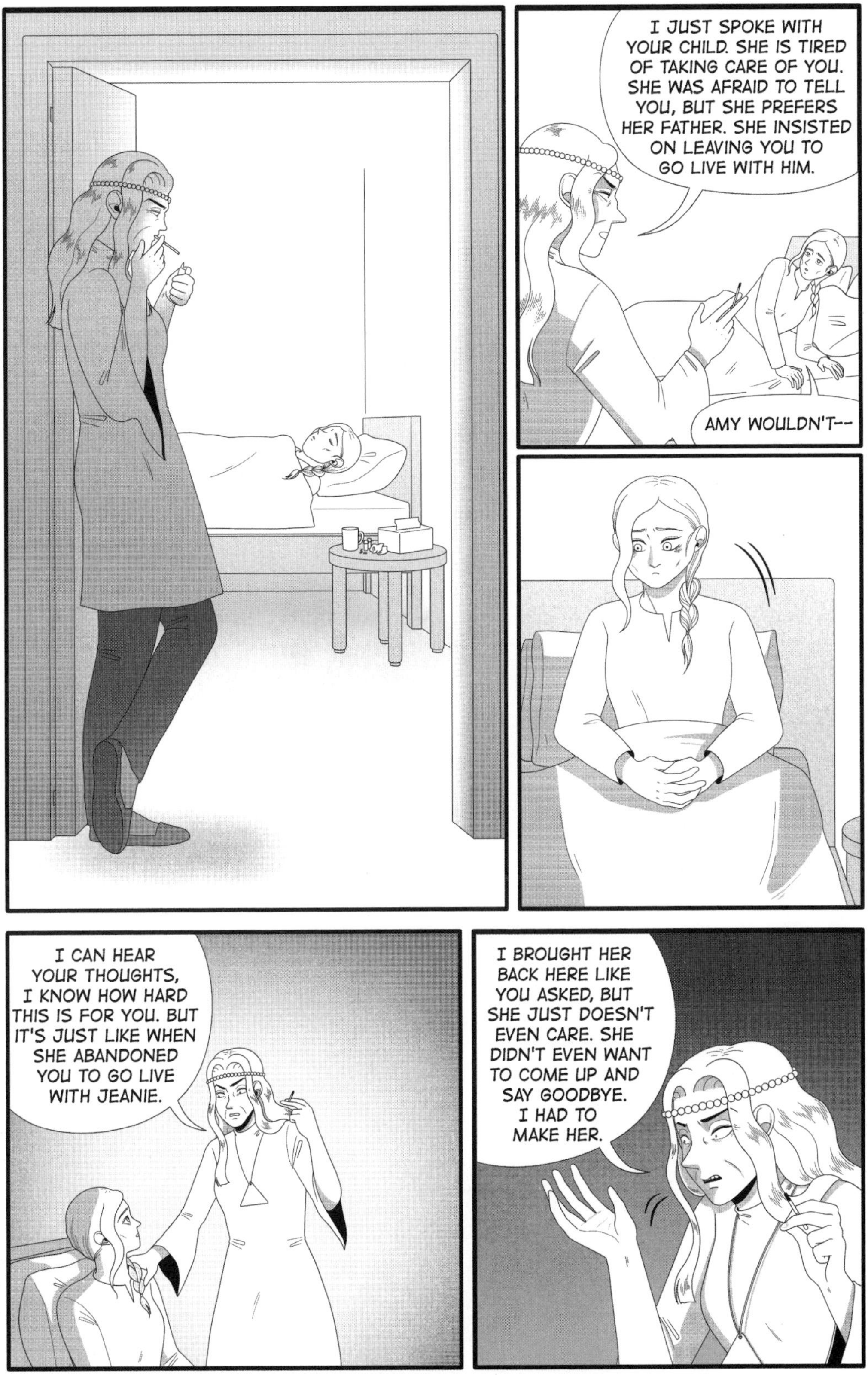
I JUST SPOKE WITH YOUR CHILD. SHE IS TIRED OF TAKING CARE OF YOU. SHE WAS AFRAID TO TELL YOU, BUT SHE PREFERS HER FATHER. SHE INSISTED ON LEAVING YOU TO GO LIVE WITH HIM.
AMY WOULDN'T--
I CAN HEAR YOUR THOUGHTS, I KNOW HOW HARD THIS IS FOR YOU. BUT IT'S JUST LIKE WHEN SHE ABANDONED YOU TO GO LIVE WITH JEANIE.
I BROUGHT HER BACK HERE LIKE YOU ASKED, BUT SHE JUST DOESN'T EVEN CARE. SHE DIDN'T EVEN WANT TO COME UP AND SAY GOODBYE. I HAD TO MAKE HER.

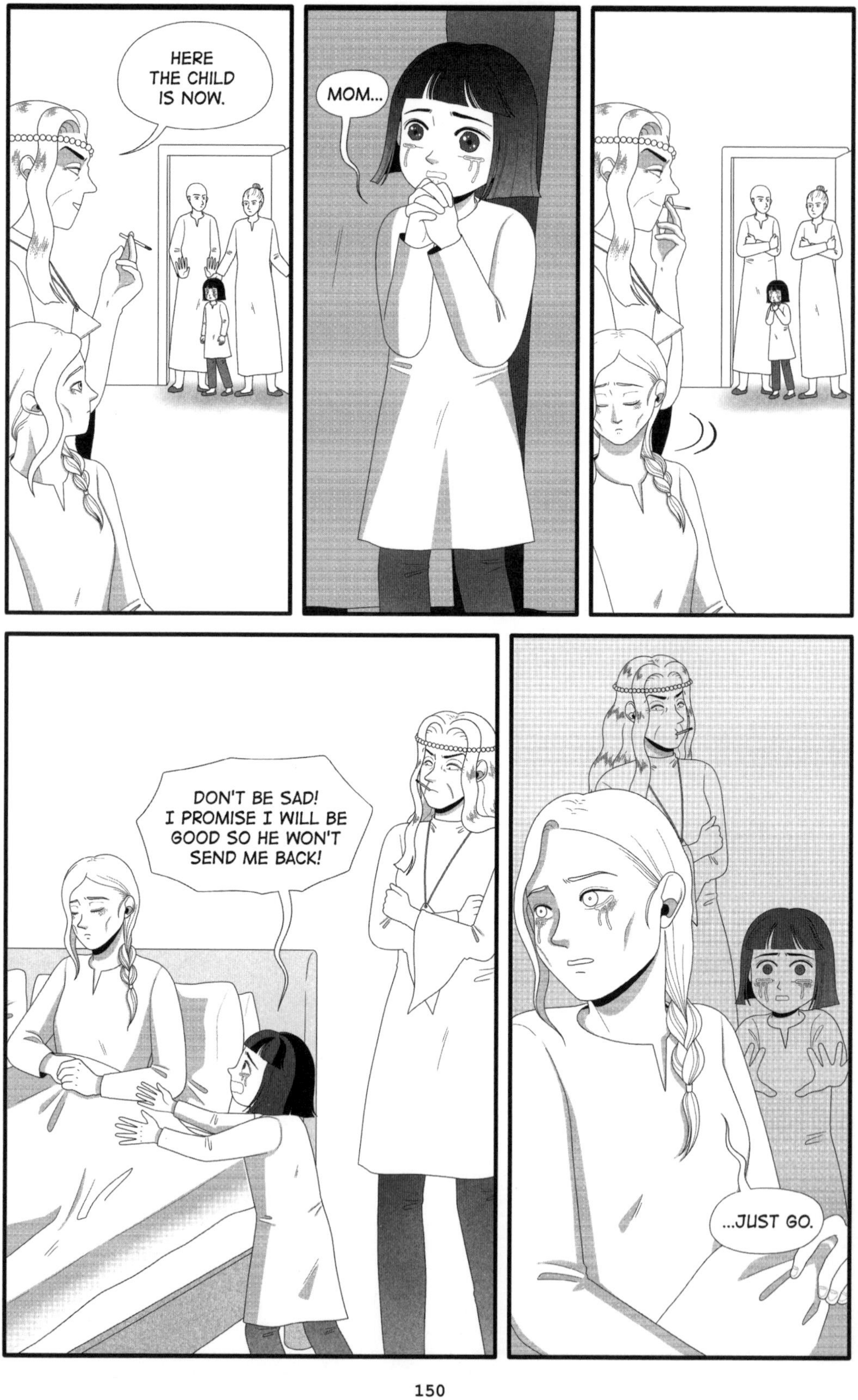
HERE THE CHILD IS NOW.
MOM...
DON'T BE SAD! I PROMISE I WILL BE GOOD SO HE WON'T SEND ME BACK!
...JUST GO.

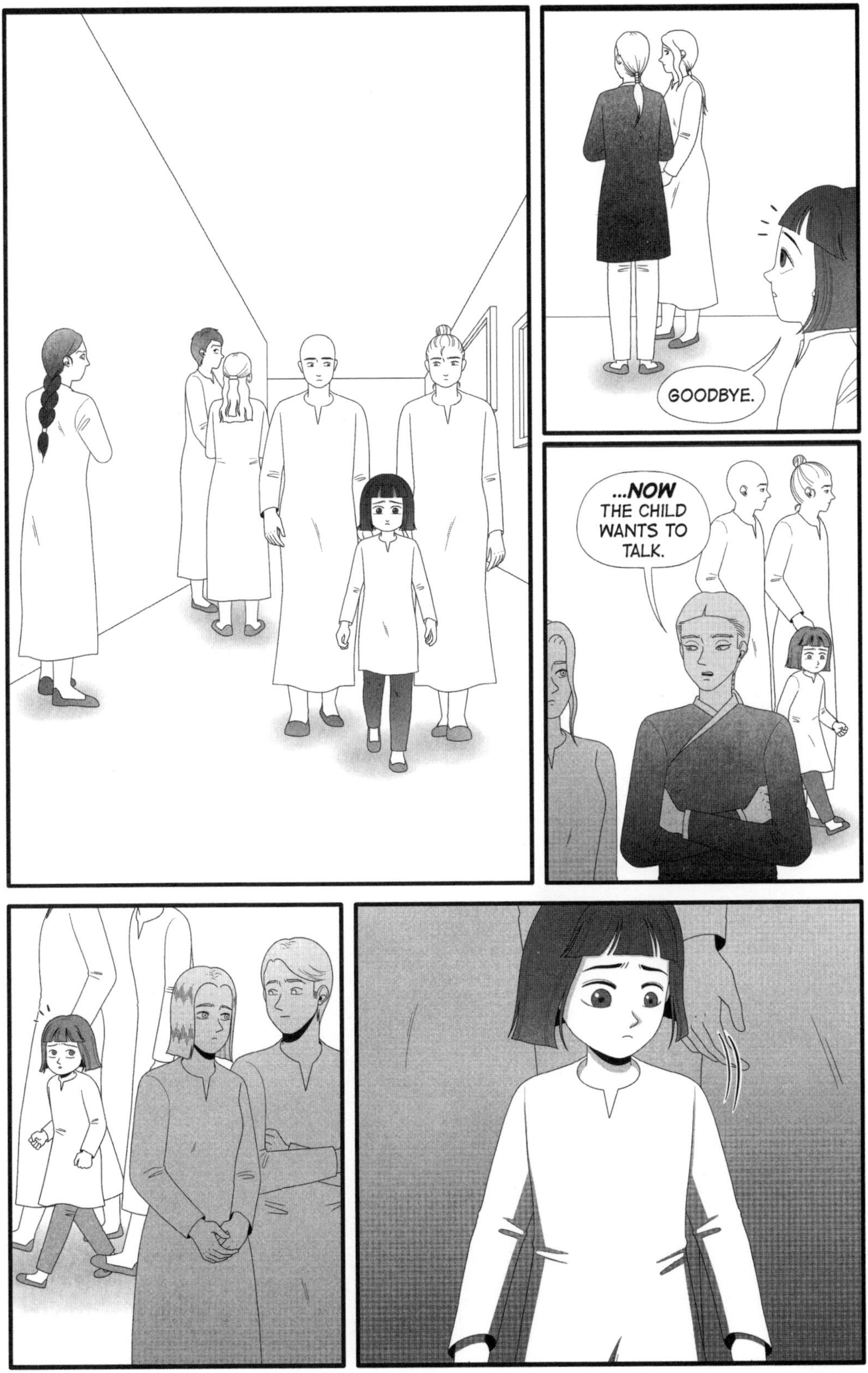
GOODBYE.
...NOW THE CHILD WANTS TO TALK.

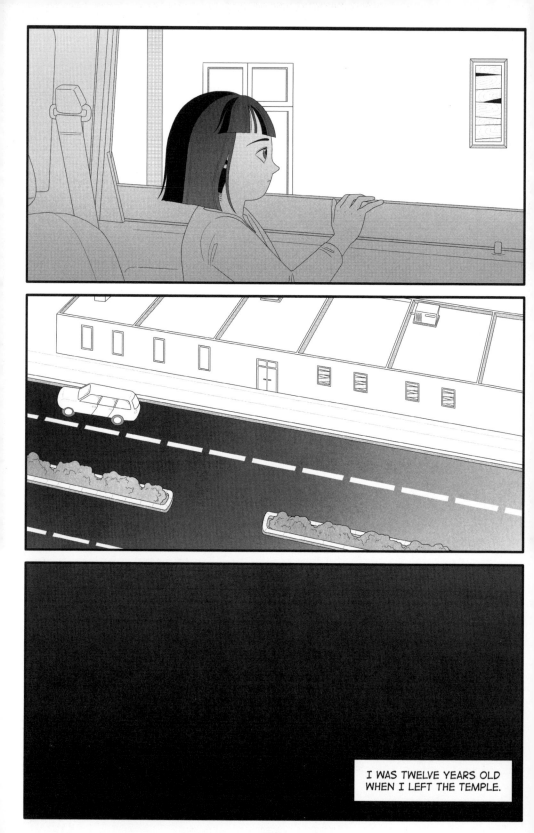

I WAS TWELVE YEARS OLD
WHEN I LEFT THE TEMPLE.

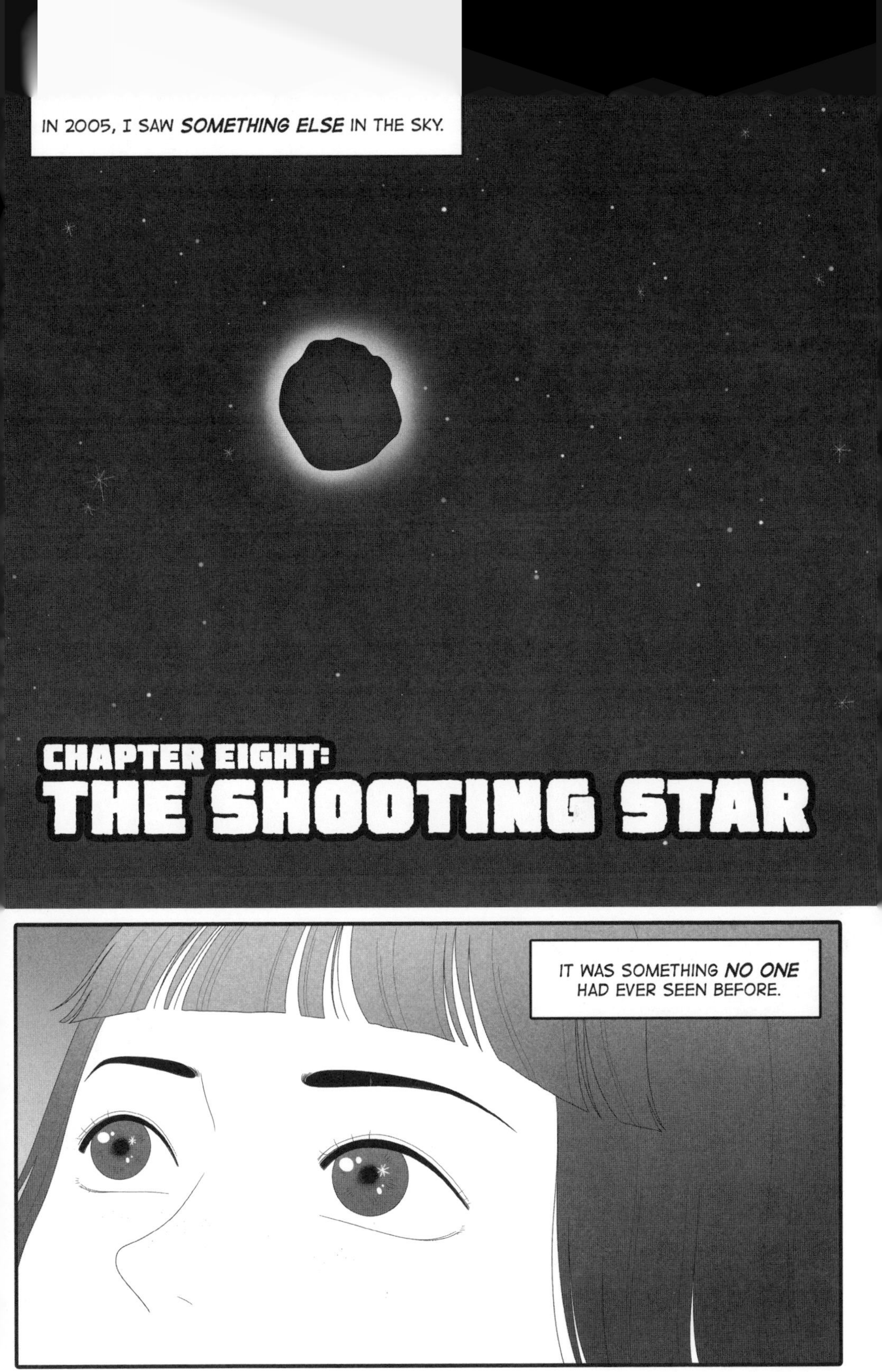
IN 2005, I SAW SOMETHING ELSE IN THE SKY.
CHAPTER EIGHT:
THE SHOOTING STAR
IT WAS SOMETHING NO ONE HAD EVER SEEN BEFORE.

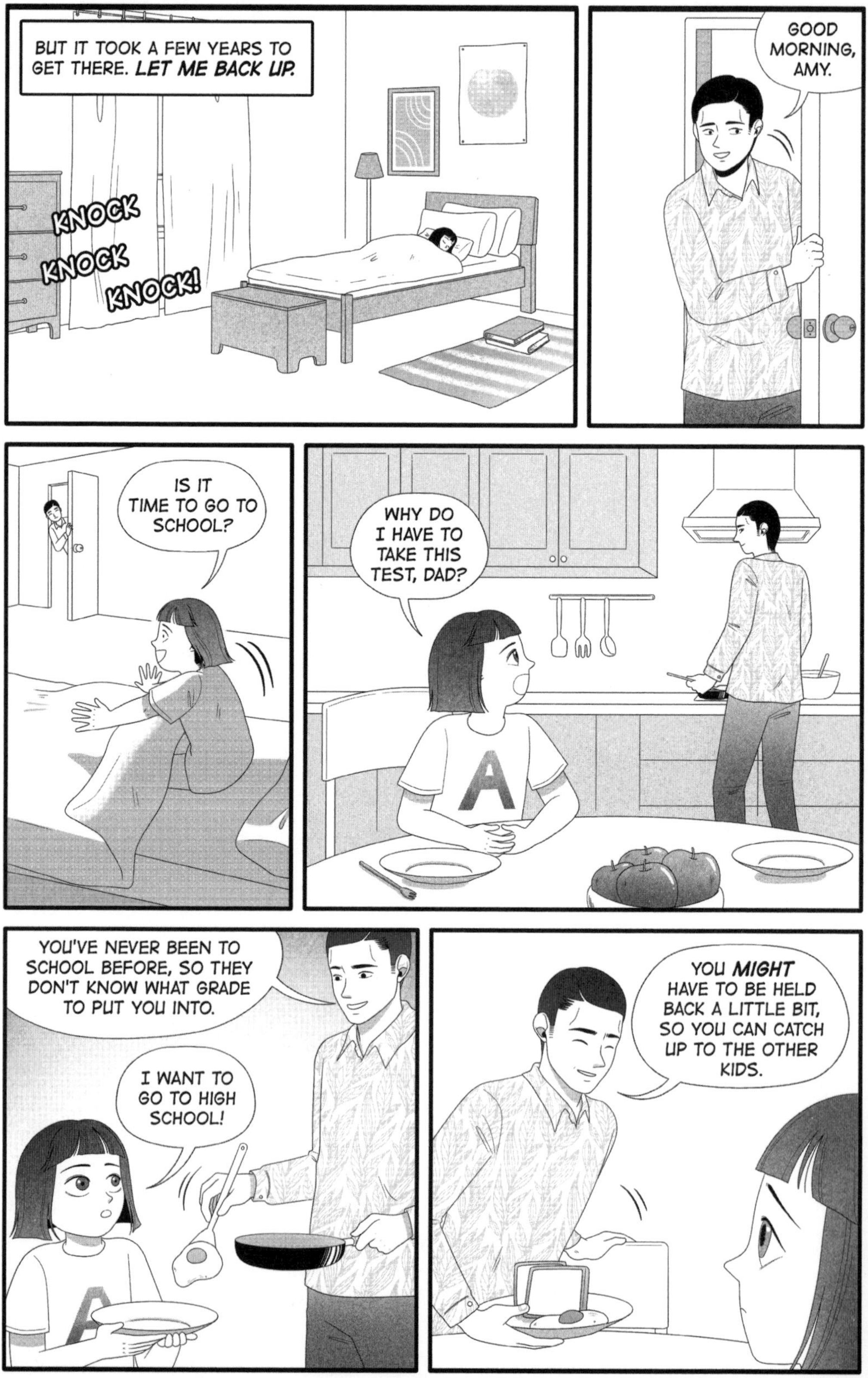
BUT IT TOOK A FEW YEARS TO GET THERE. LET ME BACK UP.
KNOCK
KNOCK
KNOCK!
GOOD MORNING, AMY.
IS IT TIME TO GO TO SCHOOL?
WHY DO I HAVE TO TAKE THIS TEST, DAD?
YOU'VE NEVER BEEN TO SCHOOL BEFORE, SO THEY DON'T KNOW WHAT GRADE TO PUT YOU INTO.
I WANT TO GO TO HIGH SCHOOL!
YOU MIGHT HAVE TO BE HELD BACK A LITTLE BIT, SO YOU CAN CATCH UP TO THE OTHER KIDS.

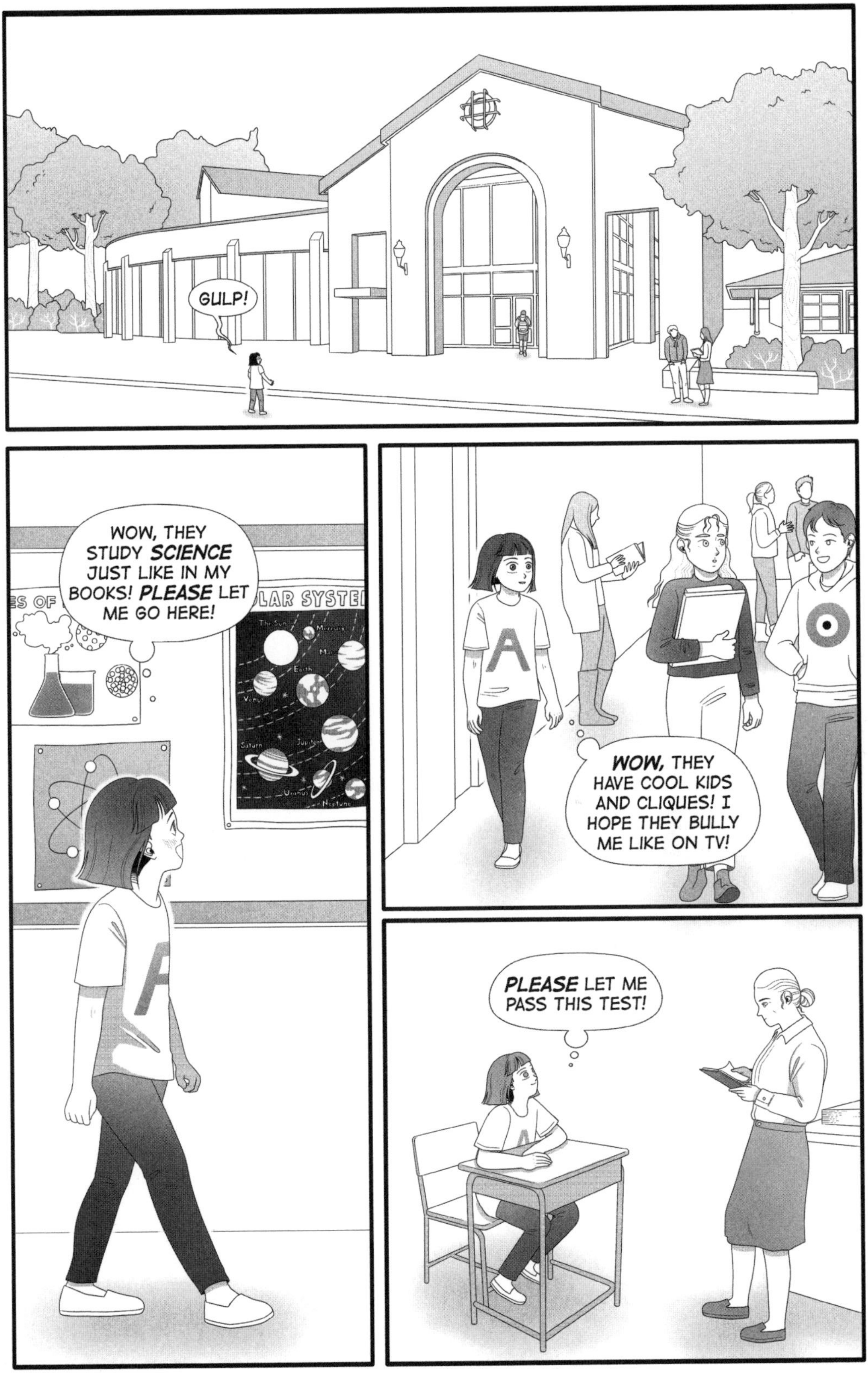
GULP!
WOW, THEY STUDY *SCIENCE* JUST LIKE IN MY BOOKS! *PLEASE* LET ME GO HERE!
WOW, THEY HAVE COOL KIDS AND CLIQUES! I HOPE THEY BULLY ME LIKE ON TV!
PLEASE LET ME PASS THIS TEST!

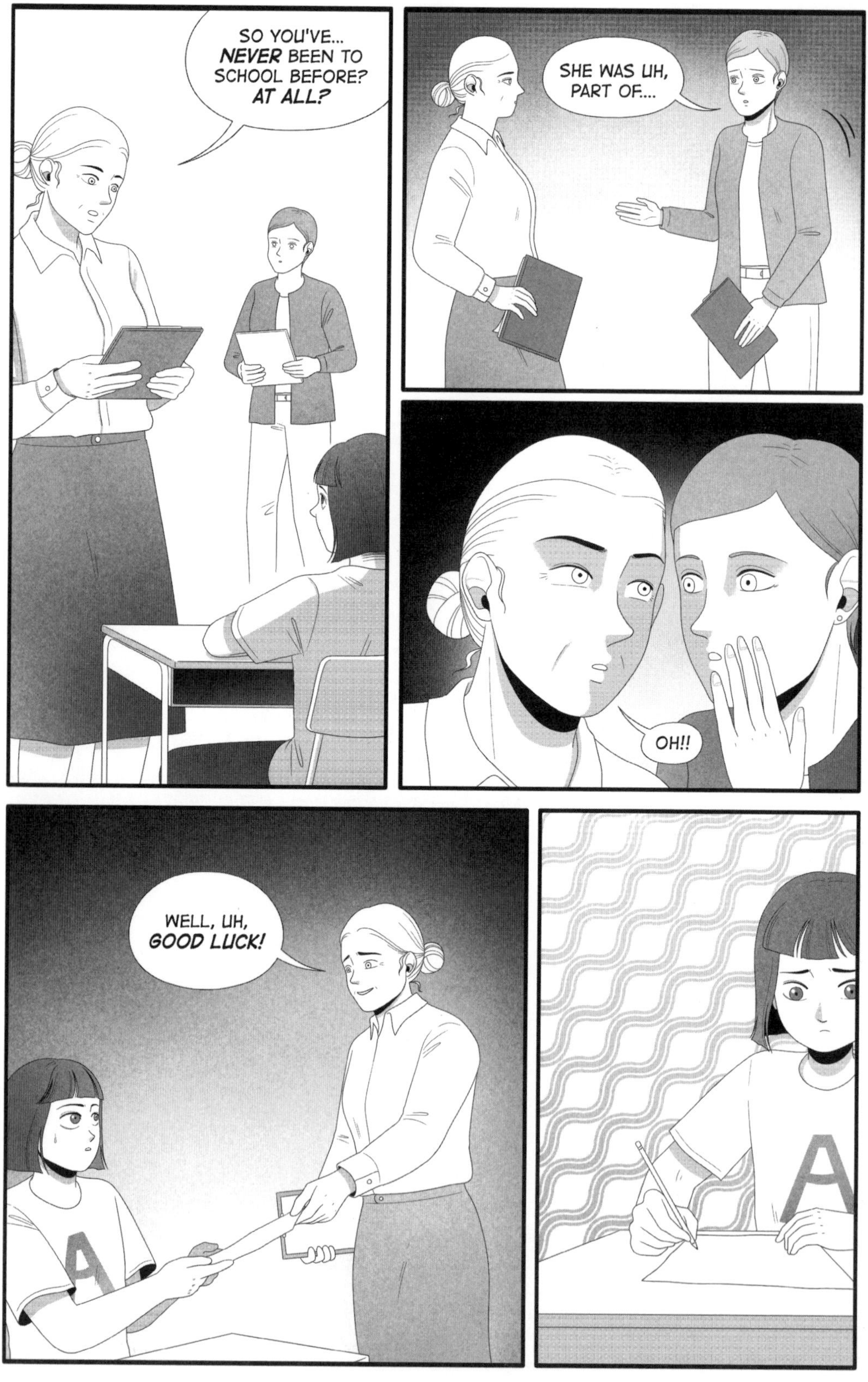

SO YOU'VE... NEVER BEEN TO SCHOOL BEFORE? AT ALL?
SHE WAS UH, PART OF....
OH!!
WELL, UH, GOOD LUCK!

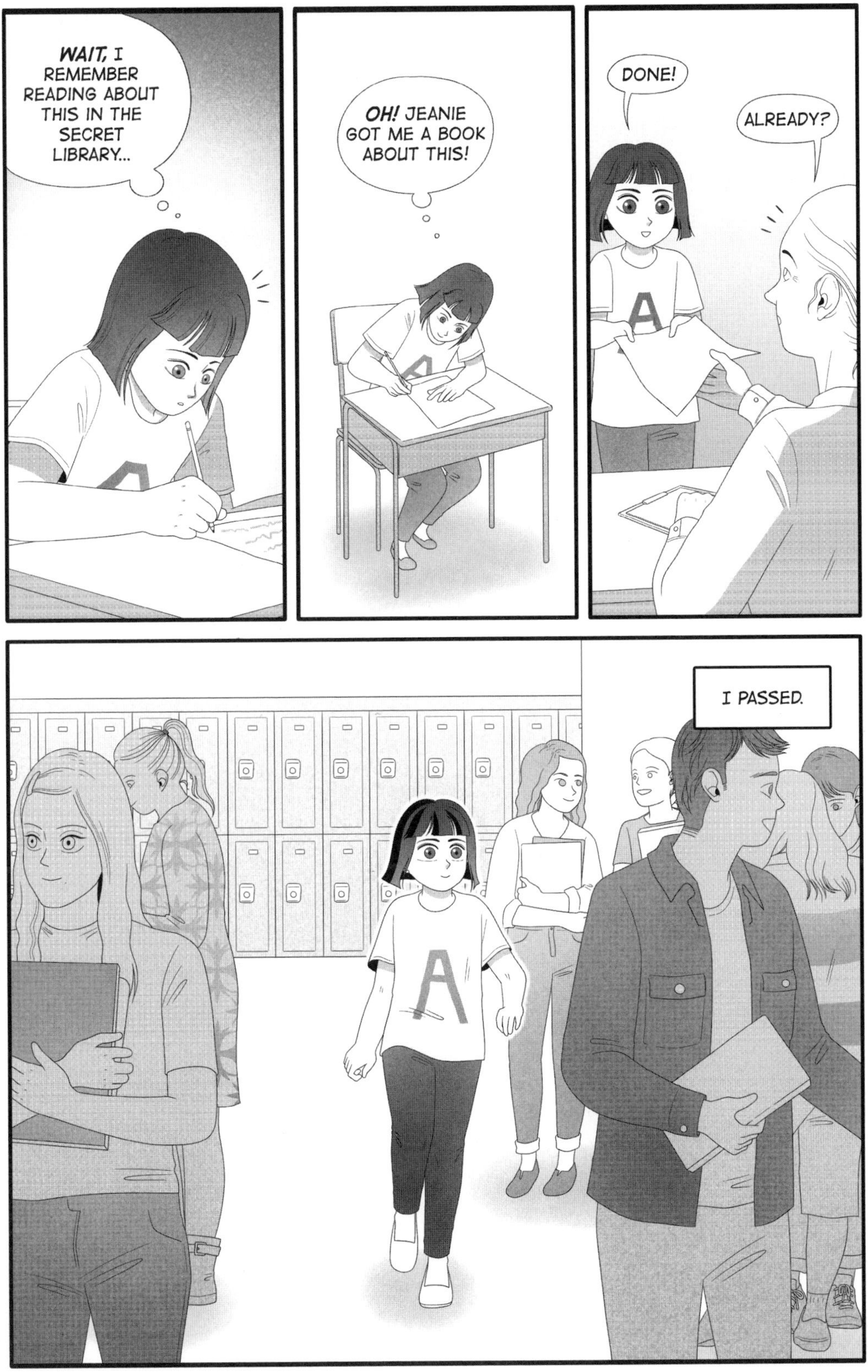
WAIT, I REMEMBER READING ABOUT THIS IN THE SECRET LIBRARY...
OH! JEANIE GOT ME A BOOK ABOUT THIS!
DONE!
ALREADY?
I PASSED.

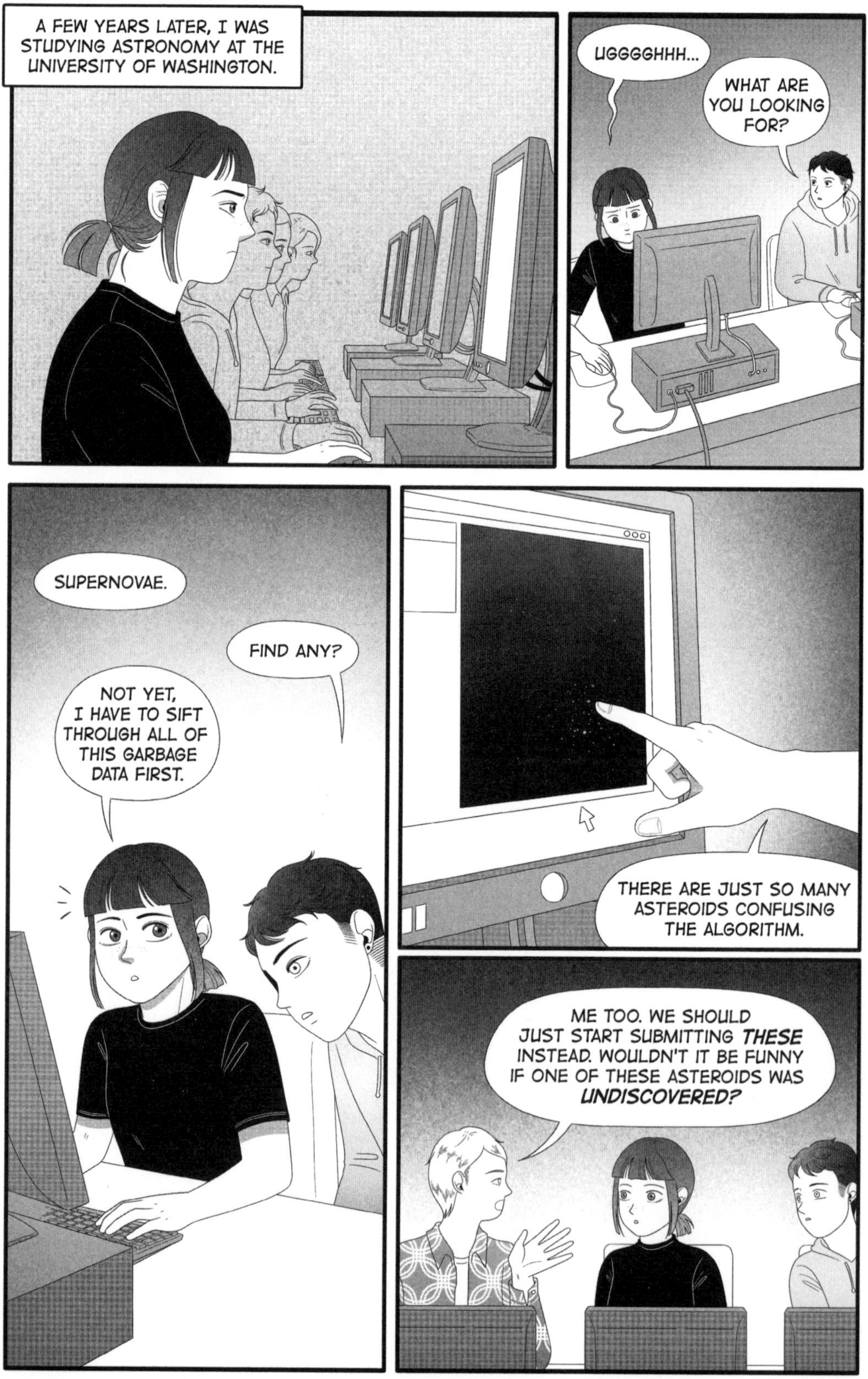
A FEW YEARS LATER, I WAS STUDYING ASTRONOMY AT THE UNIVERSITY OF WASHINGTON.
UGGGGHHH...
WHAT ARE YOU LOOKING FOR?
SUPERNOVAE.
FIND ANY?
NOT YET, I HAVE TO SIFT THROUGH ALL OF THIS GARBAGE DATA FIRST.
THERE ARE JUST SO MANY ASTEROIDS CONFUSING THE ALGORITHM.
ME TOO. WE SHOULD JUST START SUBMITTING *THESE* INSTEAD. WOULDN'T IT BE FUNNY IF ONE OF THESE ASTEROIDS WAS *UNDISCOVERED?*

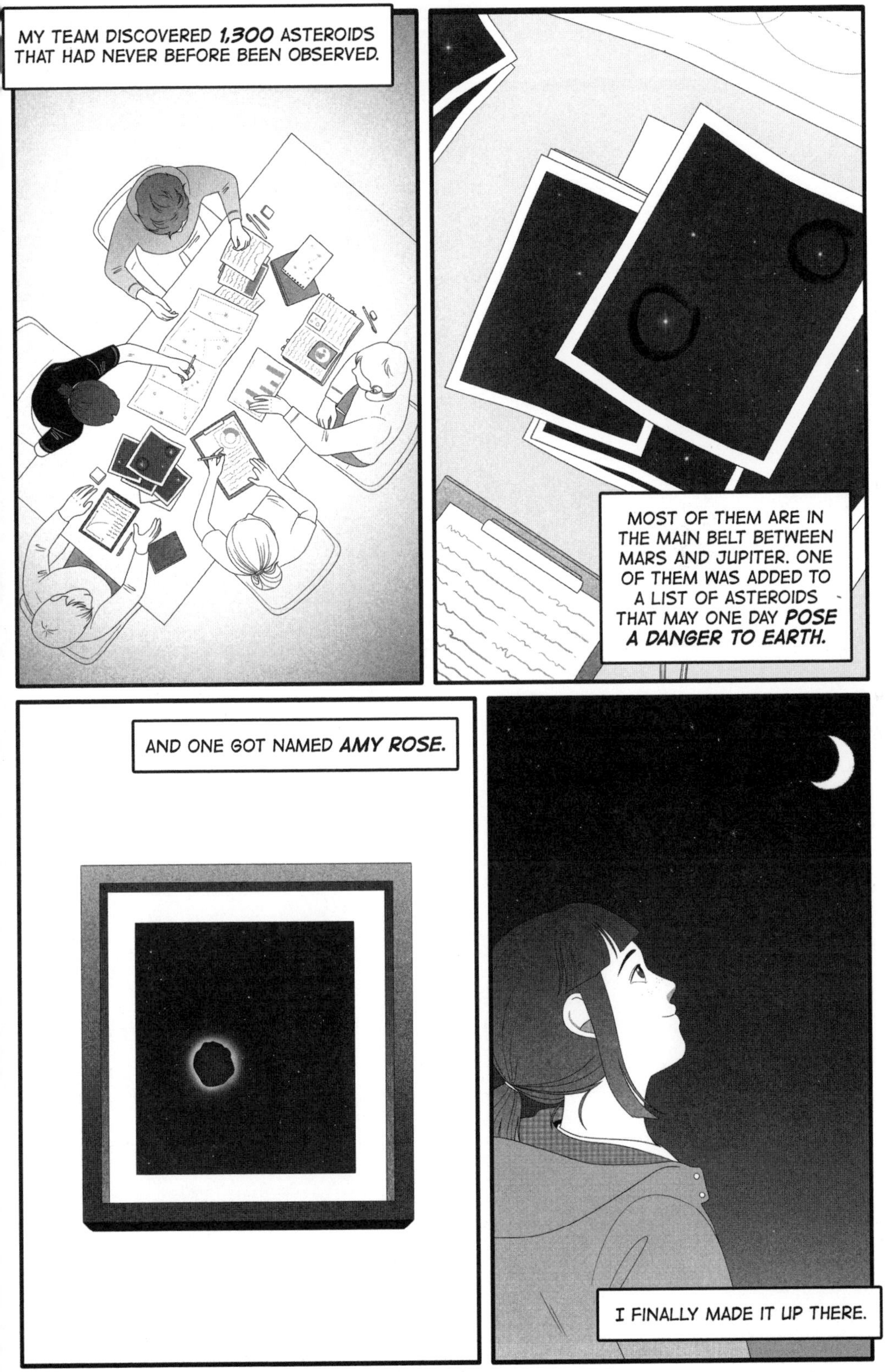
MY TEAM DISCOVERED 1,300 ASTEROIDS THAT HAD NEVER BEFORE BEEN OBSERVED.
MOST OF THEM ARE IN THE MAIN BELT BETWEEN MARS AND JUPITER. ONE OF THEM WAS ADDED TO A LIST OF ASTEROIDS THAT MAY ONE DAY POSE A DANGER TO EARTH.
AND ONE GOT NAMED AMY ROSE.
I FINALLY MADE IT UP THERE.

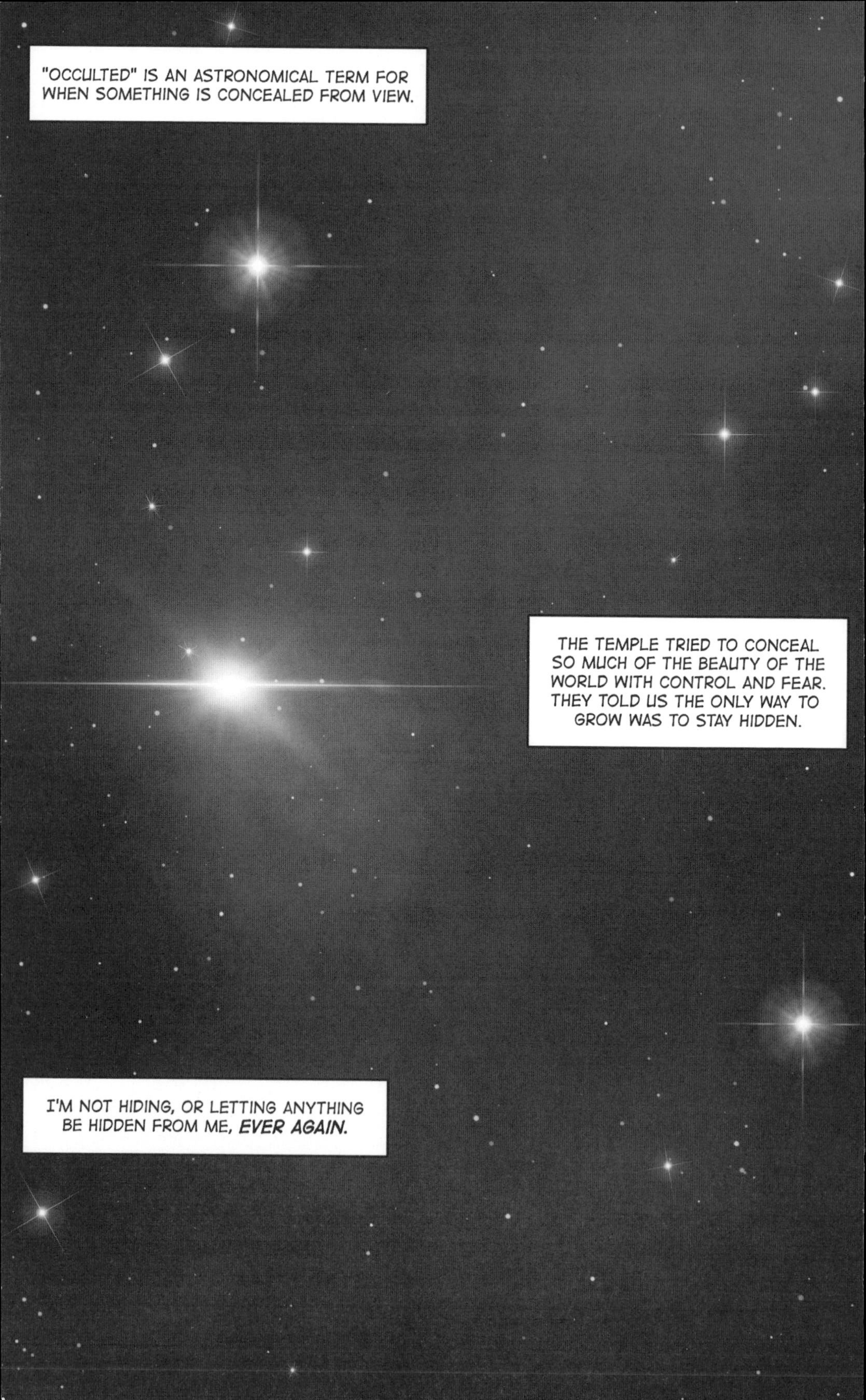
"OCCULTED" IS AN ASTRONOMICAL TERM FOR WHEN SOMETHING IS CONCEALED FROM VIEW.
THE TEMPLE TRIED TO CONCEAL SO MUCH OF THE BEAUTY OF THE WORLD WITH CONTROL AND FEAR. THEY TOLD US THE ONLY WAY TO GROW WAS TO STAY HIDDEN.
I'M NOT HIDING, OR LETTING ANYTHING BE HIDDEN FROM ME, *EVER AGAIN.*

ABOUT THE AUTHORS

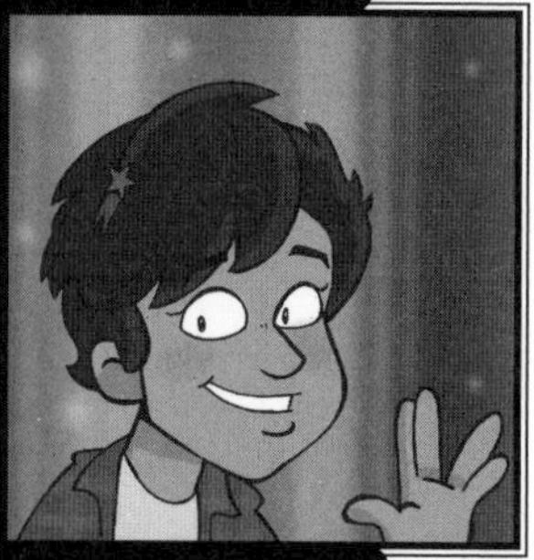

AMY ROSE is not a Sonic character, but she is just as weird. She exudes West Coast vibes no matter where she's at. Currently living and teaching in South Korea, she tries to get some writing or performing done when she isn't inspiring kids to be as strange as possible.

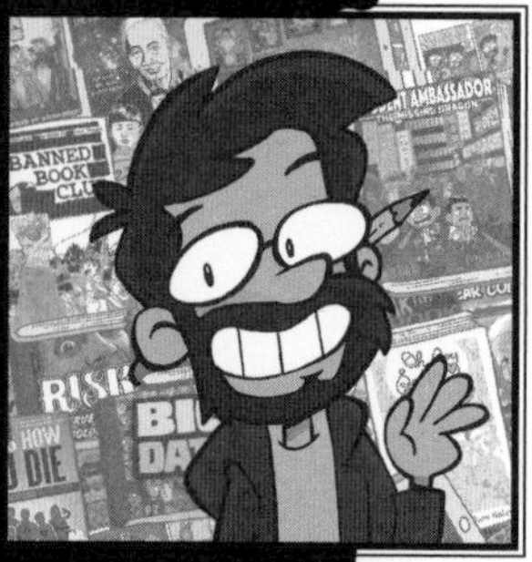

RYAN ESTRADA is an artist/adventurer who travels the world getting into trouble and making comics. He is the co-author of *Banned Book Club* and *No Rules Tonight,* and is also the creator of the *Student Ambassador* Series. He has slept on a park bench in a typhoon, was nearly eaten by lions in the Maasai Mara, and was once thrown from a moving train by the police. He deserved it.

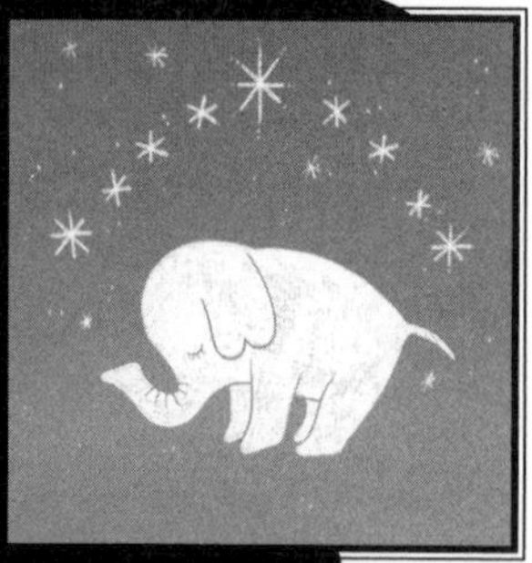

JEONGMIN LEE (a.k.a **MIN THE ELEPHANT**) is an illustrator whose work attempts to introduce a touch of dark fantasy to the mundanity of life. She draws inspiration from dreams, nature, creatures and the macabre.